The Victorian Poets

CONTRIBUTORS

Jerome H. Buckley

Frederic E. Faverty

William E. Fredeman

Park Honan

Clyde K. Hyder

E. D. H. Johnson

John Pick

Lionel Stevenson

Michael Timko

The Victorian Poets

A GUIDE TO RESEARCH

SECOND EDITION

Edited by Frederic E. Faverty

HARVARD UNIVERSITY PRESS

Cambridge, Massachusetts

1968

PREFACE TO THE SECOND EDITION

Over the past decade *The Victorian Poets: A Guide to Research* has demonstrated its usefulness. It has helped stimulate the progress in research and the new developments in criticism that make this second edition necessary. Of the original contributors to the book, two, Paull Franklin Baum and William C. DeVane, have died; and two, A. McKinley Terhune and Howard Mumford Jones, have retired from active teaching. Their places in this volume have been taken respectively by E. D. H. Johnson, Park Honan, Michael Timko, and William E. Fredeman.

The pattern of organization employed in the first edition has been retained, except that the chapter on the Pre-Raphaelites has been brought into conformity with the rest of the volume.

In the section on Arthur Hugh Clough references to a few important publications of 1967 are included. Otherwise, the material is complete to the end of 1966.

Frederick E. Faverty

CONTENTS

The Victorian Poets

Abbreviations in references are those used in the annual Bibliography, *PMLA: Publications of the Modern Language Association of America.* In addition, the following abbreviations are used.

CBEL   *The Cambridge Bibliography of English Literature*
EML   English Men of Letters series.
JWMS   *Journal of the William Morris Society*
Miles   *The Poets and the Poetry of the Century*
ZFEU   *Zeitschrift für Französischen und Englischen Unterricht*

General Materials

JEROME H. BUCKLEY

> But still, as we proceed
> The mass swells more and more
> Of volumes yet to read,
> Of secrets yet to explore.

So lamented Arnold's Empedocles—and so might complain any modern student of Arnold himself or of the other principal Victorian poets as he contemplates the great mass of scholarship that has accumulated even in the ten or eleven years since the first appearance of this guide to research. Undoubtedly the complaint would be ungrateful, for the new scholar-critics have made available more and more of the materials and approaches essential to a receptive reading of the poetry in all its abundance. But a survey of both the older criticism and the recent additions to it should help place our primary and secondary sources in clearer perspective and, by doing so, intimate some of the many secrets yet to be explored. The fact that there are already innumerable estimates should stimulate rather than discourage fresh interpretation, insofar as a living poetry yields new meanings to every new properly qualified reader. And the contributors who follow are convinced that Victorian poetry, the object of so much continuing regard, is indeed very much alive.

Since the first edition of this book no new Victorian poet has been "discovered," and few new poems have been added to the canon of the established writers. But we have had in the past decade critical and biographical studies comparable in number and in quality to the aggregate product of all the preceding years since the end of the Victorian period: book-length critiques of Tennyson, the Brownings, Clough, Hopkins, and Meredith; extended analyses of Arnold and Hardy specifically as poets; memorable editions of the letters of Swinburne and of Oscar Wilde. Our first edition called for a reappraisal of Victorian poetry. We may safely say that it has now begun with vigor and excitement.

The Victorians, of course, in a sense appraised themselves; within their own era they learned to distinguish some eight or ten major figures among the scores of contemporary verse-makers. And, though we may feel sometimes that they admired the wrong poems—or the right ones for the wrong reasons, or at least for reasons other than ours—their selection of such poets has not since been seriously challenged. Long before the age itself was over, discerning readers could recognize the pre-eminence of Tennyson, Browning, Arnold, Rossetti, and Swinburne, the real if lesser significance of Clough and FitzGerald, the quality of Meredith. Hardy's early verse, to be sure, was generally neglected, and much of it did not appear in print until the twentieth century. But the poetry of Hopkins, though for the most part still unpublished, was not entirely ignored; in the nineties, when preparing a compendious anthology, A. H. Miles paused to call particular attention to the virtually unknown Jesuit, eight of whose poems, submitted by Robert Bridges, were being given "publicity for the first time."

Yet the Victorian appraisal was by no means fixed or final, and the common agreement that Tennyson and Browning, for instance, were major poets in their own age seemed no indication that their precise place in the long history of English poetry had been at all accurately determined. At all events, the inevitable reaction of the Edwardians and the Georgians against the authority of Victorian culture left few reputations secure. By the early nineteen twenties, when in fact a good deal of disinterested research was in progress, the label "Victorian" carried an almost universal connotation of disparagement. The hostility lingered on into the forties, and rarely before 1950 could even the most dispassionate general estimate of the period and its poetry be attempted without some trace of self-conscious apology. Since that time, however, and especially in the past ten years, the revaluation of all things Victorian has proceeded with precision, intelligence, and sympathy, and Victorian literature has become one of the major areas of critical scholarship. A Victorian Studies Group has been formed at the University of Leicester, and a Nineteenth-Century Group at Cambridge; the Victorian Society of London has celebrated "the

High Victorian Cultural Achievement"; an international conference has been called at Indiana to consider all aspects of the Victorian city and the Tennyson Society has established a center for research on the Victorian laureate. The "interdisciplinary" quarterly *Victorian Studies,* a carefully edited and handsomely printed journal, began publication in 1957. *Victorian Poetry*—limited as its title suggests to one discipline, though open to many critical approaches—first appeared in 1963. Meanwhile, the *Victorian Newsletter,* having recently assumed the dignity of letterpress and attractive covers, continues to print many short papers on Victorian poetry and prose, in addition to news of concern to members of the Victorian Group of the Modern Language Association, for whom it is issued. Never before, not even in the Victorian period itself, have students been able to give the Victorian poets such informed and patient scrutiny.

I. BIBLIOGRAPHY

An extensive closed bibliography of Victorian poetry will be found in the third volume of F. W. Bateson's monumental *Cambridge Bibliography of English Literature,* which carries separate entries for over two hundred and fifty Victorian poets, great and small, and assembles a formidable array of background materials. First published in 1941, the original work lists few books appearing after 1937; but a supplementary volume (1957), edited by George Watson, brings the account down through 1954. Though indispensable as a guide to the minor verse of the period, which is nowhere else so fully tabulated, the *CBEL* is nevertheless, like most bibliographies, incomplete and sometimes misleading or even mistaken. Moreover, it is somewhat cumbersome in arrangement, ordered as it is chronologically by headings rather than alphabetically; and, despite its selectivity, it may well by its very abundance confuse the student unfamiliar with the standard works of scholarship and criticism, for by its design it is kept from passing judgment on the relative value of the titles it lists. Likewise "uncritical" is the compilation by T. G. Ehrsam, R. H. Deily, and R. M. Smith, *Bibliographies of Twelve Victorian Authors* (1936), which, citing Master's essays and doctoral dissertations as well as books and periodicals, claims—unfortunately with too much assurance—to be "complete up to July, 1934." Yet the book has a range and solidity which our recognition of some minor errors should not lead us to overlook. The twelve authors include all the more important Victorian poets except Browning, Meredith, and Hopkins; and the listing for each covers many of the Victorian reviews, signed and anonymous, of the author's works. A short, highly selective bibliography is J. H. Buckley's *Victorian Poets and Prose Writers* (1966), which includes twenty-four of the poets and lists the key recent biographical and critical studies. All of these should be supplemented by the very nearly complete *Guide to Doctoral Dissertations in Victorian Literature, 1886–1958* (1960), compiled by Richard D. Altick and William R. Matthews, a most useful index listing the general theses by genre or subject matter and the specific ones by the Victorian writers discussed.

Several "open" or continuing bibliographies report each year on current research. *The Annual Bibliography of English Language and Literature,* prepared since 1920 by the Modern Humanities Research Association, lists not only the new works of scholarship but also the scholarly reviews that appraise their worth. The bibliography printed annually in the May issue of *PMLA* has been international in coverage since 1957, and it now draws on some twelve hundred periodicals in all the major European languages. The chapter called "The Nineteenth Century and After," in *The Year's Work in English Studies* (published annually by the English Association of London), is a highly selective and eminently readable critical review of the most significant new books and articles. The "Victorian Bibliography," which appeared from 1933 to 1957 in the May issue of *Modern Philology* and has appeared since 1958 in the June *Victorian Studies,* is both inclusive and

5

descriptive: it catalogs many unexpected items bearing on the economic, religious, political, social, intellectual, and aesthetic life of the Victorians; cites key reviews of the principal monographs; and comments succinctly on the argument or importance of some of the general and specific studies. (In 1945 the first thirteen issues of this admirable compilation were edited by William D. Templeman and presented, with a convenient cumulative index, as *Bibliographies of Studies in Victorian Literature, 1932–1944;* in 1956 a similar volume, edited by Austin Wright, covered the years 1945–1954.) Taken together, these yearly lists should furnish as close a check on recent publication as we could wish. But if we are bewildered by the proliferation of research, we may welcome an essay contributed annually since 1963 to *Victorian Poetry* by R. C. Tobias, "The Year's Work in Victorian Poetry," which is both a critical survey of scholarly articles and an effort to discern the directions that scholarship is taking.

In addition to the strictly bibliographical aids, two handbooks may be helpful. *The Victorians and After,* by Bonamy Dobrée and Edith Batho, first published in 1939, offers a rapid and somewhat jaundiced general estimate of the verse, suggestive though sketchy bibliographies of the more important poets, and an interesting note on the parodies and nonsense books. *English Literature of the Victorian Period* (1949), by J. D. Cooke and Lionel Stevenson, presents with a good deal less animus a factual review of the background, a sensible commentary on the various genres, brief biographies of the major and minor writers, and lists of carefully selected secondary sources. Like the bibliographies, both handbooks should serve as reminders that Victorian poetry, however uneven its fortunes, has quickened no end of discussion and in the process has somehow survived both its admirers and its detractors.

II. ANTHOLOGIES

Most of the many anthologies of Victorian verse that appeared during the period itself have, as we might expect, been superseded by collections which enjoy the obvious advantage of a longer perspective. In view of subsequent literary history, R. H. Stoddart's *Late English Poets,* prepared in 1865, the year of *Atalanta in Calydon,* seems perceptive enough in recognizing the merit of Swinburne but at the same time singularly inept in bracketing his great "promise" with that of Robert Buchanan. A. H. Miles's *Poets and Poetry of the Century,* on the other hand, remains of value for the sheer range of its selection. Published in ten volumes between 1891 and 1897, and later (1905–1907) rearranged in twelve, it offers us biographical headnotes by well-accredited scholars on innumerable minor writers and assembles hundreds of pieces—lyrics, ballads, hymns, odes, parodies, nonsense jingles —now scarcely accessible in any other form.

Among the later anthologies designed for general reading, Sir Arthur Quiller-Couch's *Oxford Book of Victorian Verse* (1912) long remained the standard work, a tasteful and comprehensive, though rather conventional collection. Recently, however, it has been replaced by *The Oxford Book of Nineteenth-Century English Verse* (1964). Unfortunately the editor, John Hayward, though able to offer a fresh choice of the minor poetry, chooses to represent the major poets by snippets and brevities; thus two songs remain from *Idylls of the King* and four sonnets from *Modern Love,* none of Swinburne's strongest verse appears and not much of his weakest, and seven shorter pieces must suggest Arnold's total achievement. "Tennyson to Yeats," the fifth and last volume of *Poets of the English Language* (1950), compiled by W. H. Auden and Norman Pearson, is chiefly remarkable as witness to the discrimination of its editors, who are intent upon avoiding the familiar. Mr. Auden's later anthology, *Nineteenth-Century British Minor Poets* (1966), covering briefly some eighty Romantics and Victorians, makes a number of interesting discoveries or recoveries. But the most valuable contribution of the volume is the introduction in which Mr. Auden traces much of the peculiar quality of the verse to the classical training of the poets. "Struck by the contrast between the extraordinary high standards of their prosodic skill and the frequent clumsiness and inadequacy of their diction," he writes, " . . . I am inclined to attribute both the virtue and the defect to the fact that, for most of them, their first experience of writing verse was in a language syntactically and rhythmically very different from their own"; that is to say, the exigencies of translation made the verse-makers unusually conscious of prosody and at the same time ready to accept the first word that seemed to fit a metrical context. Such a suggestion carries a special weight when it comes from a critic who is himself a distinguished practicing poet.

In serviceability to the student, however, none of the "trade" anthologies compares with any of the several college texts in wide use throughout the United States: *Poetry of the Victorian Period,* edited in 1930 by George B. Woods, revised in 1955 and again in 1965 by J. H. Buckley; *Victorian and Later English Poets* (1934), edited by James Stephens, Edwin L. Beck, and Royall H. Snow; *Victorian Poetry,* edited in 1942 by E. K. Brown and revised in 1962 by J. O. Bailey; and *Victorian Poetry and Poetics* (1959), edited by Walter E. Houghton and G. Robert Stange. Each of these carries a full complement of explanatory notes, bibliographical suggestions, and other scholarly aids, and each strives, by printing a number of the key longer poems complete, to indicate the success or failure of the major writers in handling large as well as small structural units. Of the four, the Buckley and Woods, which draws on fifty poets, gives the broadest cross section of Victorian poetry as a whole, including examples of the humorous, satiric, political, and devotional verse. The Stephens, Beck, and Snow, covering some thirty writers, offers, in addition to the poetry, some prose—usually in the form of personal letters—by each of the leading poets. The Brown and Bailey, limited to fifteen poets, benefits from a sound and stimulating critical introduction. The Houghton and Stange, limited to sixteen, appends to the verse selections from eleven nineteenth-century prose writers touching on poetic theory. Still more restricted in scope is William Harvey Marshall's *Major Victorian Poets* (1966), limited to Tennyson, Browning, Arnold, Rossetti, and Swinburne. Perhaps most attractive in format is Robert Bernard Martin's *Victorian Poetry* (1964), a lightly annotated anthology including, besides the five poets of the Marshall volume, Meredith, Christina Rossetti, Hardy, Hopkins, and Housman. All six of these texts in various ways bear the authority of a disciplined scholarship.

III. BACKGROUND STUDIES

Dame Edith Sitwell admired the Victorian poets as "pure" artists and prepared her own rather odd anthology to show how they had succeeded in creating a "sheltered world," untroubled by human emotion and full of "the lovely light and colour of the rose." Most scholars, however, have seen the poets in close relation to the needs and problems of their society and have insisted accordingly on a knowledge of the milieu as essential to a cogent evaluation of their work. An ordered survey of the vast literature devoted to an elucidation of the Victorian background would scarcely be possible within the confines of this review of research, nor indeed directly relevant to our present purposes. We might, nonetheless, mention in passing a few of the general political and social histories of the period likely to prove most revealing: G. M. Trevelyan's *British History in the Nineteenth Century and After, 1782–1919* (1938); Élie Halévy's *History of the English People in the Nineteenth Century* (1949–1952); Sir Llewellyn Woodward's *The Age of Reform, 1815–1870* (1962);

R. C. K. Ensor's *England, 1870–1914* (1936); *The Age of the Chartists, 1832–1854* (1930) by J. L. and Barbara Hammond; *The Making of Victorian England* (1962) by George Kitson Clark; *The Age of Improvement* (1962) by Asa Briggs; and David Thomson's brief but well-informed *England in the Nineteenth Century* (1950). And before examining works concerned more specifically with the literature, we should consider the importance of many useful monographs bearing on the intellectual and spiritual life of the age, such as A. W. Benn's tremendous *History of English Rationalism in the Nineteenth Century* (1916); L. E. Elliott-Binns's able and objective *Religion in the Victorian Era* (1936); Alan W. Brown's detailed study, *The Metaphysical Society, Victorian Minds in Crisis* (1947); and D. C. Somervell's workmanlike though hurried survey, *English Thought in the Nineteenth Century* (1929). If the student requires a simpler introduction to the complexities of the culture from which the poetry arose, he may turn to a volume called *Ideas and Beliefs of the Victorians* (1949), edited by Harman Grisewood, the record of a remarkable series of BBC broadcasts by G. M. Trevelyan, Harold Laski, Bertrand Russell, Julian Huxley, Lord David Cecil, Basil Willey, and others, seeking in brief compass to appraise Victorian attitudes toward progress, freedom, faith, science, education, and democracy. If he demands a more systematic and less informal discussion of similar problems, he should examine *Backgrounds to Victorian Literature* (1967), edited by Richard A. Levine, a collection of fourteen essays by critics and historians, arranged under five main headings, "The Victorian Years: An Overview," "Religion and Science," "Education and the Spread of Knowledge," "Economics and Politics," and "An Epilogue." And if he wishes a somewhat closer perspective on one principal set of Victorian ideas, he might look at *The Triumph of Time* (1966) by J. H. Buckley, which draws heavily on the poetry as well as the prose to illustrate an obsessive Victorian concern with the concepts of history, progress, and decadence, and the many faces of time itself.

The Victorian Frame of Mind, 1830–1870 (1957), by Walter E. Houghton, sets out to explore "those general ideas and attitudes about life which a Victorian of the middle and upper classes would have breathed in with the air—the main grounds of hope and uneasiness which he felt, the modes of thought and behavior he followed, . . . the standards of value he held." Professor Houghton then proceeds to a categorical description of emotional, intellectual, and moral assumptions, including a discussion in considerable detail of such subjects as optimism, dogmatism, anti-intellectualism, anxiety, earnestness, love, hero-worship, hypocrisy. Though not a literary study, the book derives much of its close documentation from literary sources and, in turn, substantially increases our comprehension of themes and gestures, loyalties and prejudices, as we ourselves encounter them elsewhere in Victorian literature. In its clear and able analysis, it also prepares us to understand G. M. Young's great but difficult synthesis, *Victorian England: Portrait of an Age* (1936), a brilliant composite, urbane, ironic, infinitely allusive, the nearest approach we have to an integrated biography of the whole period in its diversity, confusion, and strength.

The importance of the social and intellectual background seemed abundantly clear to the eleven literary historians who contributed in 1950 to *The Reinterpretation of Victorian Literature*, edited by Joseph E. Baker. Though the accent throughout the essays falls on the prose writers rather than the poets, the symposium as a whole is concerned less with genres than with general trends, neglected areas of research, and new techniques of investigation. Emery Neff in particular argues convincingly for an analysis of the main currents of social thought, both English and Continental, that conditioned the vision and the performance of Victorian authors. Howard Mumford Jones suggests that a comic spirit, too often discounted by commentators, helped preserve a Victorian sanity and balance amid the peril of unprecedented change. C. F. Harrold, who writes of the Oxford Movement, and F. L. Mulhauser, who discusses the influence of Edmund Burke, warn against a too-facile reading of the true impulses behind the Victorian regard for a religious and political tradition and the parallel distrust of an ascendant "liberalism." Karl Litzenberg, assailing the myth that Victorian literature suffered from radical insularity of tone and substance, effectively demonstrates the still largely unanswered need for comparative studies which will relate the poetry and prose to a cosmopolitan context of philosophic ideas and aesthetic forms.

11

And Professor Baker in the concluding essay, "Our New Hellenic Renaissance," insists that the basic affinities between Victorian and Greek culture, often ignored, deserve our closer scrutiny.

Though much, then, remains to be done in relating Victorian literature to its setting in space and time, more than a little has already been accomplished. A number of studies, old and new, rest in various ways on an awareness of the background, a sense that art arises from—and in turn helps shape—a manifold civilization. In his characteristically paradoxical *Victorian Age in Literature* (1913), G. K. Chesterton long ago postulated his notion of "the Victorian compromise," a concept which has since been subject to the widest misinterpretation. To Chesterton the "compromise" was not a common agreement that hypocrisy was the best policy, that sex was unmentionable, or that sentiment could conceal a want of emotion. It meant, simply, on the social level, the uneasy alliance between middle-class progress and aristocratic stability and, on the spiritual, the effort to harmonize the demands of the new materialism and the values of the old faith. Whether or not the conflicts of Victorian literature can be adequately described in terms of such dichotomies, there is in both the prose and poetry evidence enough of a sincere ethical and intellectual questioning to indicate that the artist at least could accept no ready and ignoble "compromise" of principle. H. V. Routh's *Towards the Twentieth Century: Essays in the Spiritual History of the Nineteenth* (1937), an able analysis of Victorian malaise, examines a dozen major authors in the light of their quest for certainty and concludes that each, however estimable his personal victories, failed to make the requisite adjustment between the life of the spirit and the claims of modern culture. Though the pattern of his argument becomes at times rigid and even arbitrary, Professor Routh's insights are consistently stimulating, and his knowledge of nineteenth-century intellectual history is profound and acute. By comparison, the view of "Victorianism" taken by Clarence R. Decker in *The Victorian Conscience* (1952) seems stereotyped and artificial. Surveying the Victorian reception of foreign writers, especially the hostility of the popular reviews to the French naturalists, Mr. Decker assumes another sort of "compromise" to which Victorian writers apparently subscribed, a conspiracy of silence to protect a moral squeamishness. But hardly at all does he touch on the real issues of "conscience," the deeper sources of an opposition to literary naturalism, the serious sanctions behind an ethical theory of art and a spiritual view of man.

In *Nineteenth Century Studies* (1949) and *More Nineteenth Century Studies* (1956), Basil Willey seeks to interpret the Victorian religious and moral background without recourse to formula or generalization. His lucid analysis in the first volume of specific works by nine considerable prose writers from Coleridge to Matthew Arnold discloses, as we might expect, a marked fluctuation of beliefs rather than a uniformity of faith. And his sympathy in the second book with the cause of religious liberalism produces a patient appraisal of "a group of honest doubters," F. W. Newman, J. A. Froude, Tennyson, "Mark Rutherford," John Morley, and the authors of *Essays and Reviews*. If his conclusions are scarcely startling, his criticism gives us many an insight into the dilemmas of the Christian at a time when new philosophies were calling all in doubt. Drawing on some of the same materials, though for rather different purpose, *The Victorian Temper* (1951), by J. H. Buckley, attempts to present the background in terms of a literary sensibility shifting in the variable climate of ethical and intellectual opinion from the exuberant thirties through the "Decadent" nineties. In particular it strives to trace the complex relations of the artist, especially the poet, to his public and to chart the doctrine of the "moral aesthetic" which allowed the writer no retreat from social responsibility.

Several more restricted literary studies describe the actual media through which the Victorian poets found their public, the standards of taste they were expected to meet, and the levels of audience they were able to reach. Harold G. Merriam's *Edward Moxon, Publisher of Poets* (1939), for example, gives us not only a vivid portrait of one remarkable publisher but also a broad view of general publishing conditions in early Victorian England. John W. Dodds's *The Age of Paradox* (1952), a kaleidoscopic review of the 1840's furnishes a good deal of incidental information on the reception accorded poetry during that boisterous decade. Though sometimes inaccurate and often unscholarly, Amy Cruse's *The Victorians and Their Reading* (1935), which includes a chapter on readers of verse, is a useful and entertaining guide to the literary appetites of the period. Based on far more systematic research and documented with great care, *The English Common Reader* (1957), by Richard D. Altick, chronicles the growth of the mass reading public throughout the nineteenth century, correlates reading habits and the spread of a democratic education, describes the practices of the book trade, tabulates the sales of best-sellers, and estimates the significance of the many periodicals and newspapers. Thanks to Professor Altick, we now know a good deal about the readers of journals; but we have still much to learn about the contributors, most of whom remained anonymous. Recently Walter E. Houghton has begun to supply the necessary information. The first volume of the great project under his editorial direction, *The Wellesley Index to Victorian Periodicals, 1824-1900,* appeared in 1966, identifying very nearly all of the authors of some twenty-eight thousand contributions to eight periodicals (*Edinburgh Review, Quarterly, Blackwood's, North British Review, Macmillan's, Cornhill, Home and Foreign Review,* and *Contemporary*). The full *Index,* which should be of immense service in many ways, will supplement some of the monographs on journals not yet listed. Meanwhile, we may cite the following as distinctly valuable to the student of Victorian poetry: Miriam M. H. Thrall's *Rebellious Fraser's* (1934); George L. Nesbitt's *Benthamite Reviewing* (1934), on the *Westminister;* Edwin M. Everett's *The Party of Humanity* (1939), on the *Fortnightly;* Leslie Marchand's *The Athenaeum* (1941); Merle M. Bevington's *The Saturday Review* (1941); Francis Mineka's The *Dissidence of Dissent* (1944), on the *Monthly Repository;* and Katherine Mix's *A Study in Yellow: The Yellow Book and Its Contributors* (1960). And we might at least mention the great rambling *History of The Times* (by various new men of *The Times,* who still cherish anonymity), especially the second volume, *The Tradition Established* (1939), which concerns the editorship (1841–1877) of the dynamic J. T. Delane. Such studies help re-create the worlds of the reviewers whose values, prejudices, and enthusiasms shaped the first reputations of the poets and sometimes determined the course of their subsequent development.

IV. GENERAL HISTORIES OF VICTORIAN POETRY

Most studies of the Victorian literary background draw more or less extensively on Victorian verse, and all comprehensive histories of English literature give it a position of some importance. Yet there have been relatively few books concerned exclusively with the general themes and techniques of the poetry itself. In his *Ten Victorian Poets* (1940), F. L. Lucas offers what his title promises—ten provocative and discerning revaluations—but conveys no sense of a Victorian style serving as a common denominator for the diverse effort of his subjects. Though his estimates are often unsympathetic, his method of separate analyses differs little from that of such a late Victorian critic as Hugh Walker, whose *Greater Victorian Poets* (1895) approached Tennyson, Browning, and Arnold with understanding and a high reverence for their individual talents. It may be that the complexity of Victorian culture in all its changefulness and eclecticism renders difficult any sound generalization about the verse as a whole. But it should not be impossible to isolate certain recurrent patterns, motifs, or ways with words that lent the poetry a kind of multiple unity in diversity.

E. C. Stedman, the earliest to prepare a substantial critique without special bias, was less reluctant than some later critics to reach general conclusions. First published twenty-six years before Victoria's death, his *Victorian Poets* (1875) assumes that the Victorian era is virtually at an end and suggests that a new poetry, if there is to be one, must move in new directions. The Victorian poets, as Stedman sees them, have been highly self-conscious and distrustful of emotion, modern men living in an "age of prose" which has had no place for heroic sentiment. They "have flourished in an equatorial region of common-sense and demonstrable knowledge," and some of them have been beguiled by "Science,

15

the modern Circe, from their voyage to the Hesperides" and transformed "into voiceless devotees." But the best, finding in art relief from an unaesthetic time, have achieved a formal excellence much to be admired, "a peculiar condensation in imagery and thought." They have been, in short, great technicians, masters of expression; indeed, "never was the technique of poetry so well understood as since the time of Keats and the rise of Tennyson and his school." But by 1875 the virtuosity of Swinburne seems to have carried expression to its ultimate extreme, to the point of exhaustion. The vogue of idyllic and reflective verse, which has dominated the age, has apparently been exploited to the full, and the hope for poetry lies only in a return to dramatic themes.

Though Stedman failed to predict with much accuracy the shape of verse to come, his criticism, Arnoldian as it is in tone, relates Victorian poetry to the context of an analytic age and emphasizes a problem still too often neglected by the scholar: the problem of style, which in some form or other has faced all poets since the time of the Romantics. Writing at the end of the period, George Saintsbury was one of the few to extend the argument and to make the emphasis more specific. A wide-ranging chapter on the poets in his *History of Nineteenth-Century Literature* (1896) suggests that the Victorians excelled "in shorter pieces, more or less lyrical but not precisely lyrics," pieces in which they explored the distinct appeal of the polished phrase and the euphonic cadence. So far did they develop an "elaborate and ornate language" that a later generation, if it were to find an accent of its own, would have to abandon the grand style altogether and to seek other poetic effects.

Saintsbury's attention to form may have led him to neglect the themes and attitudes we have come to consider characteristically "Victorian." Yet the distinguishing marks of the poetry itself, the essential differences between Victorian verse and our own, are perhaps more stylistic than thematic; and our ultimate estimate, I think, depends largely on our acceptance or rejection of the poetic idiom. At any rate, the older studies which attempt a general survey of the content of the poetry, regardless of its form, are of little value to the modern reader seeking the basis of a critical understanding. Arnold Smith's *Main Tendencies of Victorian Poetry* (1907), for instance, identifying "tendencies" with moods, finds optimism, hope, doubt, pessimism, or yearning in each of the several major poets and concludes that the emotion of Victorian poetry was infinitely varied. Arthur Waugh's "Some Movements in Victorian Poetry," a long essay in his *Reticence in Literature* (1915), explains, not very helpfully, that "the history of Victorian poetry is the history of all art; the same eternal impulses underlie it. On the one side the spirit of beauty, on the other the spirit of humanity; on the one side Aesthetics, on the other Ethics." Yet the Victorians, says Waugh, unlike the Elizabethans, were metaphysical in aspiration: "In Elizabeth's time the concern of poetry was the life of man and his relation to his fellows, in the Victorian period it was the soul of man and his relation to his Creator." But the concern, we are told, was scarcely a joyful one; in the world of the poets, "youth and the spring morning are alike over and done with." And the source of weary disenchantment is not so much the failure of belief as the "democratizing spirit" threatening all modern culture.

Recognizing the claims of form as well as content, John Drinkwater's *Victorian Poetry* (1924) first considers the problem of poetic diction, the desire of the Victorian poet to avoid the cliché, the impossibility of his repeating many of the earlier simplicities of language, and the tendency, especially in Tennyson, to actualize, to elaborate the simple statement with precise particular detail. In subject matter, the essay continues, much of the verse is occasional (insofar as it draws at will on any occasion within the age), and its themes therefore may often seem local or accidental. Nonetheless, it remains to the credit of the Victorians that, whatever their errors of selection, they enormously widened the thematic range of English poetry, until "the actual subjects chosen ... for poetic treatment far exceeded in number the subjects that had been chosen in any age before." Later criticism tests the validity of such judgments by specific comparison and contrast of the Victorians with the two generations of Romantics who immediately preceded them.

V. THE ROMANTIC TRADITION

If the general studies of Victorian poetry are on the whole vaguer and more tentative than need be, the monographs seeking to establish particular lines of continuity from the Romantics to the Victorians and so to place the verse in a literary context are relatively precise in their formulations. In many respects the most exemplary of such books is Douglas Bush's *Mythology and the Romantic Tradition* (1937), a definitive yet always vivid examination of the classical themes and genres in Victorian as well as Romantic verse. Without forcing a thesis, Professor Bush argues from reams of evidence that, though the true myth-making faculty died with Keats and Shelley, the Victorians retained or developed a capacity to adapt old myths meaningfully to modern needs. And in the process of the demonstration he illuminates the whole problem of Romantic and Victorian Hellenism and casts brilliant critical sidelights on the general course of nineteenth-century poetry.

Studies touching on the similarities or differences between the Romantic and the Victorian sensibility depend frequently, as we might expect, on the particular concept of Romanticism held by the critic, or at least on the particular aspect of the Romantic movement he has chosen to emphasize. To Mario Praz, in *The Romantic Agony* (1933), the essential unity of nineteenth-century European verse lies in the persistence of that morbid eroticism which finds its typical expression in the voluminous literature of the femme fatale and the Byronic anti-hero. But though his insights may deepen our understanding of a part of Swinburne or Oscar Wilde, the thesis that Signor Praz labors with solemn erudition has little direct relevance to the great bulk of Victorian English poetry. C. M. Bowra, in *The Romantic Imagination* (1949), sees Tennyson and the Victorians generally as "unromantic" in what he regards as their distrust of the imaginative vision, their this-worldly and anti-mystical attitudes toward experience, and their devotion to "realism and didacticism." Yet he believes that something of the Romantic vision remained in Swinburne and the Rossettis, who held to a modified and narrowed faith in "an unseen order behind visible things," an order to be known only through the intuitive imagination. John Heath Stubbs, on the other hand, as one of the self-styled "New Romantics," considers the Pre-Raphaelites quite uninteresting and Swinburne altogether repulsive, empty, and presumably "unromantic." In *The Darkling Plain* (1950), attempting to trace "the later fortunes of . . . the Romantic Tradition in English poetry," he damns the Victorians in general for a "lack of integration, of harmony between the conscious and unconscious aspects of the personality," and praises the lonely exceptions, the rebels against a schizophrenic convention, Beddoes, Hawker, Patmore, Blunt, Thomson, and Doughty. It is well to be reminded of these poets, who are indeed too often ignored; and Mr. Heath-Stubbs sheds new light on their value. But to regard such writers, who remain after all figures of secondary importance, as the true heirs of the Romantic tradition is greatly to circumscribe the influence of Romanticism in the Victorian period and to isolate the greater Victorian poets from the poetic conventions closest to them.

Though concerned with the Victorians only in passing, Frank Kermode's *Romantic Image* (1957) sets out to describe the persistence throughout the nineteenth century of two Romantic premises, beliefs "in the Image as a radiant truth out of space and time, and in the necessary isolation or estrangement of men who can perceive it." So alienated by his private vision, the Victorian poet, like the Romantic, makes the image he has intuited the very core of his poem. R. A. Foakes, on the other hand, in *The Romantic Assertion* (1958), attempts to trace the decline of the Romantic "vision of love" and the weakening, as civilization grew increasingly urban, of the efficacy of assertive images drawn from the world of nature. In Tennyson and Browning he sees "the beginnings of a reduction of [the] vocabulary of assertion to mere rhetoric"; in Arnold, a painful inadequacy of language, "especially in the rhetoric of assertion and the rhetoric of love"; and in James Thomson, a complete inversion of "the rhetoric and images of the Romantic vision" and "an assertion of despair, the negation of that vision." Though his argument involves odd leaps from description to judgment, Mr. Foakes supports his bold generalizations with the close analysis of a few selected texts.

That the Victorians owed other and more tangible debts to their predecessors is apparent from several sound studies in the Victorian reputation and impact of the major Romantics. Samuel C. Chew's *Byron in England* (1926), though primarily concerned with the poet's vogue rather than his influence, makes it clear that the Victorians most moved by Byronic poetry frequently strove for Byronic effect. James V. Logan's *Wordsworthian Criticism: A Guide and Bibliography* (1947) carefully reviews a widespread critical interest in Wordsworth throughout the Victorian period, while Robert E. Lovelace's "Wordsworth and the Early Victorians," an unpublished University of Wisconsin dissertation (1951), analyzes in detail the Wordsworthian elements in the major Victorian poets before 1860. George H. Ford's *Keats and the Victorians* (1944) admirably combines a brief history of Keats's ever-widening fame and a sensitive examination of his influence on Tennyson, Arnold, Rossetti, and Swinburne. And Roland A. Duerksen's *Shelleyan Ideas in Victorian Literature* (1966) assesses Shelley's after-image as a dynamic political radical rather than simply a beautiful ineffectual angel. Though I know of no comparable monograph on Coleridge the poet in his relation to the Victorians, evidence of a real indebtedness should not be difficult to amass.

Books describing the various groups or coteries of the Victorian period frequently suggest that the new poetic schools were actuated by some revived Romantic ideal or impulse. Thus *The Victorian Romantics* (1929), T. Earle Welby's curiously impressionistic yet often revealing account of Rossetti and his circle, assumes a Romantic character behind the alleged Pre-Raphaelite rejection of contemporary issues and conventions, but ignores in the art those elements of "realism" which may well derive from the spirit and method of mid-nineteenth-century science. Louise Rosenblatt's *L'Idée de l'art pour l'art dans la littérature anglaise pendant la période victorienne* (1931) skillfully traces the Aesthetic Movement back to Keats and other Romantic sources, but in the process tends to ignore the Victorian intellectual conflicts that helped give rise to English aestheticism. *The Last Romantics* (1949) by

Graham Hough, concerned with the Aesthetes and others who prepared the way for Yeats, ably gauges the quality of the emotion or sensibility of a few Victorians romantically sharing "a common passion for the life of the imagination" as opposed to the materialism of their age. *Dark Passages* (1965), Barbara Charlesworth's exploration of the Decadence, detects "a consistent poetic tradition" running from the Romantics through the Pre-Raphaelites to the Decadents, all "centrally concerned with the moment of heightened consciousness." And Albert J. Farmer's appraisal of the English *fin de siècle, Le Mouvement esthétique et 'décadent' en Angleterre* (1931), argues — very much as does Holbrook Jackson's *The Eighteen Nineties* (1914) — that the "Decadence" was really a period of "Romantic" vitality and liberation, a new Romantic movement dedicated to the overthrow of "Victorianism."

Centered as they are on more or less Romantic strains, such critiques naturally do not seek to define in any detail the elements that lent Victorian poetry, whatever its debt to the past, a distinct character of its own. In a somewhat similar vein, *The Victorian Temper*, mentioned above among the general studies, recognizes a continued or rather attenuated Romanticism, especially in the work of the minor Victorians who constituted the Spasmodic School; but it stresses at the same time an "anti-romantic" impulse in the more significant poets, a self-conscious drive toward greater objectivity, which led to a repudiation and sometimes a burlesque of Romantic sentiment. George Kitchin, in his standard *Survey of Parody and Burlesque in English* (1931), describes the early Victorian period as "the great age of burlesque" and contends that "the various outbreaks of satire in this age are successive efforts to keep romantic art sane." Victorian poetry is not, of course, predominantly satiric, but it typically shares with satire a latent distrust of personal revelation, a regard for general moral and social "sanity," and, more often than most critics have acknowledged, a concern with carefully calculated technique. In an effort to estimate its essential quality, we may turn to analyses of its characteristic form and content.

VI. THE CONTENT OF VICTORIAN POETRY

Unlike the Romantics, who for the most part were able to fashion highly personal concepts of God and nature, the Victorians, whether orthodox or agnostic, were forced into a direct consideration of the framework of traditional religion as it suffered ever-increasing intellectual attack throughout the nineteenth century. If it was not invariably their first concern, man's status as a moral being, a spiritual entity, postulated by the old theology but seriously challenged by the new science, certainly supplied a central theme in much of their most representative work; and their religious assertions, compromises, and denials seemed of prime importance to troubled readers who looked to poetry for guidance and interpretation. We have accordingly a good many discussions of the spiritual content of the verse, most of them partisan, quite unscholarly, and long since badly dated, nearly all of them confusing "message" with art.

By an odd arrangement of materials that permits Browning to come last, Vida Scudder's *Life of the Spirit in the Modern English Poets* (1895), though published in the skeptical nineties, concludes that Victorian poetry has moved joyously from Romantic pantheism toward Christianity. W. J. Dawson's *The Makers of English Poetry* (1906) finds the Victorians, to whom over half the book is devoted, chiefly remarkable for their spiritual intent, their "moral power," their inspirational uplift. E. M. Chapman's *English Literature in Account with Religion, 1800–1900* (1910) likewise judges the poetry sympathetically in the light of a liberal Protestantism. A. S. Hoyt, in *The Spiritual Message of Modern English Poetry* (1924), with a heavy emphasis on the Victorians, similarly draws on standards more evangelical than aesthetic and ignores the intrinsic function of the moral values in their poetic context. Limiting himself to a single theme, Leslie D. Weatherhead, in

The Afterworld of the Poets — the Contribution of Victorian Poets to the Development of the Idea of Immortality (1929), aware that a Victorian heterodoxy may be a modern liberal orthodoxy, achieves some objective understanding of the religious conflicts of the period but remains much too literal in his reading of the poems as if they were direct transcripts of the creed of the poets.

From a very different point of view, Sister Mary Madeleva in a longish and often penetrating essay called "The Religious Poetry of the Nineteenth Century" included in her *Chaucer's Nuns* (1925), insists that the Victorians, apart from the Rossettis and a few devotional lyrists, were in no real sense religious poets. In *Christianity and Romanticism in the Victorian Era* (1957), volume IV of his wide-ranging *Religious Trends in English Poetry*, Hoxie Neale Fairchild reaches a rather similar conclusion. Impressively erudite, and acute in his criticisms sometimes to the point of excessive sharpness, Professor Fairchild begins each analysis with the clearcut assumption that true religious verse demands of the poet an unequivocal commitment to a dogmatic faith. But by the fifth volume, *Gods of a Changing Poetry, 1880–1920* (1962), he finds himself treating "a period within which poetry itself is the only religion possessed by many poets." In *The Disappearance of God* (1963), concerned with De Quincey, Browning, Emily Brontë, Arnold, and Hopkins, J. Hillis Miller brilliantly explores why "the gap between man and the divine power" seemed greater to the Victorians than to the Romantics, who could sense "a hidden spiritual force in nature." And in *Images of Eternity: Studies in the Poetry of Religious Vision from Wordsworth to T. S. Eliot* (1963), James Benziger, questioning the rigidity of Professor Fairchild's position, sees value and poetic consequence both in the Romantic faith and in the more tentative Victorian vision.

However we estimate the quality of their personal religion, Tennyson, the Brownings, Arnold, Clough, Meredith, and even Swinburne did, I believe, write poems which, traditional or not, Christian or otherwise, may be regarded as essentially religious in final effect. Despite the attention accorded the "spirituality" of the poets, we still need appraisals of the religious and ethical assumptions of the verse itself and of the symbols of faith that enrich its substance. A suggestive though rather scattered essay in such criticism is Leone Vivante's *English Poetry and Its Contribu-*

tion to the Knowledge of a Creative Principle (1950), an examination of selected passages from seventeen poets, seven of them specifically Victorian (Mrs. Browning, Tennyson, Emily Brontë, Meredith, Swinburne, Wilde, Francis Thompson). Viewing poetry as a mode of truth, Signor Vivante finds the poems and poets he analyzes each partaking in some degree of the "self-obliviousness" of the intuitive imagination, each reaching at high moments an essential creative "freedom," and so laying bare something of "the 'spirit' of life, the very life of life, its innermost soul." Though it is not his express purpose to do so, he thus reminds us that the Victorian concern with spiritual values and forces sometimes transcends the Victorian age and so remains even to us of immediate and timeless interest.

Discussion of the poetic use of ideas emanating from the new science, the source of much of the religious doubt, has been less voluminous, yet in general more scholarly and systematic. In his *Scientific Thought in Poetry* (1931), Ralph B. Crum describes ably but too hastily the struggle, experienced by all Victorians interested in science, between a naturalistic and a spiritual — or, as he calls it, "mystical" — view of the world. The poets, Mr. Crum argues, were reluctant to accept a thoroughgoing Darwinism insofar as it seemed to deprive the evolutionary process of purpose and design. In *Darwin among the Poets* (1932), Lionel Stevenson presents a short survey of evolutionary theories (not necessarily Darwinian) in Victorian verse and then turns to a more specific analysis of four or five major poets. As a whole, his exposition is lucid and convincing, though we might wish that Tennyson had been viewed with greater sympathy and that Swinburne had received closer attention. Joseph Warren Beach is stronger perhaps on the Romantics than on the Victorians, but throughout his *Concept of Nature in Nineteenth-Century English Poetry* (1936), he develops a powerful theme with impressive authority. Concerned with both philosophy and science, he demonstrates and explains the steady decline of a transcendental view of nature from the time of Wordsworth, until with Hardy at the end of the Victorian period "no trace of teleology" remained, "nature" had lost its solemn connotations, and "for the emotional effect formerly associated with nature, the poet must turn elsewhere." Douglas Bush notes the changed attitude in the stimulating fifth chapter, "Evolution and the Victorian Poets," of his *Science and English Poetry, 1590–1950* (1950), and comments tellingly that Tennyson's lingering trust in an order of nature is no less reasonable than Hardy's apparently "scientific" pessimism, which is itself but "the subjective vision of the poet, a personal assertion of the unprovable." Such an observation properly recalls us to the poetry and rebukes a too-frequent inclination to prejudge its intrinsic worth in the light or dark of our own sentimental reactions to science. Georg Roppen's *Evolution and Poetic Belief* (1956) accordingly concentrates to good effect on the precise way in which the poets adapted the evolutionary idea to their own poetic needs: "For in their intuitive search for significance and value, which is the distinctive poetic task and recognized by them as such, our writers make of their evolutionary motifs a deeply personal confession, and in so expressing their own condition they interpret the condition of mind in their times."

Though most of the background studies (see III, above) assume on the part of the poets a general interest in social and political issues as well as in the conflicts, real or apparent, between science and religion, I know of no specific analysis of the extent to which political beliefs or current social values affected the quality of Victorian verse as a whole. There have been, of course, separate accounts of the individual poets — estimates of Tennyson's conservatism, Browning's self-avowed "liberalism," Kipling's jingoism, Elizabeth Barrett's view of woman's rights, Swinburne's revolt from domesticity, and Patmore's respect for the well-ordered home. But we need a more exact knowledge of the relations between the poetry generally and the politics and social conventions of the age, and of the actual role played by the various concepts of democracy, urban living, marriage, and the family in shaping the verse.

That the Victorian poet, to his credit or discredit, did feel a peculiar social responsibility has seemed evident to readers almost from the beginning, though little effort has been made to define the sanctions of his obligation. As long ago as 1870, Alfred Austin in a peevish review of contemporary verse strove to correlate "the feminine, timorous, narrow, domesticated temper of the times, and ... the feminine, narrow, domesticated, timorous Poetry of the Period." In our own time E. D. H. Johnson's *The Alien Vision of*

Victorian Poetry: Sources of the Poetic Imagination in Tennyson, Browning, and Arnold (1952), with far greater insight and patience and far better taste, has examined the problem of the poet's social orientation, though not of his social values. Each of the three poets, according to Professor Johnson, possessed unique gifts of intuition and sensibility, an inner awareness of the demands of art; yet each was somehow driven to compromise with outer forces in the alien unaesthetic world of Victorian society; and each at last sacrificed his status as a pure poet to become a man of letters. So approached, the great Victorians appear temperamentally opposed to the "basic ideology" of an age which "assumed automatic conformity with its dictates"; they seem "lonely and unassimilated figures," able to assert their true emotion only through devious strategem, whereby their work, always on the surface "blandly complacent," at its deepest may move in dark troubled undercurrents of unconventional and indeed anti-social meaning. Professor Johnson presents a fresh and provocative reading of many poems staled by familiarity and a salutary reminder that the poets were capable of independent thought and feeling. Yet his central thesis is open to question, insofar as it presupposes a singular homogeneity in the social order, overstresses the indirection and ambiguity of much of the verse, and tends to ignore the fact that poets of every age have assailed materialism and that overt or concealed attacks on social conventions need not imply radical maladjustment to the cultural milieu. His argument should therefore, it seems to me, be weighed against that of Vivian de Sola Pinto, who works from a quite contrary premise. Concerned with the divorce of the twentieth-century poet from an inimical society, Professor Pinto, in his *Crisis in English Poetry* (1951), contends that the major Victorians, the last heirs of the great legacies of a Christian and humanistic culture, could still bridge the inner and outer worlds, could still find shared values and symbols and so achieve social communication. Like Chaucer and Spenser and Milton, Tennyson and Browning "could be 'realistic' in their poetry because the world around them, in spite of many shortcomings, was not hostile to poetry, and they could be meditative and introspective because their inner life was enriched by a great and living tradition." Though such a judgment, suggesting too high a degree of contented conformity, requires no less supporting evidence than Professor Johnson's view, it permits a more direct appraisal of the verse; it postulates a broad cultural continuity rather than a single basic social "ideology"; and it invites a sympathetic analysis of the conventions which, however private may have been the poets' vision, did help determine both the form and content of the poetry and which the poets frequently accepted without apparent constraint.

VII. THE FORM OF VICTORIAN POETRY

"The real case against mid-Victorian poetry, other than Tennyson's," writes F. W. Bateson in *English Poetry and the English Language* (1934), "is not that it rests upon a mistaken basis of theory but that it is badly written." Tennyson, Mr. Bateson concedes, did all he could with words, but his time, confusing "a language of the heart and a language of the head," was against any real precision combined with profundity. The other poets, satisfied with vague connotation where precise denotation was required, rested, we are told, in the conviction that the content of their verse, not the style, was all-important; for "the subject was the red herring of Victorian criticism." Whether or not poetic form has become at times the red herring of modern criticism, many modern readers echo the charge that Victorian poetry is formally deficient and ineffective. In a shapeless essay in his *Criticism and the Nineteenth Century* (1951), Geoffrey Tillotson explains that the poets, interested above all in change and development, had little respect for the concept of perfection and most of their work accordingly appears as but unshaped thinking in process, with "the quality of things purposefully on the move." More explicitly E. M. W. Tillyard in *Poetry Direct and Oblique* (1934) argues that the nineteenth century, with too little regard for a sound rhetorical convention, discarded the poetry of statement in order to practice the obliquities of symbolism and so broke "the general social nexus of versifying." Cleanth Brooks, on the other hand, finds Victorian poetry not too oblique but too direct, insufficiently paradoxical and ambiguous, lacking in metaphoric complexity. In an able chapter contributed to Hardin Craig's *History of English Literature* (1950), Joseph Warren Beach rejects much of the New Critical attack as unsatisfactory, yet argues that "by and large, most nineteenth-century poets made what Brooks calls the 'frontal approach' to their subject. They undertook to convey their sense directly with a verbal notation common to all discourse in prose and verse," and they therefore achieved "a dispersed and fluent rather than close-knit texture." Contradictory as they are, each of these judgments surely has at least partial basis in fact, but none extends far beyond a personal prejudice or impression; none fully acknowledges the variety of forms and styles within Victorian poetry or indicates an objective means of assessing the multiple evidence the poets have left behind.

If a defense of the manner and method of the verse is possible at all, it must counter the generalized and rather imprecise hostility with specific analyses and elucidations. Lionel Stevenson in a stimulating article, "The Pertinacious Victorian Poets" (*University of Toronto Quarterly*, 1952), has indicated the need for a much closer attention to the aesthetic values of the poetry and, working from a few definite examples, has himself attempted to show that the best poets were neither incomplete philosophers nor pretentious moralizers but essentially serious craftsmen whose "creative imagination embodied itself in significant symbols which were shaped through a mingling of personal emotion and traditional themes." It is no longer enough to declare, as did H. J. C. Grierson in his *Lyrical Poetry of the Nineteenth Century* (1929) — without giving us detailed description of the art and artifice—that Tennyson and Browning were "very great and cunning artists"; nor is it now possible to announce that "the century of the Metaphysical lyric was the nineteenth," unless one is prepared to challenge established concepts of what constitutes the Metaphysical idiom. In the general revival of interest in Victorian literature, problems of poetic form and imagery have received little dispassionate scrutiny, and the major poetic genres have been frequently slighted. We now have Elisabeth W. Schneider's highly competent prosodic analysis, "Sprung Rhythm: a Chapter in the Evolution of Nineteenth-Century Verse" (*PMLA*, 1965), and Robert Langbaum's excellent monograph, *The Poetry of Experience: The Dramatic Monologue in Modern Literary Tradition* (1957), a book as remarkable for its philosophic grasp of the mood of Victorian poetry in general as for its detailed discussions of the monologue form. But we still might learn a good deal from fresh scholarly estimates of the Victorian verse novel, the narrative poem, the elegy, and the ballad, and from prosodic analyses of standard measures. In *The Pathetic Fallacy in the Nineteenth Century* (1942), for example, Josephine Miles shows us what may be accomplished by focusing on a single poetic device as used by the Romantics and the Victorians. Drawing on statistical counts and tabulations, Professor Miles demonstrates, perhaps contrary to our expectation, a marked decline in the frequency of pathetic fallacy beginning with Tennyson and the early Victorians, a new though sharply limited use thereof, and a clear tendency to closer direct perception of nature, "a plainly developing literal vision." The Victorians, we are told, learned to state emotion by indirection, by reference to the associations of objects, and so achieved a poetry of the senses, of shapes and colors, without immediate relation to subjective feeling. Thus Ruskin, who coined the term, furthered rather than initiated the disrepute into which the pathetic fallacy fell, for "the turning point was reached practically by Tennyson before it was reached critically by Ruskin."

At the risk of promoting the "intentional fallacy," which modern critics have found even less acceptable than the pathetic, we must, I believe, consider the "intentions" of the poets, their aesthethetic principles and purposes in writing, if we are to reach any reasonable estimate of their successes or failures, or indeed if we are to understand the proportions and tensions of their work. Despite the fact, however, that we have had several sound studies of the major aestheticians (including Henry Ladd's critique of Ruskin, *The Victorian Morality of Art,* 1932), our knowledge of Victorian aesthetics remains on the whole quite inadequate. The general study by Alba H. Warren, Jr., *English Poetic Theory*

(1825–1865) *(1950)*, therefore, though it makes no pretense at startling discovery, serves as a most useful review of a large body of relevant materials. After a broad survey of the early Victorian criticism, Mr. Warren limits himself to a close analysis — by paraphrase and commentary — of nine representative essays. Behind each of these he sees the dominant influence either of Wordsworth's theory of imitation, which he describes as "Aristotelian," or of Coleridge's concern with expression and subjective idealism, which he calls "Baconian." The tenets of the critics were, he shows, frequently contradictory and inconsistent: to some art was clearly less than "reality"; to others it was in essence a revelation of the highest truth; a few saw science as the provider of new facts and new modes of scrutiny; others derided it as a complete denial of spirit; many demanded individuality of style, but nearly all feared personal eccentricity of statement. Yet there were also certain common critical assumptions and recurrent emphases. The theorists as a group believed the poet responsible not only to his own vision but to the world of men and things about him; they rejected didacticism but stressed the social value, the "morality," of art and its capacity to teach by indirection; they were accordingly less interested in formalistic matters than in psychological and moral values, in the communication of ideas and emotions; they regarded poetry, in short, as important to "the economy of the good life." Insofar as the poets presumably shared this conviction, Mr. Warren rightly assumes that an acquaintance with the theory should assist us toward a more satisfactory assessment of the verse, but he chooses merely to present the doctrine rather than to trace its literary consequences. Thus since other scholars have largely ignored the problem, the precise relation between the Victorian aesthetic and the practice of the Victorian poets remains for the most part unexplored, if not entirely unsuspected.

Whatever else it may have accomplished, our survey of the research devoted to the general themes and problems of Victorian poetry should by now have indicated that, though much has been taken — or rather given — by scholars and critics, much abides for elucidation and appraisal. In the chapters that follow we shall see how the more significant poets have fared individually under twentieth-century critical analysis. But at the outset it should hardly be necessary to remark that we are now in a position to know more of their careers and personalities than we know of any earlier literary group; for the Victorians were virtually the first children of a self-conscious modern world eager to document and publicize its activities, and as such they have left behind countless books of reminiscence, as well as official lives and authorized memoirs, reams of correspondence to, from, and about their literary masters, records of table talk and public interviews, portraits and photographs and caricatures, picture-books of the poets' haunts and homes, full and often fulsome obituaries. Yet the essential character of all but a few of the poets eludes us; we know scarcely any of them as we know, or think we know, each of the major Romantics. Sir Charles Tennyson has given us a rich and sympathetic yet wholly candid life of his grandfather; but we have had no modern lives on a comparable scale of Browning, Arnold, or Swinburne. We need fresh biographies, assimilating the many sources at our disposal, showing us the poets at work as poets, rather than merely supplying amusement through chronicles of eccentricities different from our own. For our primary concern as students of literature must rest with the poetic sensibility and the poetry itself and not with the adjuncts of literary history. We must not, of course, be unduly intimidated by the expressed desire of the major poets to detach their private lives wholly from their verse; but we may respect their sense of the autonomy of art, their will to make their performance the ultimate gauge of their value. And we may be helped toward the proper realization that their work was indeed the essence of their real selves, if we take as representative of their attitude the statement of a fellow-Victorian, who was also in his way something of the artist. "I have now mentioned all the books which I have published," wrote Charles Darwin at the close of his brief autobiography, "and these have been the milestones of my life, so that little remains to be said."

Alfred,
Lord Tennyson

E. D. H. JOHNSON

Posterity has accepted the Victorian view of Tennyson as the representative literary figure of his age and the leading spokesman of its values. As a result, the fluctuations of his fame constitute a kind of barometer for gauging the response to that age by succeeding generations of readers. With the "rediscovery" of the Victorians in the period after the Second World War, Tennyson's place among the major English poets has been increasingly acknowledged. It is with the swelling body of scholarly and critical testimony in support of this eminence that the present survey is primarily concerned. The section on Tennyson in *Bibliographies of Twelve Victorian Authors,* compiled by Theodore G. Ehrsam, Robert H. Deily, and Robert M. Smith (1936), contains a detailed and accurate listing of early Tennysonian scholarship, together with references to reviews of the more important works. Paull F. Baum's discussion of Tennyson in the first edition of *The Victorian Poets: A Guide to Research,* edited by Frederic E. Faverty (1956), assesses a number of previous studies for which room cannot here be found.

I. MANUSCRIPTS AND OTHER SOURCE MATERIAL

In England the most important repository of Tennyson manuscripts is the Library of Trinity College, Cambridge, to which Hallam, Lord Tennyson presented more than a dozen of his father's manuscript books. The use of this material remains restricted under the stringent conditions imposed at the time of the bequest in deference to the poet's opposition to the publication of what he called "chips of the workshop." An outgrowth of The Tennyson Society, founded in 1960, has been the establishment of the Tennyson Research Centre, opened in 1965 in The City Library of Lincoln. This contains a number of manuscripts and a large collection of proofs and trial copies corrected in the poet's own hand, as well as 700 volumes from his father's and 3,000 from his own library, together with a complete collection of first editions of the poems and extensive family correspondence. Included in the archive is one of the most complete manuscripts of *In Memoriam.* The Tennyson Society has also formed a Publications Board.[1]

The Cambridge University Library holds two manuscript books, subject to the same restrictions as those in force at Trinity College; and the Fitzwilliam Museum of Cambridge University is custodian of James M. Heath's Commonplace Book, the greater part of which is devoted to fair copies of pre-publication versions of early poems by Tennyson, including a number of sections from *In Memoriam.* Other manuscript material is located in the British Museum, the Bodleian Library, the Brotherton Collection of the University of Leeds, and the National Library of Scotland.

The indisputable center for Tennyson research in the United States is the Houghton Library of Harvard University, which in 1954 augmented its already extensive holdings by the magnificent collection hitherto in the possession of the poet's grandson, Sir Charles Tennyson. This acquisition is described by William A. Jackson in *The Houghton Library Report of Accessions for the Year (1954–1955)*, and more fully, with an index and first lines of poems, by Edgar F. Shannon, Jr., and William H. Bond in the *Harvard Library Bulletin* (1956). The papers, including 650 drafts of 350 poems, are contained in seventy-two notebooks, 275 folders of loose manuscripts, and forty-two additional folders largely biographical in interest. They cover the entire period of Tennyson's productive career, about three-quarters of the material appearing in the poet's autograph.

In addition to the holdings in numerous private American collections, there are manuscripts in the Yale University Library, the Pierpont Morgan Library, the Berg Collection of the New York Public Library, and the Henry E. Huntington Library. Mention should also be made of the Tennyson Collection, largely assembled

---

[1]In October 1967 The Tennyson Society published the first number of the *Tennyson Research Bulletin,* which provides a very full account of research in progress or recently completed throughout the world.

by Templeton Crocker, presented to the University of Virginia (1961) in honor of President Edgar F. Shannon, Jr., and of the seventeen consecutive editions of *The Princess* in the Duke University Library.

A catalogue of all the poetical manuscripts of Tennyson is being compiled by Rowland L. Collins and Thomas J. Collins. Edgar F. Shannon, Jr., and Cecil Y. Lang are preparing an edition of the poet's widely dispersed correspondence.

II. BIBLIOGRAPHY

The standard work on the subject remains the two volumes by Thomas J. Wise, *A Bibliography of the Writings of Alfred, Lord Tennyson* (privately printed, 1908) .[2] This bibliography must, of course, be used with caution in light of the disclosures in John Carter and Graham Pollard's *An Enquiry into the Nature of Certain Nineteenth Century Pamphlets* (1934) , and in Wilfred Partington's *Thomas J. Wise in the Original Cloth* (1946 — with an earlier version, entitled *Forging Ahead,* published in 1939) . Wise's bibliography is augmented by entries in volumes VII, VIII, and IX of *The Ashley Library: A Catalogue* (1922–1936) . For H. Buxton Forman's authorship of "The Building of the *Idylls:* A Study in Tennyson," in volume II of *Literary Anecdotes of the Nineteenth Century: Contributions towards a Literary History of the Period,* edited by W. Robertson Nicoll and Thomas J. Wise (1896) , see *Between the Lines: Letters and Memoranda Interchanged by H. Buxton Forman and Thomas J. Wise,* with an introductory essay and notes by Fannie E. Ratchford (1945) . Also

[2] A facsimile reprint appeared in 1967.

36

of interest is *Letters of Thomas J. Wise to John Henry Wrenn: A Further Inquiry into the Guilt of Certain Nineteenth-Century Forgers*, edited by Fannie E. Ratchford (1944). An appendix to this work lists the Tennyson forgeries in the Wrenn Library of the University of Texas.

Still useful are two bibliograpical studies, published anonymously by Richard H. Shepherd: *Tennysoniana: Notes Bibliographical and Critical* (1866; second edition revised and enlarged, 1879), which includes information about Tennyson's literary relationships and an appendix listing important reviews and criticisms from 1829; and *The Bibliography of Tennyson . . . from 1827 to 1894 Inclusive* (1896), with an appendix outlining a "scheme for a Final and Definitive Edition" in fifteen volumes.

The pioneer work of Shepherd and Wise will in time be superseded by the definitive bibliography under preparation by William H. Bond, Librarian of the Houghton Library of Harvard University. Essential for scholars is the extensive bibliography of Tennyson, compiled by William D. Paden and Donald Low for the new edition of *CBEL*. Also scheduled for publication is *A Tennyson Bibliography: A Selected and Annotated List of Publications in English through 1964* by Sir Charles Tennyson and Christine Fall.

D. Barron Brightwell's *Concordance* of Tennyson's writings (1869) was supplanted by Arthur E. Baker's *A Concordance to the Poetical and Dramatic Works of Alfred, Lord Tennyson* (1914, reissued 1965), and its supplement, *A Concordance to "The Devil and the Lady"* (1931). Baker also compiled *A Tennyson Dictionary* [1916].

The student of Tennyson may still consult with profit two early guides: Morton Luce's *A Handbook to the Works of Alfred, Lord Tennyson* (1895; revised edition, 1914), which takes up the poems title by title in the order of the table of contents of the one-volume Macmillan edition; and W. Macneile Dixon's *A Primer of Tennyson, with a Critical Essay* (1896 and later), including a tabulation of dates, a bibliography, and an incomplete listing of editions, translations, reviews, and other writings on the poet from 1827 through 1894. *A Tennyson Handbook* (1963) by George O. Marshall, Jr., is regrettably superficial, designed ostensibly for undergraduate use.

Jelle Postma's *Tennyson as Seen by His Parodists* (1926) contains a bibliography of parodies.

III. EDITIONS

There is no fully satisfactory edition of Tennyson's poetry. The best is the "Eversley Edition," edited by Hallam, Lord Tennyson with notes supplied by the poet (London, 1907–1908, nine volumes; New York, 1908, six volumes). This edition was subsequently issued in substantially the same form as a single volume without separate title pages, but with a Memoir by the editor (1913 and later). The "Cambridge Edition" of *The Poetic and Dramatic Works of Alfred, Lord Tennyson,* edited by William J. Rolfe (1898), does not contain the posthumous volume, *The Death of Oenone and Other Poems,* but includes many poems not printed in most standard editions, together with a bibliography of the poet's works, valuable notes, and extensive collations illustrating the extent to which Tennyson revised many of his early poems. The "Oxford Edition" of *Poems of Tennyson, 1830–1868,* edited by Sir T. Herbert Warren (1913 and later), gives the table of contents of each volume published between the dates indicated, and provides an appendix of suppressed poems. This collection should not be confused with the Oxford Standard Authors edition of *The Poetical Works, including the Plays* (1953, and later under the title, *Poems and Plays*), which, while more complete, presents an unreliable text and is without notes or bibliographical aids.

Christopher Ricks has completed for the series of Longmans Annotated Poets a much fuller edition of Tennyson (exclusive of the plays) than any previously undertaken. This establishes the texts of all of the poems, exhaustively annotated and with all of the variants in phrasing in published versions of the works, and gives a comprehensive selection of variant readings from the available manuscripts. Another edition of the poems has been undertaken by John Jones for the Oxford English Texts series.

Collected editions of Tennyson's poetry should be supplemented by two volumes of juvenile work, edited by the poet's grandson, Sir Charles Tennyson: *The Devil and the Lady* (1930), an unfinished verse drama of astonishing precocity, written at the age of fourteen; and *Unpublished Early Poems* (1932), derived from manuscripts inherited from Hallam, Lord Tennyson.[3] A facsimile reproduction of these volumes was issued in 1964, with a foreword by Rowland L. Collins. In the first half of a two-part article in *VS* (1961), William D. Paden attributes to Tennyson "upon circumstantial probability and internal evidence," eleven anonymous poems (ten printed in their entirety), which he located in the pages of the *Atheneum* for 1828–1829. A good many poems and fragments made their first appearance in the biographies of the poet by Hallam, Lord Tennyson and by Sir Charles Tennyson. Additional verses by Tennyson, hitherto unpublished, are printed by Christopher Ricks under the following titles: "Tennyson's 'Rifle Clubs!!!'" (*RES*, 1964); "Tennyson: Three Notes" (*MP*, 1964); and "Two Early Poems by Tennyson" (*VP*, 1965). In a letter to *TLS* of 3 June 1965 William Hardie gives a manuscript version of "The Charge of the Light Brigade" that differs significantly from the authorized form.

Among other editions of the poems of continuing interest to the Tennyson scholar are the following. In 1893 Hallam, Lord Tennyson issued a facsimile edition of *Poems of Two Brothers* (1827), with additional hitherto unpublished poems forming part of the 1827 manuscript. This edition contains attributions of authorship among Alfred, Charles, and Frederick. *Early Poems of Alfred, Lord Tennyson* [through 1842], edited by J. Churton Collins (1900), with a critical introduction, collations, and notes, includes an appendix which distinguishes between the poems later reprinted

---

[3]The substance of this collection Sir Charles had earlier presented with somewhat fuller notes in the first two of four articles in *Nineteenth Century and After* (March and April, 1931). The May and June issues of the same periodical print for the period after 1842 a number of unpublished poems and variants of published works.

and those which did not appear after the volumes of 1830 and 1832. In 1902 the same editor published a volume containing *In Memoriam, The Princess,* and *Maud,* with an equally full textual and critical commentary. Joseph C. Thomson edited *Tennyson's Suppressed Poems: Now for the First Time Collected* (1903) ; in the following year this volume was reissued in "The Papyrus Series" as *Suppressed Poems of Alfred, Lord Tennyson, 1830–1832. Famous Editions of English Poets,* edited by John O. Beaty and John W. Bowyer (1931), contains a reprint of *Poems, 1842.* The poet himself assisted in choosing *A Selection from the Works of Alfred Tennyson,* published in Moxon's Miniature Poets (1865).

With the increasing accessibility of manuscripts, Tennyson scholars have begun to turn to textual commentary. Noteworthy research in this vein includes the following articles. In the April, May, and June issues of *Cornhill Magazine* for 1936, Sir Charles published three instalments of "Tennyson Papers." The first of these describes in detail the contents of James M. Heath's Commonplace Book, with extensive quotations from versions of Tennyson's poems there transcribed. The two succeeding articles explore manuscript readings of the early stages of *Idylls of the King* (reprinted in *Six Tennyson Essays,* 1954), and of *The Princess.* Edgar F. Shannon, Jr.'s investigation of "The Proofs of 'Gareth and Lynette' in the Widener Collection" (*Papers of the Bibliographical Society of America,* 1947) is extended to a detailed study of manuscript changes by Joan E. Hartman in "The Manuscripts of Tennyson's 'Gareth and Lynette' " (*Harvard Library Bulletin,* 1959). In 1949 Mary J. Donahue (Ellmann) published in *PMLA* an important article, entitled "Tennyson's 'Hail, Briton!' and 'Tithon' in the Heath Manuscript." The first section relates Tennyson's early political poem, "Hail, Briton!" to *In Memoriam* and "Ode on the Death of the Duke of Wellington"; the second half argues that "Tithon" is to be regarded as the initial version of "Tithonus." A number of the readings here presented are corrected by Christopher Ricks (*RES,* 1964). Two additional articles by Mary J. Donahue (Ellmann) compare printed texts of poems with the versions in the Heath Manuscript: "The Revision of Tennyson's 'Sir Galahad' " (*PQ,* 1949) ; and "Tennyson: Revision of *In Memoriam,* Section 85" (*MLN,* 1950).

Of great interest as indicating the varieties of textual problems which confront the editor of Tennyson is William D. Paden's "A Note on the Variants of *In Memoriam* and 'Lucretius' " (*Library*, 1953). The author tabulates the changes in the printed editions of *In Memoriam* through 1884. In a letter to the Editor of *Library* (1963), Christopher Ricks augments Paden's listing by four additional variants in Tennyson's elegy; and *Library* (1965) contains a footnote to "Lucretius" also by Ricks. Edgar F. Shannon, Jr., provides a model of textual scholarship for future editors in "The History of a Poem: Tennyson's 'Ode on the Death of the Duke of Wellington' " (*Studies in Bibliography*, 1960). The writer summarizes his method and conclusions as follows: "An account of the composition, reception, and revision of the poem and an appendix of variorum readings will illustrate Tennyson's scrupulous craftsmanship and his increasing willingness, as poet laureate, to speak affirmatively to the people." Christopher Ricks contributes a correction to Shannon's findings in "A Note on Tennyson's 'Ode on the Death of the Duke of Wellington' " (*Studies in Bibliography*, 1965). The same issue of this publication prints William D. Paden's admirably detailed "Tennyson's 'The Lover's Tale,' R. H. Shepherd and T. J. Wise."

IV. BIOGRAPHY

The indispensable sources of knowledge of Tennyson's life are the official biographies by his son and grandson. *Alfred, Lord Tennyson: A Memoir by His Son* [Hallam, Lord Tennyson] (two volumes, 1897; one vol. edition with some additions, 1899) is a nobly conceived and executed work which, despite its reticence about more intimate aspects of family history, remains the most authoritative approach to the poet. For his portrait of his father Hallam drew on the still more extensive "Materials for a Life of A. T." (four volumes, privately printed [1895]), copies of which are in the British Museum and in the Lilly Library of Indiana University, as well as at the Tennyson Research Centre. The *Memoir* was supplemented by *Tennyson and His Friends,* edited by Hallam, Lord Tennyson (1911), which collects under various headings reminiscences of the poet by many of his close associates.

In writing *Alfred Tennyson* (1949), Sir Charles Tennyson utilized family papers and other private sources to throw much new light on the poet, especially his home life and early career. This is an admirably candid and well-proportioned biography, factual in emphasis but containing much judicious criticism. Sir Charles has continued to publish articles further documenting his grandfather's life, principal among which are: "Alfred's Father" (*Cornhill Magazine,* 1936); "Tennyson's Conversation" (*Twentieth Century,* 1959), with quotations from the notebook which Hallam kept while a schoolboy at Marlborough; and "The Somersby Tennysons," which appeared, together with Rowland L. Collins' catalogue of the Frederick Tennyson Collection in the Lilly Library of Indiana University, as the first publication of The Tennyson Society in the Christmas Supplement of *VS* (1963). See also Sir Charles' "The Somersby Tennysons: A Postscript" (*VS,* 1966).

The most recent biography is Joanna Richardson's *The Pre-Eminent Victorian: A Study in Tennyson* (1962). This accurate and extremely readable account of the poet's life reflects the present shift in focus from the tormented early years to the long heyday of the laureateship. The writer made use, among other unpublished materials, of about four hundred letters from Emily Tennyson to her sister and niece, Anne and Agnes Weld, as well as of Lady Tennyson's manuscript diary. The bibliography constitutes an unusually comprehensive handlist of contemporary works in which references to Tennyson are to be found. Further delightfully informal glimpses of the poet occur in "Gosse's Candid 'Snapshots'," by Paul F. Matheisen (*VS,* 1965).

Promised for the near future is a study of the relationship between Tennyson and Queen Victoria by Sir Charles Tennyson and Hope Dyson. This volume derives from unpublished letters at Lincoln and Windsor. Because the author's argument is based on the discovery of important new facts about Tennyson's early life, mention should also here be made of Ralph W. Rader's *Maud: The Biographical Genesis* (1963) , which is discussed in Section IX.

Since other accounts of Tennyson's life are, in the main, derivative and primarily important for their critical observations, they will be treated under Section VII, General Studies.

V. REPUTATION

The study of Tennyson's contemporary reputation was inaugurated by Thomas R. Lounsbury, *The Life and Times of Tennyson* [from 1809 to 1850], edited by Wilbur L. Cross (1915) . Although he left it incomplete and unrevised at the time of his death, Lounsbury's work is still worth reading for the sensitivity of its criticism and for its veracious evocation of the critical climate conditioning Tennyson's early career. His contention that the poet's revisions were dictated by artistic considerations rather than by the disapprobation of critics is reaffirmed by Joyce Green in "Tennyson's Development during the 'Ten Years' Silence' (1832–1842) " (*PMLA,* 1951) .

A somewhat different estimate of Tennyson's relation to his critics was advanced by Edgar F. Shannon, Jr.'s "Tennyson and the Reviewers, 1830–1842" (*PMLA,* 1943) . In greatly expanded form, Shannon's findings are presented in *Tennyson and the Reviewers: A Study of His Literary Reputation and of the Influence of the Critics upon his Poetry, 1827–1851* (1952) . This work, which remains definitive on its subject, argues first, that the early reviews were less hostile than had been generally assumed, and second, that, although Tennyson took his cue from critical strictures both in revising and in his choice of themes, he did so less to court popularity than from a growing disposition to subscribe to his age's belief in the prophetic role of the great poet.

Shannon extended his important research to include an exhaustive study of "The Critical Reception of Tennyson's *Maud*" (*PMLA*, 1953). On the basis of eighty-five reviews of the poem published during the three and one-half years after its publication, as well as of revisions in the text, the author reaches the conclusion that in *Maud* Tennyson misjudged his audience, projecting the theme "too deeply into the realms of abnormal psychology, politics, and opinion."

A number of other articles have taken up Tennyson's relationship to his public. William D. Paden in "Tennyson and the Reviewers (1829–1835)" (*University of Kansas Publications, Humanistic Studies,* 1940), disagrees with Lounsbury in the light of additional information. Paul F. Jamieson in "Tennyson and his Audience in 1832" (*PQ,* 1952), suggests that Tennyson found a sympathetic audience for his early poetry among the Cambridge Apostles, who were indoctrinated with Wordworth's belief that it is the function of a sympathetic literary coterie to mediate between the poet and his public. John O. Eidson in "The Reception of Tennyson's Plays in America" (*PQ,* 1956), dates the decline of Tennyson's American reputation from the stage productions of his dramas. In "The Poet as Critic: Appraisals of Tennyson by His Contemporaries" (*Tennessee Studies in Literature,* 1962), Clyde de L. Ryals marshals evidence to show that the generally adulatory opinions of Tennyson's poetic contemporaries anticipated much twentieth-century criticism. William D. Templeman devotes a long and significant article to "A Consideration of the Fame of 'Locksley Hall'" (*VP,* 1963). Because of the extensive list of works cited, this piece is, in effect, a detailed review of Tennyson's popularity and wide influence down to the present day.

Three unpublished doctoral disserations deal with issues influencing the poet's position vis-à-vis his age: Helen Pearce's "The Criticism of Tennyson's Poetry: A Summary with Special Emphasis upon Tennyson's Response to Criticism as a Factor in the Development of His Reputation," University of California (1930); Walter B. Scott's "Tennyson and His Age, 1850–1875," Princeton

University (1934) ; and Mary J. Donahue (Ellmann) 's "Tennyson: Studies in the Ten Years' Silence (1833–1842) ," Yale University (1946) . The last and most important of these advances the theory that Hallam's death may actually have stimulated Tennyson into heightened creativity.

In *Tennyson in America: His Reputation and Influence from 1827 to 1858* (1943) , John O. Eidson, who is continuing his investigations, provides a fully documented survey of Tennysons' fame in the United States during the first thirty years of his career. The author adduces testimony to show that Tennyson rose to popularity in this country earlier than in England, and that the American response was notably independent of British criticism. Appendices list the American editions of Tennyson's poems, 1827–1858, and reviews in American magazines and newspapers. Chapter six of Cornelius Weygandt's *The Time of Tennyson: English Victorian Poetry as It Affected America* (1936) gives a lively account of Tennyson's great and continuing vogue with the American reading public.

Tennyson in France (1930) , by Marjorie Bowden, traces the poet's fortunes in that country. The bibliography lists both English texts and translations, as well as critical notices.

VI. INFLUENCES

The breadth of literary reference in Tennyson's poetry has invited continuing exploration of sources, the majority of which are cited in the notes to standard editions. Research in this field has concentrated primarily on the poet's debt to the classics and to writers of the Romantic era.

J. Churton Collins' *Illustrations of Tennyson* (1891) and Wilfred P. Mustard's *Classical Echoes in Tennyson* (1904) present Tennyson's poetry against a background of reading in the classics that few modern scholars can hope to rival. A notable exception is Douglas Bush's *Mythology and the Romantic Tradition in English Poetry* (1937), chapter six of which gives the fullest recent account of Tennyson's relationship to Greek and Latin writers. In his witty and incisive discussion, an expansion of a previous article, "The Personal Note in Tennyson's Classical Poems" (*UTQ*, 1935), Bush reaches the conclusion: "In the verse of classical inspiration — and that includes hundreds of scattered lines and phases — we have less of Tennyson's weakness and more of his strength than in any other part of his work, except . . . the small body of perfect lyrics. For the classical themes generally banished from his mind what was timid, parochial, sentimental, inadequately philosophical, and evoked his special gifts and his most authentic emotions, his rich and wistful sense of the past, his love of nature, and his power of style."

Among more specialized studies the following merit attention: Sir T. Herbert Warren's "Virgil and Tennyson: A Literary Parallel," in *Essays of Poets and Poetry Ancient and Modern* (1909); and two comparisons of Tennyson and Lucretius — Katharine Allen's "Lucretius the Poet, and Tennyson's Poem 'Lucretius' " (*Poet-Lore*, 1899), and Ortha L. Wilner's "Tennyson and Lucretius" (*Classical Journal*, 1930). "Brief though Tennyson's poem is," states Wilner, "it repeats, in the form of a dramatic monologue, the great scientific and moral doctrines of the six books of the *De Rerum Natura* in such a way as to leave a true impression of Lucretius, the poet, the scientist, the moralist." In "Some Ancient Light on Tennyson's 'Oenone' " (*JEGP*, 1962), Paul Turner explores with impressive learning Tennyson's borrowings from Homer, Aeschylus, Bion, Theocritus, Virgil, Ovid, Horace, and Catullus, as well as Wordsworth, Shelley, and Keats: "Throughout the poem . . . Tennyson's method has been to pick out those images, phrases, and conventions in earlier literature which seemed to possess most poetic intensity; to refine them by eliminating prosaic or merely realistic details; and to combine them into a continuous whole."

Edna M. Robinson's *Tennyson's Use of the Bible* (1917) is the most comprehensive work on the subject. In "Alfred Tennyson as a Celticist" (*MP*, 1921), Tom P. Cross finds that "Tennyson responded as heartily to the early nineteenth-century revival of Celtic antiquities as he did to other phases of contemporary investigation," making "an honest effort to ground his *Idylls* on the most reputable authorities of his day." The poet's use of Welsh settings and literary sources is also documented by Herbert G. Wright in *Essays and Studies* (1929). J. H. Gray's " 'The Lady of Shalott' and Tennyson's Readings in the Supernatural" (*N&Q*, 1965), calls attention to the poet's knowledge of Irish fairy lore. Further evidence of Tennyson's receptivity to new ideas is supplied by Richard P. Benton, who concludes in "Tennyson and Lao-Tzu" (*Philosophy East and West*, 1962), that John Chalmers' translation of Lao-Tzu in 1868 supplied the poet not only with "certain Taoist technical terms," but also with many of "the basic tenets of Taoism" for incorporation into "The Ancient Sage." Tennyson's familiarity with Dante, while often noted, has yet to be fully examined. Sir T. Herbert Warren has a good piece on the topic in *Essays of Poets and Poetry Ancient and Modern* (1909).

Part One of George Ford's *Keats and the Victorians: A Study of His Influence and Rise to Fame, 1821–1895* (1944) presents the fullest account of Tennyson's debt to his principal Romantic progenitor. In an unpublished doctoral dissertation, "Tennyson and Expressive Art: The Relationship between Tennyson's Early Poetry and Nineteenth-Century Esthetic Theory," Princeton University (1965), James L. Hill convincingly argues that the influence of both Shelley and Keats on the youthful poet has been exaggerated. D. G. James's provocative Warton Lecture on "Wordsworth and Tennyson" (*Proceedings of the British Academy*, (1950), compares *The Prelude* with *In Memoriam* to the discredit of the latter: "Wordsworth is greater than Tennyson because in his poetry the criticism of life (which is not an affair of doctrine but of perception and vision) is profounder and a richer enablement of life." In "Tennyson, Browning, and a Romantic Fallacy" (*UTQ*, 1944), Lionel Stevenson considers Shelley's short-lived influence on the poet. Patricia M. Ball, "Tennyson and the Romantics" (*VP*, 1963), maintains that Tennyson inherited the Romantic "crisis of personality," sharing with the preceding generation of poets its "basic fascination with the issue of human identity as revealed by the individual's experience of others, of objects, and of himself in relation to these." Goethe's doctrine of *Steigerung* provides the basis for an interesting comparison between the evolutionary theories of the German poet and Tennyson by Lore Metzger in "The Eternal Process: Some Parallels between Goethe's *Faust* and Tennyson's *In Memoriam*" (*VP*, 1963).

William D. Templeman argues convincingly in an article printed in *Booker Memorial Studies; Eight Essays on Victorian Literature,* edited by Hill Shine (1950), that the central situation of "Locksley Hall" was derived from Book Two of *Sartor Resartus.* Charles R. Sanders, who notes that there is need for a study of "the full impact of Carlyle's mind on Tennyson's poetry," supplies from unpublished correspondence by Carlyle essential material towards this end in an article in *PMLA* (1961).

Surprisingly little attention has as yet been devoted to tracing Tennyson's influence on other writers. Lawrence Durrell makes a stimulating comparison between "Ulysses" and T. S. Eliot's "Gerontion" in *Key to Modern British Poetry* (1952). Writing "On the Use of Martyrs: Tennyson and Eliot on Thomas Becket" (*UTQ,* 1963), Louise R. Rehak perceptively concludes that "Tennyson's strength . . . is psychological realism and political objectivity. . . . Eliot's, his power of generality and his religious eloquence." Evidence of Henry James's debt to Tennyson's poems is adduced by Miriam Allott, " 'The Lord of Burleigh' and Henry James's 'A Landscape Painter' " (*N&Q,* 1955); and by Giorgio Melchiori, "Locksley Hall Revisited: Tennyson and Henry James" (*REL,* 1965). An article by Anna Krause in *Comparative Literature* (1956) demonstrates the "spiritual kinship" between Tennyson and Unamuno.

In a different vein is George W. Whiting's posthumously published monograph, *The Artist and Tennyson, Rice University Studies* (1964), which offers a detailed, but uncritical listing of nineteenth-century English paintings deriving their subjects from Tennyson's poetry. "The Tennyson of 1857" by Albert B. Friedman, *More Books* (1948), discusses the differing styles of the artists who prepared plates for Moxon's famous illustrated edition of the *Poems,* which, in the author's words, "inaugurates the inspired period of English illustration."

VII. GENERAL STUDIES

The critical reaction against Tennyson, as against Victorianism in general, set in soon after the poet's death and reached its culmination in the decades following the First World War. It was vigorously voiced in two book-length studies published in 1923. The more superficial of these is Hugh I'A. Faussett's *Tennyson: A Modern Portrait,* which presents its subject as an unworldly dreamer whose poetry is intellectually negligible, and who compromised his lyric genius through the vain effort to address himself to the problems of the period. Faussett significantly softens his original judgment in an essay entitled "The Hidden Tennyson" (*Poets and Pundits: Essays and Addresses,* 1947). Here the author admits: "When all that was second-rate in his philosophy, trite in his moralizing or bathos in his sentiment is forgotten, he will be remembered as the supreme lyrical poet of an age whose mortal disease he so deeply sensed and so melodiously assuaged."

In his brilliantly written and extremely influential *Tennyson: Aspects of His Life, Character, and Poetry* (1923), Sir Harold Nicolson set out to rehabilitate the essential Tennyson by pruning his work to meet the requirements of a contemporary audience. To do so, he created the image of two Tennysons: one "a morbid and unhappy mystic" who produced a small quantity of enduringly beautiful poetry; the other the laureate whose integrity as an artist was sacrificed to the demands of his public. Nicolson feels that the poet was emotionally responsive to the temper of his age, but that he was inadequate as a thinker to meet its challenge: "Tennyson is more convincing when he constructs the fabric of doubt, than when he endeavours to demolish this fabric with the tools of Faith." More recently Nicolson has reaffirmed his views somewhat less stringently in "Tennyson: Fifty Years After," *Poetry Review,* 1942 and in *Spectator* for the same year.

49

Two subsequent volumes develop Nicolson's contention that Tennyson spoke in two conflicting voices. Although he presents his evidence more objectively on the testimony of the poetry alone, C. H. O. Scaife, in *The Poetry of Alfred Tennyson: An Essay in Appreciation* (1930), reaches the conclusion: "In our time, at least, we shall never do justice to Tennyson, the poet, until we can separate our judgment from Tennyson, the Victorian." In 1948 Paull F. Baum published *Tennyson Sixty Years After*, which he called "an interim report on his ultimate position as a poet." Baum's analyses of individual poems are often felicitous in their insights, but his work as a whole is invalidated by a barely disguised antipathy to Tennyson's qualities of mind.

Concurrent with the revival of serious interest in the Victorians and notably stimulated by Sir Charles Tennyson's biography, Tennysonian studies entered a new phase in the years after the Second World War. One of the earliest attempts to reconcile historical with critical perspectives in appraising the poet was the chapter devoted to Tennyson in E. D. H. Johnson's *The Alien Vision of Victorian Poetry: Sources of the Poetic Imagination in Tennyson, Browning, and Arnold* (1952). While the author tends to push to reductive extremes his argument that the major Victorian poets sought ways of mediating between their allegiance to the life of the imagination and their sense of prophetic mission, he succeeds in identifying certain unifying motifs which recur throughout Tennyson's poetry — notably dream, madness, trance, and the quest.

The most important extended critical study of the poet which has yet appeared is Jerome H. Buckley's *Tennyson: The Growth of a Poet* (1960). This volume, the first to take advantage of the papers in the Houghton Library, and incorporating as well the most significant findings of contemporary scholars and critics, surveys the entire corpus of Tennyson's poetry in chronological order and scrupulously places it in biographical context. Buckley conclusively abolishes the argument of the Nicolsonian school that the poet's aims were divided: "Yet the distinction that his critics have repeatedly drawn between the bard of public sentiments and the earlier poet of private sensibilities is ultimately untenable. For there was no real break in Tennyson's career; from the beginning he felt some responsibility to the society he lived in, and until the end he remained obedient to the one clear call of his own imagination. . . . His response to the restless activity of his time enhanced rather than weakened his concern with the moment of insight and revelation." The author's claim that Tennyson is to be regarded as a major poet, the greatest in English between Wordsworth and Yeats, is convincingly established in terms of the following attributes: "dedication to the poet's calling, command of his medium, range of vision, capacity for growth, magnitude of performance, and place in a tradition as one who, consciously indebted to a literary past, in turn influences the course of subsequent poetry." The fourth, fifth, and sixth chapters of Buckley's earlier, *The Victorian Temper: A Study in Literary Culture* (1951) relate Tennyson's achievement to the literary history of his age.

The extent to which critical attention has shifted to the work on which Tennyson's contemporary fame rested is indicated by Valerie Pitt's *Tennyson Laureate* (1962), which devotes five chapters to the poet's career from *In Memoriam,* as against only two on the earlier poetry. The author finds that Tennyson "does not represent the Victorian age because he understood it, or was passively complacent either about its virtues or its follies, but because his response to the mood and colour of the period is fuller and more alive than that of any other contemporary poet." There are valuable sections, showing the influence of Carlyle and F. D. Maurice on Tennyson's thought; and the "retrospective shaping" through which the major poems grew into their completed form is carefully traced. "Tennyson's major problem" is shown to have been "that, although there was a body of common sentiment, there was no available poetic convention in which to express it. . . . Tennyson's laureate verse is not, then, the verse of a complacent poet working in an outworn convention, but the vigorous creation of new forms for a new national consciousness, not unlike that of the Elizabethan age." In view of its importance as a contribution to the reappraisal of Tennyson, it is unfortunate that *Tennyson Laureate* is marred by so many factual errors.

Two other recent volumes are less rewarding. Edgar E. Smith, in *The Two Voices: A Tennyson Study* (1964), surveys the poet's work as a series of unresolved tensions between art and society, sense and soul, doubt and faith, past and present, delicacy and strength. The author, who relies extensively on the work of other scholars, applies his categories too rigidly and makes insufficient allowance for Tennyson's artistic development. The title of Clyde de L. Ryals' *Theme and Symbol in Tennyson's Poems to 1850* (1964) is misleading, since the writer does not establish his claim that "Tennyson stands as the major precursor in the first half of the nineteenth century of the modern English symbolists." Ryals is guilty of indiscrimination in his desire to be all-inclusive; and he relies too extensively and uncritically on the theories of Freud and Jung and on literalistic readings of individual poems.

Although directed at the general reader rather than the scholar, J. B. Steane's little volume in the British series, *Literature in Perspective* (1966), provides a well-informed and judicious review of Tennyson's poetic achievement.

This is the place to cite a number of essays by well-known poets and critics which anticipate or confirm the attitudes toward Tennyson more expansively developed in the foregoing books. These writings, of which only a selective sampling can be given, sensitively register the ups-and-downs of Tennyson's reputation during the twentieth century. Generally the authors fall into two categories: those who hearken principally to the formal perfection of Tennyson's lyric voice, and those who emphasize the relevance of content as well.

In an essay of 1895 published in *Corrected Impressions,* and reprinted in *Collected Essays and Papers* (1923), George Saintsbury writes: "It is perhaps . . . in the combination of the faculty of poetical music with that of poetical picture drawing that the special virtue of Tennyson lies." Other early versions of Nicolson's argument occur in the following: Frederic Harrison's *Tennyson, Ruskin, Mill, and Other Literary Estimates* (1900); Oliver Elton's "Tennyson: An Inaugural Lecture" (delivered in 1902 and reprinted in *Modern Studies,* 1907), together with the same author's chapter on Tennyson in *A Survey of English Literature, 1770–1880* (1920); and John W. Mackail's "Tennyson," in *Studies of English Poets* (1926).

Much the same bias dictates the approach to Tennyson of each of the following: Lascelles Abercrombie's *Revaluations: Studies in Biography* (1931); Frank L. Lucas' *Eight Victorian Poets* (1930), and more extensively in his pamphlet on Tennyson in the series *Writers and their Works* (1957) ; and Robin Mayhead's "The Poetry of Tennyson," in volume VI of the *Pelican Guide to English Literature,* edited by Boris Ford (1958), an excessively unsympathetic treatment of the poet. W. H. Auden's introduction to *A Selection of the Poems of Alfred, Lord Tennyson* (1947) has become celebrated for the statement that "he had the finest ear, perhaps, of any English poet; he was also undoubtedly the stupidest; there was little about melancholia that he didn't know; there was little else that he did." Auden's remarks, however, include an illuminating comparison of Tennyson with Baudelaire.

Two excellent essays which forecast the recent reevaluation of Tennyson have been neglected by scholars. The first of these is Herbert J. C. Grierson's chapter in the thirteenth volume of *CHEL* (1916). "The moods to which Tennyson has given poetic expression," writes Grierson, "are as varied as his metres, and include a rare feeling for the beauty of English scenery, the mind of the peasant in many of its phases, humorous and tragic, the interpretation of classical legend, the reproduction of the very soul of some Greek and Roman poets, as Theocritus and Virgil, Lucretius and Catullus, the colour and beauty, if not all the peculiar ethical and religious tone, of medieval romance, complexities of mind and even psychological subtleties of emotion, the brooding of a sensitive spirit over the riddles of life and death and good and evil." Equally astute is Sir John C. Squire's article in the *London Mercury* (1920), which, in predicting a revival of serious interest in the poet, analyzes with great insight Tennyson's involvement in the life of his times, and the resulting "conflict between temperament and conscience, between natural genius and conviction, between the responsible Bard and the born romantic." Other early examples of efforts to give in brief compass a balanced presentation of Tennyson's total artistic accomplishment include: William P. Ker's Leslie Stephen Lecture of 1909 (reprinted in *Collected Essays,* edited by Charles Whibley, 1925); Sir Henry Jones's "Tennyson" (*Proceedings of the British Academy,* 1909, and reprinted in *Essays in Literature and Education,* 1924); and Andrew C. Bradley's "The Reaction against Tennyson," a lecture to Members of the English Association (1914, and reprinted in *A Miscellany,* 1929). John Drinkwater allots to Tennyson three chapters in *Victorian Poetry* (1923), pointing out that the poet "showed his generation, in a degree unapproached by any other poet who began writing with him, the still fresh and vital possibilities of a great traditional manner." In "Tennyson and Some Recent Critics," published in *Some Aspects of Modern Poetry* (1924), Alfred Noyes takes vigorous issue with Faussett and Nicolson, stating: "The chief indictment that has been brought against Tennyson will, in fact, be the chief ground upon which he will be praised by posterity — the fact that he did so completely sum up and express the great Victorian era in which he lived." Noyes's prediction has been authoritatively substantiated by the distinguished Victorian scholar, George M. Young in "The Age of Tennyson" (*Proceedings of the British Academy,* 1939, and reprinted in *Critical Essays on the Poetry of Tennyson,* edited by John Killham, 1960).

Arthur J. Carr's "Tennyson as a Modern Poet" (*UTQ,* 1950; and twice reprinted, in *Critical Essays,* edited by John Killham, 1960, and in *Victorian Literature: Modern Essays in Criticism,* edited by Austin Wright, 1961), has justly become something of a landmark in the Tennysonian revival. The author concludes: "In Tennyson's poetry the private and public worlds are fused." Tennyson, he finds, significantly looks forward to the thematic concerns of writers as diverse as Joyce and Yeats, T. S. Eliot and Aldous Huxley.

The belief that the poet's ability to identify his work with the crucial problems of his era constitutes a legitimate claim to greatness is a theme common to the following: Humphry House's "Tennyson and the Spirit of his Age," a talk for the B.B.C. Third Programme (1950), printed in *All in Due Time* (1955); Viscount Esher's "Tennyson's Influence on his Times," *Essays by Divers Hands* (1956), originally presented in 1953; and Aubrey De Selincourt's "Alfred, Lord Tennyson," in *Six Great Poets* (1956).

VIII. SPECIAL STUDIES

Investigation of special aspects of Tennyson's poetry conforms to the general pattern of Victorian literary research in this century. Earlier studies tend to concentrate on the poet's thought, while more recently attention has shifted to the formal properties of his art. There has, however, been continuing interest in his response to the scientific developments of his age, and especially to Darwinism.

Chapter two of Lionel Stevenson's *Darwin among the Poets* (1932) systematically outlines the development of Tennyson's evolutionary views to show that he consistently sought a compromise between science and religion. Two very solid articles explore the same subject in more technical terms. George R. Potter, writing in *PQ* (1937) on Tennyson's familiarity with pre-Darwinian speculation, comes to the conclusion that he did not embrace the theory of mutability until the publication of *The Origin of Species*. Covering some of the same ground, William R. Rutland's "Tennyson and the Theory of Evolution," in *Essays and Studies* (1941), provides evidence that Tennyson worked his way toward a meliorist faith in the cosmic process as confirming ethical evolution: "It seemed to him in his maturity that the Process visible in external Nature, which had produced Man, was also taking place in the moral nature of Man himself." In the chapter, "Evolution in the Platonic Tradition" from his *Evolution and Poetic Belief: A Study in Some Victorian and Modern Writers* (1956), Georg Roppen locates the poet's philosophic position "somewhere between the neo-Platonism of the eighteenth century and the biological theory of Nature advanced in the nineteenth." "His intuitive achievement," Roppen believes, "is to express a synthesis of the two at a time when science, in general, was striking out on a single-minded materialist track." Still broader in context is the treatment of Tennyson in the chapter, "Evolution and the Victorian Poets," from

Douglas Bush's *Science and English Poetry; A Historical Sketch, 1590–1950* (1950).

Two earlier writings by scientists testify to Tennyson's competence in handling ideas derived from many fields of scientific inquiry. In *Tennyson as a Student and Poet of Nature* (1910), Sir Norman Lockyer, the astronomer who was a friend of the poet, arranges the poems in categories to exhibit the comprehensiveness and accuracy of the knowledge they reveal. His "great achievement," the author perceptively remarks, "has been to show us that in the study of science we have one of the bases of the fullest poetry, a poetry which appeals at the same time to the deepest emotions and the highest and broadest intellects of mankind .Tennyson, in short, has shown that science and poetry, so far from being antagonistic, must for ever advance side by side." The geologist, William N. Rice, presents Tennyson's qualifications to be called "the poet of science," in *The Poet of Science and Other Addresses* (1919). A similar concept informs the Tennyson chapter of Ralph B. Crum's Columbia University dissertation, *Scientific Thought in Poetry* (1931).

Joseph W. Beach devotes a chapter of his magisterial study, *The Concept of Nature in Nineteenth-Century Poetry* (1936), to Tennyson's philosophy which, in opposition to most of the foregoing writers, he believes to be essentially dualistic:

> He wished to maintain the distinction between objective and subjective. Nature was associated in his mind with the objective world; and it gave no sure intimation of God, freedom, immortality. These were to be found only in the realm of the subjective. Hence for him the radical menace of naturalism, of evolutionism, was its growing assumption that man's conscious life was continuous with the natural process and explainable in the same terms (p. 430).

The best single study of Tennyson's philosophic ideas in relation to the Victorian religious crisis remains C. F. G. Masterman's *Tennyson as a Religious Teacher* (1900). E. Hershey Sneath's *The Mind of Tennyson: His Thoughts on God, Freedom, and Immortality* (1900), also still rewards perusal. Vilhelm Grønbech has some suggestive remarks on the difficulty Tennyson experienced in accommodating his spiritual vision to the actualities of the age, in *Religious Currents in the Nineteenth Century* (originally published in Danish, 1922, and translated by P. M. Mitchell and William D. Paden, 1964).

After a long period of reaction Paul Turner spoke out in defense of Tennyson's intellectual insight and integrity in a shrewd article entitled "The Stupidest English Poet" (*English Studies,* 1949), the title being, of course, borrowed from Auden's 1947 introduction. It is Turner's contention that the poet stood in the forefront of modern thinking on scientific and theological matters. In support of this claim he convincingly adduces examples from the writings of Bergson, William James, Freud, Russell, Jeans, and Joad.

Sir Charles Tennyson has an informative article on "Tennyson's Religion" in *Six Tennyson Studies* (1954). More controversial is Hoxie N. Fairchild's treatment of the poet in *Religious Trends in English Poetry, 1830–1880* (1957). The author aligns Tennyson with the Broad Church movement, and concludes that he "was not a mystic but an emotional pragmatist": "It is probably safe to assume that we come closest to Tennyson's real thought when he is not thinking — when he is least systematically argumentative about theology and metaphysics and relies most completely on his subjective emotions. His creed begins and ends in 'I have felt'." A similar position is developed in the chapter on Tennyson in James Benziger's *Images of Eternity: Studies in the Poetry of Religious Vision from Wordsworth to T. S. Eliot* (1962). The writer, who questions the profundity of the poet's spiritual conflict, states that "the faith advanced in the greater part of *In Memoriam* and in Tennyson's poetry generally is that of the natural inner light, the Romantic faith in individual feeling and imagination."

The implications of the approach adumbrated in Fairchild and Benziger are given philosophic definition by William R. Brashear in a suggestive unpublished doctoral dissertation, "The Concept of the 'Living Will' as an Interpretive Key to Tennyson's Poetry," Princeton University (1959). Brashear places Tennyson centrally in the stream of nineteenth-century subjectivist or vitalist thought, as it relates to "concepts of the faculty of 'will' or living principle, self-centered, that supports and shapes all that 'appears' to be." In print the author has so far applied his theory only to an interpretation of the resolution of "The Two Voices" (*VP,* 1964).

The standard discussions of Tennyson's political and social ideas have been dated by recent historical research into the Victorian scene. Worth consulting are the relevant chapters in Stopford A. Brooke's *Tennyson: His Art and Relation to Modern Life* (1894) ; Stephen L. Gwynn's unduly neglected *Tennyson: A Critical Study* (1899) ; and William C. Gordon's *The Social Ideals of Alfred Tennyson as Related to His Time* (1906). Writing on "Locksley Hall" in *Transactions of the Wisconsin Academy of Sciences, Arts and Letters* (1933), Robert K. Richardson presents evidence to show that this poem is an important document in the history of the development of the idea of progress. Of related interest is A. C. Howell's "Tennyson's 'Palace of Art' — An Interpretation" (*SP*, 1936), which presents an autobiographical reading of the poem as its author's "Protest against the narrow, hide-bound life of a university with its deadening influence upon the development of the artist. . . ." Two doctoral dissertations may also be cited here: Ernst Blos's "Die politischen Anschauungen Tennysons," Erlangen (1930) ; and W. A. Hunton's "Tennyson and the Victorian Political Milieu," New York University (1938, unpublished).

An article entitled "A Great National Poet . . . Tennyson's Mystic Imperialism," with an accompanying editorial in *TLS* for 10 October 1942, bears witness to wartime Britain's awakened receptivity to the poet's political message. More recently Sir Charles Tennyson has written on his grandfather's politics in *Six Tennyson Essays* (1954) and in the *Lincolnshire Historian* (1963). The latter piece, "Tennyson and His Times," ably demonstrates, through quotations from the poems, Tennyson's constant and well-informed interest in the political and social life of the age. Benjamin De Mott's "The General, the Poet, and the Inquisition" (*KR*, 1962, and reprinted in *Hells and Benefits: A Report on American Minds, Matters, and Possibilities,* 1962), gives, with special reference to "The Lotos-Eaters," a lively account of how Tennyson became involved in the abortive rebellion against Ferdinand VII of Spain in 1830. In a more domestic vein W. Stacy Johnson, discussing "The Theme of Marriage in Tennyson" (*VNL*, 1957), states: "It is evident that marriage, in Tennyson, represents a whole life for man, the basis for a whole society. True marriage, for him, means a balancing of aggression and passivity, of physical force and spiritual integrity." The very important findings of John Killham, in *Tennyson and The*

Princess: Reflections of an Age (1958), will be discussed in Section IX.

"Alfred Tennyson: The Poetry and Politics of Conservative Vision" by Robert O. Preyer (*VS*, 1966), breaks new ground in its examination of the aesthetic limitations of Tennyson's commitment to many of his themes. Associating the poet with the Christian humanist tradition stemming from Spenser and Milton, Preyer argues that Tennyson was unable "to utilize this great tradition as a means of clarifying and enriching his responses to contemporary life," but that in the vacillation and uncertainty of trying to do so, he composed great passages which bespeak "the suffering isolated artist, not the spokesman for the tribe." This article is especially rewarding in its treatment of Tennyson's scientific interest in "permanence and change" and of his evocation of "natural and cosmological settings" to dignify and universalize subjective states of mind.

Lately scholars have made a concerted effort to probe Tennyson's imaginative vision and to locate the unifying themes in his poetry. Robert O. Preyer, in "Tennyson as an Oracular Poet" (*MP*, 1958), writes: "The search for fantastic beauty takes place in the mindless depths of the psyche; and what it hopes to uncover there . . . is the landscape of vision and the images of a new apocalypse." The author somewhat debatably feels that Tennyson distrusted this tendency in his early poetry, and that it is in abeyance in the later work. Jacob Korg, in "The Pattern of Fatality in Tennyson's Poetry" (*VNL*, 1958), calls attention to the frequency with which the poems "fall into a pattern of sudden and disastrous change, describing power passing into impotence, ripeness into decay and maturity into death, not by the natural attrition of time, but through swift and inexplicable catastrophe." Carl R. Sonn's important article, "Poetic Vision and Religious Certainty in Tennyson's Earlier Poetry" (*MP*, 1959), takes issue by implication with the school of T. S. Eliot, finding that "Tennyson is an eminently unsuitable subject for a clinical study in disassociated sensibility," since "the very same power that afforded him the vision of the poet afforded him also the degree and kind of religious certainty that he finally attained." Sonn's conclusions are founded on a perceptive reading of a number of poems, including "The Two Voices," "Ulysses," "Tithonus," and *In*

Memoriam. Allan Danzig casts his net equally wide in "The Contraries: A Central Concept in Tennyson's Poetry" (*PMLA*, 1962), which explores the dialectic of opposites ("this double seeming of the single world") and the resulting tensions in the poet's work. Yet another thoughtful approach to this problem is provided by R. A. Forsyth in "The Myth of Nature and the Victorian Compromise of the Imagination" (*ELH*, 1964). The author associates Tennyson's poetry with the Victorian crisis in sensibility, finding it representative of "the divorce of inner and outer worlds of poet and external environment...." Sir Charles Tennyson traces a recurrent device in "The Dream in Tennyson's Poetry" and provides conclusive evidence that the dream state was for him "an essentially spiritual experience." This article, appearing in *VQR* (1964), has been reprinted as the second of the Publications of The Tennyson Society. James Kissane's "Tennyson: The Passion of the Past and the Curse of Time" (*ELH*, 1965) offers a penetrating discussion of the shaping effect of memory on many of Tennyson's best poems.

The range and complexity of Tennyson's constant experimentation with poetic forms has as yet received little specific consideration. Stopford A. Brooke has a chapter on his handling of the dramatic monologue in *Tennyson: His Art and Relation to Modern Life* (1894); and passing references to the same subject occur in Claud Howard's "The Dramatic Monologue: Its Origin and Development" (*SP*, 1910); Mungo W. MacCallum's "The Dramatic Monologue in the Victorian Period" (*Proceedings of the British Academy*, 1925); and Ina B. Sessions' "The Dramatic Monologue" (*PMLA*, 1947). More provocative is Robert Langbaum's comparison of Tennyson with Browning in *The Poetry of Experience: The Dramatic Monologue in Modern Literary Tradition* (1957). According to the author: "Tennyson ... goes much farther than Browning in dealing in his successful dramatic monologues with an emotional perversity that verges on the pathological." Nonetheless, Langbaum asserts: "Tennyson's feeling for the pathology of emotions makes for the same final effect as Browning's use of the extraordinary moral position. There is the same tension between sympathy and judgment...."

In "Tennyson and the Sonnet" (*VNL*, 1958), Dougald B. MacEachen conducts a rather prosaic review of the forty-six published examples of a form with which the poet was never much at home.

A noteworthy, though not altogether successful endeavor to associate Tennyson's narrative art with the idyll and epyllion or little epic as cultivated by the Alexandrian poets and especially Theocritus, is presented by H. Marshall McLuhan in "Tennyson and the Romantic Epic," *Critical Essays on the Poetry of Tennyson,* edited by John Killham (1960). McLuhan's theory was first advanced in more rudimentary form in the introduction to his selection of Tennyson's poetry (1956). According to R. B. Wilkenfeld in "The Shape of the Two Voices" (*VP,* 1966), Tennyson evolved in such "lyrical narratives" as "The Hesperides," "The Sea-Fairies," "The Lotos-Eaters," and "The Lady of Shalott," a poetic means for mediating the conflict between objective and subjective experience.

All students of Tennyson's poetic style will wish to refer to George Saintsbury's classic treatment of the subject in his chapter on "Tennyson and Browning," in *A History of English Prosody,* volume III (1910). The standard works still are: Roman Dyboski's *Tennysons Sprache und Stil, Wiener Beiträge zur Englischen Philologie* (1907); and J. F. A. Pyre's *The Formation of Tennyson's Style, University of Wisconsin Studies in Language and Literature* (1921). To these may be added Bernard Groom's "On the Diction of Tennyson, Browning, and Arnold," S.P.E. Tract No. 53 (1939); and Sir Charles Tennyson's "Tennyson's Versification," *Six Tennyson Essays* (1954).

Modern techniques of linguistic analysis have produced a number of extremely suggestive methods of handling Tennyson's stylistic procedures. Among the first of these was H. Marshall McLuhan's "Tennyson and Picturesque Poetry" (*Essays in Criticism,* 1951, and reprinted in *Critical Essays,* edited by John Killham, 1960). Arthur Hallam's 1831 review is made the point of departure for a subtle consideration of the "picturesque" quality of Tennyson's nature poetry, as embodied in his "habitual definition of a moment of awareness in terms of objective landscape." McLuhan's approach is further clarified in "The Aesthetic Moment in Landscape Poetry" (*English Institute Essays,* 1951).

In the chapter "Personal Style and Period Style: A Victorian Poet," from their *Three Keys to Language* (1952), Robert M.

Estrich and Hans Sperber offer the proposition: "To understand [a writer's work] ... is to see the constant interplay of literary concept and linguistic medium and to see it in both its personal and period aspects. . . ." The authors test their "theory of the complex unity of style" through a brilliant investigation of Tennyson's linguistic and prosodic manipulation of his sources in "The Revenge: A Ballad of the Fleet." Narrower in scope and somewhat less satisfactory, although thought-provoking and well-documented, is Francis Berry's discussion of "The Voice of Tennyson" in *Poetry and the Physical Voice* (1962). The writer undertakes an analysis of the reader's auditory response to the timbre of Tennyson's poetry, based on the argument that he "was haunted by sound generally and particularly within the bounds of his own voice, and that he composed in terms of his own voice. . . ." Equally prophetic of new directions in current Tennyson scholarship is Walker Gibson's "Behind the Veil: A Distinction between Poetic and Scientific Language in Tennyson, Lyell, and Darwin" (*VS*, 1958). Gibson, who contends "that Tennyson's 'poetic imagination' can sometimes be examined in terms of grammar," differentiates between the "angle" of the artist and that of the professional scientist in dealing with shared fields of speculation. Henri-A. Talon subjects to rigorous grammatical analysis Section 13 of *In Memoriam* in "Sur un Poème de Tennyson: Essai de critique formelle" (*Les Langues Modernes,* 1964), concluding: "Partout la discipline de l'art laisse deviner que le poète maîtrise son chagrin alors même qu'il paraît être le plus accablé."

A more hostile approach is represented in the following articles. Milton Millhauser in "Tennyson: Artifice and Image" (*Journal of Aesthetics and Art Criticism,* 1956), attributes a want of immediacy in Tennyson's poetry to "a shallow and apologetic use of imagery" and "a disposition to make use of terms and figures uncongenial to his own imagination." In "The Dilemma of Tennyson" (*Listener* 1957, and reprinted in *Critical Essays,* edited by John Killham, 1960), Walter W. Robson, taking off from "Ulysses," associates the decline in the later poetry to Tennyson's growing awareness of his inability to project his social conscience in a style commensurate with his artistic conscience.

Charles Wilson delightfully calls attention to an overlooked topic in "Mirror of a Shire: Tennyson's Dialect Poems," a B.B.C.

Third Programme broadcast printed in *Durham University Jour-nal* (1959) : "Save for Chaucer, no one has portrayed bucolic life with technique so consummate or knowledge so intimate."

Study of Tennyson's imagery and use of symbols has been largely confined to discussions of individual poems. The earliest, as well as the most intensive treatment of the general subject is William D. Paden's *Tennyson in Egypt; A Study of the Imagery in His Earlier Work* (*University of Kansas Publications, Human-istic Studies,* 1942). As the learned and unfailingly informative notes show, the author has exhaustively canvassed Tennyson's reading in search of the literary sources of his imagery. Although Paden is somewhat too prone to impose psychoanalytic implications on his findings, his is a valuable work which has profoundly influenced subsequent scholarship.

In "The 'High-Born Maden' Symbol in Tennyson" (*PMLA,* 1948, and reprinted in *Critical Essays,* edited by John Killham, 1960), Lionel Stevenson scrutinizes a number of related poems in which the poet developed a symbolic figure derived from Shelley. "The image of an isolated and unhappy maiden," which reappears throughout the early poetry "with a persistence amount-ing almost to obsession," is convincingly related to Jung's theory of the *anima*. Stevenson's article inspired a companion piece by Clyde de L. Ryals, "The 'Fatal Woman' Symbol in Tennyson" (*PMLA,* 1959). The writer attributes to Keatsian influence Ten-nyson's fascination with the opposing type of the femme fatale: ". . . one side of his nature cried out for sensual indulgence while the other sternly advocated the development of moral purpose. And . . . the suffering maiden and the strong woman are symbolic of this conflict, the former being the regressive symbol and the latter the aggressive symbol. Both are, to use the Jungian term, 'soul-images' of the poet."

Elizabeth H. Waterston in "Symbolism in Tennyson's Minor Poems" (*UTQ,* 1951, and reprinted in *Critical Essays,* edited by John Killham, 1960), effectively shows that the poet employed symbols with a full and sophisticated sense of their possibilities. The writer's desire to be inclusive, however, has precluded any very profound interpretation of the examples she cites. With special attention to *In Memoriam* and "The Passing of Arthur," Charles R. Sanders considers the many symbolic purposes which

Tennyson's references to hands fulfill ("Tennyson and the Human Hand," *VNL*, 1957). Howard W. Fulweiler in "Tennyson and the 'Summons from the Sea' " (*VP*, 1965), ably reviews the poet's varying uses of the sea to symbolize first, "an introspective and subjective realm of escape," second, "an outer realm of objective struggle," and third in the later poems, "a gateway to religious experience, a key to spiritual understanding." In a brilliantly original article, "The Aurora: A Spiritual Metaphor in Tennyson" (*VP*, 1965), W. David Shaw and Carl W. Gartlein demonstrate that the poet's close study of the phenomenon of the *aurora borealis* provided an important source for his imagery.

IX. INDIVIDUAL POEMS

There is space for comment only on the more important articles on individual poems, these characterizing much that is best in recent criticism of the poet. Several have been conveniently collected by John Killham in *Critical Essays on the Poetry of Tennyson* (1960), to which frequent reference has already been made. This volume is prefaced by a useful review of recent directions in Tennysonian scholarship.

The firm establishment of Tennyson in the pantheon of major English poets has led, in particular, to a renewal of interest in the more ambitious works of his maturity. John Killham's scholarly volume, *Tennyson and The Princess: Reflections of an Age* (1958), should dispel once and for all the notion that the poet was not intelligently attuned to the dominant intellectual issues of his time. Killham examines *The Princess* against a background of the feminist controversy (with special regard to higher education and the marital status of women) , socialist agitation (as influenced by the Saint-Simonians and Fourier) , and current evolutionary speculation. He also presents, à propos Tennyson's literary relationships, many new facts, the implications of which go far beyond the immediate subject of this admirably documented work. Killham writes:

> Though the topicality has gone, *The Princess,* properly understood, is a vivid reflection of an age. . . . What we have is . . . a glimpse of the aspirations of the age in the colours in which they presented themselves to a truly poetic imagination. . . . It was Tennyson's seeking for a new form of expression, one capable of representing the singular diversity of his time, that led him to forgo conventional unity in preference for a "medley" (pp. 3–4).

Students of *The Princess* should glance at Samuel E. Dawson's *A Study . . . of Alfred Tennyson's Poem The Princess* second edition, 1884) , which includes some of the poet's own comments. More recently, in "Tennyson's *Princess* and *Vestiges*" (*PMLA,* 1954) , Milton Millhauser considers Tennyson's debt to Robert Chambers, whose *"Vestiges,"* he concludes, "was a precipitant but not a determinant of Tennyson's thought." F. E. L. Priestley has some original thoughts on the complex form of the poem in "Control of Tone in Tennyson's *The Princess"* (*Langue et Littérature,* 1961) : "At the outset Tennyson frees himself from the demands of any recognized formal *genre* by the device of multiple narration. This leaves him free to choose the style. . . . The style is controlled then, so that the comic is introduced into an established serious context, made up of romantic, idyllic, and genuinely heroic elements, and is never allowed completely to become dominant. Rather it itself is more and more subordinated until it disappears." Clyde de L. Ryals' "The 'Weird Seizures' in *The Princess,*" *University of Texas Studies in Language and Literature* (1962) , offers a psychological explanation of Tennyson's additions to the fourth edition of the poem, on the basis of similar motifs in his earlier work. The poet's concern to exemplify the proper relationship between the sexes is the subject of Allen Danzig's "Tennyson's *The Princess:* A Definition of Love" (*VP,* 1966) .

Of all of Tennyson's poems the great elegy *In Memoriam* has understandably received most attention. Andrew C. Bradley's *Commentary* (1901, third edition revised 1910) remains standard and indispensable, although John F. Genung's *Tennyson's In Memoriam: Its Purpose and Its Structure* (1884) is also worth consulting. These early general studies have been ably supplemented by Eleanor B. Mattes' *In Memoriam: The Way of a Soul* (1951), which offers a reliable guide to the sources of Tennyson's ideas in the poem and suggests dates for many of the individual sections.

Studies of the elegy fall into two categories, as they relate to its intellectual content or its form. Many of these in both kinds stem from T. S. Eliot's brief estimate in *Essays Ancient and Modern* (1936, and reprinted in *Critical Essays,* edited by John Killham, 1960). Eliot, who believed that *In Memoriam* marks the "end of his [Tennyson's] spiritual development" and that thereafter he became "the surface flatterer of his own time," crystallizes a point of view first voiced by Nicolson, which has become a critical commonplace. Of *In Memoriam* he declares: "It is not religious because of the quality of its faith, but because of the quality of its doubt. Its faith is a poor thing, but its doubt is a very intense experience." For Eliot the unorthodox form of *In Memoriam* seems largely an accident of its author's temperament: ". . . it is a long poem made by putting together lyrics, which have only the unity and continuity of a diary, the concentrated diary of a man confessing himself."

Graham Hough in "The Natural Theology of *In Memoriam*" (*RES,* 1947), signalizes the growing opposition to Eliot's charge of pessimism. Believing that "Tennyson was trying to make a synthesis of the living thought of his time, in the light of a strong personal conviction," Hough discovers in the elegy "three important elements — the influence of science, transmitted especially through Lyell's *Geology;* the influence of Coleridge, experienced at Cambridge; and Tennyson's own religious intuitions, based ultimately on an unanalysable but completely cogent mystical experience." In the centennial essay, "*In Memoriam* A Century Later" (*Antioch Review,* 1950), Bella K. Milmed offers a thoughtful and widely informed discussion of the continuing implications of the poem for modern scientific and religious thought. A well-considered exploration of the meaning of *In Memoriam,* more specifically in relation to its own time, is found in Basil Willey's *More Nineteenth Century Studies: A Group of Honest Doubters*

(1956). Other briefer pieces include: J. M. Cohen's *"In Memoriam:* A Hundred Years After" (*Cornhill Magazine,* 1949); Humphry House's B.B.C. Third Programme broadcast (1950, and reprinted in *All in Due Time,* 1955); Laurence Perrine's "Tennyson's *In Memoriam"* (*Expl.,* Item 29, 1954); and Samuel C. Burchell's "Tennyson's Dark Night" (*SAQ,* 1955).

In the present decade a group of articles has sought to penetrate more precisely the nature of the religious experience recorded in *In Memoriam.* Jack L. Kendall in "A Neglected Theme in Tennyson's *In Memoriam"* (*MLN,* 1961), maintains that Tennyson achieved faith through self-renunciation: "... the spiritual predicament of the poet is such that failure and especially a certain attitude towards failure [i. e., acknowledgment of personal helplessness and hopelessness] are indispensable conditions of ultimate success." Clyde de L. Ryals in "The 'Heavenly Friend': The 'New Mythus' of *In Memoriam"* (*Personalist,* 1962), argues that Tennyson provided the "new Mythus" for which Carlyle called in *Sartor Resartus* "by substituting a symbolic and transformed Hallam for the figure of Christ." Hallam's apotheosis is related to Nietzsche's evocation of the Übermensch. In "The Mystical Implications of *In Memoriam"* (*SEL,* 1962), Stephen A. Grant amasses evidence in support of his contention that Tennyson's "mystical trances established a profound basis for his belief in God and man's purpose." A different approach is reflected in Carlisle Moore's "Faith, Doubt, and Mystical Experience in *In Memoriam"* (*VS,* 1963). The author of this excellent article develops the point first made in Buckley's *The Victorian Temper* that *In Memoriam* belongs with the nineteenth-century literature of conversion.

In *"In Memoriam:* The Way of the Poet" (*VS,* 1958), E. D. H. Johnson discusses the elegy as "a record of Tennyson's artistic development during the formative years between 1833 and 1850," and locates one of the organizing principles in the poet's "search for an aesthetic creed answerable alike to his creative needs and to the literary demands of the age." A different kind of unity is proposed in the chapter entitled "The Rhetoric of Faith" by R. A. Foakes (from *The Romantic Assertion: A Study in the Language of Nineteenth Century Poetry,* 1958), in which the writer traces the imagistic patterns through which Tennyson asserted his vision of the triumphant power of love. "Circle Imagery in Tennyson's *In Memoriam*" (*VP,* 1963), calls attention to the poet's reliance on a framework of images, which the author, James G. Taaffe, believes may have been derived from Dante.

More purely structural in its analysis is John D. Rosenberg's "The Two Kingdoms of *In Memoriam*" (*JEGP,* 1959), which sees the elegy as an attempt to reconcile evolutionary science and orthodox faith, to fuse "the myth of Progress and the Christian vision of the Kingdom of Heaven on Earth." For Jonathan Bishop, "The Unity of *In Memoriam*" (*VNL,* 1962) results from the single omnipresent theme of change. In "A Framework for Tennyson's *In Memoriam*" (*JEGP,* 1962), Martin J. Svaglic persuasively elaborates James Knowles's statement that Tennyson designed his poem in nine parts, rather than in the four parts proposed by Bradley. A fresh approach to the organic growth of the elegy informs J. C. C. Mays's important *"In Memoriam:* An Aspect of Form" (*UTQ,* 1965). Using *Piers Plowman* surprisingly but very plausibly as a basis for comparison, the author suggests that: "The form of the narrative [in *In Memoriam*] gains shape and discovers its direction, as its speaker wins through to equilibrium and stability of mind. And as he comes gradually to recognize faith in himself and in all else, so his argument, too, discovers its own coherence and significance."

Although the most controversial of Tennyson's poems, *Maud* has fared well at the hands of critics. Robert J. Mann's contemporary interpretation, *Tennyson's "Maud" Vindicated: An Explanatory Essay* [1856], remains authoritative. The writer, a physician, conducted his discussion of "the spirit and purpose" of *Maud* with great psychological insight; and his comments are, on the whole, a good deal more illuminating than the Freudian approach adopted by Roy P. Basler in "Tennyson the Psychologist" (*SAQ,* 1944, and reprinted as "Tennyson's *Maud*" in *Sex, Symbolism, and Psychology in Literature, 1948*).

Humbert Wolfe's pamphlet on Tennyson in the series, *The Poets on the Poets* (1930), belongs among the significant studies marking the turning of the tide against the post-Victorian denigration of the poet. Wolfe's masterly little volume is largely concerned with *Maud,* which the author regards as "a microcosm of Tennyson." He has no patience with Nicolson's view that the Laureate compromised with his age:

> Indeed, so far from its being true that Tennyson declined into contented domesticity of the soul, the force of *Maud* is derived not least from the internecine struggle between the man of his time, who strove to make order out of spiritual chaos, and the poet and lover for whom chaos had its own lovely and irredeemable law. It is thus that the much criticized quality of seer-in-ordinary to the British public gives its cutting edge to the heart's apprehension of beauty. The struggle — which Tennyson waged all his life — is crystallized in *Maud* and gives the poem not a little of its poignant significance (p. 50).

As a practicing poet, Wolfe skillfully shows how the prosody of *Maud* "affected the course of late English poetry"; and he is particularly acute in his remarks on the form of the poem as a precursor of *The Waste Land:* "For Tennyson here invented the new method of narrative in verse which has since passed into general use. . . . He grasped the new truth that since poetry tells its tales in lightning-flashes with no need of reboant thunder, the reader might be allowed to fill in the prose. He saw for the first time that it was enough for the poet to do a series of apparently disconnected pastels and to leave the silences between to weave the complete tapestry in the reader's mind."

The more technical aspects of *Maud* have invited continuing analysis. In a brilliant essay, "Tennyson's *Maud:* The Function of the Imagery," included in his collection, *Critical Essays on the Poetry of Tennyson* (1960), John Killham emphasizes that "The historical and psychological aspects of the action have to be related to the work considered both as drama and a series of lyrics." The writer goes on to demonstrate "that the imagery employed in the lyrics can, by its own mode of development, deepen and assist the dramatic movement." Some of Killham's conclusions are anticipated in E. D. H. Johnson's slighter "The Lily and the Rose: Symbolic Meaning in Tennyson's *Maud*" (*PMLA*, 1949). Edward Stokes, "The Metrics of *Maud*" (*VP*, 1964), comprehensively surveys the involved metrical patterns of the poem, to show "that these variations are not haphazard, but are dictated by dramatic and thematic needs."

The most detailed recent treatment of the poem is Ralph W. Rader's *Maud: The Biographical Genesis* (1963). Although the first chapter contains the fullest account of the stages through which *Maud* evolved, the principal interest of the volume, substantial sections of which had been previously published in the form of articles, resides in the new information which it presents about Tennyson's life in the period following Hallam's death, and especially in the revelation of his short-lived infatuation with Rosa Baring. Rader reads *Maud* somewhat reductively as an exercise in autobiography. His conclusions are summarized as follows:

> Biographically, *Maud* is a crucial document. It is Tennyson's purgative recapitulation of the inner and outer circumstances of his tortured early life, a deeply rooted act of spiritual self-definition and affirmation by which after the commitment initiated by marriage and the Laureateship, he moved from his earlier to his later career; it is the swan song of the bitter and troubled young poet, the inaugural hymn of the Laureate. Having objectified and judged, as accurately as he was able, the experience of his early life, he felt ready, his own salvation secure, to minister to the moral and spiritual needs of mankind at large (p. 115).

In a letter to *TLS* for 31 December 1964, Christopher Ricks substantiates Rader's hypothesis that Sir John Simeon was not the principal instigator of *Maud.*

The following additional pieces on *Maud* have appeared in recent years: Tom J. Truss, Jr.'s "Tennysonian Aspects of *Maud*" (*University of Mississippi Studies in English,* 1960) , associating the poem with thematic, prosodic, and imagistic elements in Tennyson's preceding work; Clyde de L. Ryals' "Tennyson's *Maud*" (*Connotation,* 1962) , a rather rambling exposition of the diverse themes; and George O. Marshall, Jr.'s "Tennyson's 'Oh, That 'Twere Possible': A Link between *In Memoriam* and *Maud*" (*PMLA,* 1963) .

Sharing belief in the epic pretensions of *Idylls of the King,* the latter-day Victorians produced a number of massive studies which are still informative. Tennyson's achievement within the wider context of the Arthurian tradition is set forth in two books, both of which have been dated by the discoveries of subsequent scholars: Mungo W. MacCallum's *Tennyson's Idylls of the King and Arthurian Story from the XVIth Century* (1894) ; and Stephen H. V. Gurteen's *The Arthurian Epic: A Comparative Study of the Cambrian, Breton, and Anglo-Norman Versions of the Story and*

Tennyson's Idylls of the King (1895). A more recent investigation is Ethel Bernstein's unpublished doctoral dissertation, "Victorian Morality in the Idylls of the King: A Study of Tennyson's Use of his Sources" (Cornell University, 1939). Richard Jones's *The Growth of the Idylls of the King* (1895), which includes an extensive list of variant readings and manuscript revisions, should be read in conjunction with Sir James Knowles's "Tennyson's Arthurian Poem" (in *Tennyson and His Friends,* edited by Hallam, Lord Tennyson, 1911), and Sir Charles Tennyson's "The *Idylls of the King*" (*Twentieth Century,* 1957). The fullest and most accurate account of the evolution and reception of the poem was presented by Kathleen Tillotson in a lecture at Somerville College, Oxford (1963; printed as "Tennyson's Serial Poem" in Geoffrey and Kathleen Tillotson's *Mid-Victorian Studies,* 1965). Mrs. Tillotson convincingly shows "how closely related in Tennyson's mind were the formal, the narrative, and the moral shape of his poem."

Early interpretations of the poem's allegorical meaning were proposed by Henry Elsdale in *Studies in the Idylls: An Essay on Mr. Tennyson's Idylls of the King* (1878), Albert Hamann in *An Essay on Tennyson's Idylls of the King* (1887), and Condé B. Pallen in *The Meaning of the Idylls of the King: An Essay in Interpretation* (1904, and reprinted 1965). The latter was based on an essay in *Catholic World* (1885), of which Tennyson wrote the author: "You see further into their meaning than most of my commentators have done." Mention should be made of Harold Littledale's *Essays in Lord Tennyson's Idylls of the King* (1893). Frederick S. Boas discusses the allegorical significance of the *Idylls* very sensibly in an article in *Nineteenth Century and After* (1921, and reprinted in *From Richardson to Pinero: Some Innovators and Idealists,* 1936).

The rebirth of interest in the *Idylls* in recent years dates from two notable articles. In "Tennyson's *Idylls*" (*UTQ,* 1949, and reprinted in *Critical Essays,* edited by John Killham, 1960), F. E. L. Priestley conclusively demonstrates the thematic integrity of the work as a "dramatic allegory," the sections of which are carefully articulated to produce a unified impression. Samuel C. Burchell's "Tennyson's 'Allegory in the Distance' " (*PMLA,* 1953), borrows its title from Jowett's descriptive phrase about the poem.

Burchell suggests that the *Idylls* invite a twofold interpretation. On one level it is "a rich pageant and a colorful panorama with an exciting story of sin and retribution. Beyond this, Tennyson's epic is the symbolic study of a corrupt and decadent society from its rise to its fall. . . ." A third noteworthy piece, influenced by Priestley's approach, is Edward Engelburg's "The Beast Image in Tennyson's *Idylls of the King*" (*ELH*, 1955), which points out how the poet employs a consistent pattern of imagery to reinforce his theme and to provide an additional element of dramatic unity.

William A. Madden's essay, "The Burden of the Artist" (in *1859: Entering an Age of Crisis,* edited by Philip Appleman, William A. Madden, and Michael Wolff, 1959), gives a very thoughtful discussion of the first four *Idylls* as symptomatic of the spiritual distress precipitated by the publication of *The Origin of Species*. In the important review article, "A New Look at Tennyson — and Especially the *Idylls*" (*JEGP*, 1962), Donald Smalley disputes the high praise of the poem voiced in Buckley's *Tennyson: The Growth of a Poet*. Smalley finds that the allegorical and symbolic meanings are discordant, to the detriment of the work as an organic whole. Clyde de L. Ryals pursues a related approach in "The Moral Paradox of the Hero in the *Idylls of the King*" (*ELH*, 1963). According to this author, Arthur deprives his knights of their freedom in binding them to his will. When the Arthurian ideal is brought in question by Guinevere's betrayal, they turn to other goals such as the Grail quest, and unsupported by their fealty, the king loses his own sense of identity. The growing narrative complexity of the *Idylls* mirrors the frustration of Arthur, who is at once hero and villain of the poem. Stanley J. Solomon's "Tennyson's Paradoxical King" (*VP*, 1963) takes issue with Ryals' argument, but is unsuccessful in offering a better explanation of the ambiguous n a t u r e of many of the *Idylls*. Nancy M. Engbretson's exploration of "The Thematic Evolution of *The [sic] Idylls of the King*" (*VNL*, 1964), is confusingly organized and marred by factual errors. Equally unsatisfactory is Maurice Legris' "Structure and Allegory in Tennyson's *Idylls of the King*" (*Humanities Association Bulletin,* 1965) which, in considering the interaction of narrative and allegoric elements, ignores the chronology of the sections and the poet's later additions. In "Tennyson's *Idylls of the King* as Tragic Drama" (*VP*, 1966), Henry

Kozicki makes an interesting but over-schematized attempt to present the poem "in terms of the ritual drama underlying all Greek tragedy."

A number of critiques have been devoted to single *Idylls*. One of the earliest of these was T. Sturge Moore's comparison of the differing treatments of the story of Tristram and Isolt by Tennyson, Arnold, and Swinburne (*Criterion*, 1922–1923). Arnold's version alone lives up to Moore's neoclassic requirements. In "Tennyson's Merlin" (*SP*, 1947), Gordon S. Haight arrays the literary sources which contributed to the poet's portrait of the Sage, both in the *Idylls* and in "Merlin and the Gleam." The dangers of the psycho-analytic method when incautiously applied are illustrated by Betty Miller's explication of some of the same material in her "Tennyson and the Sinful Queen" (*Twentieth Century*, 1955). In "Merlin and Vivien" the writer discovers a "pre-eminent example of that destructive attitude towards his own sex which the poet half divined, half feared in all women." John Killham's reply (*N&Q*, 1958) effectively demolishes Mrs. Miller's argument. She is on firmer ground in "Camelot at Cambridge" (*Twentieth Century*, 1958), which suggests that the fellowship of the Cambridge Apostles provided a kind of model for the Arthurian order.

Further illustrations of different critical approaches are Roy Gridley's "Confusion of the Seasons in Tennyson's 'The Last Tournament'" (*VNL*, 1962); and Boyd Litzinger's "The Structure of Tennyson's 'The Last Tournament'" (*VP*, 1963). The first explores Tennyson's handling of color symbolism for ironic purposes; the second skillfully analyzes the complex narrative and symbolic texture of this Idyll. Clyde de L. Ryals' "Percivale, Ambrosius, and the Method of Narration in 'The Holy Grail'" (*Die Neueren Sprachen*, 1963), reaches unorthodox but provocative conclusions in its examination of the only one of the *Idylls* cast in the form of a dramatic monologue. Tennyson created Ambrosius as a foil, Ryals believes, in order to alert the reader to the fact that Percivale is not a completely admirable or reliable narrator. Ambrosius represents "the humanitarian realist" in contrast to Percivale, "the sensation-seeking visionary." In an excellent analysis of "The Argument of the Geraint-Enid Books in *Idylls of the King*" (*VP*, 1964), Lawrence Poston, III, shows that the third and fourth books are so placed within the total structure of the poem as to establish many of the principal thematic motifs of the culminating Idylls. Poston has a related article, " 'Pelleas and Ettarre;' Tennyson's 'Troilus' " (*VP*, 1966). John P. Eggers presents in "The Weeding of the Garden: Tennyson's Geraint Idylls and *The Mabinogion*" (*VP*, 1964), a detailed account of the liberties taken by the poet with his principal source for this Idyll, to unite theme to narrative.

Paul Goodman's remarks on the original "Morte d'Arthur" in *The Structure of Literature* (1954) are concerned with showing that the action of this poem is analogous with its symbolic meaning. In "Tennyson's 'The Epic'; A Gesture of Recovered Faith" (*MLN*, 1959), J. S. Lawry argues that the contemporary frame of "Morte d'Arthur" is integral to the thematic significance of the narrative.

A continuing flow of writings testifies to the perennial popularity of "Ulysses." Chapter fourteen of William B. Stanford's *The Ulysses Theme: A Study of the Adaptability of a Traditional Hero* (1954) places the poet's conception of Ulysses in a tradition extending from Homer through Dante and Shakespeare to Byron. Stanford contends that Tennyson imaginatively fused these mani-fold influences into a composite portrait: ". . . what emerges in the end is a recognizably heroic, though bewildered figure, a perma-nent and influential contribution to the Ulysses myth." Earlier source studies include Albert S. Cook's "The Literary Genealogy of Tennyson's Ulysses" (*Poet-Lore*, 1891), and Giulio Bertoni's "Ulisse nella *Divina Commedia* e nei Poeti Moderni" (*Arcadia*, 1930), which stresses Tennyson's debt to Dante.

Recent discussions have been primarily concerned with the author's point of view as it dictated the form of this poem. Friedrich Brie, the first to advance the theory that the work is to be read as a soliloquy in "Tennyson's 'Ulysses' " (*Anglia*, 1935), remarks that the protagonist's artificial and melodious speech is inappropriate to his traditionally heroic role and that it is instead expressive of the Victorian spirit of compromise. In an Appendix to *Tennyson Sixty Years After* (1948), Paull F. Baum dwells on structural inconsistencies in the poem as indicative of its author's muddled thinking. Baum's attitude of disapprobation, echoed more profoundly by Walter W. Robson in "The Dilemma of Tennyson" (*Listener*, 1957), is most ingeniously countered by E. J. Chiasson in "Tennyson's 'Ulysses' — A Re-interpretation" (*UTQ*, 1954, and reprinted in *Critical Essays*, edited by John Killham, 1960). Chiasson believes that Tennyson meant Ulysses to be the exponent "of a kind of jovial agnosticism," totally opposed to the faith endorsed in *In Memoriam*. He proposes that the poem should "be read as the dramatic presentation of a man who has faith neither in the gods nor consequently in the necessity of preserving order in his kingdom or in his own life."

In contrast, Edgar H. Duncan in "Tennyson: A Modern Appraisal" (*Tennessee Studies in Literature*, 1959), accepts Tennyson's own veiled admission that the poem is a personal allegory intimately related to the circumstances of his life at the period of its composition. This judicious article is prefaced by a concise review of the leading tendencies in Tennysonian scholarship during the past generation. Yet another approach is represented by Clyde de L. Ryals' "Point of View in Tennyson's 'Ulysses'" (*Archiv*, 1962). Ryals, interpreting the poem as a *monologue intérieur*, is unconvinced that Ulysses is preparing to set forth on another quest. His address is "the utterance of a superannuated hero indulging himself in the fantasy that his beloved mariners are still alive. . . . Ulysses' majestic speech becomes, accordingly, a kind of dream, a means of escape momentarily from the uncongenial environment of Ithaca. . . ." John Pettigrew attempts to find a middle ground among interpretations in "Tennyson's 'Ulysses': A Reconciliation of Opposites" (*VP*, 1963). Taking exception to the disposition to slight the dramatic element and to treat it "as a lyric, a key, with which Tennyson unlocked his heart," he writes: "If . . . one can get rid of the beliefs that lead to the stock responses . . . and simply read it as a dramatic poem, one comes to see its speaker as a highly complex individual, drawn with such superb poetic and dramatic skill that he partakes of the web of this life, good and ill together, a figure whose strengths and weaknesses are as finely fused as in Shakespeare's Henry V." Charles Mitchell in "The Undying Will of Tennyson's Ulysses" (*VP*, 1964), also constructs his argument in reference to the form of the poem, which he calls "a soliloquy presented as a dramatic monologue." This subtle exposition develops from the theory first voiced by Robert Langbaum that Ulysses is motivated by the wish to find self-oblivion in death: "The voyage for which Ulysses is preparing is the act of dying, and his goal is spiritual reality."

Also concerned with point of view in "Ulysses" are the following: Charles C. Walcutt's "Tennyson's 'Ulysses' " (*Expl.*, Item 28, 1946) ; Georg Roppen's " 'Ulysses' and Tennyson's Sea Quest" (*English Studies*, 1959) ; Jay L. Halio's " 'Prothalamion,' 'Ulysses,' and Intention in Poetry" (*College English*, 1961) ; and John O. Perry's "The Relationships of Disparate Voices in Poems" (*EC*, 1965) .

Tennyson's exquisite lyrics have come, not always with very happy results, under scrutiny of the New Criticism, with its requirements of paradox, iron, and ambiguity. In "The Motivation of Tennyson's Weeper" (reprinted from *American Scholar*, 1944, in *The Well-Wrought Urn*, 1947, and in *Critical Essays*, edited by John Killham, 1960) , Cleanth Brooks appraises "Tears, Idle Tears." Brooks's estimate of the poet is that: "Like his own protagonist in *In Memoriam*, Tennyson 'fought his doubts' — he does not typically build them into the structure of the poetry itself as enriching ambiguities." In this lyric, however, the critic finds that Tennyson, accidentally as it were, produced a "very highly organized" work of art: "It represents an organic structure; and the intensity of the total effect is a reflection of the total structure."

Brooks's article has stirred up a lively critical give-and-take. In " 'Thought' and Emotional Quality: Notes in the Analysis of Poetry" (*Scrutiny*, 1945) , Frank R. Leavis glances unsympathetically at "Tears, Idle Tears," together with "Break, Break, Break," both of which he finds unsatisfactory in their attempt to offer "emotion directly, emotion for its own sake without a justifying situation. . . ." Frederick W. Bateson's *English Poetry: A Critical Introduction* (1950) contains the chapter, "Romantic Schizophrenia: Tennyson's 'Tears, Idle Tears'," which takes the position that the lyric functions on two levels, public and private, and that the levels fail to coalesce: "The days that are no more are at one and the same time the historic past and Tennyson's passionate, unhappy twenties. And between the two meanings no real link whatever is provided or apparently even felt necessary." In "Tears, Idle Tears" (*Hopkins Review*, 1951, and reprinted in *Critical Essays*, edited by John Killham, 1960) , Graham Hough undertakes to rescue Tennyson from the reductive mechanics of this type of criticism, by emphasizing the emotional rather than the intellectual appeal of the poet's lyric voice. Of Tennyson's "greatest successes," Hough perceptively states that they "again and again are found to lie in his power of taking an extremely vague and unspecific and objectless emotion, and giving it form, not indeed by intellectualizing it, but by embodying it, partly in images, partly in sound-patterns, of which he is one of the greatest masters in the language. Sometimes [as in 'Tears, Idle Tears'] he even so orders these private and morbid emotions that they come to correspond with the general experience of the human species."

In partial disagreement with both Brooks and Hough, Leo Spitzer brings his formidable learning somewhat irrelevantly to bear on an investigation of the meaning of "some divine despair" in "Tears, Idle Tears Again" (*Hopkins Review*, 1952, and reprinted in *Critical Essays*, edited by John Killham, 1960, and in *Essays on English and American Literature*, edited by Anna Hatcher, 1962). Frederick L. Gwynn's "Tennyson's 'Tithon', 'Tears, Idle Tears', and 'Tithonus' " (*PMLA*, 1952), convincingly relates the lyric to the early version of "Tithonus" in terms of subject matter, structure, imagery, and vocabulary. A later contextual study by Edward P. Vandiver, Jr. (*Expl*, Item 53, 1963), asserts that Brooks's claims for the lyric are even more cogent when its place in the total structure of *The Princess* is considered. In his article on "Tears, Idle Tears" in *Tulane Studies in English* (1963), Thomas J. Assad argues rather confusingly that, while the logical and prosodic ordering are at odds, the imagery reconciles the two "to produce a composite harmony."

Among Tennyson's other lyrics, "Crossing the Bar" has perhaps excited the greatest flurry of exegetical activity. Articles by the following may be cited: Lord Dunsany (*Poetry Review*, 1950); Harry W. Rudman (*Expl*, Item 45, 1950); Frederick L. Jones (*Expl*, Item 19, 1951); John T. Fain and G. Geoffrey Langsam (*Expl*, Comment 40, 1952); Thomas J. Assad (*Tulane Studies in English*, 1958); Paull F. Baum (*ELN*, 1963); James R. Kincaid (*VP*, 1965); and Milton Millhauser (*VP*, 1966). The tendency to over-anatomize Tennyson's lyric practice receives a salutary corrective in Phyllis Rackin's "Recent Misreadings of 'Break, Break, Break' and Their Implications for Poetic Theory" (*JEGP*, 1966),

77

which points out the inappropriateness of a critical approach which lets "the demand for paradox and striking metaphor obscure our vision of poems that work in other ways." The author's own very perceptive analysis of the poem's meaning is "guided . . . by the intention that emerges from the total poetic statement."

Finally, mention may be made of a scattering of articles on individual poems which further indicate the vitality and range of current Tennysonian research and criticism. Two articles by G. Robert Stange (both reprinted in *Critical Essays,* edited by John Killham, 1960), initiate investigation into the important subject of Tennyson's handling of myth. The earlier of these, "Tennyson's Garden of Art: A Study of 'The Hesperides' " (*PMLA,* 1952), suggests affinities between Tennyson and Yeats. The author reads this obscure poem as "an interpretation of the spiritual conditions under which the poetic experience comes to life. It is in essence a symbolic statement of the situation of the artist, and the inner pattern of completely associated motifs and images may all be seen to lead towards and to enforce this core of meaning." In a second article, "Demeter and Persephone (*ELH,* 1954), Stange adduces additional evidence that Tennyson anticipated "the reinterpretation of mythology which has informed some of the most distinguished poetry of our century." "The most striking achievement of the poem is the consistency with which the language of myth is used to include reflections on the nature of artistic creation, on the condition of the age, and on religious doctrine." Curtis Dahl in "A Double Frame for Tennyson's Demeter?" (*VS,* 1958), attributes to the poem the twofold purpose of incorporating Christian teaching along with a rebuttal of Swinburne's celebration of pagan virtues, especially in "Hymn to Proserpine." Tennyson, the writer believes, was undertaking to show "that the myth of Proserpine can be interpreted better as an allegory of Christian hope than as an allegory of pessimistic fatalism." In the same category with these articles belongs Lona M. Packer's "Sun and Shadow: The Nature of Experience in Tennyson's 'The Lady of Shalott' " (*VNL,* 1964), which associates the theme of the poem with Plato's allegory of the cave-dwellers.

Alan Grob makes an instructive comparison between the 1832 and 1842 versions of "The Lotos-Eaters" (*MP,* 1964). The poem, he proposes, was first conceived as a choric song in the manner of "The Hesperides," but was later revised into something like a dramatic monologue. This remodeling indicates that "Tennyson had plainly been touched by the spirit of the age. . . . Revision then meant the transformation of a troubled discourse in which the intangibles of the life of art seem finally to prevail over the urgencies of a life of action into an unqualified indictment of aesthetic irresponsibility." This interpretation receives support from Malcolm MacLaren in "Tennyson's Epicurean Lotos-Eaters" (*Classical Journal*, 1961). The writer, showing that the mariners are presented as Epicureans, extols "Tennyson's accomplishment in drawing upon one of the major philosophies of the ancient world for his statement of the artistic creed which he rejects."

Ernest C. Bufkin's "Imagery in 'Locksley Hall' " (*VP*, 1964), attempts to prove, on the basis of rather wire-drawn evidence, that this poem is constructed around three interweaving patterns of imagery, relating to time, water, and the sky. An article by Thomas J. Assad in *Tulane Studies in English* (1965) is concerned with the thematic unity of the first five poems in Tennyson's prodigiously popular *Enoch Arden* volume. The writer asserts that these "poems together reveal a similar criss-cross pattern in the handling of the common theme, which is a twofold distinction between spiritual and material wealth on the one hand and the complementary distinction between religious sentiment and religiosity on the other." Writing in *Listener* (2 April 1964), Philip Drew selects "Aylmer's Field" for a skillful analysis of the control of narrative pace which typifies Tennyson's handling of the domestic Idyls.

William Cadbury moves in significant new directions in a pair of articles concerned with problems of form. "The Utility of the Poetic Mask in Tennyson's 'Supposed Confessions' " (*MLQ*, 1963) discusses the poet's assumption of a *persona* as a means of presenting "the spectacle of ruled emotion, without sacrificing the intensity of emotional conflict." "Tennyson's 'The Palace of Art' and the Rhetoric of Structures" (*Criticism*, 1965) somewhat esoterically locates the ordering principle of this poem in a "dialectical" procedure. "By fully realizing each stage of advancing thought," the author writes, "Tennyson allows us first to see the works of the palace in the perfection he intended; then

79

to find their insufficiency and its causes in the Soul whose error distorts her response; and finally to feel the adequacy of the suggested retreat, the cottage in the vale in which she will be made whole. Because each part is self-contained, asking of the reader the acceptance of its proper tone, the structure is seen as the play of parts against each other, a dialectic which carries the reader to a synthesis of values which could not have been achieved by any other rhetorical order." In " 'The Palace of Art' Revisited" (*VP*, 1966), Joseph Sendry provides in more traditional terms a new interpretation of the theme of the poem as "a moral allegory of crime and punishment" in which "the Soul's progress towards self-awareness becomes a paradigm of universal moral experience."

Robert Browning

PARK HONAN

I. BIBLIOGRAPHY

Browning bibliographies published before 1953 must be treated warily. Since F. J. Furnivall and T. J. Wise knew the poet personally and were painstaking in their ways a few features in their eccentric works are still of interest. F. J. Furnivall's *A Bibliography of Robert Browning, from 1833 to 1881* (first published in the London *Browning Society's Papers,* 1881–1882, and separately in 1883) includes useful data in its hectic footnotes and generous extracts from contemporary notices of Browning's poems. Thomas J. Wise's Browning bibliographies must be used in the light of John Carter and Graham Pollard's disclosures in 1934. (Wilfred Partington's *Forging Ahead* — revised as *Thomas J. Wise in the Original Cloth,* 1946 — is at once a life of Wise and a bibliophile's history of Wise's forgeries, and this work summarizes Browning's relations with the man whom he called "unwise Wise.") T. J. Wise's list of "Materials" in *Literary Anecdotes of the Nineteenth Century,* edited by W. R. Nicoll and T. J. Wise (volume I, 1895), has suggestive notes and brief extracts from Victorian reviews. Without these review-extracts, "Materials" forms the basis of T. J. Wise's notorious *A Complete Bibliography of the Writings in Prose and Verse of Robert Browning* (1897). Also flawed but illuminating is T. J. Wise's later volume, *A Browning Library* (1929).

A. J. Armstrong, who established a rich collection of Browningiana at Baylor University, launched the *Baylor Browning Interests* series in 1927. Some early *Interests,* edited by Armstrong, are merely chatty newsletters, but most give short bibliographies, letters, studies or other pertinent materials.

A rigorously disciplined and comprehensive bibliography appeared in 1953 as *Robert Browning: A Bibliography, 1830–1950,* by L. N. Broughton, C. S. Northup, and Robert Pearsall. This invaluable work is the standard one. It offers exhaustive listings of Browning's manuscripts and publications, reference materials, biographical and critical studies to 1951, and representative lists of versified appreciations, parodies, and the like. Though its "Calendar of Letters" is the most extensive published census of Browning's letters it is far from complete and badly needs revision. The compilers failed to list some of Browning's short uncollected poems and verse fragments. Their lists of studies and translations in "languages not widely used or understood in the Western world" are meagre, but they refer to A. J. Armstrong's no longer timely though suggestive "Foreign" bibliographies in the *Interests* (1933), especially for T. Sone's census of Japanese Browningiana.

Two short supplements to the standard bibliography have appeared. A list of publications on Browning from January, 1951, through May, 1965, is given in *The Browning Critics*, edited by Boyd Litzinger and K. L. Knickerbocker (1965). It has a few curious inaccuracies — for example, B. Hardy's "Mr. Browning and George Eliot" (p. 399) has nothing to do with the poet. For the *Interests* (1961), Mrs. Steven Sanders has compiled a calendar of 199 Browning letters at Baylor, all but four dated after 1855, and standing for only a fraction of the poet's extant letters that are not listed in Broughton, Northup, and Pearsall.

W. C. DeVane's *A Browning Handbook* (second edition, 1955) gives mainly reliable bibliographical data about Browning's separate poems, with annotated and selected lists of editions, letter collections, biographies, and studies. Good selected lists of Browning studies are included in *Victorian Poetry,* edited by E. K. Brown and J. O. Bailey (second edition, 1962), and in *Victorian Poets & Prose Writers,* compiled by J. H. Buckley (1966).

For titles and editions of books that Browning owned, one should see the relevant sales catalogs published after his son's death. A number are listed in Broughton, Northup, and Pearsall but by far the most important is Sotheby, Wilkinson, and Hodge's catalog for May 1–9, 1913. Browning material of special interest is to be found in the Balliol, Baylor, Boston Public Library, British Museum, Folger, Harvard, Huntington, New York Public Library, University of Texas, Victoria and Albert, Wellesley, and Yale manuscript collections.

A Concordance to the Poems of Robert Browning by L. N. Broughton and B. F. Stelter (two volumes, 1924–1925) remains a standard work.

II. EDITIONS

There is no complete edition of Browning's poetry. The best modern collected editions are still *The Works of Robert Browning* or the Centenary Edition, edited by F. G. Kenyon (ten volumes, 1912; reprinted, 1966); and *The Complete Works of Robert Browning* or the Florentine Edition, edited by Charlotte Porter and Helen A. Clarke (twelve volumes, 1910). These were supplemented by F. G. Kenyon's *New Poems by Robert Browning and Elizabeth Barrett Browning* in 1914. The Centenary and Florentine editions are based mainly on the "Fourth and complete edition" of Smith, Elder, and Co., *The Poetical Works of Robert Browning* (seventeen volumes, 1888–1894), all but the last volume of which the poet supervised.

The most useful single volume is the Macmillan *The Complete Poetical Works of Robert Browning, New Edition with Additional Poems First Published in 1914,* edited by Augustine Birrell (1915). Since 1929 substantially the same edition (except that it omits line numbers and some editorial comment) has been issued by Murray in London as *The Poetical Works of Robert Browning.*

The one-volume Cambridge edition of 1895 includes Browning's essay on Shelley and ten additional lines for the epilogue to *Dramatic Idyls, Second Series,* but it leaves out a few poems that are in the Birrell.

Over fifteen versicles and fragments of poems by Browning have not appeared in any collected edition of his works. Among the more interesting are an eight-line impromptu on the Carlyles (*Alfred Lord Tennyson: A Memoir by His Son,* 1897, II, 230); a quatrain on Charles Dickens (*UTQ,* 1952, p. 181); a quatrain for Pen Browning (*N&Q,* 1966, p. 340); and three early scraps of verse on the Rev. Thomas Ready and his Peckham school (in Mrs. S. Orr's *Life and Letters of Robert Browning,* 1891, p. 56, and in *Diary of Alfred Domett,* edited by E. A. Horsman, 1953, pp. 73–74).

Little close attention has been paid to Browning's textual alterations though DeVane's *Handbook* comments on some of them. The best textual studies are A. K. Cook's "Appendix XI" in his *A Commentary upon Browning's The Ring and the Book* (1920; reprinted, 1966), and N. Hardy Wallis's *Pauline by Robert Browning: The Text of 1833, Compared with That of 1867 and 1888* (1931). As the latter shows, Browning revised *Pauline* so thoroughly in 1867 and 1888 that the final text alone (given in most of the collected editions) cannot be said to represent *Pauline* adequately.

The best notes for Browning's less-read works are in the Florentine Edition. A. K. Cook's study of *The Ring and the Book* and W. C. DeVane's study of *Parleyings With Certain People of Importance,* in effect, annotate those poems expertly, and some of Browning's shorter poems have been treated well in various anthologies and selections. Late and less-read works such as *Aristophanes' Apology* or *The Inn Album* have been wretchedly served: these usually appear in unannotated editions with columns of miniscule print and no line numbers. Even that a poem has been annotated often is no proof that it has been annotated well, as R. D. Altick's "Memo to the Next Annotator of Browning" (*VP,* 1963) reminds us with convincing examples. Browning's reading went very far afield; his allusions are often obscure and sometimes ambiguous, as readers of even so deceptively easy a poem as "Soliloquy of the Spanish Cloister" know. Helpful though occasionally sparse notes are given in A. J. Whyte's *Sordello* edition (1913) and in E. A. Parker's "school" text of *Balaustion's Adventure* (1928). E. H. Hickey's *Strafford* edition (1884) relies on a few of Browning's late comments on passages in that play.

Several promising projects are under way. John Bryson is preparing a Browning edition in two or three volumes for The Clarendon Press. Ohio University Press plans to bring out a complete and variorum edition of Browning's poems with his Chatterton and Shelley essays, under the general editorship of R. A. King, Jr. — assisted by M. Peckham, G. Pitts, and others. The thirteen projected Ohio volumes will record variants in wording, spelling, capitalization, and punctuation in Browning's surviving manuscripts and in the various English texts of each poem as published throughout the poet's lifetime, with brief factual notes on proper names, locations, and foreign and rare words.

Even so, the task of annotating Browning is likely to remain a continuing one. The need for an inexpensive edition of his complete poetry and two important essays is still great.

III. BIOGRAPHY

The standard biography by W. H. Griffin and H. C. Minchin, *The Life of Robert Browning with Notices of his Writings, his Family, and his Friends* (1910; revised edition, 1938), is restrained, judicious, factual, and offers a masterly account of early influences that helped shape the poet's career. But even Minchin's revised edition of 1938 fails to mention Julia Wedgwood, makes scant use of the poet's letters to Isabella Blagden, and has other large gaps. Mrs. Sutherland Orr knew Browning intimately and had access to important letters, from which she quotes liberally in her *Life and Letters of Robert Browning* (1891; revised edition, 1908), a valuable book. Only some of its inaccuracies were corrected in F. G. Kenyon's revised edition of this work in 1908, however. *Robert Browning, Personalia* by Edmund Gosse (1890) is even less reliable in detail but has more insight than other appreciations written just after the poet's death. Dowden's (1904) and Herford's (1905) biographies are now mainly of interest for their intelligent criticism. Lilian Whiting's *The Brownings: Their Life and Art* (1911), though effusive, illuminates Browning's later years — especially his relations with Mrs. Bronson.

Anomalies in Browning's character were noted with varying

degrees of perception and amazement in his day, and F. R. G. Duckworth studies them objectively in *Browning: Background and Conflict* (1931). Duckworth finds first, that Browning unconsciously and "to some extent" consciously dissociated his poetry from his life; second, that poetic creation was acutely distressful for him; and third, that he found great difficulty in trying to say what he intended in his own "voice" in his poems. S. W. Holmes uses Carl Jung's theories and Browning's early poems to pursue brilliantly the psychological implications of these and related ideas. In "Browning's *Sordello* and Jung: Browning's *Sordello* in the Light of Jung's Theory of Types" (*PMLA*, 1941), Holmes contends that the writing of *Pauline* helped Browning to discover and to objectify for himself his nearly psychotic condition of "unbalanced introversion" and that his seven years' work on *Sordello* had a more complex psychotherapeutic value. Browning, in effect, identified with Sordello and progressed slowly toward an enlightened condition of "unprejudiced objectivity" with the help of guiding female symbols, just as Sordello is made to do. *Sordello* prepared him for the role of the prophet-poet. But in "Browning: Semantic Stutterer" (*PMLA*, 1945), Holmes undertakes to show that this was a role Browning was otherwise unsuited for by training. The result was that he developed two personalities and became an ineffective "semantic stutterer" whenever he turned to metaphysical subjects, as in *Christmas-Eve* or *La Saisiaz*. "As metaphysician, prophet-poet, personality complex #1, he suffered and stuttered; as dramatic poet, artist, personality complex #2, he flourished and sang." Though tentative, Holmes' "neuro-semantic, neuro-linguistic" analysis has a bearing on Browning's religious poems and on his obscurity and style generally.

Two later analysts of Browning's psyche have been less sympathetic. R. D. Altick's "The Private Life of Robert Browning" (*YR*, 1951; reprinted in *The Browning Critics*, 1965), finds Browning's reputed healthiness symptomatic of mental sickness, of deep insecurity and guilt owing to his early allegiance to Voltaire's and Shelley's writings and to his later fear of speaking out and betraying "his own heart" and his philosophic illiteracy. Overprotected in childhood and lacking the training to contend with liberalism, rationalism, or science on their own terms, Browning pulled the robes of the "Seer" over his shoulders. Altick offers a salutary antidote to Browning adulation and builds shrewdly on some of Duckworth's and Holmes' ideas, but he has been challenged with partial success by K. L. Knickerbocker in "A Tentative Apology for Browning" (*TSL,* 1956; also in *The Browning Critics*). Betty Miller's *Robert Browning: A Portrait* (1952) is an irresistibly well-written biography that at times takes unbecoming liberty with quotations and incidental facts. But Mrs. Miller offers compelling psychological interpretations of Browning's relations with the important women in his life — particularly, of course, with his mother and Elizabeth Barrett, but also with Eliza Flower and Fanny Haworth, Isa Blagden, Julia Wedgwood and Lady Ashburton, and still later, Miss Egerton Smith, Mrs. Bloomfield-Moore, and Mrs. Bronson. One main thesis involves all of these. Browning's attitude of prolonged and nearly abject dependency on his mother conditioned his adult responses to the women he was fond of or loved: he needed to see them as wiser, more gifted, morally better or simply as more commanding than himself. Mrs. Miller's intuitive treatment of these relations is often brilliant. She draws on new material almost throughout and offers new — sometimes forced — readings of poems. Her account of the essay on Shelley is misleading; she neglects some aspects of the poet's intellectual life and poems that do not readily lend themselves to her thesis. But like Altick's shorter study her book destroys myths, humanizes its subject through unrelenting irony, and is likely to stimulate further realistic appraisals. Despite faults in handling detail, *A Portrait* is the best interpretive biography of Browning — and of his son as well.

J. M. Cohen's *Robert Browning* (1952; reprinted, 1964) is a brief life that concentrates less on Browning than on his poems, and has refreshingly original comments on some of the later works especially. Norman Lindsay's essay, "The Mask of Robert Browning" (*Southerly,* 1959), makes explicit what is implicit in Altick's and Mrs. Miller's probings: most Browning biographies have neglected the "off-stage part of Browning's life." Lindsay's own treatment of the poet's private life is ill-informed but his complaints are pointed. "The Death of Robert Browning" by B. R. Jerman (*UTQ,* 1965), on the poet's final months and the hubbub over his Westminster burial, implicitly criticizes Browning biographers for neglecting incidental Victorian sources. Jerman's tale "of an old man who got sick and died" is wickedly amusing, exhaustively documented, and more revealing of an epoch than of Browning. His research partly discredits Fannie Barrett Browning's slim volume, *Some Memories of Robert Browning by His Daughter-in-Law* (1928). *Forever in Joy: The Life of Robert Browning* by Rosemary Sprague (1965) is worth mentioning, I think, only for a remark it has on Wilkie Collins' novels and *The Ring and the Book*.

Good biographies of Elizabeth Barrett Browning illuminate Browning's career between 1845 and 1861. Two studies of their son help to explain Browning's outlook after 1861: "Robert Browning and his Son" by Gertrude Reese (*PMLA,* 1946) and "The Child of Casa Guidi" by Betty Miller (*Cornhill Magazine,* 1949). Both show how Pen's dismal academic failure and later career as a painter affected and involved his father. The London (but not the New York) edition of Frances Winwar's *The Immortal Lovers: Elizabeth Barrett and Robert Browning* (1950) states that Pen fathered two illegitimate children in Brittany shortly before he went up to Oxford. Mrs. Winwar's source for this remark is not clear, but M. L. G. De Courten's "Pen, il figlio dei Browning" (*EM,* 1957) — an article that synthesizes data in earlier studies of Pen — accepts the Breton children as factual, as does Mrs. Miller's *Portrait*. Gertrude Reese Hudson, at any rate, is planning a new study of the son.

More relevant to the study of his poems has been the discovery of Browning's inept proposal of marriage to the charming, impetuous, and perhaps overpowering Louisa, Lady Ashburton in either 1869 or 1870. "Browning and Lady Ashburton" by T. L. Hood (*YR,* 1932, and printed as an appendix to Hood's edition of *Letters of Robert Browning,* 1933) gives the circumstances, and Mrs. Miller's *Portrait* interprets them and traces their influence on several poems — notably "Numpholeptos." *Fifine* owes to Browning's consequent feeling that he had betrayed Elizabeth, as W. O. Raymond expertly shows in "Browning's Dark Mood: A Study of *Fifine at the Fair*" (*SP,* 1934; reprinted in Raymond's *The Infinite Moment,* 1950 and 1965). K. L. Knickerbocker's "An Echo from Browning's Second Courtship" (*SP,* 1935) reads "St. Martin's Summer" in a similar light, and DeVane's *Handbook* points to Louisa's lingering presence in "A Parleying with Daniel Bartoli." J. H. Friend's "Euripides Browningized: The Meaning of *Balaustion's Adventure*" (*VP*, 1964) is an intriguing interpretation of autobiographical elements in a poem that must have been written very soon after the affair ended.

More recently, J. M. Hitner has argued in "Browning's Grotesque Period" (*VP*, 1966) that *Red Cotton Night-Cap Country* and *The Inn Album* reflect bitterness and philosophic despair that overcame Browning in the years 1872–1875, partly owing to Louisa's rejection of him. A case of "sexual restlessness" is the gist of Barbara Melchiori's very Freudian diagnosis, in "Browning's Don Juan" (*EIC*, 1966), which analyzes the "basic sex imagery" in *Fifine*. Biographical speculations in the last two articles are interesting but based on incomplete evidence.

Still other special studies explore limited aspects of Browning's life. Sir Vincent Baddeley's "The Ancestry of Robert Browning, the Poet" (*Genealogists' Magazine*, 1938) is the best but not the definitive account of the poet's ancestry; a résumé in the 1953 *Bibliography* by L. N. Broughton, *et al*, shows how vexed this topic still is (see entry C1375).

Donald Smalley's thorough article, "Joseph Arnould and Robert Browning: New Letters (1842–50) and a Verse Epistle" (*PMLA*, 1965), gives new details about Browning's career and his close friendship with Arnould, and also about his early relations with another fellow-member of "The Colloquial" and "The Set," young Alfred Domett. Arnould, Smalley shows, was "a fierce advocate" of *A Blot in the 'Scutcheon*. And Joseph W. Reed, Jr., in "Browning and Macready: The Final Quarrel" (*PMLA*, 1960), examines Browning's revisions and Macready's proposed cuts and changes in the manuscript of this play, now at Yale, in order to establish the exact cause of Browning's quarrel with the actor-manager over *A Blot*. Reed usefully reviews Browning's and Macready's dealings from 1836 to 1843, but concentrates on what happened to the playscript during the fortnight before the play opened. This article — with Macready's *Diaries* — suggests that enough material exists for a full-length study of the important relations between the two men.

Betty Miller has written about two crucial evenings. " 'This Happy Evening' " (*TC*, 1953) concerns Browning and Macready's meeting at Talfourd's supper-party after *Ion's* performance, 26 May, 1836, when the poet's playwriting career virtually began. And Mrs. Miller's "The Seance at Ealing: A Study in Memory and Imagination" (*Cornhill Magazine*, 1957) treats Robert's and Elizabeth's attendance at D. D. Home's seance, 23 July 1855 — when Robert, perhaps, was vexed precisely because he did not catch "Mr. Sludge" at legerdemain. Both essays are convincing but add slightly to the known facts. Katherine H. Porter's *Through a Glass Darkly: Spiritualism in the Browning Circle* (1958) sketches in the social background of the spiritualism craze that possessed Elizabeth and finally led Browning to write a damning monologue about D. D. Home.

M. H. Shackford's Wellesley College monograph, *The Brownings and Leighton* (1942), focuses on Robert and Elizabeth's relations with Mrs. Orr's brother, (Sir) Frederick Leighton, their intimate friend. This work is helpful, but it treats the later London years — when Browning saw Leighton often and certainly used him for Pen's benefit — rather thinly. A primary source for Browning's later years is E. A. Horsman's splendid edition of *The Diary of Alfred Domett 1872-1885* (1953). Domett, an ex-Prime Minister of New Zealand and a poet in his own right by 1872, was a sharp and sensible observer of his old friend. He summarizes and sometimes quotes verbatim in the *Diary* from talks with Browning about the latter's past, his poems, his son, and many current activities. Two volumes of Leon Edel's thorough biography of an even more perceptive friend illuminate Browning's later social milieu in London and Venice: *Henry James, 1870–1881: The Conquest of London* (1962) and *Henry James, 1882–1895: The Middle Years* (1962). James's relations with Browning, and the character of their solicitous mutual friend, Mrs. Bronson, are well in focus. Edel confirms a conclusion in S. E. Lind's "James's 'The Private Life' and Browning" (*AL*, 1951) to the effect that the celebrated story by James about an author with a literal double existence (Clare Vawdrey in "The Private Life") is as much about James as about Browning. An implication is that James's more direct remarks about the poet may be tinted with "disguised autobiography" as well. *Robert Browning's Finances from His Own Account Book*, by R. A. King, Jr. (1947), closely examines the poet's records of his accounts during the years 1886 to 1889 for information about his habits, his reading, his pocketbook, his social engagements, and the popularity of his works at the time. This indicative little book is based on material at Baylor.

Several studies of Browning's ideas and works help to clarify h i s whole career — particularly W. C. DeVane's *Browning's Parleyings: The Autobiography of a Mind* (1927; reprinted, 1964), C. R. Tracy's succinct "Browning's Heresies" (*SP*, 1936), and Donald Smalley's edition of the Tasso review-article, *Browning's Essay on Chatterton* (1948).

Gaps in the investigation of Browning's life still exist. Studies of his reading, of his French and Italian acquaintanceships, and of his early life would be helpful. In time we may expect to learn more about his relations with a whole host of figures, including de Ripert-Monclar, Horne, Forster, Dickens, Tennyson, Arnold, George Eliot, Rossetti, Swinburne, Mrs. Orr, F. J. Furnivall, and — quite possibly — Julia Wedgwood and Lady Ashburton, to name a few. His later social years in London have been thinly sketched though often interpreted. At least two Browning biographies are in preparation: one by Maisie Ward Sheed, the other by William Irvine and Park Honan.

IV. LETTERS

Few letters Browning wrote are more revealing of his character, outlook, and ideas about art than his celebrated "love letters" to Elizabeth Barrett, first published with hers as *The Letters of Robert Browning and Elizabeth Barrett Barrett, 1845–1846* (two volumes, 1899). A glance at the index is instructive. Elvan Kintner is reediting the holographs, now at Wellesley; his edition will be published by Harvard University Press.

Three other early volumes have important Browning letters: Mrs. Sutherland Orr's *Life and Letters of Robert Browning* (1891; revised edition, 1908); *Robert Browning and Alfred Domett*, edited by F. G. Kenyon (1906); and Lilian Whiting's *The Brownings: Their Life and Art* (1911). Mrs. Orr quotes letters from every period in Browning's career. Browning's letters to Domett are richly revealing. Those he wrote in late life to Mrs. Bronson, quoted by Lilian Whiting, tend to be more bland.

Letters of Robert Browning, Collected by Thomas J. Wise, edited by T. L. Hood (1933), offers a large and indispensable collection ranging from 1830 to 1889. Hood's notes are copious and masterly, and his appendix on the Lady Ashburton affair is most useful. The volume deserves reprinting.

Two collections of minor significance appeared in 1935. H. W. Donner's *The Browning Box* has letters to T. F. Kelsall and his wife that Browning wrote from 1867 to 1874 about the Beddoes manuscripts entrusted to him. Here the poet's politeness usually conceals what he thinks. *Twenty-two Unpublished Letters of Elizabeth Barrett Browning and Robert Browning, Addressed to Henrietta and Arabella Moulton-Barrett* gives texts first edited by W. R. Benét for *Woman's Home Companion* (1935). These offer details about the Brownings' early years of marriage.

Slim and lightly annotated, *Robert Browning and Julia Wedgwood: A Broken Friendship as Revealed by Their Letters,* edited by Richard Curle (1937), is of major importance. Here Browning discusses his interest in moral evil, his intentions in writing *The Ring and the Book*, and his portrayal of Guido. Throughout he comments on his critics, on contemporary poets — showing in detail how he would rewrite "Enoch Arden" — and on his activities from 1864 to 1869. The correspondence documents his intellectual flirtation with Charles Darwin's gloomy, pious, rather philistine but not unintelligent niece, Julia Wedgwood. Curle's introduction is useful, but more data about this lady is given in C. H. Herford's prefatory "Memoir" to her posthumous *The Personal Life of Josiah Wedgwood, The Potter, by His Great-Grand-Daughter, the Late Julia Wedgwood* (1915). (A biography of Miss Wedgwood is needed.)

New Letters of Robert Browning, edited by W. C. DeVane and K. L. Knickerbocker (1950), is another general collection, supplementing Hood's of 1933, with some four hundred letters for the years 1835 to 1889. Important ones Browning wrote to Macready, Forster, Chapman, Smith the publisher, and Pen Browning are included, with ample notes and a detailed résumé of Browning's trouble with the firm of Chapman and Hall.

Dearest Isa: Robert Browning's Letters to Isabella Blagden (1951) and *Learned Lady: Letters from Robert Browning to Mrs. Thomas FitzGerald, 1876–1889* (1966) — two volumes resourcefully edited by E. C. McAleer — illuminate twenty-eight of the last thirty-two years of the poet's life. *Dearest Isa* (which supersedes A. J. Armstrong's incomplete and editorially flawed volume of Browning's letters to Miss Blagden printed in 1923) has thirty-eight letters written from 1857 to 1861 in Italy and France before Elizabeth Browning's death, and 115 more for the years 1861 to 1872. As a widower Browning wrote regularly, informally, hastily, often superficially to his sympathetic friend among the Anglo-Florentines, and yet he commented to Miss Blagden on most subjects that mattered to him: his poems, his Brittany sojourns, his contemporaries, his mourned wife, and his son. The letters of 1876–1889 collected in *Learned Lady* that he sent to the rich, generous, mildly bookish, elderly Mrs. FitzGerald are more reserved but filled with incidental details.

Letters of the Brownings to George Barrett, edited by Paul Landis and R. E. Freeman (1958), tells much about Browning's marriage and his problems later on with Pen. This volume's first section has a few letters Browning wrote among many of Elizabeth's to her brother, and the second section has thirty for the years 1861 to 1889 from Browning to his brother-in-law that are often remarkably candid: Pen's "exquisite stupidity" — and later "cleverness" — drive his father to significant self-revelation. *Browning to his American Friends: Letters between the Brownings, the Storys and James Russell Lowell, 1841–1890,* edited by G. R. Hudson (1965), gives the richly revealing letters Browning sent the sculptor W. W. Story, his wife, and their daughter, Edith. Those of the eighteen-sixties are best, but several of the 'seventies (with Mrs. Hudson's suggestive notes) are primary sources for the Lady Ashburton affair. After his proposal to that lady, Browning's relations with the Storys cooled so that his letters to them after 1872 are more conventional. The four Browning wrote to J. R.

Lowell are very slight. Browning's letter to Story from Asolo should be dated 1878 instead of 1889 incidentally (see page 193).

Only a few of the many Browning letters printed singly or in small groups can be mentioned. Four of his letters to Joseph Milsand have been published by W. Thomas in two issues of *Revue Germanique* (1921 and 1923). W. H. G. Armytage's "Robert Browning and Mrs. Pattison: Some Unpublished Browning Letters" (*UTQ*, 1952) gives a series of short letters about his social life, reading, friends, and son that Browning sent George Eliot's "Dorothea," Mrs. Emily Pattison, mainly in the 1870's. Armytage's "Some New Letters of Robert Browning, 1871–1889" (*MLQ*, 1951) merely illustrates the poet's effusiveness at its worst in excerpts from his missives to the wife and daughter of A. J. Mundella: e. g., "Again your beautiful roses, and, even better still, your beloved words!" W. H. Stone's "Browning and 'Mark Rutherford'" (*RES*, 1953) gives three rather innocuous letters, with some more interesting notes by William Hale White about visits with Browning in 1879 and 1881.

Many of Browning's letters are trivial. Yet he wrote meaningfully to the few men and women he loved or deeply respected, and John Ruskin is the latter category. His letter to Ruskin of February 1, 1856, printed in the Baylor *Interests* (1958), is concerned with *Sordello*, verse technique, Scott, and Wordsworth: "Of all my things," Browning confesses to Ruskin at one point, "the single chance I have had of speaking in my own person — not dramatically—has been in a few words in the course of 'Sordello'." His reasons for quoting brief passages from his own poem are arresting.

M. M. Bevington's "Three Letters of Robert Browning to the Editor of the *Pall Mall Gazette*" (*MLN*, 1960) reprints a letter of 1868 announcing that Elizabeth Browning was the daughter "of a private gentleman," and two of 1870 arguing that Lippi was the elder and teacher of Masaccio. Such public letters are a mild prelude to Browning's public attacks on critics who had maligned his poems or his wife, from Alfred Austin to Edward FitzGerald, in the following decades. C. T. Dougherty publishes newsy, contented, and approving letters to Pen written in 1887 and 1889, in "Three Browning Letters to his Son" (*Manuscripta*, 1962); and L. H. Kendall, Jr., in "A New Browning Letter" (*N&Q*, 1962), edits a contented one to a reviewer of *Ferishtah's Fancies* — George Barnett Smith — who, in accord with Browning's usual practice in the eighties, had been favored with advance proof sheets.

Over two dozen of Browning's letters to the Tennysons remain to be printed, and T. J. Collins is editing them. Christopher Ricks has printed two: one to the Laureate with a gloss on "A Grammarian's Funeral," and the other to Mrs. Tennyson, in 1889, in which Browning explains the circumstances that led him to write his vulgar and insulting sonnet to FitzGerald (*TLS*, 1965).

Though letters Browning received are sometimes revealing, most will interest mainly the biographer. *Intimate Glimpses from Browning's Letter File*, edited by A. J. Armstrong (1934), gives a representative selection of 181 by various persons known or unknown to the poet. Except for one letter of 1848, these are for the years 1862 to 1889; other letters and telegrams relating to offers of rectorships at Scottish universities are included. Letters to Browning from the actress Helena Faucit Martin and from the aged W. S. Landor are printed in the Baylor *Interests* (1931 and 1932). A. B. Harlan and J. L. Harlan, Jr., have edited *Letters from Owen Meredith (Robert, First Earl of Lytton) to Robert and Elizabeth Barrett Browning* (1936), documenting Browning's friendship with Bulwer-Lytton's amorous, literary, and diplomatically inclined son.

A. A. Adrian's "The Browning-Rossetti Friendship: Some Unpublished Letters" (*PMLA*, 1958) includes eleven letters from Rossetti that clarify his relations with Browning during the years 1847–1859. Nine are addressed to Browning and one is to his wife. Another letter, to Walter Deverell, establishes the fact that Rossetti first met the Brownings in 1851. C. R. Sanders' "Some Lost and Unpublished Carlyle-Browning Correspondence" (*JEGP*, 1963) includes three letters from Carlyle to Browning for 1845 and 1856, and a short reply of Browning's written in July, 1856. Sanders reviews some of the main events in this complex and most significant friendship, for which these letters supply a few fresh details.

Many letters Browning wrote to his son Pen, to de Ripert-Monclar, to R. H. Horne, to Tennyson, to Mrs. Bronson, to G. M. Smith, and to F. J. Furnivall remain to be printed. Those he wrote to Mrs. Orr have not been found. Those to Ruskin and Milsand need to be collected.

Two scholars of exceptional skill and patience, Philip Kelley and Ronald Hudson, are now preparing a massive, definitive edition of Robert and Elizabeth Barrett Browning's 11,000 letters, with 700 other letters that were sent to the two poets and 2,300 others written by their relatives, for a total of some 14,000 letters in from twenty-four to thirty-two volumes. Kelley and Hudson estimate that some 3,000 of Robert Browning's 5,000 extant letters and 4,000 of his wife's 6,000 have never been printed.[1]

It is to Philip Kelley that we owe a useful account of the poet's relations with the man who brought out his poems after 1867, "Robert Browning and George Smith: Selections from an Unpublished Correspondence" (*QR*, 1961).

V. CRITICAL AND HISTORICAL STUDIES

Browning's modern critics have been reluctant to commit themselves to generalizations about his immense, richly complex canon — generalizations of the sort late-Victorian and Edwardian critics freely indulged in. Attention has focused on rather few poems. Two of his best plays, *Colombe's Birthday* and *A Soul's Tragedy*, most of his love lyrics, the dramatic idyls, and indeed nearly all of his works dating after 1869 have been badly neglected. Approaches to Browning in the light of linguistics and stylistics,

[1]This monumental project still lacks a publisher. Information about separate Browning letters in smaller or private collections may be sent to Mr. Philip Kelley, care of Armstrong Browning Library, Baylor University, Waco, Texas 76706, U.S.A.

psychology, continental literature, and the English novel tradition (particularly pertinent to *The Ring and the Book*), are still in their infancy. We have only begun to study his structural designs, prosody, diction, imagery, and symbolism.

Browning elicits more critical and scholarly attention than any other Victorian poet, and his reputation is swiftly recovering from its nadir between the two world wars. But we have yet to estimate his artistic strengths and weaknesses convincingly for our time, and to analyze in detail his pervasive influence on twentieth-century poetry.

Handbooks and General Criticism. W. C. DeVane's *A Browning Handbook* (1935; revised edition, 1955) is still "a point of departure for further investigations" and the most useful commentary on Browning ever written, but its critical judgments need to be reexamined or set aside. DeVane's conjectures as to sources, influences, and composition dates are being modified. For its scholarly assemblage of facts for each one of the poems his *Handbook* remains invaluable. F. R. G. Duckworth has pointed to a few glaring errors of fact and interpretation in Mrs. Sutherland Orr's *A Handbook to the Works of Robert Browning* (1885; expanded and emended in successive editions), a work partly based on talks with Browning. But Mrs. Orr gives sensible, concise summaries; her weaknesses are obvious and her occasional suggestiveness is a prime asset. Far less can be said for G. W. Cook's *A Guide-Book to the Poetic and Dramatic Works of Robert Browning* (1891) or Edward Berdoe's *The Browning Cyclopaedia* (1892; reprinted as late as 1958), both of which are haphazard, crammed, and unreliable. Virtually a handbook, Arthur Symons' *An Introduction to the Study of Browning* (1886), is critically discerning.

Comments on Browning by Joseph Milsand, Walter Bagehot, Swinburne, and Pater are still suggestive, as are the *Athenaeum's* and the *Academy's* detailed reviews of his later works (in the 1870's and 1880's). The best of the early general studies of his poetry are Stopford Brooke's *The Poetry of Robert Browning* (1902), G. K. Chesterton's *Robert Browning* (1903), and W. L. Phelps's *Robert Browning: How to Know Him* (1915; revised edition, 1932). Papers of the London Browning Society — an institution whose influence on later attitudes and approaches to

Browning has been cavalierly underestimated — range from being reverently adulatory to critically sophisticated and worthwhile. The purely subjective view of Browning held by a minority of its members is still represented in the writings of Miss Dallas Kenmare, the latest of which is *An End to Darkness: A New Approach to Robert Browning and His Work* (1962).

Among modern studies, W. O. Raymond's *The Infinite Moment and Other Essays in Robert Browning* (1950; republished with new essays and one deletion in 1965) has been deservedly influential. Raymond, in his title essay, sees Browning as an impressionist and humanist of immense versatility and range, who resolved a conflict between intellect and imagination only in poems he wrote between 1840 and 1870. Browning struggled to put the infinite within the finite, as he told Ruskin, or to find adequate forms for new and complex perceptions — a struggle, as Raymond points out, that led to endless technical experimentation. E. D. H. Johnson, in *The Alien Vision of Victorian Poetry* (1952), sees Browning as an experimenter unwilling to concede to his readers' values. Poems from 1833 to 1869 are ably analyzed by Johnson to show that an intuitional psychology lying at the heart of Browning's thought placed him in strong opposition to Victorian institutions and inherited traditions, as well. Many insights result from this approach. Far less original and disciplined in method is *Amphibian: A Reconsideration of Browning* by H. C. Duffin (1956), which finds "singing" and "sermonizing" forever at odds in Browning. Even Duffin's most detailed section, "Metre and Diction," is casually impressionistic: that the poet was "in too much of a hurry to concern himself closely with diction" and that there "is no development of style" in his work are simply false notions.

In 1957 and 1961, Browning studies took a new turn with three exacting books about the dramatic monologue. The most broadly suggestive is Robert Langbaum's *The Poetry of Experience: The Dramatic Monologue in Modern Literary Tradition* (1957). Langbaum relates Browning's monologues to the empiricist and relativist tendencies that deeply inform modern literature. The monologue form, used well, elicits our sympathy for the monologuist. And since it causes us to adopt his point of view in order to judge him, our judgments will be relative ones "befitting an age which has come to consider value as an evolving thing. . . ."

Langbaum thus isolates what is "modern" in the Browning mono-
logue; the genius of the form — a tension it can create between
sympathy and moral judgment — is shown in a compelling reading
of "My Last Duchess." Equally good are Langbaum's treatments
of "Childe Roland" and that "relativist" experiment with points
of view, *The Ring and the Book*.

Roma A. King, Jr.'s *The Bow and the Lyre: The Art of Robert
Browning* (1957) brings methods of close contextualist criticism
to bear on "Andrea del Sarto," "Fra Lippo Lippi," "The Bishop
Orders His Tomb," "Bishop Blougram," and — perhaps more
controversially — on "Saul." King's interest is in how each poem's
sensuous, emotional, and intellectual elements combine with tech-
nical features to yield its "meaning." Browning's minute care as an
artist is demonstrated in King's book, and again in Park Honan's
Browning's Characters: A Study in Poetic Technique (1961),
which is concerned to show as closely as possible how Browning's
techniques of characterization were developed in his plays and
early narratives, what these techniques are, and how they operate
in twenty mature dramatic monologues dating from 1845 to 1871.
William Whitla's *The Central Truth: The Incarnation in Robert
Browning's Poetry* (1963) is rigidly schematic and almost mili-
tantly Christian in its approach, but it illuminates poems with
a more didactic religious content, from 1850 to 1869, by showing
how symbols and analogues of the Incarnation inform them.

The Browning Critics, edited by Boyd Litzinger and K. L.
Knickerbocker (1965), and *Robert Browning: A Collection of
Critical Essays*, edited by Philip Drew (1966), are handy anthol-
ogies of essays about Browning, though both err in reprinting some
available material and in neglecting French and pre-1890 Victorian
criticism. Philip Drew's volume has useful notes. Full-length
studies of Browning by Drew, by T. J. Collins, and by Roma
King, Jr., and a new essay anthology edited by C. R. Tracy, will
appear in the late 1960's.

Browning's Ideas, Interests, and Chief Sources. Few Victorian
or Edwardian studies of Browning's ideas are reliable. Those that
promulgated the myth of Browning as a Christian sage and those
that attempted to scotch the myth helped to create a climate in
which objectivity was nearly impossible. Enormously influential,
Sir Henry Jones's *Browning as a Philosophical and Religious*

Teacher (1891) is at least sane and disciplined. Arguing that Browning's ethical and metaphysical ideas and optimism were not grounded in logic, and that his poems continually insist on a correspondence between divine and human love, Jones treats the poems as metaphysical tracts — a treatment rightly objected to by Philip Drew in "Henry Jones on Browning's Optimism" (*VP*, 1964), a cogent critique of Jones's work. Santayana's "The Poetry of Barbarism" in *Interpretations of Poetry and Religion* (1900), just as influential, offers a caricature of Browning as a nearly mindless advocate of action and feeling, heedless of all consequences, with a volcanic, undisciplined talent. Far more balanced is P. Berger's brief and sophisticated *Quelques Aspects de la foi moderne dans les Poèmes de Robert Browning* (1907). A later continental study, Paul de Ruel's *L'Art et la Pensée de Robert Browning* (1929), combines sensitive poetic criticism with able discussions of the poet's thought.

The best brief study of the development of Browning's religious ideas is C. R. Tracy's "Browning's Heresies" (*SP*, 1936), which traces the influence of W. J. Fox's radical Unitarianism on a poet unwilling to abandon his early emotional bias toward Non-Conformist orthodoxy. The merit of H. B. Charlton's approach in two excellent essays, "Browning's Ethical Poetry" (*BJRL*, 1942) and "Browning as a Poet of Religion" (*BJRL*, 1943), is that it never loses sight of poetic texts. "Karshish," "Cleon," and "Saul" are closely analyzed in the latter essay to show how they explore failures in Arab, Hellenic, and Judaic thought. Browning, concludes Charlton, was "an amateur theologian" who saw "each man seeking to realise himself in satisfying his yearning after God." The poet's ethical concerns are the focus of several of W. O. Raymond's essays in *The Infinite Moment* (1950; 1965), which includes an excellent article on Browning and the Higher Criticism. Kingsbury Badger's " 'See the Christ Stand!': Browning's Religion" (*BUSE*, 1955; reprinted in *Essays*, edited by Drew) is an exacting study of the poet's very individualistic beliefs. H. N. Fairchild treats Browning from a rigidly orthodox viewpoint in *Religious Trends in English Poetry, Vol. IV: 1830–1880* (1957); and J. E. Baker in "Religious Implications in Browning's Poetry" (*PQ*, 1957) offers an acid caricature, in the Santayana vein. Neither Fairchild's nor Baker's Robert Browning is very recognizable. For Baker, he was a carnally-minded and confused poet who sanctified self-indulgence and merely vulgarized theology.

More was to come. Studies of Browning's religious and philosophical ideas proliferated in the early 1960's. James Benziger's chapter on Browning in *Images of Eternity* (1962) stresses theodicy and orthodoxy in his thinking from *Pauline* on. Benziger treats the poet's early religious position judiciously, but neglects the period of his doubts — as in *La Saisiaz* — in the 1870's. More stimulating and controversial is J. Hillis Miller's Browning chapter in *The Disappearance of God* (1963), a work that carries methods of the critical school of Georges Poulet to extremes. Context and chronology are relatively unimportant to Miller: late poems are quoted to illustrate Browning's early attitudes, and a poem of 1864 is quoted to show what he discovered "at last." But Miller's insights are often good. He sees Browning at first trying to imitate and identify with God, and then, having failed to "ape God's infinitude," attempting to reach the Creator's universality by entering into the lives and roles of dramatized characters. For Browning, according to Miller, God has withdrawn from the world and cannot be approached directly.

Equally impressionistic is N. B. Crowell's *The Triple Soul: Browning's Theory of Knowledge* (1963), which attacks a legion of critics for failing to recognize that Browning's "triple" faith in body, spirit, and mind led to a consistent theory of knowledge and saved him from distrusting man's reason. Crowell's bold thesis is not convincingly supported. *The Faith of Robert Browning* by Hugh Martin (1963) is, basically, an intelligent sermon with Browning as the text.

Among special studies, M. G. Machen's *The Bible in Browning* (1903) is a helpful guide to Browning's use of scripture — mainly in *The Ring and the Book*. Judith Berlin-Lieberman, in *Robert Browning and Hebraism* (1934), has valuable comments on the poet's use of Hebrew sources. Browning's attitude toward Catholicism is the topic of Boyd Litzinger's *Robert Browning and the Babylonian Woman* (1962), a study which documents anti-Catholic prejudice but has little to say on the artistic use of Catholics and Catholic ideas in his poems. That a strand of Plotinus and Neoplatonic thought runs through the poems is shown by Jack Matthews in "Browning and Neoplatonism" (*VN*, 1965).

Browning's passionate interest in music has been studied. Included in H. E. Greene's "Browning's Knowledge of Music" (*PMLA,* 1947) is a fascinating letter of 1887 from Browning to Henry Spaulding that suggests the poet's prosody owes much to his early musical training. Greene concludes that the training, under such masters as Relfe and Nathan, was systematic and first-rate. A running account of music references in Browning's published letters is given in R. W. S. Mendl's "Robert Browning, the Poet-Musician" (*M&L,* 1961); and W. Stacy Johnson's "Browning's Music" (*JAAC,* 1963) discusses evocations of the fugue, toccata, improvisation, and march in four poems. Also suggestive is G. M. Ridenour's "Browning's Music Poems: Fancy and Fact" (*PMLA,* 1963), especially for its comments on Browning's notion of the inadequacy of language, and the relevance of this to his poetic treatment of music.

One aspect of his interest in natural life is minutely documented in T. P. Harrison's "Birds in the Poetry of Robert Browning" (*RES,* 1956).

Browning read the ancient Greeks assiduously, borrowed from them, imitated them, translated them, often alluded to them. Among older studies, T. L. Hood's "Browning's Ancient Classical Sources" (*HSCP,* 1922) is more detailed and valuable than E. D. Cressman's "The Classical Poems of Robert Browning" (*CJ,* 1927). Robert Spindler's massive *Robert Browning und die Antike* (1930) rather stiffly explores the poet's use of both Greek and Roman sources; but Spindler's factual data is helpful to anyone attempting to annotate *Balaustion* and Browning's "Greek" works that follow it. More critically perceptive is W. C. DeVane's "Browning and the Spirit of Greece" in *Nineteenth-Century Studies,* edited by H. Davis, W. C. DeVane, and R. C. Bald (1940).

Of limited use are Karl Schmidt's *Robert Brownings Verhältnis zu Frankreich* (1908, 1909) and Richard Albrecht's *Robert Brownings Verhältnis zu Deutschland* (1912), two brief dissertations which are still the best surveys of the overall importance of France and Germany to Browning.

Too little attention has been paid to Browning's use of Shakespeare, despite the looming relevance of the subject. G. R. Elliott's "Shakespeare's Significance for Browning" (*Anglia,* 1909) is filled with precise information but leaves vast gaps. Separate studies of Browning's plays (*Luria* especially), of "Childe Roland," and of "Caliban upon Setebos" involve Shakespeare — but the influence of his style, structures, and characters on many Browning poems remains to be analyzed. Donne's vital bearing has been more thoroughly treated, notably by J. E. Duncan in "The Intellectual Kinship of John Donne and Robert Browning" (*SP*, 1953). A model of its kind, this article takes up some borrowings as well as similarities in attitudes and verse techniques.

Studies of Shelley's influence will be treated later with those of *Pauline*. Browning's relation to the Victorian age has attracted mainly biographers and students of his religion, but he was by no means immune to contemporary literary influences. His "avoidance of the bleak aspects" of industrialism is the topic of D. V. Erdman's "Browning's Industrial Nightmare" (*PQ*, 1957), which sees Elizabeth Barrett's "The Cry of the Children" as "an almost point-by-point refutation" of Browning's rosy picture of the proletariat in *Pippa Passes*. Erdman argues that "Childe Roland" is an inexplicit, nightmarish confession of the poet's guilty awareness of the Victorian wasteland he has neglected. At least he did not neglect contemporary ideas, as not only studies of his religion but C. N. Wenger's *The Aesthetics of Robert Browning* (1924) suggest. Wenger's generalities are often wearisome, but he notes Browning's relation to contemporary German philosophy and certain sharp contrasts between his notions of art and those of Romantic predecessors. The bearing of Ruskin's *Modern Painters* on three poems about painting is treated in Lawrence Poston's "Ruskin and Browning's Artists" (*EM*, 1964).

Henry James, Tillotson, Langbaum, Hugh Sykes Davies, and Rosemary Sprague comment on Browning's relation to the English novel, though briefly and generally. James's lecture on "The Novel in *The Ring and the Book*" (printed in his *Notes on Novelists*, 1914), indicating what might have happened if the OYB had been handed to the master instead of to Miss Ogle, is fanciful but splendid. M. W. Abbott's *Browning and Meredith* (1904) is almost useless, yet suggests a fascinating topic, as do Edward Dowden's fine remarks on Richardson and Browning in his *Robert Browning* (1904). Further studies linking Browning with Scott, with the Gothics from Walpole to Bulwer, and with Disraeli, Dickens, and Collins are, I think, wanted. Moreover, his wide reading in English poetry from Chaucer through Wordsworth and Byron to the Pre-Raphaelites (and in French and Italian literature) suggests that major source studies are yet to come.

Browning's Poetic Techniques. That Browning's vocabulary was vast and that he extended the range of poetic diction cannot be denied. But his artistry in words has been a battleground. His "impatient energy" and "restless activity" led him to avoid simplicity, to use technical words, compounds, a-prefixes, and Latinisms, and to adopt special vocabularies for his various monologues, according to Bernard Groom's *On the Diction of Tennyson, Browning and Arnold* (1939; reprinted with minor revisions in Groom's *The Diction of Poetry from Spenser to Bridges,* 1955). And J. A. Boulton in "Browning: A Potential Revolutionary" (*EIC,* 1953) finds him decidedly inferior to Hopkins, but achieving partial success in the "elaboration of poetic diction along the lines of colloquialism." Closer analyses of contexts suggest that characterization often minutely determines word choice. No better demonstration of the poet's painstaking care with diction and syntax exists than E. K. Brown's "The First Person in 'Caliban upon Setebos'" (*MLN,* 1951), which shows how psychological requirements, from moment to moment in a Browning poem, determine its technique. Statistical and classificatory studies of his diction include B. W. A. Massey's *Browning's Vocabulary: Compound Epithets* (Poznan, 1931) and W. M. Ryan's "The Classifications of Browning's 'Difficult' Vocabulary" (*SP,* 1963). These and other word studies draw heavily on Broughton and Stelter's invaluable *Concordance* (1924–1925).

Good special studies of Browning's imagery include J. K. Bonnell's "Touch Images in the Poetry of Robert Browning" (*PMLA,* 1922), which shows how pervasive his tactile imagery is, and C. Willard Smith's *Browning's Star-Imagery: The Study of a Detail in Poetic Design* (1941). Commenting shrewdly on many poems and on Browning's growth as a poet, Smith follows the evolution of star and light imagery through the poet's entire canon. His book is really a major study of Browning's mind and artistry.

Detailed and still valuable is H. H. Hatcher's *The Versification of Robert Browning* (1928), which supersedes earlier prosodic studies such as A. Beatty's *Browning's Verse Form: Its Organic Character* (1897). But Hatcher's work has two weaknesses: it perpetuates the myth of a ruggedly energetic and careless Browning, and neglects prosodic innovations in some lyrics. A new account of Browning's prosody would be helpful.

Earlier studies of the dramatic monologue tend to be naive, or—like R. H. Fletcher's "Browning's Dramatic Monologs" (*MLN*, 1908)—preoccupied with rigid classification schemes. Pointedly criticized by Langbaum for their rigidity, I. B. Sessions' "sub-classifications" of the form, in her article "The Dramatic Monologue" (*PMLA*, 1947), at least call attention to elements present in some Browning monologues, such as Speaker, Audience, Occasion, Interplay between speaker and audience, Revelation of character, Dramatic action, and Action taking place in the present. More concerned with the form's effects and general qualities are G. H. Palmer's "The Monologue of Browning" (*HTR*, 1918) and M. W. MacCallum's "The Dramatic Monologue in the Victorian Period" (*Proceedings of the British Academy*, 1924–1925). MacCallum's idea that the dramatic monologue "gives facts from within" strongly influences Langbaum's approach in *The Poetry of Experience*, discussed above with *The Bow and the Lyre* and *Browning's Characters*.

B. W. Fuson's monograph, *Browning and His English Predecessors in the Dramatic Monolog* (1948), sketches the history of the form in English poetry. A brief, challenging criticism of Browning's use of it is "Browning the Simple-Hearted Casuist" by H. N. Fairchild (*UTQ*, 1949; reprinted in *The Browning Critics*). In many monologues Browning resorts to an extra-dramatic "giveaway," a passage in which he coaches his readers and himself in his own oversimplifying voice, because "his simple heart could not extract sufficiently clear didactic principles from the complexities in which his subtle brain delighted." Fairchild thinks only a few monologuists are allowed to speak wholly for themselves and these coincidentally preach Browning's gospel fervently—but he notes an exception: preaching and "giveaway" alike are missing in "My Last Duchess."

William Cadbury's "Lyric and Anti-lyric Forms: A Method for Judging Browning" (*UTQ*, 1964) and Robert Preyer's "Two Styles in the Verse of Robert Browning" (*ELH*, 1965) search for central stylistic principles in Browning. Cadbury distinguishes between the song-like lyric with its single coherent vision, and the anti-lyric of character imitation, which may be cacophonous and in which the feelings expressed may be incoherent, even dishonest. The "truth of character" unifies and justifies Browning's anti-lyrics. Preyer notices that our comprehension keeps pace with our hearing or reading at the normal rate of any poem in a "simple" style; but when displacements in syntax or in time (as notoriously in *Sordello's* verse) cause comprehension to lag behind the pace suggested by a poem's rhythm, then we have the "difficult" style—that of the dramatic monologues. Both studies, at times, oversimplify. But both suggest that cacophony and "difficult" forms and "obscure" styles in Browning may be functional.

Browning's Early Poems and Plays. Domett, Mrs. Orr, Kenyon (in *New Poems,* 1914), Griffin, and DeVane comment briefly on extant juvenilia.

Pauline, Paracelsus, and *Sordello,* often enough treated as mere documents that display Browning's Shelleyan chains, early attitudes, and artistic deficiencies, are beginning to be seen as — at least partly successful—poems. Lionel Stevenson's "Tennyson, Browning, and a Romantic Fallacy" (*UTQ*, 1944) finds an autobiographical story in all three: "the painful transition of a gifted mind from egocentricity through utopianism to altruistic tolerance"—and worldly involvement. Thus, in these poems, young Browning leaves Shelley behind, in the "lofty isolation" of his Romantic ivory tower. Yet Shelley's immense influence on *Pauline* is evident enough, as F. A. Pottle's detective-like study in *Shelley and Browning: A Myth and Some Facts* (1923), of Browning's discovery of Shelley shows. Deceptively entitled, Robert Preyer's "Robert Browning: A Reading of the Early Narratives" (*ELH*, 1959; also anthologized) is mainly a "reading" of *Pauline,* with valuable notes on its relation to Romantic confession literature and "monodramas" by Shelley, Byron, and Goethe.

J. S. Mill's *Pauline* critique, fully printed in Drew's anthology, could not have changed the course of Browning's career—contrary to DeVane's statement that it did—as Masao Miyoshi's "Mill and 'Pauline': the Myth and Some Facts" (*VS*, 1965) adequately demonstrates. Miyoshi reads *Pauline* ably, but wrongly concludes that "Browning's divided will" was "repaired in the very act" of composing the poem, since *Paracelsus* and *Sordello*, after all, show the poet struggling with very similar problems. O. P. Govil in "A Note on Mill and Browning's *Pauline*" (*VP*, 1966) qualifies other remarks by Miyoshi. T. J. Collins' "Shelley and God in Browning's *Pauline:* Unresolved Problems" (*VP*, 1965) usefully explores the tentative ideas in the poem. Though W. O. Raymond's "Browning and the Harriet Westbrook Shelley Letters" (in *The Infinite Moment*, 1965) and a transcript of Browning's 1879 testimony on his Shelley essay (*ELN*, 1964) clarify his later attitudes to Shelley ("A great dramatist—almost as great as Shakespeare," Browning said of the Sun-treader in 1879), a new, full account of Browning and Shelley is needed.

F. E. L. Priestley's "The Ironic Pattern of Browning's *Paracelsus*" (*UTQ*, 1964) is a useful study of that poem's structure. *Sordello* has not been satisfactorily explicated, though David Duff's ambitious *Exposition* (1906) attempts, with some misreadings, to translate it into lucid prose, and there are numerous special studies of the great "unintelligible" work. Of lasting value are DeVane's account of its composition, "Sordello's Story Retold" (*SP*, 1930) and S. W. Holmes's "The Sources of Browning's *Sordello*" (*SP*, 1937) and his later Jungian approaches. C. M. Bowra's "Dante and Sordello" (*CL*, 1953), mainly concerned with Dante's treatment of the historical Sordello of Goito, not surprisingly concludes that Browning's hero "is largely an imaginative figure." Drawing on Holmes' Jungian articles, Earl Hilton's "Browning's *Sordello* as a Study of the Will" (*PMLA*, 1954) reads *Sordello* as a study of forces impeding or stimulating the will, and sees the hero as a Hamlet whose "sensitivity and perceptiveness" block him from action. Two attempts to vindicate Browning's methods in *Sordello* are R. R. Columbus and Claudette Kemper, "Sordello and the Speaker: A Problem in Identity" (*VP*, 1964) and Daniel Stempel, "Browning's *Sordello:* The Art of the Makers-See" (*PMLA*, 1965). The former is illuminating but overstates its case: it is hard to agree that Sordello's tale is "really well-told." Stempel's idea that the poem's language is intended to create illusions of simultaneity, as did Victorian dioramas, or transparent paintings arranged and lit so as to create three dimensional effects, is new and well-argued.

Overall surveys of the plays include A. E. DuBois's "Robert Browning, Dramatist" (*SP*, 1936), H. B. Charlton's "Browning as Dramatist" (*BJRL*, 1939), J. P. McCormick's "Robert Browning and the Experimental Drama" (*PMLA*, 1953), and Walter Federle's *Robert Brownings dramatisches Experiment* (1954). These, and sections in *The Alien Vision* and *Browning's Characters*, are at least partly concerned to show how and why Browning's stagecraft fails. DuBois finds too much irony and psychological complexity and McCormick finds Browning blocked by theatrical conventions. With more insight, Charlton's masterly essay stresses his "temperamental blindness to the group as an organic unit." Of less value are Federle's remarks on philosophic implications in the dramas. D. C. Somervell's "An Early Victorian Tragedy" (*London Mercury,* 1927) makes a case for *Strafford's* value as a play, but sounder and more useful is Harold Orel's approach in "Browning's Use of Historical Sources in *Strafford*" in *Six Studies,* edited by H. Orel and G. J. Worth (1962). Browning in 1837, Orel shows, "does not contradict known facts" of history, though his literary and dramatic failings in *Strafford* are dismal enough. G. H. Clarke vigorously argues an impossible case in "Browning's *A Blot in the 'Scutcheon:* A Defence" (*SR,* 1920), and Gertrude Reese (*MLN,* 1948) is concerned with Dickens' praise of that work.

Browning's success as a closet dramatist has been less in question but even *Pippa* has stirred debate. J. M. Purcell's "The Dramatic Failure of *Pippa Passes*" (*SP,* 1939) and J. M. Ariail's "Is *Pippa Passes* a Dramatic Failure?" (*SP,* 1940) argue its defects and merits. That Pippa and Browning's God unify the work is Margaret E. Glen's contention in her excellent study, "The Meaning and Structure of *Pippa Passes*" (*UTQ,* 1955). Also good is Dale Kramer's "Character and Theme in *Pippa Passes*" (*VP,* 1964). D. C. Wilkinson's "Comment" (*UTQ,* 1960) is merely ignorant. Two equally persuasive studies suggest that Browning borrowed far and wide for his precariously matched Jules and

Phene: F. E. Faverty (*SP*, 1941) finds Bulwer's *Lady of Lyons* and Bulwer's own French source behind the Jules-Phene episode, and C. W. Jennings (*ELN*, 1964) elaborates on parallels with Diderot's *Jacques le Fataliste* that had been noted, briefly and with truculent disapproval, by Swinburne.

Browning's Poems of 1842, 1845, and 1850. H. B. Charlton's "The Making of the Dramatic Lyric" (*BJRL*, 1953) deftly assesses theatrical elements in "Porphyria" and sees the dramatic lyric as a "form of unstaged drama." Charlton's essay and W. David Shaw's "Browning's Duke as Theatrical Producer" (*VN*, 1966) suggest that Browning never abandoned his theatrical career: instead he took the theatre to the lyric, as Dickens took it to the novel.

Shaw's article is among the better of dozens devoted to Browning's Duke of Ferrara and his hapless Duchess. J. D. Rea's "*My Last Duchess*" (*SP*, 1932), positing Gonzaga, Duke of Sabbioneta, as the chief model for the poem, is less convincing than L. S. Friedland's elaborate case in "Ferrara and *My Last Duchess*" (*SP*, 1936) for Alfonso II (1533–1598), fifth and last of the Dukes of Ferrara, who was said (perhaps erroneously) to have poisoned his seventeen-year-old wife in 1561. L. R. Stevens' "'My Last Duchess': A Possible Source" (*VN*, 1965) plausibly holds that Browning read of Alfonso in Nathaniel Wanley. Even Byron may have supplied a hint for the poem, as Lionel Stevenson (*MLN*, 1959) thinks. B. R. Jerman's "Browning's Witless Duke" and Laurence Perrine's "Browning's Shrewd Duke" (*PMLA*, 1957 and 1959; both reprinted in *The Browning Critics*) sharply debate the speaker's character, and B. N. Pipes's "The Portrait of 'My Last Duchess'" (*VS*, 1960) singles out one of the chief issues in the Jerman-Perrine debate—Frà Pandolf's portrait, which must, Pipes thinks, be taken at the Duke's own valuation if we are to read him (and the poem) correctly. There are two art-works in the poem, and George Monteiro (*VP*, 1963) discusses their relations and bearing on the Duke's "absurd vanity." These and other treatments by T. J. Assad and Stanton Millet point to the complex, subtle, intriguing qualities of Browning's monologue artistry at its best. Arnold Williams (*MLQ*, 1949), R. B. Pearsall (*MLQ*, 1952), and D. D. Waters (*MLR*, 1960) explore the "great text in Galatians" allusion in "Soliloquy of the Spanish Cloister," and P. W. Gainer (*VP*, 1963) and—more convincingly—Gordon Pitts (*N&Q*, 1966) attempt to solve the mystery of the monk's cry of "Hy, Zy, Hine." J. U. Rundle (*N&Q*, 1951) links this poem with Burns' "Holy Willie's Prayer"—which Browning certainly knew well. The most informed and compelling critical approach to it to date is M. K. Starkman's "The Manichee in the Cloister: A Reading of Browning's 'Soliloquy of the Spanish Cloister' " (*MLN*, 1960).

J. V. Hagopian's discussion of "phallic imagery" in Browning's "Count Gismond" (*PQ*, 1961) is unconvincing, though modern enough, but he sensibly challenges DeVane's taking the Countess' speech at face value. Good "new readings" of this poem by J. W. Tilton and R. D. Tuttle (*SP*, 1962) and by Sister M. M. Holloway (*SP*, 1963) see it as a casuistical companion of "My Last Duchess." Browning borrowed "sparingly and judiciously" from Scott's *Woodstock* for "Cavalier Tunes," R. L. Lowe demonstrates (*N&Q*, 1952), but few critics, other than a disenchanted Robert Graves who finds them "undeniably vulgar" (*Horizon*, 1963), have bothered with the metrically superb "Tunes." In "Touchstones for Browning's Victorian Complexity" (*VP*, 1965), Karl Kroeber shows that ostensibly simple lyrics such as "Meeting at Night" and "Parting at Morning" sometimes display the poet's intricacy and subtlety.

Longer works on the dramatic monologue treat "The Bishop Orders His Tomb" in detail. Lawrence Poston (*VN*, 1960) reads the poem as an enactment of the sacrament of Holy Communion: on the altar of his bed the Bishop is an object of worship, and his "altar-ministrants" move ritually. Among the few separate studies of *Christmas-Eve*, Phyllis J. Guskin's analysis of its meaning and structure (*VP*, 1966) is notable.

Poems in Men and Women *(1855)*. More critics have treated a poem Browning said he wrote in one day, "Childe Roland,"[2]

[2]In "The Dating of Browning's 'Love Among the Ruins,' 'Women and Roses,' and 'Childe Roland' " (*VP*, 1966), John Huebenthal reviews available evidence to show that these three poems were written, respectively, on January 1, January 2, and January 3, 1852. Huebenthal rightly maintains that the sequence of composition has implications for critics of "Childe Roland." Johnstone Parr's "The Date of Composition of Browning's 'Love among the Ruins' " (*PQ*, 1953) also challenges DeVane's *Handbook*, but interprets several statements of Browning's too literally. Evidence is, admittedly, inconclusive. But it is unlikely that Browning "began writing his poems for *Men and Women* in Florence in 1853." That is plainly too late.

than any other in his canon. Each generation of readers, one may note, has found its own favorite myths and special interests in this poem—and one awaits a socio-psychological study of its readership with some apprehension. W. C. DeVane's "The Landscape of Browning's *Childe Roland"* (*PMLA,* 1925) turns to Gerard de Lairesse (of Browning's *Parleyings*) to show that his *Art of Painting* describes an instructive "walk" through a landscape of horrible beauty. But DeVane correctly insists that Lairesse's influence on Browning was early and general. Equally valid is Harold Golder's discussion (*PMLA,* 1924) of Browning's probably unconscious borrowings from popular fairy-tales. R. L. Lowe points to a parallel in Donne's "A Valediction" (*N&Q,* 1953); C. Short finds several analogues in Keats (*N&Q,* 1953); T. P. Harrison very interestingly links "Roland" with Wordsworth's "Peter Bell" (*TSL,* 1961); Barbara Melchiori goes to Poe for the tapestry horse (*EM,* 1963); and T. J. Truss finds a vague connection with Ruskin's *Modern Painters* (*UMSE,* 1963). Myth, ritual, and especially Grail-themes concern John Lindberg (*VN,* 1959) and Victor Hoar (*VN,* 1965). Hoar brings Jessie Weston to bear on "the wasteland and the Dark Tower" and locates regeneration and initiation motifs. R. E. Hughes discovers a motif of retribution for wrong-doing (*L&P,* 1959), and Maud Bodkin briefly points to one of "challenge to the horror of death" and to a "Rebirth pattern" in the poem (*L&P,* 1960). C. C. Clarke's "Humor and Wit in 'Childe Roland' " (*MLQ,* 1962) is jumbled, but both Clarke's and E. R. Kintgen's (*VP,* 1966) articles touch on obvious but vital Shakespearian connections in "Childe Roland." Good readings of the work include John Willoughby's (*VP,* 1963) and the one in *The Poetry of Experience.*

J. A. S. McPeek's "The Shaping of *Saul"* (*JEGP,* 1945) shows that "Saul" owes partly to Wyatt's *Seven Penitential Psalms,* and M. M. Bevington compellingly argues that a reading of a Wordsworth letter may have helped Browning to complete "Saul" (*VN,* 1961). The best modern reading of "Saul" is W. David Shaw's "The Analogical Argument" (*VP,* 1964), which wisely places it in the category of visionary poems, though Ward Hellstrom's precise typological study, "Time and Type in Browning's *Saul"* (*ELH,* 1966), is very suggestive. R. C. Schweik's structural analysis of "A Grammarian's Funeral" is conventional but meticulous (*CE*, 1961), and R. D. Altick's reading of the same poem is aberrant and stimulating (*SEL*, 1963; also in *Essays*, edited by Drew). George Monteiro ingeniously shows how settling the business of Greek particles in the "Funeral" illuminates it (*VP*, 1965). Two other able studies by R. D. Altick treat "Transcendentalism" (*JEGP*, 1959), and "Master Hugues of Saxe-Gotha" (*VP*, 1965).

Moral implications of a poem in *Men and Women* that scandalized Victorians—"The Statue and the Bust"—are discussed by W. O. Raymond (*UTQ*, 1959; reprinted in *The Infinite Moment*, 1965), and again by Boyd Litzinger (in *Studies in Honor of John C. Hodges and Alwin Thaler*, 1961). The only well-informed special study of "Holy Cross Day" is by Barbara Melchiori. Her treatment of sources in "Browning and the Bible: an Examination of 'Holy Cross Day' " (*REL*, 1966) also involves "Rabbi Ben Ezra." J. C. Austin's contention that "Mesmerism" owes to the Maule-Pyncheon story in *House of Seven Gables* is supplemented by Lionel Stevenson's notion that Hawthorne himself had drawn on Browning's earlier "Porphyria" (see *VN*, 1961 and 1962). "Popularity" may allude to the Spasmodic imitators of Keats, as Jerome Thale suggests (*JEGP*, 1955) —the irony in this case being, as C. C. Watkins reminds us (*JEGP*, 1958), that *Men and Women* itself was disparaged as a Spasmodic work by contemporary critics.

The five great blank-verse monologues in *Men and Women* are treated in critical books on Browning, and William Irvine sensitively discusses ideas in four of these poems (*VP*, 1964). The best special studies of the perennially intriguing "Bishop Blougram's Apology" are by C. R. Tracy (*MLR*, 1939), F. E. L. Priestley (*UTQ,* 1946; reprinted in *The Browning Critics*), R. C. Schweik (*MLN*, 1956), and R. E. Palmer, Jr. (*MP*, 1960). C. E. Tanzy (*VS*, 1958) points to a likely source in Emerson's "Montaigne; Or, The Skeptic" of *Representative Men*. Boyd Litzinger casts doubts on the pleasant tradition that Blougram reviewed Blougram, in "Did Cardinal Wiseman Review *Men and Women?*" (*VN*, 1960), and Jose Alberich's "El Obispo Blougram" (*RL*, 1959) shows what use Unamuno has made of the poem.

"Cleon" is ably treated as a touchstone for Browning's methods by R. A. King, Jr., in "Browning: 'Mage' and 'Maker'—A Study in Poetic Purpose and Method" (*VN*, 1961; also in *Essays,* edited by Drew), an essay that begins, as so few studies of the poet's ideas do, with critical common sense: "Browning *renders* rather than writes about a subject; he is maker, not philosopher." A. W. Crawford's "Browning's *Cleon*" (*JEGP*, 1927) reasonably argues that the poem is "a companion picture and a supplement" to Arnold's "Empedocles," and E. C. McAleer's "Browning's 'Cleon' and Auguste Comte" (*CL*, 1956) sees it as an answer to the Religion of Humanity in the *Catéchisme positiviste* of 1852. Curtis Dahl (*Cithara*, 1965) offers a roster of possible sources for Cleon's name and some of his traits.

Both R. M. Bachem (*RLC*, 1964) and Barbara Melchiori (*VP*, 1966) discuss Browning's and De Musset's Andreas, but there are few good separate studies of "Andrea del Sarto." Nor of "Fra Lippo Lippi"—a poem oddly overlooked by Freudians. "Karshish" is closely examined by W. L. Guerin (*VP*, 1963) for its irony, tensions, and paradoxes; and by R. D. Altick in "Browning's 'Karshish' and Saint Paul" (*MLN*, 1957) as a "satiric comment" on anti-Christian forces. A slender case for the value of "How It Strikes a Contemporary" as a dramatic monologue is made by C. R. Kvapil (*VP*, 1966).

Poems in Dramatis Personae *(1864).* What (if anything) "Caliban upon Setebos" satirizes has been debated for a century. Few doubt that it is the finest poem in *Dramatis Personae,* but its meaning—beyond its being a glitteringly vivid motion-picture of an anthropoid's mind and vision—remains a problem. C. R. Tracy's brilliant essay (*SP*, 1938) sees "Caliban" as a sympathetic dramatization of Theodore Parker's idea that religious faith begins early in the evolutionary scale. Hence, for Tracy, the poem is not mainly a satire on either Darwinians, Higher Critics, or Calvinists. John Howard (*VP*, 1963; also in *Essays,* edited by Drew) rejects satire altogether, though L. Perrine's "Reply" to Howard (*VP*, 1964) finds it limitedly. P. Honan (*TSL*, 1964) compares what Browning took from Milton and from Shakespeare, and Michael Timko (*Criticism*, 1965) sees "Caliban's" target to be those coolly empirical theologians, Bishop Butler and Archdeacon Paley.

David Fleisher's close reading of ambiguous stanzas in "Rabbi Ben Ezra" is valuable (*VP*, 1963). Isobel Armstrong (*VP*, 1964; also in *Essays*, edited by Drew) patiently reads "Mr. Sludge," and J. V. Fleming (*AS*, 1964) examines its Americanisms. In the most detailed study so far of "James Lee's Wife," Glenn Sandstrom in " 'James Lee's Wife'—and Browning's" (*VP*, 1966) finds that it distorts and magnifies aspects of Elizabeth Barrett. Victorians, such as Furness the Shakespearian, loved "Prospice," but DeVane's estimate of its reputation no longer holds. More interesting to us is the Yeatsian "Epilogue," which W. Kirkconnell treats as a brief statement of Browning's "mature beliefs in religion and philosophy" (*MLN*, 1926; and in *Essays*, edited by Drew).

The Ring and the Book *(1868–1869)*. Indispensable for students of the magnum opus are C. W. Hodell's or J. M. Gest's translation of its chief source (The Old Yellow Book) ; A. K. Cook's minutely detailed *Commentary* (1920; reprinted, 1966) ; and DeVane's *Handbook* with thirty pages of précis and comments. DeVane does not question facts or methods in two studies. Paul Cundiff's "The Dating of Browning's Conception of the Plan of *The Ring and the Book*" (*SP*, 1941), though admirable for its time and still useful, gives an account of Browning's progress with the poem from 1864 to 1868 that needs to be emended. B. R. McElderry, Jr.'s, "The Narrative Structure of Browning's *The Ring and the Book*" (*RS*, 1943) is partly based on the mistaken assumption that poetic passages of equal length equally emphasize their respective themes. His statistics are accurate, and have some interest.

Beatrice Corrigan's *Curious Annals* (1956) gives the fullest account of the historical facts about the Franceschini. The question of how faithful Browning was to the facts that he knew is debated vigorously by Paul Cundiff, Donald Smalley, and Robert Langbaum.[3] Langbaum shrewdly sees that what matters

---

[3]See Paul Cundiff, "Robert Browning: 'Our Human Speech' " (*VN*, 1959) and "Robert Browning: 'Indisputably Fact' " (*VN*, 1960); Donald Smalley, "Browning's View of Fact in *The Ring and the Book*" (*VN*, 1959); and Robert Langbaum, "The Importance of Fact in *The Ring and the Book*" (*VN*, 1960). Also relevant is Langbaum's earlier article, a bone of contention in the debate, "*The Ring and the Book*: A Relativist Poem" (*PMLA*, 1956; included in *The Poetry of Experience*).

most is that Browning *thought* of himself as a meticulous historian. The poem owes to the Positivist climate of the 1860's, as Books I and XII and Browning's letters to Miss Wedgwood, which fairly gloat over the factual basis of the story, amply show. However, nearly all critics agree that Browning fused into the poem his own myths, ideas, beliefs, and Wimpole Street romance. Hero and heroine are as much Robert and Elizabeth as they are the historic Caponsacchi and Pompilia. DeVane's "The Virgin and the Dragon" (*YR*, 1947; also anthologized) shows how Perseus-Andromeda and St. George legends, so personal to Browning, saturate the poem.

The troubling ring-metaphor is ingeniously defended by Paul Cundiff (*PMLA*, 1948); and W. T. Going (*MLN,* 1956) and G. R. Wasserman (*MLN*, 1961) comment on the ring. J. E. Shaw's view of Pompilia as "The 'Donna Angelicata' in *The Ring and the Book*" (*PMLA,* 1926) illuminates her, and Louise Snitslàar's *Sidelights* (1934) valuably treats the two lawyers in the OYB and in Browning. Sir Frederick Treves's *The Country of "The Ring and the Book"* (1913), with many photographs, is the best study of the poem's locale. F. E. Faverty on the after-history of the Abbot Paolo (*SP*, 1939), P. E. Beichner on Fra Celestino's affidavit (*MLN*, 1943), and William Coyle on Molinos allusions (*PMLA*, 1952) are worthwhile.

A good reading by E. D. H. Johnson, "Robert Browning's Pluralistic Universe: A Reading of *The Ring and the Book*" (*UTQ*, 1961), uses William James's "pluralistic" idea, lying at the heart of his radical empiricism, that through rebellious assertions of will in opposition to perceived evils the individual grows morally and helps to redeem humanity. One sees why William James was fond of Browning. Wylie Sypher's edition of the poem (1951) is nearly useless, with small print, no notes, no line numbers, but he does relate Browning's novel-like poem to Dickens and Dostoevsky in an otherwise glib introduction. C. E. Nelson's view of the hero's and villain's "role-playing," in a context of post-Enlightenment searchings for new orientations of the "self," has merits (*VP*, 1966).

Forthcoming studies and editions by Altick and Loucks, McAleer, and others suggest that *The Ring and the Book* is quite alive; its structure, imagery, symbolism, characters and philosophic assumptions ought to be further examined. A chief glory—the Italian setting it evokes—has been neglected by critics since Henry James.

Browning's Later Poems. Will our generation, or a later one, discover that Browning did not fall asleep in 1869 to wake up only for *Fifine at the Fair?* Even that perplexing poem needs more study, though it has not lacked critics. Apart from Raymond, Hitner, and Melchiori, there is DeVane's account of *Fifine's* relation to Buchanan, Rossetti, and "Jenny," in "The Harlot and the Thoughtful Young Man" (*SP*, 1932) ; and a major article by C. C. Watkins, "The 'Abstruser Themes' of Brownings' *Fifine at the Fair*" (*PMLA,* 1959). Watkins finds that Don Juan digresses to develop relativistic views on morality, knowledge, and art that, in effect, dramatize and ridicule fashionable ideas of Pater. Watkins is less successful with image-patterns, as J. L. Kendall notes (*VN,* 1962). Watkins' "Browning's *Red Cotton Night-Cap Country* and Carlyle" (*VS,* 1964) is another able analysis of ideas in a late Browning work—the proof sheets for which, showing Browning's revisions, are assessed by L. L. Szladits (*BNYPL,* 1957).

Browning's first "parleying"—in which, to dramatize and talk over his notions of art, he summons up Euripides and Aristophanes — is really *Aristophanes' Apology,* Donald Smalley maintains in "A Parleying with Aristophanes" (*PMLA,* 1940). Smalley's methodical article discusses these notions and summarizes data in earlier studies of classical elements in the *Apology.* Its superb lyric, "Thamuris Marching," is singled out in Ridenour's analysis of Browning's music poems.

For special studies of *The Inn Album,* one must turn back to A. C. Bradley (*Macmillan's Magazine,* 1876) and to Henry James in *Views and Reviews* (1908). T. L. Hood's notes in his edition of *Letters* (1933) and N. B. Crowell's *Alfred Austin: Victorian* (1953) illuminate the title poem of *Pacchiarotto;* and K. L. Knickerbocker shows how fully Browning borrowed from an Italian manuscript to write a mere "filler" poem, "Cenciaja" (*PQ,* 1934). Good studies of one of the two late works in which the poet reveals his own thinking most directly include H. N.

Fairchild's *"La Saisiaz* and *The Nineteenth Century"* (*MP,* 1950) and F. E. L. Priestley's "A Reading of *La Saisiaz*" (*UTQ,* 1955; also in *Essays,* edited by Drew) . C. R. Tracy points to a relation between *La Saisiaz* and "Tray" (*PMLA,* 1940) . Systematically commenting on ideas in each "parleying" of 1887, W. C. DeVane's *Browning's Parleyings: The Autobiography of a Mind* (1927, 1964) is not only a useful explicatory work but an astute study of Browning's habits of thought, major literary sources, and early reading. The weakness of DeVane's book, paradoxically perhaps, is that it fails to locate the poem's structural principles and, in consequence, grossly underrates it. *Parleyings With Certain People of Importance,* though brilliantly used and explicated, after eighty years still awaits proper criticism in its own right.

Browning's Prose Works. Only two of Browning's few formal prose statements are truly important. The review-article diverging from Tasso to Chatterton's career in the *Foreign Quarterly* (1842) that he identified as the poet's own is thoroughly edited by Donald Smalley, as *Browning's Essay on Chatterton* (1948) . In his introduction, a mainly moderate sample of special-pleading itself, Smalley treats this essay as a laboratory exercise in Browning's special-pleading and shows how its methods relate to those in the mature semi-dramatic poems.

Obviously Browning's "Essay on Shelley" needs to be made more readily available; L. Winstanley's (1911) edition of the text is the best so far. Challenging DeVane's and Betty Miller's accounts, Philip Drew's "Browning's *Essay on Shelley"* (*VP,* 1963) is an able and appreciative analysis. But Drew's view that Browning sees himself as the "objective" poet, strictly faithful to commonly apprehended reality, and Shelley as both "objective" and "subjective" since Shelley also looks inward and upward to Divine reality, has itself been challenged by T. J. Collins. In "Browning's *Essay on Shelley:* In Context" (*VP,* 1964) , Collins shows that Browning's full position on Shelley in 1851 included mistrust for Shelley's lopsided subjectivity and a desire for a more harmonious subjective-objective synthesis. In "Browning's Testimony on His Essay on Shelley in 'Shepherd *v.* Francis' " (*ELN,* 1964) , P. Honan edits what Browning said about his "Essay" and about Shelley in 1879. The poet's contributions to the *Trifler* (1835), to *N&Q* (1852) and to Thomas Jones's *The Divine Order and Other Sermons and Addresses* (1884) are slight, and perhaps a computer will finally say[4] how much or how little he wrote of John Forster's *Strafford* (1836).

Browning's Reputation and Influence. T. R. Lounsbury's *The Early Literary Career of Robert Browning* (1911) is concerned to show how Browning's works from 1833 to 1846 "struck his contemporaries," but Lounsbury's research is less impressive than his insight into deficiencies in the plays and poems. Browning's reputation between 1833 and 1859 is treated in more detail by M. B. Cramer in: "Browning's Friendships and Fame Before Marriage (1833–1846)" (*PMLA*, 1940); "What Browning's Literary Reputation Owed to the Pre-Raphaelites, 1847–1856" (*ELH*, 1941); and "Browning's Literary Reputation at Oxford, 1855–1859" (*PMLA*, 1942). These articles are filled with valuable data about the poet's friendships, and show that he attracted a small, steadily growing circle of readers from 1833 on. But Cramer neglects book-sales and reviews and hence exaggerates the extent of Browning's fame. By the end of 1864, he was "in no sense popular but of considerable interest to a sufficiently large segment of the reading public," C. C. Watkins finds in "Browning's 'Fame Within These Four Years'" (*MLR*, 1958), a close study of the published reviews of *Selections* (1862), *Poetical Works* (1863), and *Dramatis Personae* (1864). Watkins holds that a "turning point" in his reputation was reached in 1863.

British reception of *The Ring and the Book* is assessed in H. P. Pettigrew's "The Early Vogue of *The Ring and the Book*" (*Archiv*, 1936) and in B. R. McElderry, Jr.'s, "Browning and the Victorian Public in 1868–69" and "Victorian Evaluation of *The Ring and the Book*" (*RS*, 1937 and 1939). Apart from a chapter in Louise Greer's comprehensive study of the reception of his poetry in the U.S.A., *Browning and America* (1952), good accounts of the Browning societies and also of Browning's reputation from 1869 to 1889 are lacking. Among general studies,

---

[4]The possibility is less fanciful than it sounds, in view of Alvar Ellegård's techniques in *A Statistical Method for Determining Authorship: The Junius Letters, 1769–1772* (1962). Browning is still believed to have written very little of Forster's biography, as DeVane holds (*Handbook*, p. 63), contrary to Furnivall.

D. C. Somervell's "The Reputation of Robert Browning" in *Essays and Studies by Members of the English Association* (1929) is the most sensible. But it is sketchy.

Boyd Litzinger's *Time's Revenges: Browning's Reputation as a Thinker, 1889–1962* (1964) lets absurdity speak for itself and is, consequently, a wryly amusing study of the persistent belief that Browning was less poet than philosopher. Yet this belief has damaged his reputation. The important related problem of Browning's influence on modern poetry has been thinly studied. A. A. Brockington's *Browning and the Twentieth Century: A Study of Robert Browning's Influence and Reputation* (1932, 1963) devotes an irrelevant page, typically, to Marshal Foch, and not a word to André Gide or Ezra Pound. Better works include G. R. Stange's "Browning and Modern Poetry" (*Pacific Spectator*, 1954), which assembles remarks on Browning by Pound and T. S. Eliot, and Robert Langbaum's more searching "Browning and the Question of Myth" (*PMLA*, 1966), which sees Browning at times using myth and symbol in a manner that links him with the generation of Yeats, Eliot, and Pound. Special studies such as M. Puhvel's "Reminiscent Bells in *The Waste Land*" (*ELN*, 1965) note analogues and influences, but no one has fully clarified Browning's relation to the great moderns. Better work on his reception in Italy, in France, and in Germany is needed.

If Browning's present reputation is suggested in the titles of two pertinent articles, "Pretense on Parnassus" by Robert Graves (*Horizon*, 1963) and "A Word for Browning" by Geoffrey Tillotson (*SR*, 1964), at least many sensitive voices are on Tillotson's side. As the late-Victorian fiction of his "message" fades, the poems, of course, remain.

Elizabeth Barrett Browning

MICHAEL TIMKO

I. BIBLIOGRAPHY

Any bibliographical listing concerning Mrs. Browning **must** begin with Warner Barnes's *Elizabeth Barrett Browning: A Descriptive Bibliography* (1968), which supersedes the heretofore definitive *Bibliography of the Writings in Prose and Verse of Elizabeth Barrett Browning* (1918) by Thomas J. Wise.[1] Barnes's bibliography not only has over five hundred books **not** cited by Wise, but also includes descriptions of first English editions, authorized first American editions, and later English editions published during the life of the author that contain new material or underwent substantial revision; posthumously printed works, including the forgeries of Wise; contributions to periodicals, newspapers, and anthologies; letters; a short-title list of all reprints to the present; and, perhaps of most importance for future research, an alphabetical list of each poem and the English editions in which it was reprinted during her lifetime, with an indication of those poems which have *substantive* textual variants. In his introduction, Barnes suggests some specific future projects to which he hopes his edition will contribute, the most urgent, perhaps, being the establishment of the text of a definitive edition of the works of, in his own words, "Nineteenth Century England's most popular woman poet." Other works which bear on this bibliographical area are Carter and Pollard's *An Enquiry into the Nature of Certain Nineteenth Century Pamphlets* (1934); Wilfred Partington's *Thomas J. Wise in the Original Cloth* (1946; *Forging Ahead,* 1939); Gardner B. Taplin's "Mrs. Browning's Contributions to Periodicals: Addenda" (*Papers of the Bibliographical Society of America,* 1950) and "Contributions to Annuals, Almanacs, Periodicals, and Series" in his *Life of Elizabeth Barrett Browning* (1957); and Robert W. Gladish's

[1] I wish to thank Mr. Barnes for allowing me to see the manuscript of his *Bibliography* and for other kindnesses shown me.

"Mrs. Browning's Contributions to the New York *Independent*" (BNYPL, 1967).

In another bibliographical area—collections of manuscripts, papers, and related materials—Wise remains indispensable; his *A Browning Library: A Catalogue of Printed Books, Manuscripts, and Autographs of R. and E. B. Browning* (1929) lists many items. The title of Aurelia Brooks's *Browningiana in Baylor University* (1921) is self-explanatory, and, although not complete, her compilation is still a valuable contribution. In this connection, publications of the *Baylor University Bulletin* and the *Baylor University's Browning Interests* should also be checked. Warner Barnes is the compiler of the *Catalogue of the Browning Collection at the University of Texas* (1966), and this work (which includes descriptions of twenty-seven literary manuscripts, a number of letters which have hitherto been unpublished or only parts of which have been published, and books and collected editions of Mrs. Browning) is an elaboration of the information found in two previous notes published in the *Library Chronicle of the University of Texas*, H. H. Ransom's "The Hanley Library" (1959) and Barnes's own "The Browning Collection" (1963). After examining these last three items, no one will be inclined to disagree with Mr. Barnes's statement that in the future "no comprehensive research on the Brownings can be undertaken without access to the collection at the University of Texas." Gardner Taplin supplies a good deal of information regarding manuscript sources and materials, especially letters, in two recent publications, "Principal Manuscript Sources" in his *Life* (1957) and "Elizabeth Barrett Browning" in "A Guide to Research Materials on the Major Victorians (Part II)" (*VN*, 1958). Of related interest are Lionel Stevenson's "The Elkins Collection, Philadelphia Free Library" (*VN*, 1953); Kenneth Pettit's "By Elizabeth Barrett Browning" (*Yale University Library Gazette,* 1959); and Martha S. Bell's "Special Women's Collections in United States Libraries" (*College and Research Libraries,* 1959), which describes the Browning Collection at Scripps College, Claremont, California.

More general bibliographies of importance are the Ehrsam, Deily, and Smith *Bibliographies of Twelve Victorian Authors* (1936), which, though useful, is incomplete and, at times, inaccurate; the supplement to Ehrsam by J. G. Fucilla (*MP*, 1939) ; and J. H. Buckley's *Victorian Poets and Prose Writers* (Golden-tree Bibliographies, 1966). The bibliographical sections in Alethea Hayter's *Mrs. Browning: A Poet's Work and Its Setting* (1963), in her *Elizabeth Barrett Browning* (Writers and Their Work, 1965), and in Gardner Taplin's *Life* (1957) are particularly good. Two bibliographies of a more specialized nature are Livio Jannattoni's *Elizabeth Barrett Browning, con un Saggio di Biografia Italiana* (1953) and *Guide to Doctoral Dissertations in Victorian Literature 1886–1958* (1960), compiled by Altick and Matthews. Finally, bibliographies of Robert Browning usually have items pertaining to Mrs. Browning; and these, especially *Robert Browning: A Bibliography, 1830–1950* (1953), compiled by Broughton, Northup, and Pearsall, and the bibliography in *The Browning Critics* (1965), edited by Litzinger and Knicker-bocker, should be reviewed.

II. WORKS AND CORRESPONDENCE

The definitive edition of Mrs. Browning's poetry is the six-volume *Complete Works of Elizabeth Barrett Browning*, edited by Charlotte Porter and Helen A. Clarke (1900). Other standard editions are *Poetical Works*, edited by F. G. Kenyon (Globe Edition, 1897) ; *Complete Poetical Works*, edited by Harriet Waters Preston (Cambridge Edition, 1900) ; and *Complete Poems* (Oxford Edition, 1904). In her own lifetime her *Poems* (two volumes, 1844) proved to be the most popular of her works, going through subsequent enlarged and revised editions in 1850 (which contained *Sonnets from the Portuguese*), 1853, and 1856 (three volumes). (In New York the 1844 edition had the title *A Drama of Exile: and Other Poems* and was dated 1845.) Other significant publications during her lifetime were *The Battle of Marathon: A Poem* (1820); *The Seraphim, and Other Poems* (1838); *Casa Guidi Windows: A Poem* (1851); *Aurora Leigh* (1857); and *Poems before Congress* (1860; in New York entitled *Napoleon III in Italy: and Other Poems*). In 1862 *Last Poems* was published posthumously, and in 1863 appeared *The Greek Christian Poets and the English Poets,* a reprint of a series of articles that had been published in 1842 in *The Athenaeum.*

Other editions of special interest include *The Poetical Works of Elizabeth Barrett Browning* (five volumes, 1866), listed as the "seventh edition" (the fifth had appeared in 1862 and the sixth in four volumes in 1864) but, as noted by Wise, essentially the first edition of her collected works; *New Poems by Robert Browning and Elizabeth Barrett Browning,* edited by F. G. Kenyon (1914); and *Hitherto Unpublished Poems and Stories,* edited by H. Buxton Forman for the Boston Bibliophile Society (two volumes, 1914). The Wise bibliography indicates that the Kenyon and Forman volumes, in spite of their titles, contain works that had already been published, and he lists the more important ones. Of further interest is another volume edited by Forman for the Boston Bibliophile Society, *The Poet's Enchiridion* (1914), which contains a preliminary draft of "Catarina to Camoëns." Two separate editions of *The Sonnets from the Portuguese* deserve mention, that edited by Charlotte Porter and Helen A. Clarke (1933), and the *Centennial Variorum Edition,* edited by Fannie Ratchford with notes by D. Fulton (1950). The latter gives variant readings from the three original manuscripts but, unfortunately, as Taplin points out in his *Life,* fails to indicate the differences among the published texts of 1850, 1853, and 1856. This task remains for future critics and students of Mrs. Browning's most popular work.

It is ironic, perhaps, but not surprising in the light of recent trends in Victorian studies, that much of the work done on Mrs. Browning in recent years has centered more on her letters than on her poetry and that she is today perhaps known by some more for her letter-writing than for her poetry. Certainly much of the present interest in her thought and life has received impetus from the published correspondence, some of it just now being discovered and/or released. There is no doubt, too, that much of the future work on Mrs. Browning will still be concentrated on the letters and related materials. To a certain extent, her letters have always had some appeal, especially to those interested primarily in her personality. The most famous and interesting of the earlier publications was, of course, the two-volume *Letters of Robert Browning and Elizabeth Barrett (1845–1846)* (1899), which reveals the story of their courtship. Earlier still were *The Letters of Elizabeth Barrett Browning Addressed to Richard Hengist Horne,* edited by S. R. Townshend Mayer (two volumes, 1877) and *The Letters of Elizabeth Barrett Browning,* edited with biographical additions by F. G. Kenyon (two volumes, 1897). As the subtitle indicates, Kenyon attempts to link the letters by means of a connecting narrative; the effect, however, is that of chronicle rather than biography. Wise, in 1916, edited *Letters to Robert Browning and Other Correspondents, by Elizabeth Barrett Browning,* the others being Isa Blagden, Sarianna Browning, and Uvedale Price.

In 1929 began a ten-year spurt of publication, four different editions being issued, the first three forming a unit concerning Elizabeth and her family. The initial volume, containing 107 letters to Henrietta, was *Elizabeth Barrett Browning: Letters to Her Sister, 1846–1859,* edited by Leonard Huxley (1929); the second, *Twenty-Two Unpublished Letters of Elizabeth Barrett Browning and Robert Browning Addressed to Henrietta and Arabella Moulton-Barrett* (1935), in effect "completes" the Huxley edition by supplying the rest of the correspondence; and the third, *From Robert and Elizabeth Browning: A Further Selection of the Barrett-Browning Family Correspondence,* introduction and notes by William Rose Benét (1936), serves as a complement to the previous work, the editor's notes and commentary providing some sort of context for the letters. The letters in this group are inclined to be gossipy ones, and they reveal many details of the family life of the newly married Brownings. The final volume of those published in this period, *Letters from Elizabeth Barrett to B. R. Haydon,* edited by Martha Hale Shackford (1939), covers the period from 1842 to 1845, and both the editor's introduction and the letters themselves indicate how Haydon widened the interests of the young woman and demonstrate how much both correspondents had in common in spite of the differences in their environments.

From 1950 on the publications of Mrs. Browning's correspondence have been varied and steady, ranging from articles publishing a single letter to important volumes of many letters that reveal new facets of her life and work. Although Edward C. McAleer's *Dearest Isa, Robert Browning's Letters to Isabella Blagden* (1951) is obviously concerned mainly with the poet himself, the work still contains many excerpts from and notes based on unpublished letters of Mrs. Browning's, and his "New Letters from Mrs. Browning to Isa Blagden" (*PMLA*, 1951) helps to complete this particular phase of Mrs. Browning's correspondence. Three more very important editions of letters were published during the nineteen-fifties. *Elizabeth Barrett to Miss Mitford:The Unpublished Letters of Elizabeth Barrett Barrett to Mary Russell Mitford,* edited by Betty Miller (1954), provides an intimate glimpse into the domestic life of Wimpole Street and the thoughts of Elizabeth herself at this vital period of her life. *Elizabeth Barrett to Mr. Boyd. Unpublished Letters of Elizabeth Barrett Browning to Hugh Stuart Boyd,* edited by Barbara P. McCarthy (1955), adds especially to our knowledge of the years at Hope End, 1827–1832, from which period Kenyon printed only three letters; we come to know through these additional letters to Boyd the literary pursuits and the personality of the young Elizabeth. This volume needs to be supplemented by two *PMLA* articles, Bennett Weaver's "Twenty Unpublished Letters of Elizabeth Barrett to Hugh Stuart Boyd" (1950) and David B. Green's "Elizabeth Barrett to Hugh Stuart Boyd: An Additional Letter" (1961). The final important contribution to the correspondence in this period of the nineteen-fifties is *Letters of the Brownings to George Barrett,* edited by Paul Landis with the assistance of Ronald E. Freeman (1958), a volume containing eighty-eight letters (fifty-eight by Elizabeth) covering the period from 1838 to 1889. Of letters by Mrs. Browning, the thirteen written from Torquay (1838–1841) are perhaps of most interest, for, as the editor points out, they show the great tension that she was under during this crucial period of her life. Of the five appendices to this volume, the second, "Diagnoses of

Elizabeth Barrett's Physicians," is noteworthy. *Browning to His American Friends: Letters between the Brownings, the Storys and James Russell Lowell, 1841–1890,* edited by Gertrude Reese Hudson (1965), the most recent addition to the canon of published correspondence, sheds more light on the life that the Brownings led in Italy and on their different interests in that country; while the main emphasis is, as the title indicates, on Browning himself, there is still enough by and about Mrs. Browning in this volume to make it an important one to know, especially if one is seeking to understand more about her relations with Italy. This is especially true in terms of the first thirty-five letters, written during a period when the Brownings and the Storys were very close friends in Italy.

It was inevitable that there would eventually be an effort to bring all of this material together, and a recent item indicates that such an attempt is being made. In "The Letters of the Brownings" (*VP*, 1963), Philip Kelley and Ronald Hudson announced that they had made a start toward publication of the definitive edition of the letters of Robert and Elizabeth Browning. They are serving as co-editors of this project that they estimate will result in a twenty-volume edition and will take about fifteen years to complete. They intend to publish "all the letters in full with the restorations, wherever possible, of passages previously obliterated and to give full bibliographical details of the letters."

III. BIOGRAPHY

In their *The Victorians and After* Edith Batho and Bonamy Dobrée note that "it is impossible to separate the biographies of the Brownings," and there is a great deal of truth in the statement. In fact, even biographies that deal ostensibly with Browning himself sometimes shed more light on Mrs. Browning than works devoted solely to her. Perhaps the best approach, therefore, is first to consider those studies that treat both figures, then take up the ones that concentrate on her alone.

Of the former, the emphasis, as might be expected, has been on their meeting, love, marriage, and life together, with great attention given to details concerning some or all phases of the relationship. This approach is found in Lilian Whiting's *The Brownings, Their Life and Art* (1911), a work which the Brownings' son invested with "cordial assent and sympathetic encouragement"; it is also found in the "eye-witness" accounts of Anne Thackeray Ritchie, *Records of Tennyson, Ruskin, and Browning* (1892), and Mrs. Anna Jameson, whose letters telling of the wedding journey are found in George K. Boyce's "From Paris to Pisa with the Brownings" (*The New Colophon*, 1950). Other items that provide more details regarding their interests and lives are H. H. Ransom's "The Brownings in Paris, 1858" (*Studies in English*, University of Texas, 1941) and Betty Miller's "The Seance at Ealing: A Study in Memory and Imagination" (*Cornhill Magazine*, 1957), a detailed account of the celebrated seance in 1855 and its aftermath. In *Through a Glass Darkly: Spiritualism in the Browning Circle* (1958), Katherine H. Porter provides a fuller study of the same subject, giving a sympathetic account of Mrs. Browning's interest in and activity concerning spiritualism. "Her's," writes the author, "was the larger hope of reclaiming man's spiritual self from materialism." Concentrating on the period preceding their marriage, Alethea Hayter in *A Sultry Month: Scenes of London Literary Life in 1846* (1965) manages not only to bring a sense of life to the now familiar story but also sheds some light on the relationship of Miss Barrett and Benjamin Haydon, whose suicide serves as the climax to one thread of this account.

Fuller treatments of their love and marriage, the titles of which suggest the common approach to the subject, are found in David Loth's *The Brownings, A Victorian Idyll* (1929), Dormer Creston's [D. J. Baynes] *Andromeda in Wimpole Street* (1929), J. P. McCormick's *As a Flame Springs* (1940), and Frances

Winwar's [Francesca Vinciguerra] *The Immortal Lovers* (1950).
Less sentimental and more concerned with the works as well as
the lives, and therefore more satifying, is Osbert Burdett's *The
Brownings* (1928). Burdett, however, sees the relationship of
the two in pretty much the same way as the authors of the
other works; it remained for Betty Miller in her *Robert Brown-
ing: A Portrait* (1952) to place it in a new perspective. Leaning
heavily on psychological interpretation, Mrs. Miller indicates that
the roles usually assigned to the two should be reversed and
that their relationship, both before and after marriage, needs
to be looked at from this point of view. A controversial study,
much of its value lies in the interest it has created in this par-
ticular area of Browning studies, and, hopefully, in the stimulus
it will give to future exploration. One example of the direction
these future studies might take is the essay by André Maurois,
"Les Browning" (*Revue de Paris*, 1953). Another, less obvious
but still pertinent, is Glenn Sandstrom's " 'James Lee's Wife'—
and Browning's" (*VP*, 1966).

Perhaps the most logical place to begin with the works that
concentrate mainly on Mrs. Browning is her own "inedited au-
tobiography," "Glimpses into My Own Life and Literary Char-
acter," written when she was fourteen and found in the first
volume of the already mentioned *Elizabeth Barrett Browning:
Hitherto Unpublished Poems and Stories* (two volumes, 1914)
and the note (dated December, 1887) by her husband to a
volume of her poems. The note was written to offset the errors
in the "Memoir" by J. H. Ingram to an edition of Mrs. Browning's
works that had appeared in the same year. Ingram the next
year expanded the "Memoir" into the first full-length biography
of Mrs. Browning in the Eminent Women Series. Even more
ambitious, and certainly more successful than this first biography
in connecting Mrs. Browning's life and poetry, are Lilian
Whiting's *A Study of Elizabeth Barrett Browning* (1899) and
Germaine-Marie Merlette's *La Vie et l'Oeuvre d'Elizabeth
Barrett Browning* (1905), both of which, and especially the
former, unfortunately are marked by occasional sentimentality
and by what Alethea Hayter calls "patronizing affection." These
faults are also present in four other more recent studies: Irene
Cooper Willis' *Elizabeth Barrett Browning* (1928); Isabel C.

Clarke's *Elizabeth Barrett Browning: A Portrait* (1929) ; Louise S. Boas' *Elizabeth Barrett Browning* (1930) ; and Laura L. Hinkley's "Elizabeth" in *Ladies of Literature* (1946). This criticism cannot be made of Percy Lubbock's considered, perceptive comments in *Elizabeth Barrett Browning in Her Letters* (1906) ; his use of the letters to bring out the character and the ideas of Mrs. Browning is an effective demonstration of what might be done by future commentators with new materials at their disposal. Lubbock also has some incisive remarks on her work.

Mrs. Browning has been fortunate in her most recent biographers, Jeannette Marks, Dorothy Hewlett, and Gardner B. Taplin. Miss Marks's *The Family of the Barretts: A Colonial Romance* (1938), using many sources, public records, and letters, provides a much-needed understanding of Mrs. Browning's background: the "home" influence, her reading, her illness and her addiction, the people she knew, the interests she had. The book also gives a full account of the relationship between her and her father and goes a long way in overcoming the "sing-song of sentimentality" that has grown up about the triangular affair of Elizabeth, Robert, and Mr. Barrett. All of this, presented with scrupulous documentation, helps to provide an accurate portrait, one needed to correct the many previous distortions. Miss Hewlett's *Elizabeth Barrett Browning: A Life* (1952) also makes use of previously unpublished correspondence and does still more to make the portrait more accurate; it is especially useful in providing details of her life and portraying her many activities. Both books, then, focus primarily on the life rather than the works, although Miss Hewlett's is less authoritative in substance and tone.

Gardner B. Taplin's *The Life of Elizabeth Barrett Browning* (1957) also has as its main purpose the life rather than the works, and it is now rightly to be regarded as the definitive biography of Mrs. Browning. Using many original sources, especially unpublished letters, Mr. Taplin's biography helps us to see and to understand even more clearly Mrs. Browning's relationship, both before and after her marriage, with her father, and it supplies new details about the Brownings' life in Italy. It also provides what might be regarded as a corrective to the Freudian emphasis of Mrs. Miller's book and the excessive adulation found in so many other biographical studies. Combining knowledge, insight, and discrimination, Mr. Taplin has made a genuine contribution to the understanding of Mrs. Browning.

IV. CRITICISM

Although Mrs. Browning's poetry was highly regarded in her own day and her husband insisted that she had genius while he was only a clever person by comparison, criticism since her death has tended to concentrate on qualities other than her art. In the words of Alethea Hayter, there has been "overemphasis on her womanly sweetness and purity, undervaluation of her language and prosody, exaltation of the *Sonnets from the Portuguese* over the rest of her work, and in general a patronizing affection for this impetuous, sheltered, high-minded but unrealistic little woman." There may be a bit of exaggeration in this generalization, but many of the critical studies of Mrs. Browning reflect at least one and often more of these tendencies. This is certainly true of such earlier ones by Peter Bayne in *Two Great Englishwomen: Mrs. Browning and Charlotte Bronte* (1881); A. C. Benson in *Essays* (1896), in which he talks of the "passionate spirit that beat so wildly against the bars"; and G. K. Chesterton in *Varied Types* (1903), the main point of which is that Mrs. Browning's chief poetic curse was her Elizabethan "luxuriance and audacity." In *Elizabeth Barrett Browning and Her Poetry* (1918), Kathleen E. Royds emphasizes Mrs. Browning as representative of the "woman poet" who takes the "world, herself, and her mission eminently seriously." In the same vein, Marjory Bald in *Women-Writers of the Nineteenth Century* (1923) writes that Mrs.

Browning was acutely conscious of her sufferings, her sex, and her vocation as artist.

Recent studies have been intent on examining the poetry itself, and the results have been somewhat more satisfactory in terms of evaluating Mrs. Browning's work. Martha Hale Shackford's *Elizabeth Barrett Browning, R. H. Horne: Two Studies* (1935) is mostly on *Aurora Leigh,* but she makes some valid comments on the earlier poetry, as does Frederick S. Boas in his *From Richardson to Pinero* (1956). Alethea Hayter's two critical studies have already been mentioned for their bibliographies; her *Mrs. Browning: A Poet's Work and Its Setting* (1963) and *Elizabeth Barrett Browning* in the Writers and Their Work series (1965) indicate a possible renewal of interest in Mrs. Browning. The first is, in her own words, concerned with Mrs. Browning as a writer of rhymes, not as a personality. She does, on the whole, succeed in keeping the poetry and the poet in focus, following the work chronologically and tracing the development of Mrs. Browning's theory and practice. What is lacking, though, is a consistent critical evaluation or even a tentative comparative judgment of much of the poetry. The discussions remain descriptive and expository rather than analytical and explicatory. For the author, there seem to be no qualitative distinctions; her comments, sometimes shrewd and even discerning, often raise more questions than they answer and suggest possible directions never fully explored. What, for instance, of Mrs. Browning's influence on the Pre-Raphaelites? However, her discussions of the prosodic theories of Mrs. Browning and of the possible effect of opium on her poetry are especially rewarding, and her final chapter on the need for a reassessment is one that all those interested in Mrs. Browning and her work ought to know. The same might be said of Mrs. Hayter's brief study of Mrs. Browning in the Writers and Their Work series. Here Mrs. Hayter concisely and most clearly indicates much more discriminatingly the chief strengths of Mrs. Browning as a poet and those qualities that make her poetry of interest to us today. Her comments on Mrs. Browning's command of "striking and original imagery," for instance, are both illuminating and suggestive of future lines of investigation. The same is true of her comments on Mrs. Browning's ability to "shock" in her poetry, her willingness to say anything on paper.

More specific studies have centered on such subjects as the influence of Mrs. Browning on others, the nature of her religious thought, and her relationship with other countries. Two studies are concerned with Mrs. Browning and Emily Dickinson: the first, Rebecca Patterson's "Elizabeth Browning and Emily Dickinson" (*Educational Leader,* 1956), finds that there was indeed a subtle but real influence of the Englishwoman on the American; while the second, Betty Miller's "Elizabeth and Emily Elizabeth" (*Twentieth Century,* 1956), emphasizes the dissimilarity of the manner, matter, and quality of their poetry, but stresses the fundamental affinity of their temperaments, especially their shyness. Two other studies attempt to show the influence of Mrs. Browning on her husband. J. W. Cunliffe in "Elizabeth Barrett's Influence on Browning's Poetry" (*PMLA,* 1908), as the title implies, sees the direct influence of his wife's ideas and personality in Browning's poetry. William T. Going in "The Ring and the Brownings" (*MLN,* 1956) suggests that the possible "rough ore" for the ring metaphor in *The Ring and the Book* possibly came from Mrs. Browning's poem "The Ring," not published until after her death. He shows the ambivalent public-private implications of the piece. In his chapter on Mrs. Browning in *Religious Trends in English Poetry* (IV, 1957), Hoxie N. Fairchild indirectly presents a rejoinder to Cunliffe's claim of Mrs. Browning's influence on her husband's religious ideas. Fairchild shows that, far from "retarding" Browning's own religious development towards a subjectivist theism, Mrs. Browning herself became less Evangelical and narrow after her marriage, and her interests became more humanitarian and ethical. She can be classified as Broad Church, if one needs to classify her. David B. Green reminds us once again of Mrs. Browning's keen interest in the United States and its literature in "Elizabeth Barrett and R. Shelton Mackenzie" (*Studies in Bibliography,* 1961). Her interest in Italy and Italian affairs is the subject of Giovanna Foà's *Elizabeth Barrett Browning and Italy* (1954); Guiliana A. Treves's *Anglo-Fiorentine de Cento Anni Fa* (Florence, 1953; translated by Sylvia Sprigge, *The Golden Ring: The Anglo-Florentines, 1847–1862,* 1956); and Edward C. McAleer's "Pasquale Villari and the Brownings" (*Boston Public Library Quarterly,* 1957). The first two, as might be expected, concentrate on "Casa Guidi Windows," Foà calling it her best poem on a political subject.

Her other longer poems—*Sonnets from the Portuguese* and *Aurora Leigh*—have received surprisingly little critical attention, an omission that ought to be noted by those interested in Mrs. Browning's work. The early enthusiastic reception of the *Sonnets* (Gosse in *Critical Kit-Kats*, 1896, called it an example of the highest art of which Mrs. Browning was capable) has turned into general acceptance on the basis of the biographical interest and the love story found in the work, as the many editions and various translations attest. Of the translations, that by Rilke has inspired two articles, Helmut Rehder's "Rilke und Elizabeth Barrett Browning" (*JEGP*, 1934) and Norbert Furst's "Rilke's Translations of English, French, and Italian Sonnets" (*SP*, 1942). Rehder concentrates more on the ideas, while Furst is more concerned with the art of translation. He takes Sonnet XXV and analyzes it in detail, concluding that the strength of the German version lies in the "Rilkean form." The bibliographical matters concerning the series of sonnets and the various manuscripts are taken up in an article in *TLS* (1947) and in Fannie Ratchford's introduction to the *Centennial Variorum Edition* (1950). Dorothy Hewlett provides the biographical background of the work in her introduction to the edition of the *Sonnets* published by the Folio Society of London (1962). Osbert Burdett in his *The Brownings* and Alethea Hayter in her *Elizabeth Barrett Browning: A Poet's Work and Its Setting* have some critical observations to make on the form and imagery of the sonnets, but, as indicated earlier, much still needs to be done in the way of incisive commentary on them.

The same must be said of *Aurora Leigh*, which has attracted attention but not analysis. Swinburne in his introduction to the poem (1898) stated that although it is one of the longest poems in the world, there "is not a dead line in it." Subsequent criticism has tended to be less enthusiastic. Virginia Woolf, in what is still probably the best essay on *Aurora Leigh* (*Yale Review*, 1931), writes of the obvious imperfections of the poem, but concludes that it is "a book that still lives and can still be read." For her, it is a failure as a novel, but successful as a poem conveying a sense of life. Most criticism, however, has been directed to the autobiographical or feminist aspects of the poem. "Elizabeth Barrett Browning's Heroine," by Mildred Wilsey (*College English,* 1944), is a discussion of the autobiographical elements in the poem. Paul Turner, "Aurora Versus the Angel" (*RES,* 1948), views the poem as an answer to Patmore's ideas on women and their relationship to men as revealed in his *Angel in the House.* Most recently, Joyce M. S. Tompkins in her *Aurora Leigh* (Fawcett Lecture, 1961) has also emphasized the auto-biographical elements of the poem, seeing as its master-theme "the woman with a vocation"; the poem reflects Mrs. Browning's ideas on the rival claims of marriage and a vocation.

It is clear from the above that what remains in the area of criticism is the need for genuine critical treatments, perceptive and discriminating, of much of Mrs. Browning's work, especially of the longer poems. The basis for this, of course, would be the integration of her ideas on poetry and life, something which can be approached much more readily because of the great amount of material, especially letters, now being published. Future critics will have no lack of matter on which to base their studies, and these studies, hopefully, will help to reveal those qualities, artistic and intellectual, on which Mrs. Browning's fame will finally come to rest.

Edward FitzGerald

MICHAEL TIMKO

I. BIBLIOGRAPHY

There is an apparent need for bibliographical work on Fitz-Gerald, work that would incorporate the recent discoveries and writings about him. Of the older bibliographies and collations of his writings, those by W. F. Prideaux, *Notes for a Bibliography of Edward FitzGerald* (1901), and George Bentham, editor, *Variorum and Definitive Edition of the Poetical and Prose Writings of Edward FitzGerald* (seven volumes, 1902–1903; the bibliography is in the seventh volume), are full and very useful. The *Notes* is annotated, but the annotations vary in the degree of helpfulness, sometimes being merely the reaction of Prideaux himself to the particular item. Of the older general bibliographies, the Ehrsam, Deily, and Smith *Twelve Victorian Authors* (1936), supplemented by Fucilla (*MP*, 1939), is the most complete and the most accessible. This last point, unfortunately, cannot be made of the bibliography (three volumes in typescript) compiled by Charles Van Cise Wheeler before the sale of his FitzGerald collection in 1919, copies of which are now in the Library of Congress (the original) and the Newberry Library in Chicago (the carbon). In this connection see also *The Important Private Library of Charles V. Wheeler* (1919), the catalog of the auction.

More selective general bibliographies are found in A. McKinley Terhune's *The Life of Edward FitzGerald* (1947), which occasionally corrects errors in older bibliographies and has helpful annotations on several items; Joanna Richardson's *Edward FitzGerald* (Writers and Their Work, 1960), which also contains brief annotations on selected items; and J. H. Buckley's *Victorian Poets and Prose Writers* (Goldentree Bibliographies, 1966). More specialized in nature are Terhune's "Edward FitzGerald" in "A Guide to Research Materials of the Major Victorians (Part I)" (*VN*, 1957) and Altick and Matthews' *Guide to Doctoral Dissertations in Victorian Literature, 1886–1958* (1960).

With FitzGerald, of course, one needs to be aware of the Rubáiyát literature, and, fortunately, there are several excellent bibliographies, old and more recent, on the subject: Ambrose G. Potter's *A Bibliography of the Rubáiyát of Omar Khayyám* (1929) and Nathan Haskell Dole's *Rubáiyát of Omar Khayyám, Multi-Variorum Edition* (two volumes, 1896; the bibliography is in the second volume, pp. 438–544). Potter's is the most comprehensive listing of all materials relating to the *Rubáiyát,* but his arrangement by version and publication makes it a little difficult to use. The "Check-List of the *Rubáiyát* Collection Now in the Colby College Library" compiled by James Humphry for Carl J. Weber's *FitzGerald's Rubáiyát, Centennial Edition* (1959) might be regarded as a limited supplement to the Potter bibliography, and the chronological listing is certainly the more practical one. Two hundred and fifteen *Rubáiyáts* from 1859 to 1959 are listed, over two-thirds of these being American editions; and full information, including place, publisher, date, pagination, version, illustrator, the Potter number, and the provenance, if known, is supplied for each. In addition, there is a census of the eighteen extant copies of the 1859 edition now in American libraries. Finally, another centennial publication, Arthur J. Arberry's *The Romance of the Rubáiyát* (1959), also contains a useful bibliography on the *Rubáiyát* and related materials.

II. WORKS, CORRESPONDENCE, AND BIOGRAPHY

The definitive edition of the works is the seven-volume *Letters and Literary Remains of Edward FitzGerald,* edited by W. A. Wright (1902–1903), which includes all the FitzGerald material published previously by the editor up to this time. The only other edition that bears comparison with the Wright is the seven-volume *Variorum and Definitive Edition of the Poetical and Prose Writings*, edited by George Bentham, with an introduction by Edmund Gosse (1902–1903). As the title of the latter implies, this edition pays more attention to the different versions of FitzGerald's works (Wright prints only the first four editions of the *Rubáiyát*) and contains more of them. It does not, however, contain the correspondence, but it includes "extracts" of letters that have some bearing on the different writings. The Bentham edition, as has already been noted, also has a good bibliography and a useful index. Other editions worth special notice are the two-volume *Works,* published by Bernard Quaritch (1887), and *FitzGerald: Selected Works,* edited by Joanna Richardson (1962). Miss Richardson's selections are representative and the volume serves as an excellent introduction to FitzGerald's work.

The *Rubáiyát,* of course, is the work for which FitzGerald is now known, but mention should at least be made of other writings published in his lifetime that for special reasons still retain interest. *Euphranor: A Dialogue on Youth* (1851) provides an insight into both his educational ideals and prose style. *Six Dramas of Calderon, Freely Translated* (1853) illustrates his efforts to convey the spirit of the Spanish plays, and *Salámán and Absál* (1856) represents the first results of his study of Persian. The latter has been treated very fully recently by Arberry in his *FitzGerald's Salámán and Absál: A Study* (1956). Professor Arberry reprints two versions of FitzGerald's translation and a literal one, together with excerpts from previously unpublished letters between FitzGerald and Edward Cowell concerning the translation and publication. The publication in 1876 of FitzGerald's *Agamemnon* (privately distributed earlier in 1868) represents still another area in which his interest lay and which later criticism, concentrating mainly on the *Rubáiyát,* has tended to ignore too much.

The fact remains that the *Rubáiyát* has been the one work of FitzGerald's that has received the greatest critical attention, as well as the most popular acclaim. Published in four different versions in his own lifetime (1859, 1868, 1872, and 1879; a fifth, with minor changes, was published posthumously), it has since been reprinted many times and translated, imitated, and parodied in many languages. All but one of the works that are most helpful in providing the important texts have already been mentioned: Wright's *Literary Remains,* Bentham's *Variorum and Definitive Edition,* Dole's *Multi-Variorum Edition of the Rubáiyát,* the Weber *Centennial Edition,* and the Arberry *Romance of the Rubáiyát.* Also very useful is E. Heron-Allen's *Edward Fitz-Gerald's Rubáiyát of Omar Khayyám with Their Original Persian Sources* (1899).

Of these, the Dole, as the title indicates, is the most ambitious, and contains not only the five versions of the *Rubáiyát* along with other translations, but also extensive annotation and commentary. The Arberry *Romance,* however, is the most authoritative and helpful. Using previously unpublished correspondence between Cowell and FitzGerald, the editor is able to show fully and effectively FitzGerald's attitude towards his manuscript sources and his approach to the whole matter of translation. He shows that FitzGerald did not "toss off" the work in his spare hours, but labored over it. Arberry prints the first edition, and in the notes provides the Persian source and gives variants of the other editions. All this and a scholarly appendix dealing with technical matters of the manuscripts and points brought up in the correspondence make this edition the definitive one of this most famous work of FitzGerald's. Professor Weber also provides the first edition and the variants, a helpful introduction, and useful notes (although nothing like the ones in Arberry's *Romance*), but the important feature of his work is the bibliographical one, already discussed in the section on bibliography. Perhaps here, too, is the proper time to mention Professor Weber's story of the "discovery" of the poem by Whitley Stokes, told in the introduction to this edition, and in two other places: *Colby Library Quarterly* (1959) and *The Library Chronicle of the University of Texas* (1963). For a pithy reply to Weber's argument see Terhune's remarks in his review of Weber's edition (*VS,* 1960). A related article is Michael Wolff's "The *Rubáiyát's* Neglected Reviewer: A Centennial Recovery" (*VN,* 1960). Other noteworthy works concerning the *Rubáiyát* are *The Golden Cockerel*

Rubáiyát (1938) , FitzGerald's "Monk-Latin" version (see Arberry's "corrected" version in his *Romance*) , and *A Concordance to FitzGerald's Translation of the Rubáiyát* (1900) by J. R. Tutin.

Like Mrs. Browning, FitzGerald is becoming as well known for his letters as for his other works, and critics are beginning to pay more attention to his correspondence, which helps shed light on both the man and poet. There is, as yet, no definitive edition of his correspondence, and one is badly needed; there are, however, several collections. William Aldis Wright's seven-volume *Letters and Literary Remains* devotes four volumes to the letters. From the letters with such correspondents as Fanny Kemble, the Cowells, George Crabbe, and Bernard Barton we begin to sense FitzGerald's full personality, especially his genius for friendship and his love of nature. These and other aspects of his character are brought out in *Some New Letters of Edward FitzGerald*, edited by F. R. Barton (1923; in New York, 1924, *as Edward FitzGerald and Bernard Barton); Letters from Edward FitzGerald to Bernard Quaritch, 1853 to 1883,* edited by C. Quaritch Wrentmore (1926) ; and *A FitzGerald Friendship,* edited by N. C. Hannay in collaboration with C. B. Johnson (1932). Quaritch was FitzGerald's publisher and the letters to him are concerned, as one might expect, with matters pertaining to the works; *A FitzGerald Friendship* contains his correspondence with William Bodham Donne, a close and dear friend, and the correspondence is accordingly much more personal. Another side of FitzGerald is revealed in James Blyth's *Edward Fitz-Gerald and "Posh": "Herring Merchants"* (1908) , a correspondence that tells of FitzGerald's days as the owner of a lugger in partnership with Joseph Fletcher, a Lowestoft fisherman, whose habit of getting "fuddled" on beer caused FitzGerald no end of concern. More recent collections are J. M. Cohen's *Letters of Edward FitzGerald* (1960) , and Joanna Richardson's *Selected Works* (1962). Although Miss Richardson publishes some new letters, she depends heavily on W. A. Wright, and Cohen depends solely on him, so that there is nothing substantially new in these. However, they both serve a useful function in making available in convenient collections the letters of the poet. Perhaps they will also serve as spurs to badly needed studies of FitzGerald's prose style, artistic and literary ideas, and personality. Cohen states flatly that FitzGerald wrote "the best letters of his age," and that he "stands with Gray, Cowper, Horace Walpole and Lamb among the supreme masters of this humble branch of literature." Miss Richardson in her introduction to the letters emphasizes the extent to which they bring out his "Keatsian, Elian humour" and "childlike innocence." Elizabeth Drew's section on FitzGerald in *The Literature of Gossip: Nine English Letterwriters* (1964) is a brief survey of his character and ideas as seen in his letters, with emphasis on his "Chekovian melancholy."

The standard biography of FitzGerald is A. McKinley Terhune's *The Life of Edward FitzGerald* (1947), the first " authorized" one. In his "Foreword" Terhune states that he tried to be "objective and impersonal" because of his belief that a biographer should not "intrude between his subject and the reader." The result of his success in this respect is that the *Life*, based on much material not available to others and, consequently, much more authoritative than previous ones, gives a great deal of new information about FitzGerald's life and thought; it does not, however, convey as effectively as one would wish what Tennyson called his "fine and delicate wit" and what Joanna Richardson calls his "Keatsian, Elian humour." This is not to imply that Terhune is not sympathetic to FitzGerald, for the opposite is evident throughout the work. The "impersonal" approach, however, and the evident concern to be informative and factual rather than critical lessen somewhat the result that one is led to expect from the correspondence and the works of FitzGerald himself.

What was the standard biography until Terhune's study, Thomas Wright's *The Life of Edward FitzGerald* (two volumes, 1904), although less comprehensive and less reliable than Terhune's, does have the virtue of containing much first-hand information that helps to develop those facets of personality not brought out in Terhune. Wright's biography is still an indispensable item for information on FitzGerald. Less indispensable, but still of some value, is Francis H. Groome's *Two Suffolk Friends* (1895). Three other works containing some inaccuracies but still useful are John Glyde's *The Life of Edward FitzGerald*, with an introduction by Edward Clodd (1900); Morley Adams's *Omar's Interpreter. A New Life of Edward FitzGerald* (1909); and Peter de Polnay's *Into an Old Room: A Memoir of Fitz-Gerald* (1949). The last book, written in a casual, breezy style, is of interest if only as an example of what happens when one attempts to emphasize FitzGerald's "eccentricity" and "genius" above all else. Another "exercise" of this kind is found in James Turner's *The Dolphin's Skin: Six Studies in Eccentricity* (1956). Of biographical interest also is Paul F. Mattheisen's "Gosse's Candid 'Snapshots,'" (*VS*, 1965), which prints a short excerpt from Gosse's notebook for January 3, 1903, indicating that FitzGerald felt a deep obligation to marry Lucy Barton. It seems clear from the above that FitzGerald still needs a study that will take up where Terhune's admirable one left off: a critical-biographical one that will reveal the complex relationship between his art and life. To do this, the critic will need what is the second great *desideratum* in FitzGerald studies, one that has already been mentioned—a definitive edition of the correspondence.

III. CRITICISM

Most criticism of FitzGerald sooner or later takes up the subject of his translation of the *Rubáiyát* and the success or failure of his attempt. There are, however, a few general essays covering both his life and work that deserve special notice. The one by Hugh Walker in *The Literature of the Victorian Era* (1910) certainly belongs in this category, as does that by Oliver Elton in his *Survey of English Literature, 1780–1880* (IV, 1920).

Elton's remarks on FitzGerald are brief but meaty, and he emphasizes FitzGerald's good taste and his genius as a translator in all of the works that he touched. He also has some perceptive comments on the possible influence of Dryden on FitzGerald. Two other noteworthy general critiques are A. Y. Campbell's "Edward FitzGerald" in *The Great Victorians*, edited by H. J. and E. Massingham (1932), and Joanna Richardson's pamphlet on FitzGerald for the Writers and Their Work series (1960). After briefly surveying FitzGerald's life, Miss Richardson has some pertinent and sensible things to say on FitzGerald in the sections she calls "The Man of Letters and Translator" and "The Letter-Writer." Like Elton, she emphasizes his unerring taste, but she then goes on to stress those aspects of his character and writing that are now receiving and deserve further attention: "his *mal du siècle*, his pastoral and exotic interests, his morbidity, his humour and chivalry." In short, she insists that FitzGerald, like all great artists, cannot be neatly classified.

The criticism of the *Rubáiyát* itself has revolved mostly around the extent to which FitzGerald remained faithful both in language and spirit to the original. From this has arisen the question of Omar's own religious position. Was he a Sufi mystic, or was he more in keeping with FitzGerald's translation, an Epicurean? In the preface to his *Les Quatrains de Khèyam* (1867; reprinted in translation in *The Sufistic Quatrains of Omar Khayyám*, introduction by Robert Arnot, 1903), J. B. Nicholas insists that Omar was a mystic and that the poem must be interpreted in this light. Arnot, in the general introduction to *The Sufistic Quatrains*, supports this position, as do many others, including J. E. Saklatwalla in *Omar Khayyám as a Mystic* (1928) and E. G. Parrinder in "Omar Khayyám: Cynic or Mystic" (*London Quarterly and Holborn Review*, 1962). FitzGerald himself, of course, took the opposite view, as do such critics as Arthur Christensen, *Critical Studies in the Rubáiyát of Omar Khayyám* (*Historisk-Filologiske Meddelelser*, 1927), A. McKinley Terhune in his *Life*, and Professor Arberry, whose opinion must, of course, carry great weight, in his *Omar Khayyám: A New Version* (1952). Arberry, however, indicates that FitzGerald, while correct in refuting the view of Omar as a mystic, did not fully understand Omar's thought; in his translation FitzGerald did not clearly convey and "perhaps did not apprehend" the whole of Omar's philosophy. Characterizing Omar as a poet of "rationalist pessimism" who never takes himself or his views too tragically and whose style is enlivened by a "delicate sense of humour," Arberry tries to convey with "greater accuracy and fidelity" in his own translation those qualities and ideas that he finds in Omar's work, what he calls Omar's "whole message."

This point leads logically to the second part of the problem: the faithfulness of the FitzGerald translation. If FitzGerald did not "apprehend" the whole of Omar's philosophy, was he able to capture in any measure the style, language, and spirit of the poem? "There were those," wrote T. E. Welby in a brief article on FitzGerald (*Back Numbers*, 1929), "an intolerably industrious tribe, who would not content themselves with the consummate paraphrase by FitzGerald, but would pester us with disquisitions on the relation between the Persian and the English poem." One of the "tribe," Edward Heron-Allen, in *Edward FitzGerald's Rubáiyát of Omar Khayyám* (1899), compared FitzGerald's verses with the original Persian ones and concluded, along with other critics, that FitzGerald did not depart drastically from his sources and his translation remained close enough to them to be called faithful.

Arberry, however, does not agree in this matter either. He does not deny that FitzGerald worked long and hard at the task of translation; indeed, in both *The Romance of the Rubáiyát* and *FitzGerald's Salámán and Absál* he establishes once and for all the extent of FitzGerald's devotion to scholarship. Still, by his introductory remarks and by his notes to the works themselves, he indicates that FitzGerald sometimes erred in the understanding of the texts and that he consequently did not capture the spirit of the originals. Arberry shows (especially in his *Salámán and Absál* and *Omar Khayyám: A New Version*) that FitzGerald did not care for literalness in translation and preferred to have his translations "orientally obscure" rather than "Europeanly clear." This desire to have a "live Sparrow" rather than a "stuffed Eagle," together with his own notion of "mashing" together many of the quatrains of the *Rubáiyát* to fit a preconceived pattern of following one day and thus "tesselating" a very pretty eclogue out of them, resulted in what Arberry calls "that most unfaithful but loveliest of translations—the *Rubáiyát of Omar Khayyám.*"

While not taking up the question of Omar's mysticism or Epicureanism, John Draper does treat the matter of FitzGerald's faithfulness to the *Rubáiyát* in style and spirit, and he disagrees with the conclusions reached by Arberry. In a long and important article that could well serve as a model for further studies on FitzGerald's other translations as well as the *Rubáiyát,* "Fitz-Gerald's Persian Local Color" (*West Virginia University Bulletin Philological Papers,* 1964), Draper examines the style and symbolism of the quatrains, analyzes FitzGerald's additions of Persian folklore, popular science, scenery, customs, and religion, and finds that, on the whole, FitzGerald retained accurately the "local color" of the poem. Of more than fifty additions, only five or six are "misleading." FitzGerald was using, Draper concludes, the "eclogue" form very successfully to unite the East and the West into a coherent whole. He then goes on to suggest Major Thomas H. J. Hockley, a neighbor of FitzGerald, as a possible source for the information that FitzGerald so skillfully used for "local color."

Although Arberry and Draper disagree on the faithfulness of FitzGerald's translation of the *Rubáiyát,* they do share (more implicitly than explicitly, perhaps) a common thought that would seem to suggest a significant area of exploration for future studies—namely, FitzGerald's concern to express in all of his translations, but especially in the *Rubáiyát,* the *mal du siècle* that he felt. "He belongs to, and stands apart from, his age," Joanna Richardson writes, and it is this close connection with the growing changes about him and his various reactions to these changes that warrant further analysis. In his desire to bridge opposing, seemingly conflicting, ideas and civilizations, he is both Victorian and modern, and critics have already begun to center their attention on both his thought and art in this respect. In using Omar as a *persona* to express his own fears, doubts, and disillusionments about his own time, FitzGerald was prefiguring both the methods and the thoughts of the "moderns."

A. W. Benn sees the *Rubáiyát* as a "rationalistic" doctrine (*The History of English Rationalism in the Nineteenth Century,* two volumes, 1906); May Harris views him as being "imprisoned in an alien age" (*SeR*, 1926); and Augustus Ralli stresses the opposition that FitzGerald felt to his age, particularly his fear of the ideas and manners of the commercial classes (*Critiques*, 1927). In more recent criticism, the transitional aspect of his work and his influence on modern writing have been stressed. In his introduction to *The Rubáiyát, Euphranor,* and *Salámàn and Absál* (G. F. Maine, editor, 1953), Laurence Housman sees the *Rubáiyát* as illustrating the conflict between FitzGerald's liberalism and the Victorian influence, and he comments on FitzGerald's success in "this fortunate paraphrase" of "deceiving us, making either the East seem West, or the West seem East, in a sympathy of thought and feeling." Closer to our own time, Arthur F. Beringause shows, somewhat tentatively to be sure, a possible influence of FitzGerald's *Rubáiyát* on the *Waste Land*, particularly in Eliot's use of themes, symbols, and "general plan of development" (*SAQ*, 1957). William A. Madden in his essay "The Burden of the Artist" (*1859: Entering a Year of Crisis*, 1959) suggests what one might do in the way of analyzing the *Rubáiyát* (and other translations of FitzGerald's) in terms of his "subjective style" and the connections of this style to his own thoughts and to the temper of his age. Madden discusses the mid-Victorian artists' need for a new mythology to express the conflict of the age, and he sees FitzGerald as a transition figure (along with Browning) leading eventually to Yeats, Eliot, and Pound. Along with Draper's study, Madden's article demonstrates clearly the need for seeing FitzGerald as an artist in his own right and as an important figure in the development of the twentieth-century poetic mode.

Arthur Hugh Clough

MICHAEL TIMKO

I. BIBLIOGRAPHY

The most complete bibliography of works by and about Clough is *Arthur Hugh Clough: A Descriptive Catalogue* (1967), edited by Richard M. Gollin, Walter E. Houghton, and Michael Timko, published originally in the *Bulletin of the New York Public Library* (1960; 1966–1967). Part I, "The Poems of Clough," has (except for translations) a listing of Clough's unpublished poems, separately published poems, and editions of his poetry; and it prints partly or completely many poems not contained in the definitive 1951 edition. Part II, "The Prose of Clough," notes many prose items still in manuscript. Part III, "Biography and Criticism," contains not only books and articles about Clough, but also includes references to him in contemporary letters and diaries. All three parts have descriptions of most of the entries and in many instances provide significant quotations from both unpublished and published material. In an Appendix to his *Selected Prose Works of Arthur Hugh Clough* (1964), Buckner B. Trawick prints "A Chronological List of Clough's Prose Works" that is based on Part II of the *Descriptive Catalogue;* and in his *Innocent Victorian: The Satiric Poetry of Arthur Hugh Clough* (1966), Michael Timko has a bibliographical section with many items from Part III. H. F. Lowry, A. L. P. Norrington, and F. L. Mulhauser, the editors of the *Poems of Arthur Hugh Clough* (1951), supply much bibliographical matter concerning Clough's poetry in the preface and the notes to that edition, including helpful information about the various manuscripts that have survived. Of bibliographical interest, too, is the "Catalogue of All Known Letters" in the second volume of the two-volume *Correspondence of Arthur Hugh Clough,* edited by F. L. Mulhauser (1957), a listing of 1,311 letters from which the selections for the *Correspondence* were made. Good general bibliographies are also found in *Twelve Victorian Authors* (1936), Goldie Levy's

BIBLIOGRAPHY

Arthur Hugh Clough (1938), Paul Veyriras' *Arthur Hugh Clough* (1964), and Isobel Armstrong's *Arthur Hugh Clough* (Writers and Their Work, 1962). The Levy and Veyriras bibliographies are especially valuable for items dealing with background, especially contemporary activities, movements, and thought.

II. WORKS AND CORRESPONDENCE

Clough did not publish much in his lifetime, and his work certainly did not receive the popular acclaim accorded Mrs. Browning's. Besides some individual poems printed in scattered places, his "major" publications include the poems in the *Rugby Magazine* (1835–1837), the *Bothie of Toper-na-Fuosich* (1848), *Ambarvalia* (with Thomas Burbidge, 1849), and *Amours de Voyage* (*Atlantic Monthly*, 1858). He gained recognition through the posthumous publications, the more important volumes of which were *Poems by Arthur Hugh Clough* (1862), with a "Memoir" by F. T. Palgrave (published in Boston in an almost identical edition with a "Memoir" by C. E. Norton as the *Poems of Arthur Hugh Clough); Letters and Remains of Arthur Hugh Clough* (For Private Circulation Only, 1865), which included the "Easter Day" poems and *Dipsychus;* and the *Poems and Prose Remains of Arthur Hugh Clough* (two volumes, 1869), volume two of which included more than half again as many poems as had been previously published. This volume, as Gollin points out, had nine reissued versions between 1871 and 1885, a publishing record which is testimony enough to Clough's popularity during the years following his death. The 1951 edition of Clough's *Poems* must be regarded as the "definitive" one, for the editors did provide texts of previously unpublished poems, textual notes, variant readings, and valuable commentary on manuscripts; however, it does have some shortcomings, the most glaring being the omission of previously unpublished poems, and, consequently, it must be used with caution. Most pertinent in this connection is Richard M. Gollin's "The 1951 Edition of Clough's *Poems: A Critical Re-examination" (MP, 1962)*.

"Considering their importance for the study of his poetry and of Victorian social and literary criticism," Walter Houghton wrote some years ago, "the prose works of Clough have been unwisely neglected." This situation is becoming rectified and Clough's prose writings, including his correspondence, are now starting to receive the attention they deserve. One significant reason, of course, is that more texts are now available. Until 1964, for instance, the only sources for Clough's essays were the first volume of the 1869 edition of *Poems and Prose Remains* and the *Prose Remains* (1888). The first of these had eleven prose items, some of which were incomplete, and the second was identical to the first except that it omitted Clough's review of F. W. Newman's *The Soul.* In addition to these, there were also Clough's prose contributions to the *Rugby Magazine.* In 1964 *Selected Prose Works of Arthur Hugh Clough,* edited by Buckner B. Trawick, printed thirty-three items, ten of which had never before been published and from two of which only extracts had appeared. Professor Trawick's edition, which groups the essays according to topics — "On Language and Literature," "On Economics and Politics," "On Religion and Ethics," "On Miscellaneous Topics"—thus provides for the first time a substantial enough body of Clough's prose writings to enable scholars and critics to judge both style and content, studies sorely needed.

The history of the correspondence parallels roughly that of the prose writings. Until 1957 a limited selection of Clough's letters could be found in the 1865 *Letters and Remains,* the first volume of the 1869 *Poems and Prose Remains,* and the 1888 *Prose Remains,* all of these being heavily and at times poorly edited by Mrs. Clough. Also available was the *Emerson-Clough Letters,* edited by H. F. Lowry and R. L. Rusk (1934). In 1957 Professor F. L. Mulhauser edited the *Correspondence of Arthur Hugh Clough* (two volumes), printing complete or in extract 571 of 1,311 letters. As these figures reveal, far too much had to be omitted, especially many important letters that had been included in the earlier editions no longer readily available; but the quantity is still large enough to be useful to those interested in studying Clough's personality, work, and life. Like FitzGerald, however, Clough needs a complete edition of correspondence and prose works.

III. BIOGRAPHY

Although there have been recent studies of Clough, a satisfactory biography that would synthesize the various and often disparate elements in his life and work still needs to be written. For the biographical details, one has to begin with the "Memoir" by Mrs. Clough in the 1869 edition of *Poems and Prose Remains,* which contains, as one might expect, much first-hand information, but is also, as one might not expect, free from excessive sentiment or adulation. Unfortunately, the "Memoir" served to strengthen the tradition that stresses Clough's unfulfilled promise, his life cut off before he could accomplish his "significant" work.

Other sources of first-hand biographical material are the memoirs, diaries, and collections of letters listed in Part III of the *Descriptive Catalogue* (1967); the "Memoirs" to the 1862 volume of *Poems* by Palgrave and Norton; notices by R. H. Hutton and Thomas Hughes in the *Spectator* (1861) and by A. P. Stanley in the London *Daily News* (1862); *A Memoir of Anne Jemima Clough* (1897), by Blanche Athena Clough; and "Arthur Hugh Clough: A Sketch" in *The Nineteenth Century and After* (1898), by Thomas Arnold. Samuel Waddington's *Arthur Hugh Clough:*

A Monograph (1883), the first full-length work devoted to Clough, lacks objectivity, insight, and thoroughness and is, on the whole, a disappointing work. The same might be said of James I. Osborne's *Arthur Hugh Clough* (1919), which, although a generally sympathetic study, may be regarded at best as a useful general introduction to Clough's life and writings.

Later studies have been more satisfactory for various reasons. H. F. Lowry's introduction to *The Letters of Matthew Arnold to Arthur Hugh Clough* (1932) has some perceptive observations on the relationship between the two. Goldie Levy's *Arthur Hugh Clough: 1819–1861* (1938) is of no critical value but utilizes much contemporary material and supplies copious details about Clough's movements and activities during his lifetime. In *Arthur Hugh Clough: The Uncommitted Mind* (1962), Lady Katharine Chorley, also making extensive use of contemporary sources and, in addition, much previously unpublished material (especially the correspondence between Clough and Blanche), presents even more detailed information about Clough's life, thought, and writings. An important biographical study, her book is especially valuable for its treatment of the experiences and actions of Clough's life and the social and historical context in which these occurred. Lady Chorley is able, through her graceful and lively style, to bring to life many events and places that have remained vague or have become dulled by repetition, most particularly the Oxford of the forties and Clough's life in London and University Hall. The chief weakness of the study lies in its acceptance of the tradition that sees Clough as a failure and the explanation of that "failure" in psychological terms. For Lady Chorley, Clough's principal difficulty lay in "longing with all the force of his hidden instinctive drives for complete and exclusive possession of his mother." However, Lady Chorley is not able to support convincingly this thesis. A more detailed discussion of this and other flaws of Lady Chorley's biographical study may be found in Richard Gollin's "Clough Despite Himself" (*EC*, 1962). The most recent biographical study is Paul Veyriras' *Arthur Hugh Clough (1819–1861)* (*Paris, 1964,* but making its appearance in 1965). Monsieur Veyriras depicts Clough as vacillating, sensitive, and introspective, very much like one of his own fictional characters, tormented by conscience, utterly unable to resolve the dilemma posed by the World and the Spirit. The chief asset of the book is the author's careful, indeed meticulous, examination and tracing of the various incidents of Clough's life and the main directions of his thought. He is even more successful than Lady Chorley in evoking the milieu in which Clough lived and wrote. Wendell V. Harris has completed a study of Clough for the Twayne series of English authors, and this work is due to be published shortly.

IV. CRITICISM

That there has been in recent years a resurgence of interest in Clough is evident by the increasing number of critical studies dealing with his life, thought, and art. This resurgence is due partly to the greater amount of material now available for study; it is also due partly to the changed atmosphere in which these studies are taking place—one much more conducive to fresh attempts to overcome the "traditional" critical attitudes toward Clough that prevailed for so long and are so ably discussed by Walter Houghton in the first chapter of his *The Poetry of Clough: An Essay in Revaluation* (1963). The most prominent development is the serious attention now being given to Clough's poetry in terms of his own poetics and those of his age, rather than as evidence to support or refute a thesis. Discussion has more and more come to center on the specific characteristics of the poetry, the particular techniques and qualities revealed in specific poems, and, in the light of these new critical directions, the need to recognize the "modernity" of his thought and art and the positive nature of his achievement. Besides the chapter in Houghton's

The Poetry of Clough, two other essays of special interest on this subject are F. Bowers' "Arthur Hugh Clough: Recent Revaluations" (*Humanities Association Bulletin,* 1965) and Paul Veyriras' "Un Regain d' Intérêt pour Arthur Hugh Clough" (*Études Anglaises,* 1958).

Some of the earlier essays—notably Walter Bagehot's in the *National Review* (1862), David Masson's in *Macmillan's Magazine* (1862), J. A. Symonds' in the *Fortnightly Review* (1868), R. H. Hutton's in the *Spectator* (1869), and Henry Sidgwick's in the *Westminster Review* (1869)—do provide illuminating criticism about Clough's poetry, but it is not until much later that the tenor of the changing critical approach becomes noticeable. In contrast to the "traditional" view—typified by Stopford A. Brooke in his *Four Victorian Poets* (1908) and F. L. Lucas in his *Eight Victorian Poets* (1930; *Ten Victorian Poets,* 1940, published originally in 1929 in *Life and Letters Today*) — J. M. Robertson in *New Essays towards a Critical Method* (1897) and Desmond MacCarthy in *Portraits* (1931) and "The Modern Poet" (Sunday *Times,* London, 1938) insisted that Clough's contribution to English poetry was real and significant. MacCarthy particularly denied the so-called failure of Clough and, as the title of his 1938 article (actually a review of Goldie Levy's biography) indicates, insisted that Clough's poetry was worth serious attention and emphasized the similarities between modern poetry and Clough's, especially in technique and tone. "There are passages in his verse which in their irony, their double irony... forestall the social conscience-qualms of many poets today," MacCarthy wrote.

MacCarthy's main points—the need to evaluate Clough's poetry on its own terms and to see Clough as a poet writing at a certain time and prefiguring a later one—have been treated in various ways. Michael Roberts in the "Introduction" to *The Faber Book of Modern Verse* (1936) wrote of resemblances in tone, intention, and "metaphysical" quality between Clough's poetry and the poetry of Pound and Eliot. The reviewer of Clough's *Poems* (*TLS,* 1951) stressed Clough's modernity, particularly in diction and technique; and Geoffrey Tillotson, reviewing the *Correspondence* (*TLS,* 1957), characterized Clough as "one of the most searching thinkers of his time." The modernity of Clough's poetry, especially the tone, is also the central thesis of "Arthur Hugh Clough: The Modern Mind" (*SEL*, 1966) by Frederick Bowers, who cites passages in Clough's poetry that are similar to many found in Eliot, Pound, and Auden. Clough's poetry, states Bowers, in attitude and tone "anticipates the best of twentieth century poetry" and also represents "a return to the intelligence of the line of wit which runs on to Eliot."

Three recent lengthy studies are concerned mainly with the question of Clough's poetic theory and practice, and all are largely in agreement in their conclusions. Isobel Armstrong in *Arthur Hugh Clough* (Writers and Their Work, 1962) sees Clough as a "Janus-like" poet: some aspects of his work make it possible to view him as a poet within the eighteenth-century tradition, and yet he is, in some ways, "a precursor of twentieth century poetry." Michael Timko, in his *Innocent Victorian* (1966), also discusses the modern elements in Clough's poetry, especially his techniques and attitude, and views the satiric poetry as being the chief means by which Clough was able to reveal his positive attitudes with impressive force and artistry. Walter Houghton, in his important *The Poetry of Clough* (1964), first examines the context in which Clough was writing and then shows by close analysis of many of the poems the characteristics and techniques that make Clough's poetry especially meaningful for modern readers. Houghton stresses the "contemporary relevance" of Clough's poetry, particularly his "double vision," the "intellectual character" of his verse, and the "idiomatic style." "Clough," he concludes, "is not only one of the best of the Victorian poets, he is also perhaps the most modern."

The increased attention being given to Clough is also apparent in the studies dealing with the individual longer poems and the shorter lyrics. *Amours de Voyage* has been treated by V. S. Pritchett (*New Statesman and Nation*, 1951), J. D. Jump (*English*, 1953), and James Bertram (*Landfall*, 1963) as one of Clough's finest poems. All three use the poem to demonstrate Clough's "modernity," Jump viewing Claude as a prototype of Eliot's Prufrock and the whole poem as an example of the "serio-comic" vein Clough used in deliberate defiance of the nineteenth-century tradition of "elevated" poetry. Bertram points out that in creating poetry "out of the very form and pressure of the times," as he did in the *Amours,* Cough succeeded where Arnold, Tennyson, and Browning failed; he discerns Clough's originality in his depiction of Claude, for in using this "civilized" protagonist Clough was anticipating the complex art of Henry James, "in which fineness of perception and personal intuitions of good and evil reverberate far beyond the immediate circle of a few fictional characters."

Clyde De L. Ryals also stresses the positive nature of Clough's achievement in "An Interpretation of Clough's *Dipsychus*" (*VP,* 1963); he views that poem not as a study of failure but, on the contrary, an ironically humorous dramatization of human development, in which Clough "half ridicules" the spiritual anguish of his youth. To read the poem as a story of moral failure is to miss the point altogether. Clough's ability to view himself in an ironic manner is also discussed by Masao Miyoshi in "Clough's Poems of Self-Irony" (*SEL,* 1965). John Yeoman (*TLS,* 1951) points out the similarities of the *Bothie* and MacNeice's *Autumn Journal,* characterizing both as "quietly charming and occasionally moving," and expresses puzzlement as to why so few people seem to appreciate either. Finally, Doris Dalglish in "Arthur Hugh Clough: The Shorter Poems" (*EC,* 1952) regards as unfortunate the neglect into which Clough's shorter poems have fallen and attempts to show that although the "sheer solidity of thought" in the lyrics demands concentrated reading, one is rewarded for the effort. Like the other critics, she is especially concerned with showing the contemporary relevance of Clough's poetry and stressing the need for a reconsideration of his role in Victorian literature.

In this connection certainly one future direction of Clough studies will be that of examining the various versions and stages of the poems, and some fruitful work has already been done in this area. In "Clough's 'Love and Reason'" (*MP,* 1945), F. L. Mulhauser uses three unpublished versions and the final one to shed some light on Clough's method of poetic composition and to demonstrate the process by which the poem became transformed in both diction and intent from a personal consideration of the best time for a young man to marry to an intellectualized discussion of love and reason. F. G. Townsend's "Clough's 'The Struggle': The Text, Title, and Date of Publication" (*PMLA,*

1952) ; M. A. F. Borrie's "Three Poems of Arthur Hugh Clough" (*British Museum Quarterly*, 1963) ; and Evelyn Barish's "A New Clough Manuscript" (*RES*, 1964) take up different problems in this general area and all contribute toward a better understanding of Clough's methods and the poetry itself. Miss Barish shows how four additional previously unpublished stanzas of *"Solvitur Acris Hiems"* change the tone of the published three-stanza poem and illustrate still more concretely the "modern" quality of his poetry.

Another direction in critical studies is the discussion of the poetry in terms of Clough's religious and social attitudes, and here too the traditional view is being strongly challenged. There is still need for investigation, however, particularly in assessing the exact nature of Clough's relationship to people and movements of his time (J. H. Newman and the Oxford Movement, the higher criticism, laissez-faire) and the extent of his commitment to these. In two significant articles, "Was Clough a Failure?" (*PQ*, 1943) and "The Bearing of Science on the Thought of Arthur Hugh Clough" (*PMLA*, 1944), Francis W. Palmer found that Clough was well aware of the scientific thought and the higher criticism of his time and that he held positive moral and social convictions. The positive nature of Clough's religious and social thought is also emphasized by Timko in the chapter entitled "Clough's Thought" in his *Innocent Victorian* (1966), by Clyde Ryals in his article (already mentioned) on *Dipsychus* (*VP*, 1963), and somewhat more indirectly by Kenneth Allott in "Thomas Arnold the Younger, New Zealand, and the 'Old Democratic Fervour' " (*Landfall*, 1961).

The view of Clough as one overcome by doubt still persists, however. Kingsbury Badger states that Clough allowed the "destructive force of reason" to play too large a role in his life, letting it become "tyrannical" over the other elements of his own nature, including his "intuitive faith in life" ("Arthur Hugh Clough as Dipsychus," *MLQ*, 1951). In his chapter on Clough in *Religious Trends in English Poetry* (IV, 1957), Hoxie N. Fairchild examines the poetry and finds that it is, with few uninteresting exceptions, the record of a hopeless struggle to be simultaneously religious, romantic, rational, and realistic. More recently, A. O. J. Cockshut, devoting a chapter to "Clough: The

Real Doubter" in his *The Unbelievers: English Agnostic Thought 1840–1890* (1964), depicts Clough as one who "never developed any coherent attitude to religion, to marriage, to work or to life itself."

Other recent essays on Clough illustrate various subjects now receiving attention and deserving still more consideration. Professor Trawick's introductory essay to the *Selected Prose Works* (1964) is suggestive rather than comprehensive, and the only other essays that deal exclusively with the prose are two earlier ones, which arrive at opposing conclusions. S. T. Williams in *Studies in Victorian Literature* (1923) characterizes Clough's prose as stylistically undistinguished and conventional, and he considers the essays themselves deserving to be remembered only for the light they cast on Clough's thought. J. M. Beatty, Jr., in "Arthur Hugh Clough as Revealed in His Prose" (*SAQ,* 1926), finds them considerably more substantial and praises Clough's prose style for its intellectual cast, balance, impeccable taste, and equability of temper. Clough's ideas on translation are given some attention by Trawick in his introduction to the *Selected Prose Works* and by Geoffrey Tillotson in *TLS* (1954).

The influence of Carlyle on Clough still needs to be thoroughly explored. In "Teufelsdröckh in Hexameters" (*Nineteenth Century and After,* 1922), Maurice Hewlett points out the Carlylian elements in the *Bothie;* and in "Clough's 'Epi-Strauss-ium' and Carlyle" (*VP,* 1966), C. Castan suggests that the main image of the poem may have been derived from a passage in *Past and Present.* Emerson's relationship to Clough also needs to be investigated, since the only essay thus far is the unsatisfactory "Incredible Recoil: A Study in Aspiration" (*American Scholar,* 1936) by Townsend Scudder, who pictures Emerson's high hopes for Clough, aroused by his reading of the *Bothie,* being thoroughly crushed by his friend's later "failure." Indeed, Clough's entire relationship with America and his American friends needs detailed study.

One other significant subject that deserves closer study is Clough's relationship to the Arnolds, especially the extent of the influence on Clough by Dr. Arnold and the personal, intellectual, and artistic obligations of Matthew Arnold and Clough to each other. In an essay on Clough in *The Eighteen-Sixties* (1932)

Humbert Wolfe ascribed Clough's difficulties to the struggle of his "innate satirical genius seeking in vain to rid itself of the swaddling-clothes of Arnoldism." Stephen Spender, writing in the London Sunday *Times* (3 November 1957), tends to agree with Wolfe as far as the influence of the Arnolds is concerned, for he sees Clough's main poetic theme being a kind of "underground protest against them and their ideas about duty and beauty." However, two recent studies—Frances J. Woodward's *The Doctor's Disciples* (1954) and Isabella Black's "Was It Arnold's Doing? A Psychological Study of Arthur Hugh Clough" (*Psychoanalysis and the Psychoanalytic Review*, 1961)—attempt to show that it was not so much Arnoldism as "Momism" that was to blame for Clough's later difficulties. Miss Black insists that, contrary to earlier criticism, Clough's admiration for Dr. Arnold was a positive influence on him and that for the source of Clough's "recognized limitations" one must look to "the inadequacies of his relationships in his early home life."

That Matthew Arnold and Clough were important to each other has always been known, but exactly how much each owed to the other still needs clarification. In his important introduction to *The Letters of Matthew Arnold to Arthur Hugh Clough* (1932), H. F. Lowry not only contributed much factual material toward a better understanding of their relationship, but he also made the point that Clough's influence on Arnold is perhaps greater than most critics have realized. This latter idea is expanded on by Michael Timko in "Corydon Had a Rival" (*VN*, 1961) and Roger L. Brooks in "Matthew Arnold's Revision of *Tristram and Iseult:* Some Instances of Clough's Influence" (*VP*, 1964). Opposed to the concept of any influence of Clough on his younger friend are Lionel Trilling in his *Matthew Arnold* (1939) and Sidney Coulling in "Matthew Arnold's 1853 Preface: Its Origin and Aftermath" (*VS*, 1964); both Trilling and Coulling regard Arnold and Clough as having opposing ideas about poetry. Wendell Stacy Johnson demonstrates that both poets were important to each other in his "Parallel Imagery in Arnold and Clough" (*English Studies*, 1956).

Concomitants of this whole question are the important matters of the poetic reputations of both and the present significance of their poetry. R. H. Hutton, comparing the two in the *Spectator*

(1882), ranked Clough with Arnold as "having found a voice for this self-questioning age" and asserted that Clough's popularity would be as great as Arnold's, for his "rapture and exultation, when they reach their highest points, are beyond the rapture and exultation of Arnold's." Reviewing Arnold's poems in the *Academy* (1891), Lionel Johnson contrasted Arnold's meditative poems with their true humanism to Clough's "mournful, homesick, desultory" ones. In 1932 Lowry insisted that it had too often been forgotten that "Corydon once *had* a rival, and a very good one!" Basil Willey, reviewing the 1951 *Poems* in the *New Statesman and Nation* (26 January 1952), compared Clough's poetry with Arnold's to the former's disadvantage. In 1957 Stephen Spender in the London Sunday *Times* praised Clough's use of a language which "exactly conveys his temperament and meaning, and which is idiomatically modern" as achieving a kind of success not gained by Tennyson and Browning, whose very perfection of forms "inhibited them from using a contemporary idiom in which to convey contemporary experience or a discussion of disturbing current ideas." James Bertram calls the *Amours*, with all its human frustrations, not defeatist, as Arnold's *Empedocles* was defeatist (*Landfall*, 1963). In *The Poetry of Clough* (1963) Walter Houghton in the final chapter claims that "for us he belongs with Tennyson, Browning, Arnold, and Hopkins, intrinsically and relevantly." On this point critics and scholars will no doubt have much to say in the future.

Matthew Arnold

FREDERIC E. FAVERTY

I. BIBLIOGRAPHY[1]

Additions are still being made to the canon of Arnold's works. Thomas Burnett Smart's *Bibliography of Matthew Arnold* (1892 and 1904), with its list of the poems in each volume, its record of exclusions and republications, its "synoptical index," and its chronological arrangement of critical material concerning Arnold, has been supplemented but not superseded. As Marian Mainwaring in "Notes toward a Matthew Arnold Bibliography" (*MP*, 1952) has shown, Smart's work is neither complete nor quite accurate. It omits American editions of his writings, though they were sometimes the first to appear. Miss Mainwaring also corrects and supplements T. H. V. Motter's "A Check List of Matthew Arnold's Letters" (*SP*, 1934). Her record of Arnold's Oxford orations and occasional speeches is in turn corrected by R. H. Super's "Arnold's Oxford Lectures on Poetry" (*MLN*, 1955). Super's list "presumably completes" the one provided by E. K. Brown in *Matthew Arnold: A Study in Conflict* (1948).

Using Arnold's personal account books as a guide, Fraser Neiman in "Some Newly Attributed Contributions of Matthew Arnold to the *Pall Mall Gazette*" (*MP*, 1957) and R. H. Super in "Arnold's Notebooks and Arnold Bibliography" (*MP*, 1959) have made significant additions to the canon. Neiman identifies as Arnold's a "number of unsigned book reviews, miscellaneous articles, and pseudonymous letters." He shows that Arnold reviewed books much more frequently than has previously been known. In periodicals other than the *Pall Mall Gazette* Super finds "four hitherto unrecorded Articles." The internal evidence

[1] At the 1966 convention of the Modern Language Association of America, the Victorian Literature Group approved a project for a book on the Victorian prose essayists to serve as a companion volume to *The Victorian Poets: A Guide to Research* and *Victorian Fiction: A Guide to Research*. The announcement came too late for a complete revision of the present chapter on Arnold, but it has been possible to omit or curtail comment on much of the material dealing exclusively with Arnold's prose works.

used by Neiman in the identification of four articles is made conclusive by evidence in Arnold's unpublished diaries, as Roger L. Brooks indicates in "Matthew Arnold and the *Pall Mall Gazette*" (*MP*, 1961). Brooks also ascribes two articles in the *London Review*—for March and April, 1963—to Arnold in "Matthew Arnold and the *London Review*" (*PMLA*, 1961) and in " 'A Septuagenarian Poet': An Addition to the Matthew Arnold Bibliography" (*PQ*, 1962) identifies as Arnold's a review of William Bell Scott's *A Poet's Harvest Home* in the *St. James Gazette*.

Two important additions to the bibliography are Kenneth Allott's "A Birthday Exercise by Matthew Arnold" (*N&Q*, 1958), and "Matthew Arnold's Original Version of 'The River' " (*TLS*, 28 March 1958). The exercise is "Natalis Dies Bonzensis," a Latin birthday poem for Arnold's sister Fan, whose nickname was "Bonze." To the 1852 version of "The River" Allott restores six stanzas probably cut out by Arnold because they gave a too-intimate self-revelation. The six stanzas definitely link the poem to Miss Wightman. Roger L. Brooks, in "The Publication of Matthew Arnold's Early Volumes of Poetry" (*VN*, 1962), suggests approximate dates for Arnold's first three volumes on the basis of announcements in the *Publisher's Circular*, periodical advertisments, published correspondence, and dated inscriptions in extant volumes of each collection. In "A Census of Matthew Arnold's *Poems* (1853) " (*PBSA*, 1960), Brooks gives the location for forty-six copies of *Poems* (1853), the 1853 volume being rarer today than the two that preceded it.

Roger L. Brooks makes a beginning toward a history of the American publication of Arnold's prose and verse in "Matthew Arnold and Ticknor & Fields" (*AL*, 1954), carrying the account to 1867. In "A Neglected Edition of Matthew Arnold's Poetry and a Bibliographical Correction" (*PBSA*, 1961) Brooks shows C. B. Tinker and H. F. Lowry (*Commentary*, 1940) to be wrong in their description of the 1856 American edition of Arnold's *Poems*. The text was actually made up of the 1853 and 1855 editions of *Poems*, and it "represents the first attempt anywhere at a complete edition of Arnold's poetry." William E. Buckler's "An American Edition of Matthew Arnold's *Poems*" (*PMLA*, 1954) establishes the 1878 edition of *Poems* as the basic text for subsequent editions. The first American text of "Literature and Science," differing from other versions chiefly in the opening and closing paragraphs, appeared in *The Manhattan: An Illustrated Monthly Magazine,* as James K. Robinson proves in "The First Published Text of Arnold's 'Literature and Science' " (*VN,* 1961).

A few items on Arnold's *Diaries* and *Note-Books* deserve mention. Kenneth Allott's "Matthew Arnold's Reading-Lists in Three Early Diaries" (*VS,* 1958) shows the extent of Arnold's reading in philosophy during the years 1845 to 1847. Assuming that the *Note-Books* much be dated before they can be used in tracing the development of Arnold's mind, Richard C. Tobias, in "On Dating Matthew Arnold's 'General Note-Books' " (*PQ,* 1960), tries to prove that the first collection of "General Note-Books" was made from 1860 to 1865, the second, from 1876 to 1888. Roger L. Brooks in "Some Unaccomplished Projects of Matthew Arnold" (*SB,* 1963) gives an annotated list of twenty-one projects that Arnold presumably never completed.

All students of Arnold's poetry are heavily indebted to C. B. Tinker and H. F. Lowry for *The Poetry of Matthew Arnold: A Commentary* (1940). Drawing on all materials, published and unpublished, available before 1940, they bring together in compact and manageable form the necessary information for an understanding of every poem—sources, influences, biographical details, dates, and the editorial history of each work up to 1890. In view of the sanity and good judgment displayed in the occasional literary evaluations, it is to be regretted that the plan of the book ruled out interpretation. Also to be regretted is the absence of an overall discussion of Arnold's aesthetics.

Stephen M. Parrish's *Concordance to the Poems of Matthew Arnold* (1959) adds Arnold to the list of more than thirty English and American poets for whose works concordances are now available.

II. EDITIONS

Arnold is fortunate in his recent editors. Along with Boswell he has been adopted by Yale University, and out of the great Yale Collection of manuscripts, papers, and volumes printed by Arnold have come four noteworthy editions and the *Commentary*. The first of these is H. F. Lowry's edition of *The Letters of Matthew Arnold to Arthur Hugh Clough* (1932). No single work has contributed more to the twentieth century study of Arnold. It presents a mine of new critical and biographical material. The editor's introductory essays and the notes are invaluable for tracing Arnold's development from 1845 to 1861. *The Poetical Works of Matthew Arnold* (1950), edited by C. B. Tinker and H. F. Lowry, supersedes the Oxford editions of 1909 and 1945. For the first time, the complete poetical works are given and are edited by modern standards. The only objection thus far raised to the edition is that it follows Arnold's own order and classification of the poems rather than the more convenient chronological arrangement of the Oxford editions. The monumental *Note-Books of Matthew Arnold* (1952), edited by H. F. Lowry, Karl Young, and W. H. Dunn, includes only literary items. All references to his finances and official engagements are omitted. Students who expect the intimate revelations of a journal will be disappointed, for the *Note-Books* record only what Arnold read, and tell us little about his reactions to his reading. The editors have identified most of the thousands of quotations from six literatures. When so much has been given, it is perhaps ungrateful to complain that there is no index for seventy-seven pages of reading lists, and that the editors did not find it "appropriate to attempt any detailed essay on the significance of the note-books or their bearing on Arnold's own work." William Bell Guthrie's edition of *Matthew Arnold's Diaries, the Unpublished Items* (Ann Arbor: University Microfilms, 1959) gives a transcription of the forty-four diaries Arnold kept from 1852 through 1888. The headnotes relate the entries to his letters and works, the information being arranged under personal matters, literary projects, finances, educational problems, miscellaneous material, and school reports. The editor is justified in his claim that "Access to the full diary entries, here first transcribed, would seem to be essential to any future biographer of Arnold or to any student of Arnold's life in relation to his work."

The first fully annotated edition of Arnold's poems is *The Poems of Matthew Arnold* (1965), edited by Kenneth Allott. By the inclusion of most of Arnold's poetic *juvenilia*, of his poetic drafts and fragments, of his previously uncollected translations from Homer, and by the first printing of an unmutilated text of "The River," the editor can justly claim that the edition is "more nearly complete than any earlier edition" of the poetry.

The arrangement of the poems by order of composition makes it possible for the student to follow the development of Arnold's mind and art, but unfortunately, as Allott realizes, the exact date of composition cannot always be established, and the chronological order breaks up such sequences as the *Switzerland* and *Faded Leaves* groups.

The headnotes are remarkable feats of compression and illumination, presenting all known information necessary to an understanding of the composition and publication of the poems, and of the historical and biographical backgrounds. In the footnotes, Allott has "explored a little further than earlier commentators Arnold's poetic debt to the Greek and Latin classics and to German literature," but the parallels drawn with many other writers such as Byron, Carlyle, and Gray, are sometimes unconvincing. In final tribute to this edition, one need only say that it is worthy of a place beside R. H. Super's impressive edition of Arnold's prose works.

Louis Bonnerot's *Matthew Arnold, Empedocle sur l'Etna: Étude critique et traduction* (1947) is valuable for its ninety-page introduction, tracing sources and influences and drawing comparisons with other dramatic poems such as "Manfred," "Paracelsus," and "Dipsychus."

That a critical edition of the prose works was badly needed was demonstrated by E. K. Brown in his *Studies in the Text of Matthew Arnold's Prose Works* (1935). Brown's book is an attempt, a successful one, "to illuminate Arnold's personality, thought and art by a study of his revisions." Arnold's major changes in text, editorial and stylistic, give proof of his improving architectonic sense, and of his intellectual honesty. Brown's running commentary is invariably suggestive, sensitive in offering the right clues to Arnold's motives in revision. The book is a rich source for further deductions and an excellent example of the method by which purely technical matters can be humanized and be given wider significance.

Merle M. Bevington's edition of *England and the Italian Question* (1953) and Kenneth Allott's *Five Uncollected Essays of Matthew Arnold* (1953) were followed by Fraser Neiman's edition of *Essays, Letters, and Reviews by Matthew Arnold* (1960), which is a collection of "articles signed by Arnold that have not been reprinted since their original publication in the nineteenth century, largely in periodicals of the day; articles not collected in the Edition de Luxe of 1903–1904, but which, though gathered into one or more small collections since then, are now either out of print or accessible only in scattered volumes; articles that Arnold contributed anonymously or pseudonymously to various journals and which have been ascribed to him only recently." Neiman's annotation is excellent, though his index leaves something to be desired.

Most of the material in the three foregoing editions will eventually be incorporated in R. H. Super's massive and indispensable edition of *The Complete Prose Works of Matthew Arnold*. Of the ten or more projected volumes, five have already appeared: *On the Classical Tradition* (1960), *Democratic Education* (1962), *Lectures and Essays in Criticism* (1962), *Schools and Universities on the Continent* (1964) and *Culture and Anarchy* (1965). In the collation of texts and in the commentary the highest standards are set. For the most part, the writings are "printed in the order of their first appearance," although Super confesses that the arrangement does some violence "to Arnold's final order when he collected his essays into books." The critical and explanatory notes, exemplary in their scholarly thoroughness and compression, "are provided to explain Arnold's topical references and to indicate his sources and throw some light on the way he worked."

William E. Buckler's edition of *Passages from the Prose Writings of Matthew Arnold: Selected by the Author* (1963) is the first reissue of the 1880 anthology made by Arnold from his own works.

III. BIOGRAPHY

Although Arnold seems to be the first of the great Victorians to have his works properly edited by modern standards, he evidently will be the last to receive adequate treatment in biography. The chief biographical contribution of the last thirty-five years is that provided by *The Letters of Matthew Arnold to Arthur Hugh Clough* (1932). Most writers since 1932 have leaned heavily on this volume. Alan Harris in his informative "Matthew Arnold: the 'Unknown Years'" (*Nineteenth Century and After*, 1933), and W. S. Knickerbocker in "Semaphore" (*SeR,* 1933), for example, use the letters in an attempt to reconstruct the relationship with Clough. Much more baffling is the Marguerite episode, on which almost every commentator has exercised his ingenuity. Where the facts are few, the field is open to conjecture. Tinker and Lowry have rummaged among the tombstones of Thun, but the grave retains its secret. The 1848–49 register of the Hotel Bellevue has been destroyed. Thus we are thrown back on Arnold's letters and the internal evidence of the poems. On the basis of these, a number of critics (for example, W. S. Knickerbocker in "Thunder in the Index," *SeR*, 1939, and A. S. Cairncross in "Arnold's 'Faded Leaves' and 'Switzerland,'" *TLS*, 28 March 1935) conclude that Marguerite was not a real person. T. S. Eliot in *The Use of Poetry and the Use of Criticism*

(1933) finds her a mere shadow, a "pretext for lamentation." Another group—more numerous and including H. A. Garrod in *Poetry and the Criticism of Life* (1931), E. K. Chambers in his Warton lecture on English poetry (*Proceedings of the British Academy,* 1932), Iris Sells in "Marguerite" (*MLR,* 1943) and P. F. Baum in "Arnold's Marguerite" (*Booker Memorial Studies,* 1950; reprinted in his *Ten Studies in the Poetry of Matthew Arnold,* 1958)—is inclined to believe that the episode is auto-biographical. They also are agreed that in renouncing Marguerite, Arnold renounced passion and poetry and emerged into the light of common day. Louis Bonnerot in "La Jeunesse de Matthew Arnold" (*Revue Anglo-Américaine,* 1930) goes even further. He deplores the puritanical attitude of the English critics regarding this very important phase of Arnold's development. In Bonnerot's view, Arnold is haunted for the rest of his life by this memory of his youth. To Marguerite, Bonnerot attributes many significant later developments: the accentuation of the tendency toward elegiac poetry, the theme of isolation so important in Arnold's work, even some of Arnold's philosophical and religious attitudes. Mention should also be made of Isobel Macdonald's fictional treatment of Arnold's relationships with Marguerite and with his future wife, Lucy Wightman, in *The Buried Self: A Background to the Poems of Matthew Arnold, 1848–1851* (1949).

The best full-length treatment of the Marguerite problem since P. F. Baum's judicial survey of the evidence in 1950 is A. Dwight Culler's in *Imaginative Reason: The Poetry of Matthew Arnold* (1966). Involved in the controversy is the Marguerite canon: "The high tide of Marguerite idolatry," as Culler says, "attributed to her some twenty or twenty-five poems, whereas most scholars now would give her about a dozen."

Of the two book-length biographies (Louis Bonnerot, *Matthew Arnold, Poète: Essai de biographie psychologique, 1947,* and E. K. Chambers, *Matthew Arnold, A Study,* 1947), that by Chambers is the slighter. Coming from so eminent a scholar, it is a disappointment. It is done evidently with his left hand in the intervals of his severer labors in earlier periods of English literature. For this reason, perhaps, he provides no documenta-tion at all. He is content with a brief, brisk factual account, unimpeded and unrelieved by much in the way of criticism and interpretation. As a factual account, however, it is the best and the fullest that thus far has been made. Bonnerot attempts more, more also that is open to question. He calls his work "an essay in psychological biography." Many of Arnold's contemporaries, neurotic, exotic, and erotic (Carlyle, Ruskin, D. G. Rossetti, etc.), have fallen prey to the psychologists. Even Arnold could not elude them forever. Bonnerot's main thesis is that Arnold suffers from pathological doubt, a disease of the affections. From this spring his various dualities, oscillations, wanderings between worlds. Although Bonnerot fails to convince the reader that Arnold suffers from a psychoneurosis, the psychological interpretations do suggest new and deeper meanings for many of the poems. The subtle reading of "Tristram and Iseult" is a case in point. Based on a thorough knowledge of all Arnold's works, and the literature on them, the book, in spite of its extravagant central thesis, is the most impressive attempt yet made to explain Arnold's personality.

A scattering of articles provides some new information on the years at Winchester, Rugby and Oxford. John P. Curgenven's "Theodore Walrond: Friend of Arnold and Clough" (*DUJ*, 1952) traces the career of Walrond who was Arnold's Rugby and Balliol classmate and his life-long friend. Arnold later sponsored Walrond unsuccessfully for the headmastership of Rugby and, according to Lucy Whitridge, "never really got over the shock" of Walrond's death. Kathleen Tillotson's "Rugby 1850: Arnold, Clough, Walrond and 'In Memoriam'" (*RES*, 1953) makes a strong case for the ninth chapter of the Rev. Arthur Gray Butler's *The Three Friends: a Story of Rugby in the Forties* (1900) as a factual account and a contribution to the biography of Arnold. Arnold's later strictures on Tennyson, she says, were the result of his attempt to resist the attraction that Tennyson always had for him. R. H. Super shows in "Matthew Arnold's Rugby Prizes" (*N&Q*, 1955) that Arnold won prizes for two other compositions in addition to the well-known one for "Alaric at Rome." John P. Curgenven in "Matthew Arnold in Two Scholarship Examinations" (*RES*, 1946) presents evidence that Arnold won second place in the competition for the Balliol Scholarship in 1840, and the Hertford Latin Scholarship in 1842. William S. Knickerbocker's "Matthew Arnold at Oxford: the Natural History of a Father and Son" (*SR*, 1927) gives an account of Arnold's years at Winchester, Rugby, and Oxford, emphasizing the influence on him of Dr. Thomas Arnold and Newman. J. G. Watson in "Arnold and Oxford" (*QR*, 1956) treats Arnold the student and the Professor of Poetry, but adds nothing new beyond the statement that Arnold is in part responsible for "a flourishing School of English Language and Literature" that eventually developed.

Arnold's anthology of Byron was suggested to him in 1881 by Lord Beaconsfield. And Edmund Gosse derived the method of his *Critical Kit-Kats* from Sainte-Beuve and Arnold, as Paul F. Mattheisen demonstrates in "Gosse's Candid 'Snapshots'" (*VS*, 1965).

IV. LETTERS

That there is as yet no adequate biography of Arnold is due in part to his family's early observance of his request that there be none, but even more to the lack thus far of a full collection of his correspondence. In spite of the labors of numerous scholars over the years, such a collection still seems to be a decade or more in the offing.

The fullest and perhaps most important collection to date is *Letters of Matthew Arnold,* edited by G. W. E. Russell in two volumes (1895). The volumes represent Russell's selection from the family's selection of letters available. Excisions by family and editor in "deference to living susceptibilities" detract from the reliability of the texts. With no introduction, no index, and annotation that is wholly inadequate, the collection badly needs reediting. Arthur Kyle Davis, Jr. (*VN*, 1962) has indicated that he may undertake the task.

Only a small number of copies of *Letters of Matthew Arnold to John Churton Collins* (1910) were printed and the volume is generally unavailable. In the brief collection *Unpublished Letters of Matthew Arnold* (1923) the editor, Arnold Whitridge, provides notes when they are necessary, but no index. Most of the letters are addressed to members of the Arnold family. H. F. Lowry's impeccable editing of *The Letters of Matthew Arnold to Arthur Hugh Clough* (1932) has already been commented on under "Editions." The letters are of particular significance because of the discussions of literary and aesthetic problems, in which Arnold lays the groundwork for much of his poetry and prose. Frederick L. Mulhauser's edition of *The Correspondence of Arthur Hugh Clough* (1957) provides supplementary material for Lowry's volume in that many letters to and from Arnold's brother Thomas are included. In these letters frequent references are made to the entire family, and particularly to Matthew. Another work, too frequently overlooked, is *The Life and Correspondence of John Duke Lord Coleridge* (1904), edited by Ernest Hartley Coleridge, which contains almost a score of Arnold letters, some of them concerned with Arnold's writings.

The frequent reliance of scholars on William E. Buckler's *Matthew Arnold's Books: Toward a Publishing Diary* (1958) shows that the book is a definite contribution to our knowledge of Arnold and his affairs. From a collection of some 300 Arnold letters to his two major publishers, Buckler has taken what he considers of literary importance and has presented it as "a publishing diary, in which passages from Arnold's letters and (where available) from the letters of his correspondents which pertain to specific Arnold publications are given chronologically according to title." By this arrangement he enables the reader "to follow, with the least possible interruption, the evolution of Arnold's major works during the last twenty-five years of his life." An eighteen-page introduction is informative on "The Author-Publisher Relationship."

Over the past thirty-three years scholars have been busy in an attempt to coordinate Arnold's scattered correspondence. An admirable history of these endeavors is to be found in "Letters of Matthew Arnold: A Supplementary Checklist," by Roger L. Brooks (*SP*, 1966). T. H. V. Motter begins the project with "A Check List of Matthew Arnold's Letters" (*SP*, 1934). This is followed in 1947 by Louis Bonnerot's *Matthew Arnold: Poète,* in which he printed eight of Arnold's letters to Sainte-Beuve, along with Sainte-Beuve's replies. He also included a list of other Arnold letters, particularly those published in periodicals. R. H. Super in "Documents in the Arnold–Sainte-Beuve Relationship" (*MP*, 1963) lists the documents in chronological order and brings Bonnerot's basic scholarship up to date. In "Notes toward a Matthew Arnold Bibliography" (*MP*, 1952), Marian Mainwaring lists Arnold letters written for publication and personal letters published before his death. In "A Project for a Check-List of Matthew Arnold's Letters" (*VN*, 1953) and "Matthew Arnold's Letters: A Progress Report on a Descriptive Checklist" (*VN*, 1962), Arthur Kyle Davis says that in his attempt to "identify, locate, assemble, and describe all the known letters of Matthew Arnold" he has accumulated a list of 2,172 letters to 349 different correspondents. "The total includes unpublished, published, and partially published letters." Roger L. Brooks, one of the most active scholars in this enterprise, has made three significant additions to the checklist. The first, "Matthew Arnold and his Contemporaries" (*SP*, 1959), catalogs "unpublished letters in the libraries of England and the published letters in the works of Arnold's contemporaries or their biographers." The second, "Matthew Arnold's Correspondence" (*MP*, 1962), lists "unpublished letters in the libraries of the United States." The third, "Letters of Matthew Arnold: A Supplementary Checklist" (*SP*, 1966), describes forty-five unpublished letters in private collections, and sixteen letters published by Arnold's contemporaries or their biographers. From the C. B. Tinker Collection at Yale University another list of forty-three letters to thirty-seven correspondents is added by Robert F. Metzdorf in *The Tinker Library: A Bibliographical Catalogue of the Books and Manuscripts* (1959).

As Roger L. Brooks indicates, a great deal of work remains to be done: "The sale and auction catalogues identify scores of letters that have not been located. Then, too, collections prob- ably in Germany and Italy have not yet been discovered, not to mention the letters in the hands of private collectors."

Limitation of space prevents the listing here of the numerous articles during the past twenty-five years in which single letters or small collections are published.

V. CRITICAL STUDIES

From the mass of general and introductory material only a few items have been selected for comment. The wealth of such material in the Arnold literature is really a sign of its poverty. What is needed are more studies that give thorough considera- tion to particular aspects of his work. The very excellence of some of the general studies lessens the need at present for more works in this kind. The worst general introduction is probably "Hugh Kingsmill's" *Matthew Arnold* (1928). The best are cer- tainly Lionel Trilling's *Matthew Arnold* (1939; new edition, 1949) and A. Dwight Culler's *Imaginative Reason: The Poetry of Matthew Arnold* (1966). Somewhere between these extremes lie modest summaries such as those by Harvey and Duffin and illuminating critiques such as those by Garrod, Chambers, Stanley, Kathleen Tillotson, and Gottfried.

As prelude to a consideration of the books by Trilling, Garrod, and the others, a few words should be said of the verdict of the twenties on Arnold. From this decade there is a considerable body of comment, most of it without benefit of scholarship. The critics adventuring among Arnold's masterpieces try to determine whether he is greater as a poet or as a writer of prose; from what ultimate sources his melancholy springs; and where and how he failed as an artist. None of the commentators speaks with final authority, but taken together they do establish a perspective necessary for evaluation of the later book-length studies.

Arnold's turning from poetry to prose is explained very simply, and inadequately, by Sir Arthur Quiller-Couch in *Studies in Literature* (1919). It is "testimony to the perfect development of a life which in due season used poetry and at the due hour cast it away, to proceed to things more practical." In spite of his frequent poetic clumsiness, his overworking of interjections, his use of italic type for emphasis, his occasional bad ear for rhyme, his lack of the bardic, the architectonic gift, Arnold does have a vein of "the most real and rarest poetry." And his sense of natural atmosphere and background deserves high praise. In "The Second-Order Mind" (*The Dial*, 1920) T. S. Eliot mildly regrets Arnold's desertion of poetry for the writing of editorials, but concludes that the temptation was probably irresistible. Sir Walter Raleigh in *Some Authors* (1923) also prefers the poetry, for it "deals only with the great things," the themes which though they are invoked as memories and appealed to as standards in the prose, are distant there "as they are never distant in the poems." Further, the prose takes on a tone of mockery. C. H. Herford in "Matthew Arnold as a Prophet" (*Living Age*, 10 February 1923) is chiefly concerned with Arnold's role as apostle of culture, but the same fundamental characteristics are observed of the poet as of the prophet. It is the "stoic exaltation" that appeals to Herford, "the hidden ground of thought and impassioned resignation," which even more than the radiant form account for the vitality of his poems. On Arnold's melancholy there are two articles: C. R. Elliott's "The Arnoldian Melancholy" (*PMLA*, 1923; republished in *The Cycle of Modern Poetry*, 1929); and Douglas Bush's "The Varied Hues of Pessimism" (*Dalhousie Review*, 1929). In Elliott's view, Arnold's mood has its source in differentiated emotional currents which give a sense of deep oppositions. Bush finds that both Arnold and Hardy are inspired by "a kind of melancholy that is more universal than that of religious disillusionment." In *Studies in Victorian Literature* (1923), S. T. Williams devotes a chapter to "Three Aspects of Arnold's Poetry"—the mastery of mood-creating detail, the habitual sacrifice of narrative to philosophical details, and the particular type of Hellenism.

Lionel Trilling's *Matthew Arnold* has been so widely acclaimed as one of the finest examples of recent American scholarship and criticism that it need not be discussed here at any length. It is at once an exposition, a vindication, a criticism, and an interpretation; it is admirable alike for its tone and erudition. As Harold Nicolson says, he gives us "not only Arnold's mind, but also the mind of an age." The chief charge that has been brought against Trilling's book is that it deals less than adequately with Arnold the poet. C. H. Harvey's *Matthew Arnold: A Critic of the Victorian Period* (1931) is in the main an industrious paraphrasing of Arnold's prose works. The tone throughout is one of eulogy. It is a useful but not very important book. With H. W. Garrod's *Poetry and the Criticism of Life* (1931), E. K. Chambers' Warton lecture on Arnold in *Proceedings of the British Academy* (1932), and Carleton Stanley's *Matthew Arnold* (1938), however, we move on a higher level. All three men are perceptive, discriminating critics. They are persuasive spokesmen for Arnold. Stanley, writing after the appearance of the letters to Clough, can speak with more factual authority. Garrod's voice, however, is more commanding, better to listen to. Chambers is much interested in the Marguerite episode, but also discusses Arnold's poetic theory and practice.

In the general revaluations of the thirties and the forties, Arnold the poet receives higher praise than Arnold the writer of prose. Even Garrod admits that the critical writings are going out of fashion. According to Edmund Blunden ("Matthew Arnold," in *The Great Victorians*, edited by H. J. Massingham and H. Massingham, 1932), the prose covers fields that are too technical for the treatment Arnold gave them, fields that have now been taken over by expert treatises and monographs. Louis Kronenberger, in "Re-reading Matthew Arnold" (*SRL*, 15 September, 1934), is more damning: Arnold's social and religious criticism has dwindled to nothing; much of the literary criticism will follow. Only his style will remain. And in the same vein of detraction, T. S. Eliot remarks (*The Use of Poetry and the Use of Criticism*, 1933) that in philosophy and theology Arnold is an undergraduate, in religion a Philistine. For all these views authority and precedent can be found among the nineteenth-century critics of Arnold—Frederic Harrison and George Saintsbury, for example. T. S. Eliot's unflattering comments on Arnold's philosophy and religion are echoes of the earlier strictures by F. H. Bradley and J. M. Robertson.

On Arnold's poetry the general verdict is more favorable. But there are reservations. He is too intelligent to be a great poet (Harold Nicolson, "On Re-Reading Matthew Arnold," in *Essays by Divers Hands: Being the Transactions of the Royal Society of Literature,* 1948). His poetry is academic in the best sense (T. S. Eliot, *The Use of Poetry and the Use of Criticism*). He is a little bleak, too serious, too melancholy, too much the preacher (F. L. Lucas, *Ten Victorian Poets,* 1940). A number of critics—T. S. Eliot; G. L. Strachey in "Victorian Critic," *Characters and Commentaries* (1933); and J. W. Cunliffe in "Mid-Victorian Poets," *Leaders of the Victorian Revolution* (1934) — object to Arnold's moral prepossessions, and to the definition of poetry as a criticism of life. Garrod's reply to such charges is that Arnold was merely giving sharp expression to what had passed as a truism for centuries. That it is not the business of a great writer to teach virtue is an absurdly modern thesis; we ought to get over the feeling that a moral idea will bite us. With another group of critics (Chambers, Blunden, and Stanley) Arnold's greatest success is in his elegiac poetry, and in bringing to mind the English landscape. It is not mere acceptance and resignation that the poetry reflects, however. There is also the note of courage. And in any case, his philosophy is infinitely preferable to Browning's. At his best he is better than Tennyson.

Arnold scholarship and criticism before 1950, with the exception perhaps of Tinker and Lowry's *Commentary,* in its treatment of the poetry is concerned chiefly with content, with the philosophical and religious, the sociological and psychological ideas. From 1950 to the present day, a shift is discernible. Some attention is paid to form and technique: structure, imagery, symbolism, prosody and diction. A rather pedestrian beginning is made in *Das Meer als Gleichnis bei Matthew Arnold* (1951), by W. Oxenius, which treats the sea as a symbol of Arnold's many polarities—life and death, freedom and restraint, eternal change and eternal law. The book is a development, with numerous citations, of the statement by E. K. Chambers that "the metaphor is not always consistently used, but a sense of the flux of things is always recurring in Arnold's mind." W. Stacy Johnson's "Parallel Imagery in Arnold and Clough" (*ES*, 1956) presents evidence that similar images and groups of images appear in the works of the two poets, and that the symbolic use to which the imagery is put is also similar. The similarities in fact are so striking that the two poets seem to be responding to each other, carrying on a kind of interchange. Drawing on Tennyson, Browning, Arnold, Swinburne, and Thomson for proof, Curtis Dahl in "The Victorian Wastleland" (*CE*, 1955; reprinted in *Victorian Literature: Modern Essays in Criticism*, edited by Austin Wright, 1961) shows that the wasteland is hardly a modern discovery, though "The wasteland of the Victorian poets is on the whole more dignified, more static in significance, more restrained in regard to sex, more specifically social rather than individual, and more nostalgic toward the past than that of most twentieth century poets." A more important contribution is P. F. Baum's *Ten Studies in the Poetry of Matthew Arnold* (1958). Baum's versatility is displayed in the wide range of problems undertaken: detailed exegesis, as in "Shakespeare" and "Mycerinus"; source studies, as in "Tristram and Iseult"; metrical analysis, as in "The Two Laments," "Dover Beach," and "Empedocles on Etna"; and biographical studies, as in "Arnold's Marguerite." Unlike Tennyson and Browning, Arnold as yet has had no monograph devoted to his versification. On the technique and craftsmanship of his poems there have been fewer studies than on other aspects of his work. Baum's metrical analyses, therefore, take on added significance.

Over several works on Arnold's poetry during this period falls the shadow of Dr. F. R. Leavis. A confessed disciple, J. D. Jump (*Matthew Arnold*, 1955) echoes Leavis in making a harsh assessment of the poems in contrast to the high value placed on the prose. In the one chapter of his book devoted to "The Poet," Jump maintains that "too much" of Arnold's "work consists of uncreative ruminations and academic exercises. His good poems are regrettably few. Only once did he fully exploit a symbolic landscape in the service of his deeper, Empedoclean impulses;

and on that occasion he wrote his one great poem, 'Dover Beach.' "
Citing Jump frequently in support of his views, Pietro de Logu
(*La Poetica e la poesia di Matthew Arnold,* 1962) discovers
weaknesses in all but a few of Arnold's poems.[2] The love poems
deal not so much with love as with an attempt by Arnold to
understand his own personality. "Empedocles on Etna" becomes
genuine poetry only occasionally when Arnold's own feelings
show through. The narrative poems are in the main a failure:
"Sohrab and Rustum" because it is an application of a theory;
"The Sick King in Bokhara" because it is too obvious and didac-
tic; "Tristram and Iseult" because it shows a greater interest in
philosophical problems than in the story. In "The Forsaken
Merman," however, Arnold for once abandons his intellectual
concerns and presents his personal problem successfully through
fantasy and symbol. Most of the elegies are impaired by an
excessive concern with intellectual and critical problems. Only
in "The Scholar Gipsy," "Thyrsis," and "Rugby Chapel," where
his emotions are fully involved, does Arnold achieve authentic,
inspired poetry. In his discussion of Arnold's poetics, particularly
the idea of poetry's future as a substitute for religion, Logu,
following the lead of T. S. Eliot, credits Arnold with being a
forerunner of the aesthetes and decadents at the close of the
century. Other reasons for Arnold's comparative failure as a poet
are adduced by Gerhard Müller-Schwefe in *Das personliche
Menschenbild Matthew Arnolds in der dichterischen Gestaltung*
(1955). Arnold's language is better suited for intellectual than
for aesthetic purposes. It lacks the capacity to call up images. His
subjects, whether ancient or modern, are almost always aspects
of himself. And his interests center too largely on moral and
intellectual questions. As a critic, too, Arnold is found to be
wanting by John S. Eells, Jr., in *The Touchstones of Matthew
Arnold* (1955). Eells concludes that "in the selection of the
touchstone passages Arnold was influenced, even dominated, by
states of mind habitual to him." Arnold therefore becomes guilty
of the personal estimate against which he protests. Furthermore,
the touchstones are "not widely enough representative," limited

[2]An Italian study as well informed as Logu's but more sympathetic is
Vittorio Gabrieli's *Il Mirto e l'Alloro: Studio sulla Poesia di Matthew Arnold*
(1961).

as they are to "an attitude of profound earnestness toward the grimness and darkness of the human adventure."

In reaction to the severity of judgments such as the foregoing, and in the belief that from 1930 to 1962 Arnold has been viewed chiefly as a prose writer on social, ethical, and religious themes, Henry C. Duffin (*Arnold the Poet*, 1962) tries to revive critical interest in what he thinks is Arnold's most important activity— the poetry. Duffin is by no means blind to Arnold's failings, but he believes them to be sufficiently outweighed by his virtues to establish him solidly as the third of the great Victorian poets. Duffin's best chapter, though even so a rather superficial one, is "The Art of Arnold's Poetry," in which he analyzes diction, metrics, imagery, and the indebtedness to Keats.

For perception and thoroughness in the study of sources and influences, Kathleen Tillotson ("Matthew Arnold and Carlyle," *PBA*, 1956; reprinted in *Mid-Victorian Studies,* 1965) and David J. DeLaura ("Arnold and Carlyle," *PMLA*, 1964) deserve particular mention. Kathleen Tillotson's thesis is that Carlyle the preacher exerts a strong influence on Arnold's early work ("Cromwell," the sonnets, and "Empedocles on Etna"), but is rejected finally when Empedocles disavows his own creed, which is recognizably the creed of *Sartor Resartus*. But Carlyle the poet never loses his attraction. "His style and feeling" haunt Arnold's poems and prose till the end of his career. Fraser Neiman in "The Zeitgeist of Matthew Arnold" (*PMLA*, 1957) shows that in the 1840's and 1850's, the period of the Arnold-Clough correspondence, Carlyle also influences Arnold's conception of the Zeitgeist, "the current fashionable opinion, especially as opposed to ascertainable critical absolutes," the spirit of the times from which the artist must escape to preserve his integrity. DeLaura's article confirms the Tillotson-Neiman findings and goes beyond them to a consideration of Arnold's critical writings, especially those of the 1860's. His study, remarkably probing and solidly documented, proved that "At the heart of Arnold's attitude towards Carlyle is a persistent ambivalence, one half of it a remarkable bulk of conscious and half-conscious borrowings of ideas and key expressions, the other half a seemingly fixed need to depreciate Carlyle, combined with something very close to concealment of his influence."

Only in the last decade has Arnold's relationship with the Romantic movement received the attention it deserves. William A. Jamison's monograph, *Arnold and the Romantics* (1958), opens with a chapter on a subject that still awaits definitive treatment—Arnold's poetics. He then gives a chapter, methodical in pattern though also somewhat mechanical and monotonous, to each of Arnold's five Romantic poets. For the most part, Jamison's conclusions are the generally accepted ones: that Arnold was at his best in his treatment of the poets he most admired, Wordsworth, Byron, Keats; at his worst with Shelley; and at his weakest with Coleridge. D. G. James's *Matthew Arnold and the Decline of English Romanticism* (1961) is a lively and irresponsible attack on Arnold the person, the poet, and the critic. James sets up his own questionable, twentieth-century definition of Romanticism and then takes Arnold to task for not conforming to it. His witty marshaling of Arnold's many inconsistencies, however, is provocative. Both Jamison and James limit their discussion almost entirely to Arnold's prose, the critical essays. By drawing on the verse as well as the prose, Leon Gottfried (*Matthew Arnold and the Romantics*, 1963) is able to explore and evaluate "the full range of Arnold's reactions to the major Romantic poets over his whole career: the nature and extent of their poetical, critical, and personal influence upon him, and the quality and limits of his critical reaction to them." In Gottfried's view, Arnold is "both continuator and severe critic of the Romantic tradition," attracted to the tradition temperamentally, repelled by it intellectually. And in the lifelong contest temperament is finally triumphant. The chapter on Wordsworth is of especial significance, for, as Gottfried says, "a study of Arnold's criticism of Wordsworth becomes, in effect, a survey of Arnold's life." Gottfried's book is the best informed and most discerning treatment that Arnold's relationship with the Romantics has yet received.

Although the idea of measuring the effectiveness in Arnold's poetry of T. S. Eliot's three voices (*The Three Voices of Poetry*, 1953), and a fourth voice, that of the narrator, seems promising, the results are disappointing in W. Stacy Johnson's *The Voices of Matthew Arnold* (1961), an elaboration of his article, "Matthew Arnold's Dialogue" (*UKCR*, 1960). The categories in Johnson's classification of the poems are not very sharply differentiated; the voices too frequently are intermixed. And we have already met in earlier criticism the conclusions to which Johnson comes: that the oracular and narrative poems are the weakest, and that the soliloquies, monologues, and dialogues, in which Arnold's tensions and feelings are dramatically involved, present him at his best.

Two attempts have been made to trace underlying themes in Arnold's verse: R. A. Donovan's "Philomela: A Major Theme in Arnold's Poetry" (*VN*, 1957) and Herbert R. Coursen's " 'The Moon Lies Fair': the Poetry of Matthew Arnold" (*SEL*, 1964). The Philomela theme is defined as the inevitable association of isolation and pain with the poetic vision. Because of his compulsion to "see life steadily and see it whole," the poet is more nearly allied to the philosopher and the prophet than to the painter and the musician. Such "integral vision" involves pain, loss of illusions, even loss of identity. According to Coursen, however, "Arnold's poetry can be defined as an attempt to revisit the Wordsworthian scene and find there the transcendent significance which revealed itself to Wordsworth." The power of his poetry lies in the tension created between his yearning for perfection symbolized in the Wordsworthian landscape, and his tough-minded realization of the illusory nature of all fair appearances.

A. Dwight Culler's *Imaginative Reason: The Poetry of Matthew Arnold* (1966) provides a fitting climax for discussion of general works on Arnold's poetry. Solidly based on all relevant preceding scholarship and criticism, it gives for the total body of Arnold's poetry a genuinely fresh interpretation, which deepens and enlarges our conception of Arnold's imaginative world. Arnold's poetic works are conceived of as "one large complex myth," made real and visible through character, landscape, and action.

> It is a world divided into three regions which we may call the Forest Glade, the Burning or Darkling Plain and the Wide-Glimmering Sea. The first is an idyllic region in which youthful figures live joyously in harmony with nature; the second is a region of mature suffering and isolation; and the third is a region in which suffering subsides into Calm and then grows up into a new Joy, the joy of active service in the world. Connecting these three regions is the River of Life or Time, and the thought is that man, whether in his individual life or in human history, moves from childhood

faith and joy, through a period of skepticism and the understanding to a final synthesis that reconciles the two.[3]

An especially valuable feature of Culler's interpretations is the biographical background included. Though he omits a considerable number of poems from his discussion and sometimes seems to wander off on interesting tangents from his central theme, his is the most comprehensive and illuminating critique that Arnold's poetry has thus far been given.

Having employed the myth to such good effect in explaining the poetry, Culler then uses it less successfully to explain the arrangement of *Essays in Criticism* in "No Arnold Could Ever Write a Novel" (*VN*, 1966). To make his formula work he has to do violence to the final essay, "Marcus Aurelius," which hardly provides the culminating joy that he attributes to it. More convincing explanations of the arrangement of the essays can be found in Robert A. Donovan's "The Method of Arnold's *Essays in Criticism*" (*PMLA*, 1956), and in William E. Buckler's "Studies in Three Arnold Problems" (*PMLA*, 1958).

Early Poems. Except for the sonnet on Shakespeare, Arnold's early poems have not been given much attention in the learned journals during the past twenty-five years. Frazer Neiman, in "Plotinus and Arnold's 'Quiet Work'" (*MLN*, 1950), believes that there is less affinity than is commonly supposed between Arnold's and Wordsworth's concepts of nature. A more likely source than Wordsworth for "Quiet Work," he suggests, is the third *Enneid* of Plotinus.

The sonnet "Shakespeare" has been subjected to exegetical scrutiny by a number of scholars. F. R. Leavis judges the poem harshly in *Education and the University* (1943; revised edition, 1948): it is a piece of mere versifying, vague, inappropriate, and clumsy in its imagery, so formless in its thought that it becomes "an unwitting confession of vacuity." P. F. Baum's interpretation in *Ten Studies in the Poetry of Matthew Arnold* (1958) is more temperate and acceptable. After a review of suggestions in Tinker and Lowry, and of other brief comment-

[3]A. Dwight Culler, "No Arnold Could Ever Write a Novel" (*VN*, Spring 1966, p. 2). Earlier versions of this world, as Culler indicates, are developed in his own edition, *Poetry and Criticism of Matthew Arnold* (1961), and in Alan H. Roper's important article "The Moral Landscape of Arnold's Poetry" (*PMLA*, 1962).

aries (*N&Q,* 1942, and *Expl,* 1946, Item 47), he gives his own paraphrase. Shakespeare is like a great mountain. His wisdom surpassing human knowledge he reveals only to the stars. Thus, we mortals "seek in vain to learn from his works." Like the mountain, he is aloof and independent of ordinary life. Only his serene countenance reveals his human sufferings and his victory over them. The point of the sonnet is the aloofness from "the eternal mundane spectacle." Another reading is provided by Robert A. Greenberg in "Patterns of Imagery: Arnold's 'Shakespeare'" (*SEL,* 1965). The mountain, he thinks, is not equated with Shakespeare. It is, as in so many of Arnold's poems, a mountain to be climbed. Shakespeare has climbed it and so stands inviolate among the stars. The sestet emphasizes Shakespeare's looking within himself, mastering himself, an introspection paralleled in many of Arnold's poems. If Greenberg's explication seems a bit contrived, the article by T. T. Truss, "Arnold's 'Shakespeare'" (*Expl,* May 1961, Item 56) is even more so. Truss regards the sonnet as a typical example of Arnold's practice of grafting "an idea to a landscape," and making "the landscape do his talking for him."

In "Matthew Arnold's 'The New Sirens' and George Sand" (*VP,* 1963), Kenneth Allott suggests that "The New Sirens" may have been inspired by George Sand's Lélia between 1843 and 1845, being reprinted by Arnold in 1876, the year of George Sand's death, as homage to her memory. To her influence Allott, in "Matthew Arnold's 'Stagirius' and Sainte-Marc Girardin" (*RES,* 1958), also ascribes the title "Desire" given in 1855 to the poem published in 1849 as "Stagyrus" and from 1877 on as "Stagirius." Girardin had described Stagyre as a romantic who sought peace but found only dissatisfaction in austerity and renouncement. Arnold's poem, then, is an exploration of his own romantic weakness. The title "Stagyrus" is used to disguise the autobiographical element in the poem.

W. Stacy Johnson thinks that earlier critics have been misled by the title of "In Utrumque Paratus." He reads the poem, in "Arnold's 'In Utrumque Paratus'" (*Expl,* May 1952, Item 46), as an "antithesis between man's moral (and proud) isolation from material nature and his sympathetic identification with it."

Taking issue with Johnson and others, Jan B. Gordon, in "Disenchantment with Intimations: a Reading of Arnold's 'In Utrumque Paratus' " (*VP*, 1965) , interprets the first three stanzas of the poem as a Wordsworthian explanation of the origins of the world, and the last three stanzas as an exposure of the inadequacy of the Wordsworthian explanation. The poem is therefore a "subtle inversion of the Wordsworthian retreat: instead of finding the long sought 'healing power,' Arnold's protagonist finds a nature which at best is morally neutral."

Robert A. Greenberg's "Matthew Arnold's Mournful Rhymes: A Study of 'The World and the Quietist' " (*VP*, 1963) explains "The World and the Quietist" as Arnold's apology for his own kind of poetry—"the dialogue of the mind with itself." Arnold omitted the poem in the 1869 collection because he was no longer a quietist, but a reformer. And in 1877 he restored it, when he and his public "had found their accomodation."

Narrative Poems. Scholarly investigations of the narrative poems have been relatively few in recent years. Such criticism as the poems have received stresses mainly their failure. Melvin L. Plotinsky's "Help for Pain: the Narrative Verse of Matthew Arnold" (*VP*, 1964) is representative. In Plotinsky's view the central problem of all Arnold's verse is "the divided mind." In his best verse he leaves the questions in suspense. But in many poems and particularly in the narrative poems he gives the impression that "he has solved the problem of the divided mind, and insofar as the poems attempt to embody that solution they fail as poems whether or not the solution is in any way acceptable."

For the oriental coloring of "Sohrab and Rustum" sources have been found in the works of Captain Sir Alexander Burnes (Jennie E. MacNeill in *TLS*, 11 April 1936; 15 January 1938) and of Marco Polo (R. L. Brooks in "A New Source for Matthew Arnold's 'Sohrab and Rustum,' " *PQ*, 1963) . Arnold's epic similes in the poem have been attacked by J. B. Broadbent in "Milton and Arnold" (*EIC*, 1956) as being merely decorative in contrast to Milton's similes with their moral meaning. John Holloway in "Milton and Arnold" (*EIC*, 1957) charges Broadbent with working only on the periphery when he should have attacked the center: "Sohrab and Rustum" fails for lack of a great action and because it has no firm relation to "life's general fabric." The best defense of the similes and of the poem as a whole is that by A. Dwight Culler in *Imaginative Reason* (1966).

For most commentators the major appeal of *Sohrab and Rustum* lies not in the classical objectivity that Arnold intended, but in the personal significance. Maud Bodkin in *Archetypal Patterns in Poetry* (1934, pp. 65–68) suggests that the "foiled circuitous wanderer" is Arnold himself, and she sees in the flowing of the Oxus into the Aral Sea an expression of the death wish, death being a release from conflict and tension. Lionel Trilling in *Matthew Arnold* (1939) interprets the slaying of the strong son by the "mightier father" as a symbol of Arnold's sacrifice of youth and poetic talent to maturity and "the creation of a character." What Trilling implies, W. H. Auden ("Matthew Arnold," in *Another Time*, 1940) states positively: Arnold sacrificed his poetic gift to become his "father's forum." The autobiographical element is most fully developed by Kenneth Burke (*A Rhetoric of Motives*, 1950, pp. 7–10), who links "Empedocles on Etna" and "Sohrab and Rustum" as expressions of self-abnegation, Sohrab's death particularly symbolizing Arnold's "pious deference to the authority of his father." J. D. Jump ("Matthew Arnold," in *From Dickens to Hardy*, edited by B. Ford, 1958) views "Sohrab and Rustum" as "in part an unconscious imaginative projection of the conflict, concerning which we have independent biographical evidence, between Matthew Arnold and his formidable father, Dr. Arnold of Rugby." The biographical evidence is supplied in some detail later in Patrick J. McCarthy's *Matthew Arnold and the Three Classes* (1966), p. 25. W. Stacy Johnson (*The Voices of Matthew Arnold*, 1961, pp. 127, 128) recognizes the psychological significance of the Persian material, but adds that "presumably the son and poet was not fully aware of his motive in selecting this material." A. Dwight Culler (*Imaginative Reason*, 1966, p. 229) discusses the final battle scene as an expression of the Oedipus complex. However tempting all these theories may be, K. Muir ("Arnold and the Victorian Dilemma," in *The Penguin New Writers*, no. 31, 1947) and K. Allott (*Matthew Arnold*, in *British Writers and Their Work*, 1962, p.52) recommend some reserve in accepting them, because most poets die young however long the man may survive, and in whatever sacrifice Arnold made to the memory of his father, love and admiration as well as antipathy were involved.

Several unsuccessful attempts have been made to revive interest in "Balder Dead." Frederick Page in "Balder Dead" (*E&S*, 1942) tries, as he says, to "read *Literature and Dogma* into *Balder Dead*." He interprets the poem allegorically. "Balder is Christianity as it has fared among men. Lok is the critical spirit, 'the all-corroding, all-dissolving skepticism of the intellect in religious inquiries.' Hoder . . . is popular opinion . . . that indifference to religion that Arnold so much deplored." Clyde De L. Ryals' "Arnold's 'Balder Dead' " *VP* (1966), which presents Balder as the modern poet, the sport and target of those he soothed, and Hoder's blindness as emblematic of society's inability to appreciate the singer's worth, is too far-fetched and fanciful to win acceptance.

On "Tristram and Iseult" the comment, if often unfavorable, is more extensive. By critics of the thirties and forties the autobiographical interpretation is widely accepted. E. K. Chambers (*PBA,* 1932) detects the Marguerite affair in the theme of the poem. H. W. Garrod calls the 1852 volume Marguerite's book, "Tristram and Iseult" in particular, as a tale of separated lovers, being written for her. F. L. Lucas sees in the poem Arnold's struggle of renunciation, the triumph of his puritanism. What emerges from the poem for Trilling is not the suffering of any of its three characters, but the despair of the poet himself. Bonnerot finds exact biographical parallels: Tristram is Arnold, Iseult of Ireland is Marguerite, Iseult of Brittany is Lucy Wightman. Iseult of Ireland represents youth, passionate love, and the lyric impulse in Arnold's poetry. Iseult of Brittany represents domesticity, Arnold's prosaic life, and the suppression of his lyric impulse. Although the romantic elements, the Keatsean and Byronic influences in the poem are pointed out by most critics, the prevailing opinion is that the poem dispels the romantic dream, the Wordsworthian conception of "the healing power" of nature.

To the frequent charge that the poem's "coda," the Merlin and Vivien story, is irrelevant, J. L. Kendall, in "The Unity of Arnold's 'Tristram and Iseult' " (*VP*, 1963) attempts an answer. The best interpretation of the Merlin story, he believes, is that which regards it as a reflection of the insight and sensibility, not of Arnold himself or even of Iseult of Brittany, but of another *persona*, the character-narrator, perhaps a Breton bard. Thus interpreted, the story is not the vehicle for Arnold's heavy underlining of moral message: the folly of passion. The pronouncements are made by the *persona*, the Breton bard, whose judgments are in keeping with the reflective spirit of the poem. A similar use of the narrator device is made by Robert A. Greenberg, in "Matthew Arnold's Refuge of Art: 'Tristram and Iseult' " (*VN*, 1964), to explain the retention of the poem in Arnold's 1853 volume in which "Empedocles on Etna" was omitted. As "Memorial Verses" illustrates, Goethe in Europe's dying hour achieves his wide and luminous view through art. Arnold in "Tristram and Iseult" finds a similar refuge. The narrator, not Arnold, explains, mediates, and as artist transforms by grouping or shaping according to his vision. Whether or not the narrator device is completely successful, it "answered to the criteria of 1853." Robert L. Brooks, in "Matthew Arnold's Revision of 'Tristram and Iseult': Some Instances of Clough's Influence" (*VP*, 1964), discovers eleven changes made by Arnold in the 1853 edition of the poem, all because of Clough's criticism in the *North American Review*. In "The Intellectual Background and Structure of Arnold's 'Tristram and Iseult' " (*VP*, 1963), M. G. Sundell argues that the basic purpose of the poem is to depict "the insufficiency of any single idea to interpret experience." Arnold presents three methods for meeting life's terrible events and making them bearable: that of Iseult of Brittany, who turns the events of her life into a legend; that of the narrator, who organizes his views into an oration on the destructive power of passion; and that of Tristram, who converts life into a dream.

Following the lead of several earlier scholars who read "The Forsaken Merman" as autobiography, Howard W. Fulweiler in "Matthew Arnold: The Metamorphosis of a Merman" (*VP*, 1963) emphasizes the conflict between the land which represents conventionality and restriction and the sea which represents youth, wonder, and art. In Margaret's return to the land Arnold depicts his own relinquishment of art, poetry, and the life of the imagination for security, marriage, and an inspectorship of schools. The awkward shift in sex seems to be no obstacle for Fulweiler in this interpretation. The plight of the Forsaken Merman is pictured again by Arnold in the first version of "The Neckan." But by the addition of the budding staff incident in the 1853 text of the poem Arnold implies a promise of ultimate salvation. To this involved psychological interpretation of the Merman poems Kenneth Allott takes exception in "Matthew Arnold's 'The Neckan': The Real Issues" (*VP*, 1964). Sufficient explanation for the budding staff incident is found, he thinks, in Arnold's unquestioned source: Thorpe's *Northern Mythology*. In his view Fulweiler's interpretation of "The Forsaken Merman" is "closer to imaginative fiction than to literary criticism." In a reply, "The Real Issues in Arnold's 'The Neckan'" (*VP*, 1964), Fulweiler insists that Allott's new source does not discredit but rather confirms the symbolical reading.

Lyric Poems. It is appropriate that for Arnold's almost perfect lyric, "To Marguerite—Continued," an almost perfect scholarly criticism should be available. In less capable hands, the study might have become a routine tracking down of verbal parallels in Horace, Lucretius, Donne, Keble, Carlyle, Wordsworth, Thackeray, Browning, and Collins. But Kathleen Tillotson, in "Yes: In the Sea of Life" (*RES*, 1962; reprinted in *Mid-Victorian Studies*, 1965), weaves together the seemingly tenuous associations, the "airs and floating echoes" to form a solid biographical and intellectual background for a deeper reading of the poem. She proves that "The subject of 'Yes: in the sea'; is human life; and 'the same heart beats in every human breast.' The poem draws part of its strength from the common stock of experience; it represents Arnold's own multiform experience of what was read and thought as well as what was proved upon the pulses." One of her provocative conclusions is that the continuing arguments over which are "Marguerite" poems is artificial, since for Arnold Marguerite became an inseparable part of the experience which is basic to all his poems.

In "Matthew Arnold's 'The Strayed Reveller'" (*RES*, 1960) and in *Matthew Arnold and the Romantics* (1963), Leon Gottfried develops new and persuasive explanations for the title "The Strayed Reveller," the use and conception of Circe, and Arnold's choice of a poem so highly charged with romanticism as the title piece of his first volume. In Gottfried's opinion, the poem is ironic and allegorical. The youth has "gone astray," has fallen into the hands of Circe, who has lost none of her ancient and sinister powers of seduction. Drunk with her wine, the youth sees without pain those poetic visions which come to the "wise bards," not drunk with Circe's wine, only through labor and pain. The youth, a romantic sensualist, lacks any centralizing idea with which he can prevail over the world's multitudinousness. He is like Keats: his dramatic utterances, though rich and evocative, are ununified. "Arnold, both attracted and repelled by the wine of the sensuous, the passionate, the varied, the ornate, has created in *The Strayed Reveller* not only a dramatic representation of certain romantic attitudes toward art and the self, but also has implied in the structure and diction of the poem a subtle allegorical critique of them." In reaction to such attempts to make of the poem "a versified essay in criticism," M. G. Sundell, in "Story and Context in 'The Strayed Reveller' " (*VP*, 1965), contends that the statements on the nature of art and artists are subordinate to the story and the atmosphere. Arnold fuses thought and story by means of striking devices: "internal narration, complementary characters, metrical and rhetorical emphasis, limited but highly significant imagery, and above all a central story-line which somehow manages to hold the poem together while fostering illuminating commentary on the events."

The accepted source of the closing battle-by-night incident in "Dover Beach," Arnold's most famous lyric, is a passage in Thucydides' *History of the Peloponnesian War,* a work all Rugby students would have known in Dr. Thomas Arnold's translation. It is suggested, however, by Paul Turner, in " 'Dover Beach' and the 'Bothie of Tober-na-Vuolich' " (*ES*, 1947), and by B. Trawick, in "The Sea of Faith and the Battle by Night in 'Dover Beach' " (*PMLA*, 1950), that Arnold may have had his memory of the passage refreshed by Clough's version of it in the "Bothie." Turner presents evidence, too, for the possibility that Arnold wrote the closing nine lines of "Dover Beach" as a criticism of Clough's view of life in the "Bothie." There are evidences also, as shown by D. A. Robertson in " 'Dover Beach' and 'Say Not the Struggle Nought Availeth' " (*PMLA*, 1951), and by P. F. Baum, in "Clough and Matthew Arnold" (*MLN*, 1952), that Clough's "Say Not the Struggle Nought Availeth" in turn was written as a reply to

"Dover Beach." According to Kenneth Allott, in *The Poems of Matthew Arnold* (1965), however, Arnold's adoption of the passage from Thucydides "is more likely to have been influenced by Newman's sermon of Jan. 1839, *University Sermons* (1843)" than by Clough's "Bothie." A close comparison of "Dover Beach" with Empedocles' *On Nature* and *Purifactions* convinces Sidney Feshback, in "Empedocles at Dover Beach" (*VP*, 1966), that "The last lines of the poem may be derived from Thucydides, Clough, or Newman, but more certainly they owe something to Empedocles' Fragment 121."

Adopting R. Delasanta's idea, in "Arnold's 'Dover Beach'" (*Expl*, October 1959 Item 7), that the poem's theme is the melancholy awareness of the incompatability between illusion, expressed through light imagery, and reality, expressed through auditory imagery, Murray Krieger, in " 'Dover Beach' and the Tragic Sense of Recurrence" (*University of Kansas City Rev.*, 1956), sees the shift in light imagery as an expression of the endless battle between sea and land, the Nietzschean sense of tragic recurrence. In the versification, too, and in the parallel structure of three of the stanzas he finds an indication of "the unprogressiveness of man's ever-repetitive circular history."

In one of the better readings of the poem, "Dover Revisited: the Wordsworthian Matrix in the poetry of Matthew Arnold" (*VP*, 1963), W. C. Knoepflmacher draws attention to the similarity in situation between "Dover Beach" and Wordsworth's sonnet " 'Tis a Beauteous Evening." And he interprets Arnold's poem as an inversion of Wordsworth's "Near Dover, September, 1802." "Just as in 'Resignation' Arnold discredits the 'healing power' of a Wordsworthian landscape, so, in 'Dover Beach,' he stresses the unreliability of a Romantic belief in the visual." But Arnold's attitude is ambivalent: he rejects Wordsworth intellectually, yet tries to conserve the power to feel. Since nature provides no basis for the Wordsworthian vision, he turns to the dissemination of "culture." Even so, in 1879 he edits a volume of Wordsworth's poetry to preserve Wordsworth's "joy."

Norman H. Holland's "Psychological Depths and 'Dover Beach'" (*VS*, 1965) is an unconvincing interpretation of the poem and of Victorian culture as a whole in terms of sexual symbolism. And an objection of little weight is raised in "Missing

Persons on Dover Beach" (*MLQ*, 1965) by Gale H. Carrithers, who thinks that the poem is weakened because our knowledge of the speaker and of the person addressed is so limited.

In proof of the generally held opinion that "Growing Old" is an answer to Browning's "Rabbi Ben Ezra," Conrad A. Balliet in " 'Growing Old' Along with 'Rabbi Ben Ezra' " (*VP*, 1963) points out that Arnold's poem "inverts not only the optimism and assertions of Browning, but the stanzaic structure itself." In writing "Growing Old," Arnold may also have been "attacking Tennyson's passion for the past in 'Tears, Idle Tears,' " as John Hubenthal demonstrates in " 'Growing Old,' 'Rabbi Ben Ezra,' and 'Tears, Idle Tears' " (*VP*, 1965) .

Elegiac Poems. "The Scholar-Gipsy" has been a subject of considerable controversy during the past fifty years. S. P. Sherman in *Matthew Arnold: How to Know Him* (1917) presents a view of "The Scholar-Gipsy" and "Thyrsis" to which a number of later critics subscribe: "the thought in these much-praised elegies is a bit too thin to bear triumphantly the weight of all the flowers which Arnold has strung upon it. He presents, in them both, an unwonted appearance of dallying by the wayside, of digressing, of indulging in a moral holiday." In answer, E. K. Brown's " 'The Scholar-Gipsy': An Interpretation" (*Revue anglo-américaine*, 1935) defends the nature descriptions as an aid in illuminating the character of the Scholar-Gipsy. Also answering Sherman, L. Perrine, in "Arnold's 'The Scholar-Gipsy' and 'Thyrsis' " (*Expl*, February 1957 Item 33) , defends the thought of the poems on the ground that the Scholar-Gipsy is a "quester" in the devoted and single-minded pursuit of truth. Perrine lays the responsibility for the misinterpretation of the Scholar-Gipsy on Arnold himself, his use of such descriptive terms as "wanderer," "truant," "roam," and "stray."

If F. R. Leavis is not always a good critic himself, he is often the cause of good criticism in others. His unfavorable analysis of "The Scholar-Gipsy," in *The Common Pursuit* (1952) , as a "charming" poem weakened by confusion and "intellectual debility," and of the Scholar-Gipsy as on "an eternal week-end," has stimulated much expostulation and reply. The first of these replies and by all odds the best, indeed the most thorough and perceptive critique the poem has had, is " 'The Scholar-Gipsy':

A Study of the Growth, Meaning and Integration of a Poem"
(*Litera*, 1955 and 1956) by J. P. Curgenven. His contention is
that the poem is "both a vision and a critique," not just a section
of biography or a place poem. It is really a criticism of life,
with man, not the Oxford country, as its main theme. He is
particularly successful in showing the fusion of Part I, the natural
description, with Part II, the meditation. And in a very helpful
analysis, he demonstrates that both in form and thought Arnold's
critique is a culmination of Romanticism: the deepening rift
between sensibility and environment; the rift between creative
and non-creative levels of personality; the dream world "with
which sensibility can wholly identify itself; the craving for soli-
tude, withdrawal, death; the themes of wandering and quest-
ing; the tone of angst"; the attacks on reason and philosophy;
the new synthesis in the "cult of inwardness," expressed in the
exaltation of imagination and in the cultivation of a "heart that
watches and receives, a wise passiveness, the holiness of the
heart's affections," a diligent indolence, a negative capability.

The Scholar-Gipsy is by no means on an "eternal week-end,"
according to G. Wilson Knight in " 'The Scholar Gipsy': An
Interpretation" (*RES*, 1955). He is in pursuit of a deeper, darker,
Dionysian wisdom, the intuition of the Orient, which the Gipsies
and the Tyrian trader represent. He is fleeing from the barren
intellectualism of Oxford, which is its heritage from Greece and
Rome. The poem thus becomes a plea for the refertilization of
Western Europe "from the cool depths of the 'Dionysian,' the
more darkly feminine and Eastern powers." To Wilson's inter-
pretation, A. E. Dyson provides a refutation in "The Last En-
chantments" (*RES*, 1957). Subjective views such as Wilson's
might have been taken, he says, by Carlyle, or Blake, but not
by Arnold. It is not Oriental mysticism, but enlightenment,
Hellenism, and Hebraism, that Arnold stands for. Though he
loves Christian and medieval thought forms for their beauty and
joy, their emotional and moral value, he can no longer accept
their intellectual basis. "The Scholar-Gipsy" therefore represents
the Victorian predicament: the rejection by the mind of the
heart's desire. It is a poem of unbelief. V. S. Seturaman in " 'The
Scholar-Gipsy' and Oriental Wisdom" (*RES*, 1958) rejects Dyson's
reading. Seturaman believes that the Scholar-Gipsy has found

dry, rationalistic Victorian intellectualism unsatisfying and is in search of a new kind of awareness in which intellect and faith will be joined: the peace, the integrated ideal that Arnold found in the *Bhagavad Gita*. In "Hebraism, Hellenism and 'The Scholar-Gipsy'" (*DUJ*, 1962), Paul Edwards takes issue with Seturaman. The poem is confused and ineffective, Edwards believes, because its central purpose, the reconciliation of Hebraism, or action, and Hellenism, or thought, is not achieved. The Scholar-Gipsy lacks intellectual and physical energy. The poem is too passive. And the passivity is the result of Arnold's enthusiasm for the *Bhagavad Gita*.

For the Tyrian trader passage at the close of the poem, sources are claimed in Thucydides by R. H. Super (*N&Q*, 1956), in Herodotus by Kenneth Allott (*TLS*, 18 October 1963), and in the Bible by E. E. Stevens (*VN*, 1963).

On "Thyrsis" the learned articles have been few, and except for J. P. Curgenven's "Thyrsis" (*Litera*, 1957), of little significance. Curgenven puts "Thyrsis" in the period of Arnold's decline as a poet. He finds it, compared and contrasted with "The Scholar-Gipsy," slower in tempo, lower in key. The tensions are loosened. There is more emphasis on landscape and less on meditation. The poem is not concerned primarily with remembrance of things past, but with the quest of truth. And this "central parable" is carried by two symbols: the Tree, and Light which increases as the poem progresses. Though the Greco-Roman pastoral is successfully fused with the Oxford landscape, the pastoral tradition itself seems outworn and out of place applied to modern issues and to a man so complex as Clough.

For the description of the school chapel with which "Rugby Chapel" opens, W. S. Peterson in "'Rugby Chapel' and *Tom Brown's School-Days*" (*ELN*, 1966) discovers a possible source in the closing paragraphs of *Tom Brown's School-Days*. Kathleen Tillotson, in "'Rugby Chapel' and 'Jane Eyre'" (*N&Q*, 1948), thinks the "long, steep journey" over mountains in snow may have been inspired by a passage in *Jane Eyre*. And Lilian H. Hornstein, in "'Rugby Chapel' and Exodus" (*MLR*, 1952), presents Moses of Exodus as a possible original for Dr. Thomas Arnold, the leader. According to H. Kerpneck's "The Road to Rugby Chapel" (*UTQ*, 1964), the poem is not simply a reply to Fitzjames Stephen's 1858 attack on Dr. Thomas Arnold. It is an 1866 summation and restatement of Arnold's own spiritual progress. It is the climax of a series of spiritual poems, involving the quest motif: "The Scholar-Gipsy," "Stanzas from the Grande Chartreuse," and "Thyrsis." The same kind of imagery, Kerpneck believes, is used in all these poems. The series shows a continuous spiritual development, culminating in "Rugby Chapel," and incomplete without it.

Dramatic Poems. In the scholarship of recent years, no poem of Arnold's has excited more spirited controversy than "Empedocles on Etna."[4] The result of the critical attention has been an increased respect for the poem as one of the major long poems of the nineteenth century. The Tinker and Lowry analysis, in the *Commentary*, is a good indication of the attitude toward the poem before 1940. After a discussion emphasizing the faults— that the poem as a whole is verbose, and that the philosophical sections are prosaic in expression and superficial in thought— they indicate, nonetheless, that future criticism may support T. Sturge Moore's opinion that *"Empedocles* more and more appears the most considerable poem of comparable length by a Victorian."

In assuming that Empedocles is Arnold's spokesman, and finding the philosophy of Empedocles unsatisfactory, most critics before 1940 conclude that the poem is a failure. Trilling in his book (1939) opens up a new avenue of approach, however, which becomes the course of later criticism: *"Empedocles* is a philosophical poem and very explicit; but it is also a dramatic poem and its drama lies not so much in the internal struggle of its hero or its resolution as in its juxtaposition of two kinds of poetry," that of the rational Empedocles and that of the intuitive Callicles.

Douglas Bush (*Mythology and the Romantic Tradition in English Poetry*, 1937), too, recognizes the importance of Callicles in the drama, the basic theme being "the relative value of and the conflict between two ways of life and art, that of sensuous emotion and intuition and that of elevated and disciplined thought." So strongly is the presence of Callicles felt that the

---

[4]For valuable suggestions on "Empedocles on Etna" I am indebted to Professor Thomas Deegan of St. Xavier College, Chicago, Illinois.

entire poem becomes in a way "an anti-intellectual affirmation on the side of simple feeling, sensuous intuition." But Arnold cannot surrender completely to this side of himself, and "the dilemma remains a dilemma." In this dramatization of the problem, with no attempt at a solution, later critics see the modernity of the poem. A. Dwight Culler (*Imaginative Reason*, 1966), for example, dissociates "Empedocles" from representative Victorian poems like Tennyson's "In Memoriam" and Browning's "Saul," in which tensions are resolved and idealistic answers proposed.

In his biography of Arnold (1947), Bonnerot views Empedocles and Callicles as the two sides of Arnold's own nature. He provides a more searching analysis, however, in his translation of the poem (1947) with its long introduction. In this he points out the poem's lack of unity, the architectonic quality that Arnold himself demanded, and the lack of grandeur or originality in the stoic philosophy presented. The secret of "Empedocles," he thinks, lies in its unresolved tensions, more moral than metaphysical, which reflect the search for equilibrium as the major problem of life.

E. D. H. Johnson (*The Alien Vision of Victorian Poetry*, 1952) interprets "Empedocles" as a dramatization of Arnold's own creative problem: "Fear of the Zeitgeist, on one hand, and distrust of his own innate perceptions, on the other," which give to his poetry "its characteristic tone of indecision." Johnson is the first critic to regard Callicles as a more authoritative spokesman than Empedocles for Arnold. In the dialogue of the songs of Callicles and the speeches of Empedocles, the solutions to Empedocles' problems are suggested in the songs. And Callicles' final song, "a serene and joyous acceptance of things as they are," is the final judgment on Empedocles.

If at one extreme, Johnson presents Empedocles as a failure, Frank Kermode (*The Romantic Image*, 1957), at the other, presents him as victorious. Callicles is seen as a naive Wordsworthian, whose joy in nature Empedocles rejects because he knows its grounds are not true. Empedocles is the Romantic artist who in the battle against society and his own dwindling powers heroically chooses suicide in preference to compromise. In Kermode's words, "the poem, designed with extraordinary care, a professional job of architectonics, is a system of tensions which deliberately excludes all movement save the suicide of the hero. The poem is a victory."

Avoiding the extremes of autobiographical and symbolical interpretation, Walter E. Houghton, in "Arnold's 'Empedocles on Etna'" (VS, 1958), is content to regard Empedocles as a dramatically conceived character making his confession. The form of the poem is dictated, Houghton says, by Arnold's desire to portray "modern thought" in Act I and "modern feeling" in Act II. To avoid further contamination by the world or the complete domination of his faculties by the intellect, Empedocles leaps heroically into the crater, and thereby preserves the better elements of his nature.

P. F. Baum's treatment of "Empedocles" in *Ten Studies in the Poetry of Matthew Arnold* (1958) has little new to offer as an analysis of the drama, but is to be commended for its close analysis of the metrics. In calling "Empedocles" a dramatic poem, not a poetic drama, W. Stacy Johnson (*The Voices of Matthew Arnold*, 1961) makes an important distinction. The poem, in his view, is a series of monologues visualizing and giving limited dramatic form to the disparities between the views of Empedocles and Callicles, but lacking the resolution and synthesis that a playwright would have to provide. Warren D. Anderson, in *Matthew Arnold and the Classical Tradition* (1965), agrees with the earlier critics that the strength of the poem lies in the tensions between Empedocles and Callicles. Yet he maintains that one of the views must be more valid, and "while Arnold may not arrive at a rationale, he clearly makes a choice between the two ways of responding to life... It is the way of Callicles that Arnold chooses as an ideal." Anderson also regards "Empedocles" as the culmination of Arnold's development toward an ordered conception of classicism. From this point on Arnold will not allow the classical spirit to penetrate him. He "now takes refuge in externals—first Homeric and then tragic form, but always form of some kind."

A. Dwight Culler (*Imaginative Reason*, 1966) suggests that "Empedocles" was written in a mood of "supreme Promethean defiance." In Culler's symbolic landscape, Callicles is associated with the forest glade, Pausanias with the cities, and Empedocles with the barren cone. Callicles as a poet of youth and joy in nature, and Pausanias as a slave to religion and superstition represent stages which Empedocles has outgrown and to which he cannot return. The "creed" Empedocles propounds is meant for Pausanias' benefit and is not one by which Empedocles himself could live. The suicide, Culler says, "is a complex act which cannot be interpreted wholly one way or another." It is not "the act whereby the Romantic hero transcends limitation." Neither is it wholly a defeat. "The total meaning of the drama, of course, does not lie in Empedocles alone, but in him in relation to Pausanias and especially to Callicles."

Source studies of "Empedocles" subsequent and supplementary to those of Tinker and Lowry have been made by a number of scholars. Warren D. Anderson traces the classical sources of Callicles' songs. Marie C. Menger, in "Matter Versus Man: Or Régnier's Lyrical Integration, Hugo's Dream of Triumph and Arnold's Abdication" (*FR*, 1955), analyzes Arnold's treatment of the Marsyas legend. Kenneth Allott, in "Arnold's 'Empedocles on Etna' and Byron's 'Manfred' " (*N&Q*, 1962), shows similarities with "Manfred" in dramatic structure, incidents, phrasing, and rhythms. For the influence of Carlyle's *Sartor Resartus* on Empedocles' "creed," Kathleen Tillotson presents strong evidence in "Matthew Arnold and Carlyle" (*PBA*, 1956). In Empedocles' rejection of his "creed" she sees Arnold's own rejection of Carlyle's teachings. And the presentation of contradictory attitudes toward Carlyle accounts for the poem's failure. In spite of his thesis that there are "numerous verbal echoes," "many parallel themes and images," and a "profound similarity in the entire structure of the two dramas," Fred L. Burwick, in "Hölderlin and Arnold: Empedocles on Etna" (*CL*, 1965), is unsuccessful in trying to prove that Arnold was familiar with Hölderlin's work on Empedocles. Though he does indicate some possible influences, S. Nagarajan, in "Arnold and the *Bhagavad Gita:* A Reinterpretation of 'Empedocles on Etna' " (*CL*, 1960), is unconvincing in his overall conclusion that "the intellectual frame of reference in *Empedocles on Etna* is substantially derived from the *Bhagavad Gita*."

The tone of the criticism on "Merope" is set very early by Swinburne's remark: "The clothes are well enough, but where has the body gone?" Later critics find fault, however, even with the clothes. To Tinker and Lowry the choruses in the play seem very Greek and very dull. They fail to capture John Bailey's interest ("Ancient Tragedy and Modern Imitations," in *Poets and Poetry*, 1911), because they contain too much vague legendary matter, and too many long complicated genealogies. Even their defender, J. Churton Collins, in his edition of the play (*Matthew Arnold's Merope*, second edition 1917), has to confess that they fall short of Milton's standard in his choruses. Lionel Trilling calls the verse of the play "wooden." Warren Anderson (*Matthew Arnold and the Classical Tradition*, 1965) regrets that Arnold in seeking elevation so often becomes stilted. "The compound epithets that he was to bar from translations of Homer are here in full force . . . on a few occasions the poem seems to parody itself. Syntax and diction twist into strange paths from time to time and take on a Latinate air or a pre-Elizabethan antiquity." The play has no unity of action, for, as Tinker and Lowry charge, our interest shifts from Merope to Polyphontes. There is no real hero in the classical sense. Trilling thinks that the subject matter is not truly agitating, and that the recognition scene between Merope and her son is "buzz saw melodrama." Other commentators find the true classical spirit lacking. Bonnerot points out the absence of the Gods who play such a central part in Greek drama. Ruth Goldmark (*Influence of the Classics on English Literature*, 1918) notes the lack of attention to Fate, and the excessive self-analysis as being violations of the Greek spirit. According to Pietro de Logu (" 'Merope': Tragedia Neo-Classica di Matthew Arnold," in *English Miscellany*, 1960, edited by Mario Praz, and in *La Poetica e la poesia di Matthew Arnold*, 1961), Arnold chose the Greek dramatic form not for aesthetic reasons, but as an effective medium for his moralistic message. He is too little the artist and too much the preacher. He also employs the Greek form in opposition to the Romantic revival of Elizabethan tragedy. In Leon Gottfried's view (*Matthew Arnold and the Romantics*, 1963), the Greeks achieved tragic grandeur by showing how man could achieve dignity in an alien world, whereas "Arnold's feeling does not advance beyond disillusionment." A. Dwight Culler (*Imaginative Reason*, 1966) defines the theme of the play as "the complexity of the moral situation and the difficulty of choosing between a pragmatic and an absolutistic ethic." Thus Arnold departs from Greek practice in which values are made clear and issues are sharply defined. Most critics grant, however, that the play is not wholly a failure. Tinker and Lowry discover "some noble and lofty rhetoric," "a fine Sophoclean irony," and "a certain pathos and humanity given to Merope's character." Ruth Goldmark recognizes in the play classical seriousness and the clarity of arrangement and the lack of ornamentation that Arnold admired in the Greeks. Logu is impressed by the severe beauty of the verse. And Culler admits that there is at least one truly poetic passage in the poem, the drowning scene as described by AEpytus. For the preface to "Merope" the best reference work is R. H. Super's *On the Classical Tradition* (1960).

VI. SPECIAL STUDIES

Arnold and France. In the field of comparative literature there is no more fascinating topic than Matthew Arnold and France. On this theme we should have a work like C. F. Harrold's *Carlyle and German Thought*, in which sound and thorough scholarship is combined with critical insight and good judgment. Instead we have *Matthew Arnold and France* (1935), by Iris E. Sells, which gives too much, and *The Critic's Alchemy* (1953), by Ruth Z. Temple, which gives too little significance to Arnold's relationship with France. Iris E. Sell's book, which is mainly concerned with Arnold's debt to Quinet, Sénancour, and George Sand, has met with an unfavorable reception because of her fanciful and sentimental recreation of the Marguerite episode, and her inability in source studies to distinguish between a parallel and an influence. A similar defect is apparent in Joseph W. Angell's study, "Matthew Arnold's Indebtedness to Renan's 'Essais de morale et de critique'" (*Revue de Littérature Comparée*, 1934). Angell too often attributes to a single work and a single author ideas that were generally current and could have been derived from many writers. More temperate and in every way more impressive than Angell's source study is Lewis W. Mott's "Renan and Matthew Arnold" (*MLN*, 1918). But Sidney M. B. Coulling in "Renan's Influence on Arnold's Literary and Social Criticism" (*Florida State University Studies*, V, 1952) contends that Mott and Angell have greatly exaggerated Renan's influence on Arnold's critical writings. Further evidence of this influence on Arnold's literary and social criticism and particularly on the religious writings is supplied, however, by F. E. Faverty in *Matthew Arnold the Ethnologist* (1951). Joan N. Harding's "Renan and Matthew Arnold: Two Saddened Searchers," (*HJ*, 1959), contributing nothing new or original, is a general comparison of the ideas of the two writers on religion, education, morality, Hellenism, Celticism, and other topics.

The severest indictment to date on Arnold as an apostle of French culture is that delivered by Ruth Z. Temple in the first three chapters of *The Critic's Alchemy: A Study of the Introduction of French Symbolism into England* (1953). She insists that "his service to the cause of his countrymen's appreciation of French literature and especially French poetry was dubious at best." With the masterpieces of French prose his acquaintance was neither wide nor deep nor sympathetic. Echoing Emile Legouis, E. K. Brown, Lionel Trilling, and others, she condemns him as a critic of French poetry for his indifference to the qualities of the language, and his failure to appreciate the music of the alexandrine. His errors in judgment she attributes partly to his lack of information, partly to the bizarre application of his touchstone system. In "Matthew Arnold and Sainte-Beuve" (*PMLA*, 1938), Arnold Whitridge emphasizes the similarities between the two critics: their agreement that French poetry was second-rate, that criticism must be combined with charm; their intellectual conscience, and dislike of pedantry; and their aristocratic preference for subtlety, distinction, and refinement rather than pure genius. Yet, Whitridge says, there is a fundamental difference.

Arnold is a moralist for whom literature is a matter of ethics. Sainte-Beuve is more catholic in taste and understands the values of things of the mind for their own sake. On the basis of this chief difference, Miss Temple concludes that "Arnold's criticism has no real resemblance in theory, in spirit, or in practical method to that of his great contemporary." Miss Temple also believes that Arnold's likeness to Renan has been overemphasized. Arnold, she says, lacks epigram, eloquence, elegance, wit, even the power to persuade—all distinguishing traits of Renan. The only French critic with whom he has any real kinship is the dogmatist Edmond Scherer. Not content with robbing Arnold of his claims as an intermediary between France and England, Miss Temple denies him eminence as a critic of any literature, including his own. Three French influences on Arnold—George Sand, Sénancour, and Marguerite—are discussed by Florence Wickelgren in "Matthew Arnold's Literary Relations With France" (*MLR*, 1938). She attempts to reconstruct the visit to George Sand in 1846, and to show what Arnold had in common with Sénancour. The influence of the affair with Marguerite she believes has been over-stressed by Iris E. Sells.

In her brief section on Arnold in *From Gautier to Eliot: The Influence of France on English Literature* (1960), Enid Starkie summarizes some of the generally accepted views on Arnold's relationships with France: the influence on him of George Sand, Sénancour, and Sainte-Beuve; his neglect of Racine, Hugo, and Baudelaire; his inability to appreciate the real quality of French poetry; and his shift late in life to sympathy with Germany, because of the French deficiency in morality. F. J. W. Harding's *Matthew Arnold the Critic and France* (1964) is an examination of Arnold's prose works to balance "the complementary work of I. E. Sells, *Matthew Arnold and France: The Poet.*" It displays sounder scholarship, however, and better judgment than its counterpart and "is concerned rather with his interpretation of France, than with the French influences upon Arnold the critic; although these latter will in part emerge from an assessment of the sources he used for his essays and remarks upon French writers." *The View of France: From Arnold to Bloomsbury* (1965), by Christophe Campos, is based on the questionable assumption that "the image of a nation" is formed "not when the leaders of thought read foreign books, but when they travel to another country with the more or less direct intention of criticizing their own." Ignoring political, economic, and social factors that may play a significant part in determining views toward a foreign nation, Campos attributes to the influence of Arnold and his Bloomsbury disciples the views that twentieth-century England holds of France. Campos is frequently wrong in his statements about Arnold's life and career. Arnold's knowledge of France, he thinks, "is gained mainly at second hand," and needs qualification and correction. And finally, in their criticism of France, Arnold and his successor, Clive Bell, pandered too much to English pride. In effect, they "merely played 'Rule Britannia' in a minor key."

Arnold and Germany. Although there is sufficient material to justify a monograph on Arnold and Germany, none has yet appeared in English. The subject has been treated, however, in a number of German doctoral dissertations (Margarete Lassen, *Matthew Arnolds Verhältnis zu den Deutschen und zur Deutschen Literatur*, 1923; Johannes Renwanz, *Matthew Arnold und Deutschland*, 1927; Paul Wilhelm Zorn, *Matthew Arnold und seine Beziehung zu Deutschland*, 1924). Of these, Renwanz's *Matthew Arnold und Deutschland* is representative. With what Arnold calls "the steady humdrum habit of the creeping Saxon," Renwanz has extracted from Arnold's published works the leading references to Germany and has arranged them neatly in their proper categories: descriptions of German districts in the verse and correspondence; the use of the German people as examples of Philistinism; the relationship between Arnold's liberal republicanism and his unfavorable view of Prussian monarchy; his praise of W. von Humboldt and the German educational system; his unflattering comments on the German language and his mixed views on German literature; his adoption of Goethe's conception of Spinoza; his references to the Reformation, his indebtedness to the higher critics of the Bible, and, in his attempt to free Christianity from Semitism, his dependence on Schleiermacher, W. von Humboldt, and Bunsen; his scattered comments on German music and the plastic arts. Unfortunately, Renwanz does not often or for very long allow himself any higher function than that of a cataloguer. Walther Fischer's "Matthew Arnold und Deutschland" (*GRM*, 1954) is a brief but informative study of Arnold's knowledge of the German language and literature: his partial reliance on Carlyle for views on Goethe; his indebtedness to Goethe for ideas on form, art, morality, and Classicism; his half correct, half erroneous interpretation of Heine; and his interest in German political development.

Helen C. White's preliminary tracing of the general outline of Goethe's influence on Arnold, in "Matthew Arnold and Goethe" (*PMLA*, 1921), leads to J. B. Orrick's fuller and more critical analysis, "Matthew Arnold and Goethe" (*PEGS*, 1928). Arnold's idea of Goethe, Orrick says, was derived secondhand from Carlyle. And like Carlyle, Arnold transformed and sometimes misinterpreted what he found. Orrick traces Arnold's admiration for Goethe in the numerous allusions, in the incidental criticism of Goethe's works, in the essays that have special reference to him, and in the passages reminiscent of Goethe. On Arnold's estimate of three writers in particular—Byron, Heine and Spinoza—Goethe's influence is paramount. And in all three cases it is Goethe qualified or misinterpreted. From this critical but nonetheless sympathetic survey Orrick concludes that Arnold learned no habits or methods from Goethe. For Arnold, Goethe was primarily a standard of reference and a perpetual source of inspiration.

Recent scholarship, however, takes issue with Orrick's conclusions (see particularly W. Robbins, *The Ethical Idealism of Matthew Arnold*, 1959; *The Poems of Matthew Arnold,* edited by Kenneth Allott, 1965; and two important books that appeared too late for full treatment in the present chapter, G. Robert Stange's *Matthew Arnold: The Poet as Humanist,* 1967, and William A. Madden's *Matthew Arnold: A Study of the Aesthetic Temperament in Victorian England,* 1967). Robbins insists that Goethe was largely responsible for the ruling idea in Arnold that "established customs, beliefs, creeds, and intellectual patterns must come before the joint tribunal of general culture and cumulative human experience." Questioning Carlyle's importance as intermediary, Madden emphasizes the independence of Arnold's ideas on Goethe and tries to show that "the point of view that informed his criticism" in his many "essays on the aesthetic education of man" was "the one that Goethe had formulated:

Whoever has art, has religion." Allott in his annotations on, and Stange in his analyses of the poems demonstrate that Goethe's influence was more profound and pervasive than earlier scholars had thought. Stange finds that "of the four major ideas which I regard as the organizing centers of Arnold's poetry, three seem to be conscious extensions of Goethe's insights."

On Arnold's treatment of Heine in the poem and in the essay a rather harsh verdict is rendered by Elsie M. Butler ("Heine in England and Matthew Arnold," *GL&L*, 1956), Arnold's translation, she thinks, is poor at best, and often incorrect. Goethe's mantle did not fall on Heine. Arnold skipped a great deal in Heine's works. And he was definitely wrong in his opinion that Heine "wanted love." The poem, she says, denies Heine even the "charm" that the essay granted. A more sympathetic account of both the poem and the essay is to be found in Sol Liptzin's "Heine, the Continuator of Goethe: A Mid-Victorian Legend" (*JEGP*, 1944; reprinted in *The English Legend of Heinrich Heine*, 1954).

Arnold and America. Turning to Arnold and America, we again have a topic that deserves but has not yet received a comprehensive treatment. Thus far we have only an unpublished doctoral dissertation by C. H. Leonard: *Arnold in America: A Study of Matthew Arnold's Literary Relations with America and of His Visits to This Country in 1883 and 1886* (1932); John Henry Raleigh's admirable *Matthew Arnold and American Culture* (1957), limited to a study of Arnold's influence in America; and scattered articles: William T. Beauchamp's "Plato on the Prairies (Matthew Arnold at Galesburg)" (*Educational Forum*, 1941); Walter E. Bezanson's "Melville's Reading of Arnold's Poetry" (*PMLA*, 1954); John B. Hoben's "Mark Twain's 'A Connecticut Yankee': A Genetic Study" (*American Literature*, 1946); Harriet R. Holman's "Matthew Arnold's Elocution Lessons" (*New England Quarterly*, 1945); H. M. Jones's "Arnold, Aristocracy, and America" (*American Historical Review*, 1944); E. P. Lawrence's "An Apostle's Progress: Matthew Arnold in America" (*PQ*, 1931); John P. Long's "Matthew Arnold Visits Chicago" (*UTQ*, 1954); James Dow McCallum's "The Apostle of Culture Meets America" (*New England Quarterly*, 1929); R. H. Super's "Emerson and Arnold's Poetry" (*PQ*, 1954); W. D. Tem-

pleman's "A Note on Arnold's 'Civilization in the United States' "
(*MLN,* 1944). On C. H. Leonard's excellent dissertation Trilling
has drawn heavily in the last chapter of his *Matthew Arnold.* Most
of the articles attempt to discover the causes of Arnold's failure
with his American audiences. J. D. McCallum distinguishes be-
tween the receptions given Arnold by the literary class—highly
favorable—and by the general public—highly unfavorable. Para-
doxically, the general public thought him lacking in humor, yet
was offended by his witticisms. E. P. Lawrence finds Arnold
himself entirely to blame. His inaudibility in New York, his tact-
less depreciation of Emerson in Boston, his supercilious attitude,
priggishness, unconscious rudeness, and lack of a sense of humor
made his message unpalatable. A similar comment is made by
W. T. Beauchamp on Arnold's appearance in Galesburg, Illinois.
His self-absorption, cold formality, affectation, monotonous de-
livery, and egotism alienated his audience. But the audience in
this case was also at fault, for in its sturdy Midwest Philistinism
it was incapable of receiving or understanding Arnold's spiritual
kinship with the aristocracy, his instinctive feeling that the
majority is always bad and usually wrong. His doctrine of culture,
according to Jones, rested on a deep distrust of the people. Fur-
thermore, it was closely bound up with racial snobbery and anti-
democratic political action. Harriet Holman shows that Arnold
took as a matter of course, and spoke with marked condescension
of, the elocution lectures which the Reverend J. W. Churchill
offered as a favor. With no sense of public address, none of the
instincts of a speaker, Arnold was more heavily indebted to
Churchill than he cared to admit for whatever success he
achieved on the American lecture platform. In his interesting and
informative article, John P. Long for the first time has brought
together all the materials on Arnold's visit to Chicago in 1884.
His article is based on F. W. Gookin's *The Chicago Literary
Club* (1926) and on the files of four Chicago newspapers: the
Daily Inter-Ocean, the *Tribune,* the *Daily News,* and the
Evening Journal. Long's most significant contributions are the
story of Eugene Field's aversion to Arnold, and "The Matthew
Arnold Hoax," a full account of the *Tribune's* altercation with
Arnold, or Joseph Medill's "melancholy experience with the
apostle of sweetness and light."

According to John B. Hoben, however, Arnold's American visit had in one instance, at least, a good effect. The raging Anglophobia which Arnold inspired in Mark Twain awakened him from a literary lethargy and evoked the spirit which transformed an unpromising sentimental romance into the satirical *A Connecticut Yankee in King Arthur's Court*. R. H. Super explores "large areas of correspondence between Emerson and the young Arnold . . . intimating how many of Emerson's specific ideas were congenial to him." Walter E. Bezanson analyzes all Melville's marginal comments in his copies of *Poems* and *New Poems*. The analysis reveals that Melville was profoundly impressed by "Empedocles on Etna." In his struggles with the spiritual dilemmas of the nineteenth century he found Arnold a helpful guide. In J. H. Raleigh's words (*Matthew Arnold and American Culture*), "No other foreign critic, and perhaps few native ones, have acquired such a reputation and exercised such a palpable influence on American culture." In the development of that reputation and influence the leading figures, Raleigh indicates, were Henry James, William Brownell, Stuart P. Sherman, T. S. Eliot, and Lionel Trilling. In his discussion of these major figures and many minor ones, he shows that "although a great deal of Arnold's impact as a critic in the English-speaking countries can be accounted for by the fact that he had offered the age precisely what it wanted and needed, there were also certain elements in his thought that made his writings permanently congenial to Americans in particular."

Arnold and the Classics. According to Ralph E. C. Houghton in *The Influence of the Classics on the Poetry of Matthew Arnold* (1923), Arnold's classicism "consists in the production of the same kinds of effect upon our minds that the Classics produce." In determining the extent of the classical influence on Arnold, Houghton notes detailed resemblances in style and in spirit.

Arnold's style, Houghton believes, is full of classical reminiscences. In "Sohrab and Rustum" and "Balder Dead" the epic similes and the catalogs of place names show Homeric influence. "Sohrab and Rustum" lacks Homeric "rapidity," but possesses the other qualities Arnold listed as Homeric—"simplicity" and "nobility." The classical device of style — *Epanalepsis* — is detected in "Alaric at Rome" and in "The Scholar Gypsy." Arnold's ex-

Matthew Arnold

amples of English hexameters are regarded as unfortunate. His unrhymed lyric poems often imitate the rhythms of the Greek choral odes in a wooden way, without sufficient regard for the genius of English. And finally, Arnold's insistence on design and unity is classical. On Arnold's spirit the influence of the classics is even more marked. Houghton finds the works permeated with the classical feeling of sanity, sincerity, and reticence. And there is a Roman *gravitas* in Arnold's character and judgments.

With many of Houghton's judgments on individual poems Douglas Bush in *Mythology and the Romantic Tradition in English Poetry* (1937) disagrees. Most of Bush's predecessors in the field[5] had devoted themselves to the study of sources and to tracing Homeric adaptations and echoes in Arnold. Although Bush in his footnotes does justice to these subjects, he is mainly concerned with other matters. Arnold, he thinks, is "a prophet and preacher" seeking intellectual and spiritual discipline in the classics. For Arnold classical mythology serves as a refuge, a partial escape from the perplexities and disharmonies of his own era. But it also ministers to his desire for the reign of law in nature and in himself. In some of his best lyrical and ethical poems it is the classical symbol that gives distinctness, unity, and noble connotations to the presentation. The classical doctrines expounded in Arnold's prose essays, particularly in the preface of 1853, Bush finds valid today as yesterday. But the classicism of the longer poetic works—"Merope," "Sohrab and Rustum," and "Balder Dead"—he thinks is synthetic and academic.

Although R. H. Super's *On the Classical Tradition* (1960) is an edition of prose works, his annotation for the Prefaces to *Poems* (1853) and (1854), for the Preface to "Merope," and

[5]*Matthew Arnold's Merope: To Which Is Appended the Electra of Sophocles Translated by Robert Whitelaw*, ed. J. Churton Collins, 2d ed. (1917); John Bailey, "Ancient Tragedy and Modern Imitations" [*Merope*], *Poets and Poetry* (1911); Frank L. Clark, "On Certain Imitations or Reminiscences of Homer in Matthew Arnold's 'Sohrab and Rustum'" (*Classical Weekly*, 1923–1924); Milo G. Derham, "Borrowings and Adaptations from the 'Iliad' and 'Odyssey' in Matthew Arnold's 'Sohrab and Rustum'" (*University of Colorado Studies*, 1909–1910); Ruth I. Goldmark, *Studies in the Influence of the Classics on English Literature* (1918); W. P. Mustard, "Homeric Echoes in Matthew Arnold's 'Balder Dead'" (*Studies in Honor of Basil Lanneau Gildersleeve*, 1902); T. S. Omond, "Arnold and Homer" (*Essays and Studies by Members of the English Association*, 1912); John A. Scott, "Matthew Arnold's Interpretation of *Odyssey* iv. 563" (*Classical Journal*, 1920–1921).

for *On Translating Homer* are helpful in the study of Arnold's poetry. In "Arnold and the Classical Tradition" (*Arion,* 1962), H. A. Mason argues that Arnold's lectures on Homer reveal him to be "radically inadequate both in his conception of translation and in his formulation of the claims that may be made on Homer's behalf." Henry Ebel's "Matthew Arnold and Marcus Aurelius" (*SEL,* 1963) is mainly a digest of the content of "Marcus Aurelius," but in the memorable conclusion of Arnold's essay, Ebel maintains, "it is not Marcus Aurelius who 'yearns' but Arnold himself, the Arnold of 'Dover Beach' and 'Stanzas from the Grande Chartreuse,' the Arnold of 'Obermann Once More' (with its flat, weak, and unconvincing ending), the Arnold who, within a few years, will undertake the mission of imbuing the world with a joy which he himself cannot feel."

Warren D. Anderson's *Matthew Arnold and the Classical Tradition* (1965) is a major contribution to the field. The opening chapters are concerned with the poetry. For Anderson the chief interest of the early poems lies in Arnold's struggle between an intellectual commitment to Classicism and an emotional leaning toward Romanticism, a struggle that reaches its culmination and supreme expression in "The Strayed Reveller," in which the two forces are held in balance. Thereafter Classicism begins to dominate and Arnold's career as a poet moves toward its end. The second peak in Arnold's development is "Empedocles on Etna," in which the Appolonian and Dionysian elements in Classicism contend. With the triumph of the Appolonian forces in Arnold's poetry a dreary formalism sets in, which leads finally to the abandonment of poetry. The remaining chapters, devoted mainly to Arnold's prose, develop the thesis that for all his advocacy of Classicism, Arnold never allowed himself to be completely possessed by its spirit, and the Hellenic world he pictured was a distorted one, the product of his own imagination. Anderson, also, includes a nine-page tabulation of classical sources. His unusually full annotation of the text provides an excellent summary of critical opinion on Arnold.

Political Ideas. More than thirty years ago J. Dover Wilson called for some competent student of politics to assign Arnold his true place in the role of English political thinkers. The call is still unanswered. In the early thirties it was possible for Leonard

Woolf (*After the Deluge,* I, 1931) to condemn Arnold as a reactionary authoritarian, and for R. H. Tawney (in chapter two of *Equality,* 1931) to claim him as a champion of democracy. On the Irish question, Arnold as against Gladstone, later writers like Carleton Stanley (*Matthew Arnold,* 1938) and W. Robbins ("Matthew Arnold and Ireland," *UTQ,* 1947) continued to hold diametrically opposite views, Stanley as exponent of Arnold's prophetic insight and Robbins as defender of Gladstone and home rule. Although we have B. E. Lippincott's long chapter (somewhat slanted toward the liberal side) in *Victorian Critics of Democracy* (1938), Lionel Trilling's acute observations in his chapter, "Culture or Anarchy" in *Matthew Arnold,* and Otto Elias' full, well-balanced but at the same time pedantic and heavy-footed discussion in *Matthew Arnolds Politische Grundanschauungen* (1931), the definitive work on Arnold's politics remains to be written. Arnold's hitherto not readily available pamphlet on the Italian question has now been published in a separate edition (Merle M. Bevington, *Matthew Arnold's England and the Italian Question,* 1953). Bevington supplies an introduction and notes, and in an appendix, James Fitzjames Stephen's *Saturday Review* article on the pamphlet. Of more recent studies, those most deserving mention are: Geoffrey Carnall's "Arnold's 'Great Critical Effort' " (*EIC,* 1958), listed only because of its extreme position, its intemperate attack on Arnold's social criticism as "commonplace"; Martha S. Vogeler's "Matthew Arnold and Frederick Harrison: The Prophet of Culture and the Prophet of Positivism" (*SEL,* 1962), which shows the importance of Harrison and his ideas to any proper understanding of *Culture and Anarchy;* N. N. Feltes's "Matthew Arnold and the Modern Spirit: A Reassessment" (*UTQ,* 1962), which regards the religious essays of the seventies as a "watershed separating the period of Arnold's approval of the workings of the modern spirit from that of his fear of its evil effects"; Sidney M. B. Coulling's "The Evolution of *Culture and Anarchy*" (*SP,* 1963), an exhaustive and enlightening account of the backgrounds of *Culture and Anarchy;* C. LeRoy Gaylord's "Arnold and Aselgeia" (*BNYPL,* 1963), a brief attempt to explain Arnold's shift in political attitudes; Michael Wolff's "The Uses of Context: Aspects of the 1860's" (*VS, Supplement,* 1965), which discusses *Culture and Anarchy*, along with works by other authors, against the background of the reform crisis of the sixties; P. J. McCarthy's *Matthew Arnold and the Three Classes* (1965), a lively, straightforward study of Arnold's political and social criticism, with many fresh, if sometimes questionable interpretations, and particularly valuable for the biographical information it brings to bear on problems concerned; and Edward Alexander's *Matthew Arnold and John Stuart Mill* (1965), a thorough, well-organized, but not very perceptive comparison between Arnold, the advocate of humanism, and Mill, the advocate of liberalism.

Education. Since politics and education are not unallied, it need cause no surprise that the best brief work on Arnold's politics is J. Dover Wilson's "Matthew Arnold and the Educationists," in *The Social and Political Ideas of Some Representative Thinkers of the Victorian Age,* edited by F. J. C. Hearnshaw (1933). In the field of education proper, W. F. Connell's book, *The Educational Thought and Influence of Matthew Arnold* (1950), supersedes all other work. It is a systematic and thorough analysis. It places Arnold's theories against the contemporary educational background and illuminates both. In view of the importance that Arnold attached to education, it is fitting, perhaps, that this particular aspect of his work should be the first to receive anything like definitive treatment.

Philosophy and Religion. Among Victorian philosophers the redoubtable F. H. Bradley in his scornful treatment of Arnold's theology (*Ethical Studies,* 1876; revised and expanded, 1927) delights T. S. Eliot, who in *For Lancelot Andrewes* (1928) compliments Bradley on the finality of his criticism and the wit of his performance—an aping of Arnold's methods and tricks of speech. T. Sturge Moore, however, in "Matthew Arnold" (*E&S,* 1938), takes Bradley severely to task for distortion of Arnold's meaning, for basing his criticism on a single chapter of *Literature and Dogma,* and for misconception of the purpose of Arnold's books on theology. The work on Arnold's stoicism by John Hicks in *Critical Studies in Arnold, Emerson, and Newman* (1942), by J. Hicks, E. E. Sandeen, and Alvan S. Ryan, is still of value for students of the poetry as well as the prose. Basil Willey, in *Nineteenth Century Studies: Coleridge to Matthew Arnold* (1949), regrets that Arnold's religious books are now little read, for they contain matter of importance for those who are concerned with preserving a rational religion. It is Willey's opinion that religion was Arnold's chief and central interest—all his efforts in criticism, politics, and education really led up to it. In his chapter "The Poetry of Doubt and of Despair," in *The Darkling Plain* (1950), John Heath-Stubbs contends that Tennyson and Browning were fundamentally dishonest, whereas Arnold "at least, saw more truly the sickness of the Age and had the courage to record his vision." In his analysis of Arnold's poetry he has a number of insights that later scholars document and develop more convincingly. *The Ethical Idealism of Matthew Arnold* (1959), by William Robbins, is the most ambitious and successful attempt thus far to explain and justify Arnold's religious ideas. After a presentation of the ideas and their background, chiefly Continental, he analyzes particular aspects of Arnold's thought, and concludes, in agreement with Basil Willey, that Arnold's religious books offer much helpful guidance even for the present age. Robbins' leading thesis is that Arnold was intellectually a radical, but temperamentally a conservative. Citing "Empedocles on Etna," and some of the narrative poems, Allan Brick, in "Equilibrium in the Poetry of Matthew Arnold" (*UTQ*, 1960), concludes that for Arnold "the discovery of reality is the discovery of self vis-à-vis the outer world. It comes at a point of equilibrium between, on the one hand, engagement in society, in love, in ideals, and, on the other, isolation from action, from passion, from principle, indeed, from life itself." Although J. Hillis Miller's chapter on Arnold in *The Disappearance of God: Five Nineteenth-Century Writers* (1963) has been criticized for its muddled chronology, its confusion of the man with the poet, its use of quotations out of context resulting in misrepresentation, its "ugly jargon," and its "dubious assertions," it does establish a case for its conclusions. In summation, Miller says: "All the ways of escape from these damned times have failed. Not the exploration of time or space, not the acceptance of society, not love, not passion—no way will work, and whichever way Arnold turns he is thrown back on himself, and on his usual state of isolation and fluctuation." Arnold's last strategy is self-dependence, which means withdrawal from practical involvement. By this strategy "he attains at last what he has sought from the beginning. Arnold's final platform is the absence of God." Miller leaves Arnold hovering in the void, still criticizing his era for its cultural failings, but also waiting for the dawn to come. Graham Hough's "Coleridge and the Victorians," in *The English Mind: Studies in the English Moralists, Presented to Basil Willey* (1964), treats Arnold as "the most obvious successor of Coleridge as a religious thinker." But the point is made that Arnold's views are narrower, that he divests Coleridge's teaching of its "philosophical armament." In his chapter "Matthew Arnold: Conservative Revolutionary," in *The Unbelievers: English Agnostic Thought, 1840–1890* (1964), A. O. J. Cockshut develops the theme stressed earlier by William Robbins that Arnold is a revolutionary intellectually and a conservative in his feelings. Arnold, in Cockshut's analysis, draws his moral system from the Old Testament rather than the New; rejects a personal God, dogma, and miracle; likes the Church of England because it has a sense of style; and rejects Christian doctrine but loves the liturgical traditions and the accumulated moral wisdom of Christendom. David J. DeLaura's exhaustive "Matthew Arnold and John Henry Newman: the 'Oxford Sentiment' and the Religion of the Future" (*Texas Studies in Language and Literature,* 1965) is concerned with Arnold's prose but has relevance also for the poetry in that "Arnold's interest in Newman the man and the thinker is intense at every period of his life." DeLaura supports Dennis Butts's argument (*N&Q,* 1958) that Arnold's famous passage on the substitution of poetry for religion was anticipated in Newman's "Prospects of the Anglican Church" (1839).

Arnold and Science. On Arnold and science very little work has been done. Fred A. Dudley has contributed an exploratory article, "Matthew Arnold and Science" (*PMLA,* 1942), valuable for its definition of terms. Arnold used the word science in two senses. Of one he always approved: a thorough and systematic knowledge in any field, as opposed to irrational prejudice. Of the other he did not approve so uniformly: science in reference to a particular branch, such as physics or biology. F. E. Faverty's *Matthew Arnold the Ethnologist* (1951) is a discussion of Arnold's racial theories in the light of nineteenth century classifications of the Celts, the Teutons, the Semites, and the Indo-Europeans. The title of the book is too restrictive, however. Many Victorian writers beside Arnold are treated and wider concepts are examined than those identified with the science of ethnology. The theme, in fact, is the whole confused but significant doctrine of cultural and racial traits which colored much nineteenth-century thinking. On one particular branch of science, anthropology, Arnold has made a definite impact, as is explained by George W. Stoking in "Matthew Arnold, E. B. Tylor, and the Uses of Invention," *American Anthropologist* (1963). E. B. Tylor's *Primitive Culture* (1871), one of the earliest and most influential works in the development of anthropology, used "culture" in its title, according to Stoking, because of the currency given it by Arnold. Tylor "made Matthew Arnold's culture evolutionary," for in Arnold's view "primitive culture" would have been a contradiction in terms. Arnold's culture was above all an inward perfection, progress in which does not go hand in hand with progress in techniques and artifactual manifestations such as those Tylor arranged in evolutionary and hierarchial sequence. Tylor, therefore, was answering Arnold, as well as Richard Whately, the "degenerationist," who believed that barbarous tribes had degenerated from a higher culture conferred by divine intervention.

Literary Theory and Practice. Although the consideration given to sociological and metaphysical aspects of Victorian poetry in the first half of the twentieth century has been disproportionate, a few scholars and critics have devoted some attention to artistry. E. K. Brown sets an example. His book, *Matthew Arnold: A Study in Conflict* (1948), following a lead from Geoffrey Tillotson's perceptive essay, "Matthew Arnold: the Critic and the Advocate" (first in *Essays by Divers Hands*, edited by Gordon Bottomley, 1943; later included in G. Tillotson's *Criticism and the Nineteenth Century*, 1951) shows how often Arnold failed to practice the disinterestedness he preached. And where he failed to be disinterested, he failed as an artist. This is most apparent in the social essays. But the divided mind and spirit are evident in all the genres that Arnold practices. In the poems, the conflict accounts for "the extraordinary success and extraordinary failure within the bounds of a single work," the beautifully accomplished style breaking suddenly into pieces. A similar view of Arnold's disinterestedness is taken by Everett L. Hunt in

"Matthew Arnold: The Critic As Rhetorician" (*Quarterly Journal of Speech*, 1934). For all his praise of the objective critic and his attacks on the rhetoricians, Arnold himself was primarily a rhetorician, attempting to persuade through intuitive rather than logical methods. It was the general reader for whom Arnold wrote with a learning greater than that of twentieth-century journalists, but less than that of twentieth-century professors. With increased specialization and the disappearance of the general reader, Arnold has lost his audience. Today he is reduced to the inglorious level of introducing college freshmen to culture. W. J. Hipple's "Matthew Arnold, Dialectician" (*UTQ*, 1962) describes Arnold's method of analysis and synthesis as Platonic. He is a dialectician in his manipulation of such "contraries" as Hebraism and Hellenism, and pagan and medieval religious sentiment.

Arnold's poetic diction and his prose style have also been analyzed by the critics. John Drinkwater, in *Victorian Poetry* (1923), discovers in Arnold's poetic diction a seventeenth-century quality, something of the magic of Vaughan and Marvell. According to Bernard Groom, in *On the Diction of Tennyson, Browning, and Arnold* (1939), Arnold's diction is "classical" as distinguished from the "traditional" and the "eccentric" diction of Tennyson and Browning respectively. And Arnold's habit of repeating expressions suggests limitation. The severest judgment on Arnold's diction is found, however, in F. W. Bateson's *English Poetry and the English Language* (1934). Bateson thinks that all mid-Victorian poetry, Tennyson's alone excepted, is badly written. And Arnold's verse specifically is deficient in poetic originality. "The sensibility is not of Arnold himself but of his age, and the style is an amalgam of the language that was then available for poetry. And what a language it was." Allen Tate in "Literature as Knowledge: Comment and Comparison" (*SoR*, 1941) maintains that in Arnold's poetic theory, language is of secondary importance to subject. R. A. Foakes, in *The Romantic Assertion: A Study in the Language of Nineteenth Century Poetry* (1960), develops his theory that the "failure of language in the rhetoric of assertion and the rhetoric of love reflects the most terrible feature of Arnold's poetry, the disintegration of the Romantic vision." Richard Lloyd Jones, in "Common Speech—A

Poetic Effect for Hopkins, Browning, and Arnold" (*Dissertation Abstracts*, 1956), believes that Arnold's "rhythms frequently are lightly stressed, and the conventional metrical pattern is lost beneath a more significant pattern of syntax, which by means of pauses and subtle groups of sounds establishes a quiet rhythm of speech." In "Matthew Arnold and Cacophony" (*VP*, 1963), Park Honan undertakes a defense of harsh and grating passages that have usually been considered defects in Arnold's poetry. "Cacophonous and euphonic verses," he says, "are 'grouped' in counter-balancing structures to produce designed effects." Cacophony in the sonnets of 1849 and 1867 is meant to suggest the discord of the age.

A full-scale study of Arnold as a stylist in prose is worthy of a book. Three perceptive treatments of the subject are Lewis Gates's in the introduction to his *Selections from the Prose Writings of Matthew Arnold* (1897), E. K. Brown's *Matthew Arnold: A Study in Conflict,* and John C. Major's "Matthew Arnold and Attic Prose Style" (*PMLA*, 1944). Gates and Brown distinguish at least four styles in their author. But the fullest and most helpful analysis thus far is John Holloway's in his chapter on Arnold in *The Victorian Sage: Studies in Argument* (1953).

H. W. Garrod's "Matthew Arnold's 1853 Preface" (*RES*, 1941) is a significant contribution. Arnold's narrow poetic theory, Garrod argues, accounts for his failure in poetic practice. In attacking Keats and Shakespeare, he repudiated the influences that go to make up his own best poems. Between the "Scholar Gipsy" (1853) and "Thyrsis" (1866) lie "the 'Preface' and the desert." Douglas Bush underlines a similar paradox: that Arnold repudiated the Romantic Age while actually drawing nourishment from it *(Mythology and the Romantic Tradition).* George H. Ford, in *Keats and the Victorians: A Study of His Influence and Rise to Fame, 1821–1895* (1944), devotes three chapters to Arnold. His thesis is that Arnold acts both as destroyer and preserver of Keats's reputation and influence. The 1853 Preface sets up standards in opposition to the practice of Keats and his Victorian successors. But in the *Study of Celtic Literature* and in the essay on Maurice de Guérin, Arnold pays Keats the highest tribute, ranking him with Shakespeare in natural magic, the Celtic strain in English poetry. In style and content Arnold's poetry as a whole is a deliberate departure from the Keats tradition. Among the Romantic poets Keats served as his "principal whipping-boy in matters of style." Arnold's chastened verse is a reaction to Keatsian exuberance. Furthermore, he minimized sensuousness, even to the point of excluding color. His verse-music also is a reaction to the smoothness of style established by Keats and developed by Tennyson. For their harmonies he substituted "a simpler, more intellectualized conversational style." All this holds true for the bulk of Arnold's minor work, yet in his best poems, "The Scholar Gipsy" and "Thyrsis," and in the uneven poems, "Tristram and Iseult" and "The Church of Brou" the influence of Keats is pronounced. Thus Arnold turns on himself, and ironically, the chief opponent of the Keats tradition himself succumbs. Indeed, Arnold's poetry is "the most convincing manifestation" of the importance of Keats's influence on Victorian literature. A. H. Warren's *English Poetic Theory, 1825–1865* (1950) provides an excellent study of the Aristotelian elements in the 1853 Preface and traces the origins of many of the ideas to the Arnold-Clough correspondence. In his indispensable "Matthew Arnold's 1853 Preface: Its Origin and Aftermath" (*VS*, 1964), S. M. B. Coulling has amassed evidence to show that in the Preface Arnold is making a general attack on critics in contemporary journals and a specific attack on two of those critics; a general condemnation of romantic excesses in poetry and a specific attack on Alexander Smith and his predecessors; a general reply to reviews of the 1849 and 1852 volumes and a specific reply to Clough and other Oxford friends; a general defense of his own poetry and a specific defense of his choice of a classical subject, and his refusal to be a mere spokesman for his age. Coulling also discusses "The Modern Element in Literature" and the Preface to "Merope" as sequels to and modifications of the 1853 Preface.

In *The Alien Vision*, E. D. H. Johnson maintains that the dialogue of the mind within itself is a characteristic feature of Arnold's poetry. "The protagonists of his poems are invariably lonely and isolated figures, alien to their environment." Arnold accepts alienation and makes a virtue of it—the way of the Romantic poets. Alternating in his early poetry between involvement in and aloofness from his environment, Arnold failed to resolve his conflict. Some of his early poems and many of the letters to Clough attempt to "develop the aesthetic aspect of alienation." In the 1853 Preface, according to Johnson, Arnold rejects the content and form of his earlier poetry and turns to objectivity and *architectonicè*. Poetry hereafter is regarded as a cultural agent. "The Empedoclean dialogue of the mind with itself was to be replaced by an outward communion between the artist and his public conducted on a no less elevated plane." In his final chapter Johnson discusses the transformation of the artist into the man of letters. If the age required an intellectual deliverance, it was Arnold the critic, not Arnold the poet, who would have to supply it. Yet even in the critical essays the subjects he preferred were the "foil'd circuitous" wanderers. In his prose no more than in his poetry was Arnold's conflict to be resolved.

Each of Johnson's main points had been made in the earlier literature on Arnold. His contribution lies in bringing all these theories together and in applying them to a considerable part of Arnold's work. The result is often a "seeing more deeply into the poet's mind." The rift between society and its artists, however, is hardly peculiar to the early and mid-nineteenth century. Certainly the rift becomes more pronounced in the latter part of the nineteenth century and the early part of the twentieth. Johnson's thesis, therefore, becomes more convincing when applied, as in *The Last Romantics* (1949) by Graham Hough, to later authors. In modification of Johnson's conclusions, John M. Wallace, in "Landscape and 'The General Law': The Poetry of Matthew Arnold," *Boston University Studies in English* (1961), contends that it is "misleading to lay special emphasis on conflicts within the mind or on his alienation from society." Arnold believed that it was the general law, or natural law, that proscribed the free expression of deep feeling in all men. In his earlier poems he rebelled against the law, but in his later ones he learned to accept it. As a result, poems like "Thyrsis" end on a note of affirmation.

In "Corydon Had a Rival" (*VN*, 1961), Michael Timko reviews the long and close association between Clough and Arnold to show that in their early discussions of poetry Arnold was an advocate of form, the beautiful, and Clough an advocate of content, but that later Arnold was converted to Clough's view and himself became a champion of content. Arnold was also converted to Clough's opinion that the style of modern poetry should be severe, direct, and plain.

Reputation and Influence. Swinburne's literary career and fame were properly chronicled some thirty years ago by C. K. Hyder. Arnold's reputation and influence offer materials even larger and more attractive in scope. As preliminary studies indicate, his battles with the periodicals on social, political, and literary questions were lively encounters, calling forth his best powers in irony and satire. In his controversies with the hosts of the orthodox over his religious heresies he gave better than was sent. E. K. Brown in "The French Reputation of Matthew Arnold" (*Studies in English by Members of University College, Toronto,* 1931) supplies evidence in plenty to support a basic law that between their foreign detractors and their eulogizers nations show more interest in their detractors. Arnold, the great friend of France, has been given far less consideration in that country than Carlyle. In an important article, "Matthew Arnold and the *Academy:* A Note on English Criticism in the Eighteen-Seventies" (*PMLA,* 1953), Diderik Roll-Hansen shows that Arnold "had been consulted and had approved of the general plan of the new journal." It is one of the major ironies of his career, however, that because of his professional duties and his commitments to other periodicals, Arnold was able to contribute only a few articles to the *Academy,* the distinguished journal realizing his dream of a national organ which should bring about "a more centralized effort in intellectual matters," and carry England into the current of Continental thought. In *The Name and Nature of Poetry* (1933), A. E. Housman acknowledged his dependence on Arnold the critic, but he was indebted also to Arnold the poet, as E. H. S. Walde and T. S. Dorsch ("A. E. Housman and Matthew Arnold," *Boston University Studies in English,* 1960) show in their comparison of the two writers. They list thirty-three parallels with or echoes and reminiscences from Arnold in Housman's poetry.

T. S. Eliot's charge that Arnold fathered the Decadents, Pater and his disciples ("Arnold and Pater," *Bookman,* 1930) has met with agreement in some, with protest in other quarters. Geoffrey

Matthew Arnold

Tillotson ("Arnold and Pater: Critics Historical, Aesthetic and Unlabelled," in *Criticism and the Nineteenth Century,* 1951) demonstrates how Pater takes one of Arnold's basic ideas, interprets it in his own fashion, and ends by differing widely from Arnold. In "Pater and Arnold" (*EIC,* 1952) Kenneth Allott presents evidence for Arnold's influence on *Marius the Epicurean.* Clyde de L. Ryals ("The Nineteenth Century Cult of Inaction," in *Tennessee Studies in Literature,* 1959) links Arnold with Oscar Wilde, whose cult of inaction was an outgrowth of the teachings of Arnold as well as Pater. David J. DeLaura's "The 'Wordsworth' of Pater and Arnold: 'The Supreme Artistic View of Life' " (*SEL,* 1966) points out the irony in Arnold's denunciation of "the new aestheticism and immoralism" which he had done much to found. Leonard Brown ("Matthew Arnold's Succession: 1850–1914" *SeR,* 1934), however, emphatically disagrees with Eliot's idea that through Pater, Wilde can be traced to Arnold. Arnold's noblest bequest, according to Brown, was not his opinions but his attitudes, and these the Decadents ignored. His true heirs were the poets who had direct contact with his skepticism and therefore faced life with honesty and courage—Swinburne, Meredith, Hardy, De la Mare, and T. S. Eliot himself. That Eliot *is* a lineal descendant of Arnold is the contention also of M. L. S. Loring in "T. S. Eliot on Matthew Arnold" (*SeR,* 1935). Although Eliot himself will own no connection with Arnold, Loring feels that they are much alike, particularly in their views on the social purpose of criticism and the purpose of art. In a number of respects Eliot is a latter-day Arnold. Eliot's strictures on Arnold in *The Use of Poetry and the Use of Criticism* (1933) —that he is an undergraduate in philosophy and theology, a Philistine in religion; that he is an academic poet; that he is insensitive to style; that his definition of poetry as a criticism of life is meaningless—seem, therefore, to take on the nature of paradox. In a series of illuminating parallels, Douglas Bush (chapter fifteen of *Mythology and the Romantic Tradition*) summarizes the relationships between Eliot and Arnold. The disillusionment and pessimism of the two poets, he thinks, have the same origins. And in revolt from the mechanized and commercialized present, from "arid and ugly actuality," both turn to classic myth. In "Eliot, Pound, and the Conservative Tradition" (*History of Ideas*

News Letter, 1957) R. D. Spector says that Eliot and Pound continue Arnold's conservative tradition but without his sense of social obligation, since they withdraw from the world.

As early as 1897 Andrew Lang in "The Celtic Renaissance" (*Blackwood's*) traced the origin of the Celtic Revival to Renan and Arnold, the Moses and Aaron respectively of the movement. Further evidence on Arnold's part in this Renaissance is supplied by John V. Kelleher in "Matthew Arnold and the Celtic Revival" (*Perspectives of Criticism*, 1950) and F. E. Faverty in the fifth chapter of *Matthew Arnold the Ethnologist*. Rachel Bromwich's *Matthew Arnold and Celtic Literature: A Retrospect, 1865–1965* (1965) gives an excellent critique of Arnold's Celtic studies and their backgrounds in the light of twentieth-century knowledge, and recognizes the importance of Arnold's contribution, direct and indirect, toward the development of Celtic studies.

Arnold was also the Patron Saint of Irving Babbitt and his circle, the American Neo-Humanists of the 1920's, as Everett L. Hunt convincingly demonstrates in "Matthew Arnold and His Critics" (*SeR*, 1936). Irving Babbitt, Norman Foerster, and Paul Elmer More were disciples of Arnold in their attitude toward Romanticism and in their defense of absolute standards of taste. Following Stuart P. Sherman's rehabilitation of Arnold (*Matthew Arnold, How to Know Him*, 1917) the Neo-Humanists developed the ethical side of his criticism to such an extreme that Arnold himself would probably have called them "Hebraists" (W. S. Knickerbocker, "Asides and Soliloquies: Farwell to Neo-Humanism," *SeR*, 1930). And for the last forty years, university departments of English, American ones particularly, have been accused of deriving most of their critical opinions from one source—Matthew Arnold. Indeed, he "may even be said to have established the teaching of English as an academic profession" (Lionel Trilling, "Literature and Power," *Kenyon Review*, 1940). All these developments are presented more authoritatively and in their proper context by John Henry Raleigh in his *Matthew Arnold and American Culture*. The place, importance, and influence of Arnold's concept of culture in the long tradition from the late eighteenth century to the present is indicated in *Culture and Society, 1780–1950* by Raymond Williams. Since the publication of *Culture and Anarchy* a flood of articles and books has appeared on the subject of culture. And Arnold's is the chief name invoked either in praise or censure. Two twentieth-century works illustrate the extremes. F. R. Leavis' *Mass Civilization and Minority Culture* (1930) in its very title shows the indebtedness to Arnold. Indeed, the book begins with a quotation from *Culture and Anarchy* and is, by the author's admission, simply an application to the contemporary scene of Arnold's principles. At the other extreme is Sir Herbert Read's *To Hell with Culture: Democratic Values Are New Values* (1941). Read will have nothing to do with Arnold's "saving remnants," the elite, and the small circle of the privileged. The whole of our present culture, he says, "is one immense veneer: a surface refinement hiding the cheapness and shoddiness at the heart of things."

Commenting in the mid-fifties on Arnold's reputation as a poet, Kathleen Tillotson ("Matthew Arnold in our Time," *Spectator*, 1954; reprinted in *Mid-Victorian Studies*, 1965) was able to say, "During the last decade no other English poet of the nineteenth century, or earlier, can show so many reprintings—except the poet who died the year after Arnold, Gerard Manley Hopkins ... On bibliographical evidence, then, Arnold is something of a popular poet." His technical defects, she thinks, are outweighed by his virtues, for "Arnold is one of the really powerful emotional forces that have found expression in our poetry." Lionel Stevenson ("Matthew Arnold's Poetry: A Modern Appraisal," *TSL*, 1959) is less sanguine in his estimate of Arnold the poet: "In the last few years there has been a perceptible revival of respect for Arnold's prose works, but its extension to his poetry cannot be confidently affirmed. He is being recognized as a significant forerunner of some influential modern critics, as an evangelist of the Hellenic and Celtic revivals, as a key figure in the trouble-making theories about races and cultures ... His poetry has not received anything like the same attention." Stevenson then cites the decline of interest in Arnold's long poems which are "technically impeccable but emotionally cold"; Arnold's "constricted inventive power" evidenced in the frequent sequels to his own poems and in the few recurring symbols; and "the small bulk and narrow range" of his poetry. "Tristram and Iseult" and "Empedocles on Etna," he grants, still excite interest and command admiration because of "the urgency of personal feeling" involved. Arnold's frequent use of the "coda" device, he thinks, is very effective; and his experiments with form helped to prepare the way for twentieth-century free rhythms in poetry. The continuing appeal of Arnold's poetry he attributes to the fact that it expresses "the dilemma of the modern intellectual, who can find satisfaction neither as a recluse in a cloister nor as a participant and policy-maker in public affairs." Finally, he ranks Arnold as a major poet on the basis that "his individual voice, subdued though it is, stands out distinct and unmistakable in the midst of an era when English poetry was as varied, fecund, and technically accomplished as ever in its history." Some of Stevenson's judgments would perhaps have been more favorable had he had the benefit of Kenneth Allott's and A. Dwight Culler's recent contributions in scholarship and criticism.

In conclusion it can be said that Arnold's power to incite dissent is as strong today as ever. Everett L. Hunt in "Matthew Arnold and His Critics" shows that he is denounced and praised for different reasons by each critic. The basic quarrels of the critics are not with Arnold, but with each other, over the very nature of literature, criticism, religion, and society. Excellent illustrations are provided in Theodore Morrison's "Dover Beach Revisited. A New Fable for Critics" (*Harper's Magazine*, 1940), and in the 1953 exchange of asperities between F. W. Bateson ("The Function of Criticism at the Present Time," *Essays in Criticism*) and F. R. Leavis ("The Responsible Critic: Or the Function of Criticism at Any Time," *Scrutiny*). The title, *Essays in Criticism*, is singularly appropriate for a periodical published by Arnold's own university.

A glance at the bibliographies for the last few decades reveals that Arnold's reputation in one or another of its facets has been assigned almost annually at some American, English, or Canadian university as a dissertation for an advanced degree. On at least four of these, though they are still unpublished, scholars have already levied tribute. Marian Mainwaring's *Matthew Arnold's Influence and Reputation as a Literary Critic*, a Radcliffe College doctoral dissertation (1949), presents a great deal of new information on Arnold the poet as well as on Arnold the critic, for, like most commentators on Arnold, she finds an absolute separation of his two major activities impossible. Sidney M. B. Coulling's *Matthew Arnold and His Critics,* a University of North Carolina dissertation (1957), much of which is now available in articles, is a thorough investigation of Arnold's controversies with the periodical press. Charles T. Wilkins' *The English Reputation of Matthew Arnold* (University Microfilms, 1959), and Satyaprasad SenGupta's University of London doctoral dissertation *The Reception of Matthew Arnold as Poet and Critic, 1849–1871* (1961) are particularly valuable for the bibliographical information they provide.

If all these scattered materials on Arnold's reputation and influence were brought together by some practiced hand, the result would be a fascinating and instructive account of the changes in culture and literary taste of the last one hundred years.

Algernon Charles Swinburne

CLYDE K. HYDER

I. BIBLIOGRAPHY

Since 1956, when *Victorian Poets: A Guide to Research* appeared, Thomas J. Wise's pilfering of title pages from around 150 plays in the British Museum to complete copies that later became a part of his own library or of the Wrenn Library has come to light; but little has been added to the list of Swinburne pamphlets branded as spurious or under suspicion by Carter and Pollard and others—*Dead Love, Dolores, Siena* (one of the English editions), *Laus Veneris, Cleopatra, An Appeal to England against the Execution of the Condemned Fenians* (the pamphlet), *A Word for the Navy* (Wise's edition, not George Redway's), *The Question, The Jubilee,* and *Gathered Songs.* In addition, *Grace Darling, The Ballad of Bulgarie, Robert Burns: A Poem,* and *A Sequence of Sonnets on the Death of Robert Browning* are suspected to be piracies (Wilfred Partington, *Forging Ahead,* 1939). Obviously, one cannot trust all statements in Wise's bibliography of 1919–1920 (Bonchurch Edition, XX, 1927) or in his *Swinburne Library* (1925, based mainly on his earlier *Ashley Library*). These works are nevertheless useful sources of information, supplanting older bibliographies by Wise (1897), Shepherd, Thomson, Vaughan, and O'Brien.

Students await eagerly the new bibliography being prepared by John S. Mayfield, Curator of Manuscripts and Rare Books at the Syracuse University Library, whose own remarkable collection of Swinburniana—including, for example, seventy-two copies of the first edition of *Atalanta in Calydon,* recorded by Swinburne as having consisted of only five hundred copies—was recently his generous gift to that library. Mayfield plans to include a census of manuscripts.[1] Incidentally, he has recently discov-

[1]William B. Todd discusses "Swinburne Manuscripts at Texas" in *TQ* (1959). The manuscripts in the Ashley Library collection in the British Museum are being recatalogued.

ered the two missing leaves of *Lesbia Brandon,* restoring whole-
ness to that work.

II. EDITIONS AND TEXTS

Unfortunately, a large part of Swinburne's work is still acces-
sible only in the Bonchurch Edition (1925–1927), the text of
which is both incomplete and shockingly corrupt. Without ex-
planation Gosse and Wise capriciously changed the order of
some poems and omitted others, as well as extensive prose pas-
sages.[2] While the Bonchurch Edition is convenient for reference,
one should be wary of quoting from it on the assumption that
one is quoting accurately. The text of the first collected edition
of the poems and dramatic works, brought out in the poet's
lifetime, is far more dependable.

An outstanding work of Swinburne scholarship, Cecil Y. Lang's
The Swinburne Letters (six volumes, 1959-1962), has supplanted
the unsatisfactory selections earlier assembled by Gosse and
Wise, Mrs. Disney Leith, and Hake and Compton-Rickett. It
contains about two thousand letters. Most are Swinburne's, but
some addressed to him, as well as an occasional extract from
contemporary memoirs, are included—for instance, a letter from
Baudelaire or Browning, or Admiral Swinburne's letter to Ruskin
and Ruskin's reply. The net result is a more balanced portrait.
Though one is reminded of the poet's tiresome obsessions and
his unfortunate conditioned reflexes, evidences of his intellectual

[2]Among the omissions were passages on Congreve, Charles Wells, Webster,
and Tourneur, as well as "Sir Henry Taylor on Shelley" and the *Dedicatory
Epistle.* Cf. Chew's *Swinburne,* notes on pp. 151, 154, 286, 291.

energy and keen discernment are abundant. His intelligent interest in the world of affairs, his friendships, his sensible literary opinions and pursuits, and his beliefs and loyalties are revealed with detail no biography can match. In spite of occasional wit and charm and the excellence of many letters, the editor does not rank Swinburne among the great letter-writers, but, as he points out in his introduction, even the perfunctory and sometimes curt letters to Andrew Chatto have their interest "not only as a chronicle of the poet's querulousness and an index to much of his reading, as a partial record of his finances, of his difficulties with proofs, of his deficiencies as a proofreader, but also as a portrait of a shrewd and imperturbable publisher." Though any reader can appreciate the editor's zeal and assiduity, whether in collecting or transcribing and interpreting the letters, scholars, for whom the work has been and will continue to be a stimulus, will best appreciate Lang's careful identification of persons and allusions. An incidental result of the publication, as indicated by J. C. Maxwell's three short articles (*N&Q*, 1960, 1961), is the disclosure that the poet used about fifty words not recorded in the O. E. D. Words like *sprucification, Oxonicules, merdiloquent, Popification, subporcine, theophagy, and copromania* are eloquent reminders of Swinburne's linguistic inventiveness and of his outlook.

New Writings by Swinburne, also edited by Lang (1964), contains morsels particularly attractive to the knowledgeable literary epicure and the devoted Swinburnian. "Duriesdyke," a ballad whose restored form is due to the perceptive research of Miss Anne Henry, now Mrs. Ehrenpreis (*Harvard Library Bulletin,* 1958), is the most interesting of the ten poems, three of which are in French. "The Ballad of Villon and Fat Madge" also has its admirers. Among the five critical writings, "The Chaotic School," a forceful diatribe aimed at Browning's worst stylistic weaknesses, was written in anger and neglects merits of which Swinburne later showed himself aware. "Changes of Aspect," which C. K. Hyder had earlier edited for *PMLA* (1943), is an essay in which Swinburne defended himself from charges of inconsistency, particularly in his estimates of Byron, Tennyson, Arnold, Blake, FitzGerald, and Whitman. "The Monomaniac's Tragedy, and Other Poems," the first of the hoaxes in the volume, is, like "The Early English Dramatists," reprinted from *Under-*

graduate Papers. It is an exceedingly clever satire of the Spasmodic poets. Also included are the hoaxes Swinburne planned to publish in the *Spectator*—hoaxes in which he quotes passages from a supposititious French poet, Félicien Cossu, and a writer whose chief aim is to "justify the ways of Satan to man," Ernest Clouët. The editor's lively commentary enables readers to enjoy the full flavor of such works.

On a larger scale are two incomplete satires composed entirely in French. *La Sœur de la reine,* a drama, portrays, not a man in an iron mask, but a twin sister of Queen Victoria who was to be branded as an impostor by the Archbishop of Canterbury's perjury. Rumors in regard to the play delighted not a few of Swinburne's acquaintances. As yet undiscovered is Queen Victoria's confession of "a lapse from virtue" after hearing Wordsworth read the more seductive passages of his *Excursion.* The final burlesque, *La Fille du policeman,* is a novel in which the Queen appears again, along with Prince Albert ("le prince prolétaire"), "Sir Bright," and others. "Hideous disclosures of English society" follow the pattern of French writers on English life. The editor states that Victor Hugo's portrayal of the English in his historical plays reads almost like the work of a parodist, and he indicates that here, as in Swinburne's French poems, Hugo was a source of inspiration.[3]

These satirical works broaden our awareness of Swinburne's powers of satire and parody. The poet possessed the novelist's insight and portraying hand, even though he may not have created great fiction. In his introduction to *The Novels of A. C. Swinburne* (1962), Edmund Wilson finds that as a novelist Swinburne excels in realistic portrayal of contemporary life and character. This volume contains *Love's Cross-Currents* and the so-called *Lesbia Brandon.* The latter, never published by Swinburne, has been edited by Randolph Hughes.[4]

The centenary of *Poems and Ballads* was the occasion for *Swinburne Replies* (1966), in which C. K. Hyder included *Notes*

[3]See *The Victorian Poets: A Guide* (1956), pp. 141–142, for a note on G. Lafourcade's *Swinburne's "Hyperion" and Other Poems* (1927), casting light on Swinburne's study of Keats, and also p. 141, note 3.

W. D. Paden's "A Few Annotations by Swinburne" (*N&Q*, 1961) mentions the poet's comments written on copies of the *Oxford and Cambridge Magazine.* Cecil C. Seronsy's "An Autograph Letter by Swinburne on Daniel and Drummond of Hawthornden" appeared in *N&Q* in 1965.

[4]See *The Victorian Poets: A Guide* (1956), pp. 142–143 and notes, for discussion of Randolph Hughes and of some uncollected writings by Swinburne.

on Poems and Reviews, Under the Microscope, and the *Dedicatory Epistle* of 1904. For most readers the first two were accessible only in the grossly inaccurate text of the Bonchurch Edition; the third, Swinburne's only extended comments on his own work, was omitted entirely, apparently because of Gosse's dislike of Watts-Dunton, to whom it was addressed. The introduction concerns the background of the three works. Textual notes cite variant readings from the manuscripts of the first two, and explanatory notes deal with all three.

Clearly, the textual study of Swinburne has been neglected, and a critical edition of his poetry and important prose seems a hope of the distant rather than the immediate future.[5] Few problems of attribution remain. Robert H. Tener (*TLS*, 1959) proved that the review of Part I of *Les Miserables*, attributed to him by Gosse and Wise, was not Swinburne's. W. D. Paden's "Swinburne, the *Spectator* in 1862, and Bagehot" (in *Six Studies in Nineteenth-Century Literature and Thought,* edited by Harold Orel and George J. Worth, 1962) disproves the attributions Samuel C. Chew considered likely (*MLN*, 1920). Cecil Y. Lang has indicated that Lafourcade's attribution of a self-criticism to the poet, in the *République des Lettres,* must be rejected.[6]

III. STUDIES PRIMARILY BIOGRAPHICAL

Gosse's *Life* (1917; slightly revised for the Bonchurch Edition), skillfully written by a friend of the poet, has greatly influenced

[5]For an earlier list of selections from Swinburne's poetry, see *The Victorian Poets: A Guide* (1956), p. 144, note 7. A volume edited more recently by Edith Sitwell is chiefly of interest for its disclosure of the editor's taste; her selections come mostly from *Atalanta* and *Poems and Ballads.*
[6]Cf. *ibid.,* p. 145, note 10.

subsequent biographies. Since its publication many inaccuracies have come to light and a number may still be undetected. Gosse's carelessness was chronic.[7] The limitations of his experience did not enable him to understand a personality so complex as Swinburne's. His reticences, the importance of which some commentators have overestimated, were in part due to literary conventions that his generation accepted. No doubt it was to compensate for these reticences that he wrote the manuscripts now in the British Museum, first published in the sixth volume of Lang's *Swinburne Letters*. Gosse's statements would have been sensational if they had appeared before the revelations of Georges Lafourcade.

A comparison of Gosse's account of certain episodes with Lafourcade's underlines Gosse's tendency to embellish for the sake of vividness and readability. Though Lafourcade's work also contains some errors of detail, the first volume of *La Jeunesse de Swinburne* (1928) gave a fuller treatment than Gosse's of Swinburne's family background, education, and friendships. It dealt frankly with the poet's algolagnia. The same author's later *Swinburne: A Literary Biography* (1932), though less important, supplies some new material. In this and the earlier work, Lafourcade sometimes supplements and corrects Gosse—for instance, in regard to the poet's travels and the date and occasion of "Sir John Franklin." His discussion of *Songs before Sunrise* and of Swinburne's later career is more illuminating than Gosse's.

Humphrey Hare's *Swinburne: A Biographical Approach* (1949), which drew heavily on Lafourcade, is today of little independent value. Lafourcade was sometimes led astray by formulas; Hare oversimplifies what he found in Lafourcade. For instance, he interprets *Atalanta in Calydon,* one of Swinburne's greatest achievements, as "intellectualized algolagnia," alleging that after *Poems and Ballads* "the synthesis is abandoned and with it the theory of Art for Art's sake, . . . its necessary moral justification." Swinburne modified his theories about art but did

---

[7]Cf. *ibid.,* note 9. Besides the garbled Swinburne texts in *Posthumous Poems* and in the Bonchurch Edition, consider his editorial handling of Gray's letters. Cf. R. W. Ketton-Cremer's remarks in *The Familiar Letter in the Eighteenth Century,* ed. Howard Anderson, Philip B. Daghlian, and Irvin Ehrenpreis (Lawrence, 1966), pp. 153–154.

not abandon any of them; his interest in Italy was older than his interest in the Marquis de Sade.

Hare unduly minimizes Swinburne's later work. In his earlier "Swinburne and 'Le vice anglais' " (*Horizon*, 1947; compare this title with that of an appendix in Praz's *The Romantic Agony*), Hare does not take into account the effect of the poet's isolation (which did not diminish with years that often bring a loss of poetic power) or even of his increasing deafness. Hare decided to attribute Swinburne's decline to the abandonment of "the algolagnic synthesis." Gosse fostered the impression that Swinburne was overshadowed by Watts-Dunton's personality, and Hare repeats the charge (*Horizon*, 1949) that his friend caused the poet to turn against his youthful idols, such as Whitman and Baudelaire. But Swinburne's early opinion of Whitman was not one of unqualified approval,[8] and his alleged repudiation of Baudelaire, with whom, he said, he never had much in common, probably seemed to Swinburne a mere statement of fact; doubtless, too, he had resented being linked with Baudelaire by such persons as Robert Buchanan, who charged that the English poets of "the fleshly school" were mere imitators of the Frenchman.

Of the accounts of Swinburne and Watts-Dunton, the most delightful is still Max Beerbohm's "No. 2. The Pines," a work of art even if, like the pictures in his *Rossetti and His Circle* (1922), something of a caricature. Alfred Noyes's *Two Worlds for Memory* (1953) is more factual. Clara Watts-Dunton's *The Home Life of Swinburne* is naive, and, like C. Kernahan's *Swinburne As I Knew Him* (1919), mostly anecdotal. As Mrs. Disney Leith's reminiscences do, it characterizes Swinburne as pleasant in his personal relationships. H. G. Wright's "Unpublished Letters from Theodore Watts-Dunton to Swinburne" (*RES*, 1934) illustrates Watts-Dunton's tact, showing that it was in 1872 that he took over the management of his friend's business affairs. L. A. Marchand's "The Watts-Dunton Letter Books" (*Journal of the Rutgers University Library*, 1953) states that "the tendency if not the aim" of Watts-Dunton's last years with Swinburne "was to tame the wild bear he was proud to exhibit and to channel

[8]See the citations in *The Victorian Poets: A Guide* (1956), p. 146, note 11, and Swinburne's discussion of Whitman in *Under the Microscope*.

the poet's energies and his writing into safe and conventional paths."

Watts-Dunton has been accused of grooming Swinburne for the poet-laureateship—a position he would not have accepted. A behind-the-scenes account by P. Knaplund (*UTQ*, 1937) explains that Lord Acton called Gladstone's attention to the moral aspects of *Poems and Ballads*, as well as Swinburne's anti-Russian writings and advocacy of tyrannicide.

Various writers have touched on Swinburne's other friendships. Helen Angeli has written on that with D. G. Rossetti. P. M. Grosskurth's "Swinburne and Symonds: An Uneasy Relationship" (*RES*, 1963) and Lona Mosk Packer's "Swinburne and Christina Rossetti: Atheist and Anglican" (*UTQ*, 1963) summarize the evidence on what is known about the relationships of these writers. J. Pope-Hennessy's *Monckton Milnes: The Flight of Youth* (1951) modifies the picture of Lord Houghton and his influence as given in Lafourcade's *La Jeunesse*, emphasizing Swinburne's macabre sense of humor, as illustrated by his extravagant references to "the divine Marquis" even before he read the books lent to him by Lord Houghton.[9] Alfred Werner's "The Sad Ballad of Simeon Solomon" (*KR*, 1961) seems highly speculative, being undocumented.

Gosse's story of the supposed central episode of Swinburne's emotional history has been widely accepted. Evidence of its falsity was first cited by John S. Mayfield in "Swinburne's Boo" (his early mimeographed statement, 1953, appeared in *English Miscellany*, IV, and as a separate publication). Jane Faulkner was only ten years old in 1862, when, according to Gosse, Swinburne proposed to her, and was not married till 1871. It remained for Cecil Y. Lang, in his important article "Swinburne's Lost Love" (*PMLA*, 1959) to outline the reasons for identifying the poet's cousin, Mary Gordon, as the object of his deep affection. "Thalassius," "A Leave-Taking," and, above all, "The Triumph of Time"—poems reflecting this emotional experience—indicate that "the speaker did *not* declare his love, and the innominata *had no suspicion* of its existence," in spite of Gosse's absurd misreading of the third poem. Interpretation of the poems agrees

[9]See *ibid.*, p. 147, note 12.

with the facts known about Mary Gordon's marriage to Colonel Robert William Disney Leith.

The role of a woman fond of roles, Adah Menken, has been exaggerated or described inaccurately. With no evidence that Swinburne could have met her before the poem was composed, Falk's revised edition of his journalistic, sentimental, and undocumented biography of Menken (1952) assumes that "Dolores" was inspired by her, though it was obviously rooted in the poet's imagination and sensibility. Falk even assumes that Swinburne's disavowal of "Dolorida" was a personal betrayal, whereas the poet was correct in saying that he had not contributed to an annual edited by A. M. Moore the lines in question, which appear in *Lesbia Brandon* and which were apparently copied as an inscription in Adah Menken's album. The title "Dolorida" had been used for a poem by Alfred de Vigny, and the name Dolores (in Latin, "pains," "sorrows") is an appropriate one for Swinburne's Anti-Madonna, "Our Lady of Pain."

A sketchy biographical study, *Algernon C. Swinburne* (1964), by John A. Cassidy, adds little that is both new and factual. Though the book may contain an occasional perceptive or even enthusiastic judgment, the author did not find his subject congenial. A review in *Victorian Poetry* (1966) does not attempt to list all the errors and conjectures. Robert A. Greenberg's "Answer to an Inquiry," a response to Cassidy's reply to Greenberg's earlier review (all three in *VS*, 1966), specifies a considerable number. Two or three other points may be mentioned here. When one reads that "The Poet and the Woodlouse" is a parody of Mrs. Browning's "poem of the same title," one supposes that the author must have in mind Mrs. Browning's "A Poet and a Bird." In interpreting Buchanan's "The Session of the Poets" as describing an actual scene, has the author forgotten Buchanan's explanation at the *Examiner* trial that the poem refers only to "literary matters"? Some readers of *Under the Microscope* will hardly agree that in it Swinburne admits writing a passage in *Notes on Poems and Reviews* with Buchanan in mind. Did the publisher of Cassidy's book impose limitations that led to neglect of Swinburne's criticism and of some important poems, like *The Tale of Balen*? Regretfully, one must conclude that the book contributes more to the Swinburne legend than to knowledge of his life and work and that there is still room for a scholarly biography.

IV. SOURCES OF INSPIRATION

Swinburne thought of books as living things; to consider them as sources of inspiration which are in a category separate from that of experience would have seemed to him arbitrary. The sale catalog of his library and his letters on "The Hundred Best Books" (see *The Swinburne Letters*, V, 131–136), as well as numerous literary allusions, bear witness to the breadth and catholicity of his reading.

His debt to both the Hebrews and the Greeks was vast. His debt to the Bible and the Book of Common Prayer has not been adequately appraised, but Swinburne's Hellenism has interested many students. Douglas Bush's treatment of Swinburne in *Mythology and the Romantic Tradition in English Poetry* shows command of the relevant scholarship and cites more references than can be mentioned here.[10] W. R. Rutland's *Swinburne: A Nineteenth Century Hellene* (1931) deals at length with the Meleager myth and with the relation of Atalanta to Greek drama, as well as with "the Hellenistic poems." Rutland is less accurate and polished than Bush but more generous in critical judgments. C. M. Bowra, a distinguished Greek scholar who is unschooled in revelations of Lafourcade or Praz and, it may be, is on that account less biased in critical emphases, has praised *Atalanta* (*The Romantic Imagination*, 1949) as "profoundly and inescapably Greek," though pointing out that the author's love of the sea and of wild places,

---

[10]*Ibid.*, p. 149, note 13. I do not find H. A. Hargreaves' "Swinburne's Greek Plays and God, 'The Supreme Evil' " (*MLN*, 1961) convincing.

his delight in childhood and family affections, his imagination and genius for language were important in shaping the play. In many ways Swinburne's experience was wholesome, even "normal," and Bowra's admirable criticism makes us wonder whether too much attention is not given to one component of that experience.

Like the Romantic poets of whom he was an heir and like the other members of his literary circle, Swinburne was attracted to the medieval world. Lafourcade's *La Jeunesse* discusses the poet's study of Dante and of Villon (for the latter, see also Lang's *New Writings by Swinburne*). For the sources of the Arthurian poems, the student may turn first to S. C. Chew's *Swinburne* (1929). An early paper by C. K. Hyder on Swinburne and the popular ballad (*PMLA*, 1934) concerned one of the poet's earliest and most enduring enthusiasms. Anne Henry Ehrenpreis' "Swinburne's Edition of Popular Ballads" (*PMLA*, 1963) makes important observations on *Ballads of the English Border* (1925), wretchedly edited by William MacInnes and containing the text of twenty-six popular ballads reconstructed by Swinburne on the assumption that one may combine passages from variant versions. Mrs. Ehrenpreis' paper illustrates the fruitful results of going directly to manuscripts. She shows that Swinburne's so-called introduction was not an introduction at all, having been written as part of a projected answer to Andrew Lang's claim for the superiority of Scottish over English ballads. Swinburne had begun his experiment in ballad-editing perhaps thirty-five years earlier; indeed, since the ballads Swinburne edited are more Scottish than English, the realization of that fact may have been why he left his answer to Lang incomplete. In addition to correcting "the errors of Wise compounded by the errors of MacInnes," Mrs. Ehrenpreis makes a careful study of the texts, showing that, besides choosing passages from various versions in a way no modern editor would approve, Swinburne composed some lines of his own for certain ballads (in doing this could he have had in mind Sir Walter Scott's handling of "Kinmont Willie"?). In writing his own literary ballads, Swinburne used tricks of ballad diction which he well understood but sometimes overemphasized, such as the removal of relative pronouns, the use of repetition, and the simplification of language.[11]

Swinburne's interest in the Renaissance was discussed by Randolph Hughes in *Lucretia Borgia: The Chronicle of Tebaldeo Tebaldei* (1942).[12] Its chief literary manifestation was, of course, in his books on Elizabethan drama and his non-Hellenic plays. G. C. Spivey's "Swinburne's Use of Elizabethan Drama" (*SP*, 1944) lists literary devices thought to be borrowed from the Elizabethans; not all the parallels mentioned are convincing. Chew's chapter on the dramas considers sources. B. Ifor Evans, in *English Poetry in the Later Nineteenth Century* (1933; second edition, 1966), includes some specific statements about the sources of *The Queen-Mother* and the plays on Mary Stuart.[13]

Swinburne's early verse shows his study of the eighteenth-century poets. His obligations to the Romantics need little comment. The author of *Hellas* and *Prometheus Unbound* was an object of lifelong enthusiasm to the author of *Songs before Sunrise,* as nearly all books on the latter explain. Also well known is the influence, personal and literary, of D. G. Rossetti and his circle. Several of the early poems now accessible, as well as some in *Poems and Ballads,* show the influence of Rossetti and the more tangible influence of Morris. Differing views on the so-called Pre-Raphaelite phase of Swinburne's work are presented by Lafourcade and by T. E. Welby in *The Victorian Romantics, 1850–70* (1929).

Personal contacts and letters quickened Swinburne's devotion to his three great teachers—Landor, Hugo, Mazzini. W. B. D. Henderson's *Swinburne and Landor* (1918) perhaps claims too much in attributing to Landor "the passionate love of liberty and

[11]For notes on "Laus Veneris" and "The Leper," see *The Victorian Poets: A Guide* (1956), pp. 149–150, note 14.

[12]*Ibid.,* p. 142.

[13]Some relevant titles are listed in note 15, *ibid.,* p. 150. To these I add Curtis Dahl's "Autobiographical Elements in Swinburne's Trilogy on Mary Stuart" (*VP,* 1965), which may go too far in tracing parallels between Swinburne's life and and the plays.

Eben Bass's "Swinburne, Greene, and 'The Triumph of Time' " (*VP,* 1966) seems to be bolstered chiefly by a coincidence of title, since it adduces no conclusive similarities between the two writers. In regard to the title, one may recall that Petrarch's poem "The Triumph of Time" is part of a series of once famous *trionfi.*

contempt of tyrants which is one characteristic of *The Queen Mother*," though Henderson may be right in supposing the elder poet to have been responsible for Swinburne's advocacy of tyrannicide. Henderson identifies the foster-father of "Thalassius" as Landor. (When, during his visit to The Pines, Paul de Reul asked Swinburne who the old man of that poem and of the "Prelude" to *Songs before Sunrise* was, the poet replied, "Je ne sais pas . . . plutôt Landor.")

Like other critics, notably Lafourcade and Chew, Henderson also touches on the influence of Mazzini on *Songs before Sunrise*. H. W. Rudman's *Italian Nationalism and English Letters* (1940) offers a broad perspective, though Rudman rather tantalizingly raises questions which he does not solve, such as the exact role of Swinburne's teacher at Oxford, Aurelio Saffi. Mazzini, whose charm and moral force won many disciples in England, perhaps more than Hugo imparted to Swinburne the vision of the universal Republic, the goal towards which humanity was believed to be moving.

The subject of Hugo's influence has been discussed at some length by Reul (*L'Œuvre de Swinburne*, 1922) and more briefly by Lafourcade and Chew. Parallels between *Les Châtiments* and *Songs before Sunrise* and *Songs of Two Nations* have been noted. Similarities have been found in the two poets' denunciations of Louis Napoleon and of the Pope. In rhyme and vocabulary, Swinburne's French songs are remarkably close to some passages in Hugo. G. Jean-Aubry's "Victor Hugo et Swinburne" (*Revue Bleue*, 1936) is mainly concerned with personal relations and correspondence. Jean-Aubry errs in declaring that Swinburne's only translation of Hugo was that of "Les enfants pauvres." Ruth Marie Faurot (*N&Q*, 1954) points out that "Love" translates a song in *Ruy Blas*.[14]

Ludwig Richter's *Swinburne's [sic] Verhältnis zu Frankreich und Italien* (1911) is sketchy and superficial in its discussion of the relation between Swinburne and such writers as Hugo and Baudelaire. Swinburne himself thought that Reul, whose *Swinburne et la France* appeared in the poet's lifetime, had overemphasized Baudelaire's influence; a similar criticism has been made of a recent work, F. Delattre's *Charles Baudelaire et le jeune Swinburne* (1930). Harold Nicolson's "Swinburne and

---

[14]See also Cecil Y. Lang's notes in *New Writings by Swinburne*.

Baudelaire" (*Essays by Divers Hands,* edited by G. K. Chesterton, 1926) compares the two poets' literary qualities. Swinburne's debt, especially in *Lesbia Brandon,* to other French writers (particularly Dumas, Balzac, and Gautier) is discussed in two longer works edited by Randolph Hughes. Ruth Z. Temple in *The Critic's Alchemy* (1953) stresses Swinburne's indebtedness to Gautier and the relative soundness of his appreciation of French poetry. Lafourcade has dwelt upon the poet's borrowings from Sade, especially in "Dolores," "Anactoria," *Atalanta,* and *William Blake.* Cecil Lang finds that "Song before Death," in *Poems and Ballads,* translates a song in Sade's *Aline et Valcour.* Martha H. Shackford's "Swinburne and Delavigne" (*PMLA,* 1918), not quite convincingly, proposes "Les Limbes" as the source of "The Garden of Proserpine." K. L. Knickerbocker's "The Source of Swinburne's *Les Noyades"* suggests that Carlyle, not Louis Blanc as Richter thought, supplied the legend used in the poem. Eileen Souffrin (*Revue de littérature comparée,* 1950) writes on "Swinburne et Banville" (see also her article cited in the concluding section). A few other articles on Swinburne's relations with foreign authors are listed in F. Baldensperger and W. P. Friederich's *Bibliography of Comparative Literature* (1950).

Since the study of sources has little value unless it helps one to explain or to evaluate an author's work, the mere fact of "sources" is less significant than the use made of them. Furthermore, no complete survey of Swinburne's sources is possible: clearly such a survey would embrace more than his reading. Mrs. Disney Leith tells of the effect of Handel's music during the composition of *Atalanta.* Swinburne's interest in Wagner is also acknowledged. More than one writer has speculated on Wagner as a possible stimulus for the use of leitmotifs in *Tristram of Lyonesse,* which John R. Reed ("Swinburne's *Tristram of Lyonesse:* The Poet-Lover's Song of Love," *VP,* 1966) effectively analyzes as "an elaborate song of love in which all creation, its contradictions and joys, is seen as a supreme music." Though the influence of painting is manifest in such poems as "A Ballad of Life," "A Christmas Carol," "Before the Mirror," "Erotion," and "Cleopatra," no systematic study of it exists.[15]

[15]T. E. Welby, whose *Victorian Romantics* includes a few pages on Simeon Solomon, seems correct in believing that Swinburne's "At a Month's End" preceded the design by the painter, despite a statement in the *DNB* article on Solomon.

V. SWINBURNE'S THOUGHT AND ART

Swinburne's relations to his contemporaries and his use of contemporary ideas were complex for a poet sometimes said to have lived in isolation. The topic will repay study. A lecture by W. K. Clifford (*Lectures and Essays*, 1879) has influenced subsequent criticism of *Songs before Sunrise*. Clifford used "To Walt Whitman in America" and other poems to illustrate "cosmic emotion"—"emotion felt in regard to the universe or sum of things." He explains how Swinburne links evolution with freedom and with the ideal Republic. To a few later critics, Swinburne's describing man as "the master of things," in the "Hymn of Man," seems unforgivable; impressed with social chaos in the contemporary world, they agree with Emerson: "Things are in the saddle, and ride mankind." One answer could reflect a point of view like that of Gilbert Murray, who declares that the Positivist venerates "not everything that is characteristic of Man, but that quality, or that effort, by which Man is morally and intellectually higher than the beasts" (quoted from "What is Permanent in Positivism," in *Stoic, Christian, and Humanist,* 1950). Moreover, the Positivist's disinterested altruism, which hopes for no reward, is much like that memorably expressed in Swinburne's "The Pilgrims."

J. W. Beach's *The Concept of Nature in Nineteenth-Century English Poetry* (1936) gives a sympathetic exposition of Swinburne's outlook, though excluding from consideration his descriptive poetry and those poems, such as "A Nympholept," in which he deals with the more primitive feelings toward nature. For Beach, Swinburne is an English poet who has so well assimilated evolutionary ideas that he "has already invented a highly poetical vocabulary in which to render what is for him the spiritual gift of evolution, its bearing upon human conduct and destiny."

By a curiosity of criticism, the poet who mainly grounded his views in what he considered fundamental realities has been charged with lacking an "internal centre"; it is ironical that Meredith's phrase, applied to Swinburne before he had written any of his greater works, should have become fashionable, for Meredith's outlook is remarkably similar to Swinburne's. (What Meredith actually wrote was, "I don't see any internal centre.") Welby and others find the poet's "internal centre" to be his devotion to freedom. Herbert Dingle in *Science and Literary Criticism* (1949) thinks that it is "the passion for immersion in an infinite and indefinite environment." These definitions seem more tangential than what Cecil Y. Lang has said in his introduction to *The Swinburne Letters:* that Swinburne's "poems of enduring appeal nearly always endeavor to explore" his own psyche, "the relationship between this natural experience and the external world."

As a critic, too, Swinburne had his "internal centre," and several recent writers have recognized his importance as such. "Swinburne's Mature Standards of Criticism," by Ruth C. Child (*PMLA,* 1937), collects passages indicating that he reserved his highest admiration for loftiness of thought and power of emotion—not merely skill of expression. Thomas E. Connolly's *Swinburne's Theory of Poetry* (1964) is a workmanlike outline of the poet's views, stressing "the solid core of principles" that form the basis of his criticism. The highest poetry, Swinburne believed, is concerned with the "attainment of a spiritual harmony with the divine, universal essence of things," Swinburne's "inner music" being rooted in insight into nature. Robert L. Peters, who earlier had written "Algernon Swinburne and Use of Integral Detail" (*VS,* 1962), "Swinburne's Idea of Form" (*Criticism,* 1963), and "Swinburne and the Moral Design of Art" (*VP,* 1964), in 1965 published *The Crowns of Apollo: Swinburne's Principles of Literature and Art: A Study in Victorian Criticism and Aesthetics.* One of the aims of this work is "to correct the reputation of a great and neglected essayist," whose aesthetic theories and practice, here treated sympathetically and with due respect for their flexibility, anticipated those of such later writers as Pater, Wilde, and Yeats. Peters observes that while Swinburne says much of detail and is concerned with synaesthesia and the interrelationship of the arts—a concern he shared with the Romantics and the Symbolists—he was also concerned, like Arnold and Pater, with the structure of the whole. Both Connolly and Peters controvert the mistaken view that Swinburne's criticism is "exclusively aesthetic." Peters, however, pays more attention to Victorian artistic theory, considering the poet's criticism of art along with his criticism of literature and including several appropriate illustrations. Though it apparently neglects the *Dedicatory Epistle* and though some passages may create the impression that Swinburne was more schematic than he would have admitted, the book is the most extended and skillful discussion of Swinburne's criticism yet published. A. J. Farmer's *Le Mouvement aesthétique et "décadent" en Angleterre* (1931) and J. H. Buckley's *The Victorian Temper* (1951) also deal with Swinburne's historic position in the "aesthetic movement." A. A. Löhrer's *Swinburne als Kritiker der Literatur* (1925) merely catalogues the poet's opinions of authors. The citations referring to Americans may be supplemented by Cecil Y. Lang's "Swinburne and American Literature: With Six Hitherto Unpublished Letters" (*AL*, 1948). Some of the longer studies listed in the final section below also discuss Swinburne's criticism.

The more technical aspects of Swinburne's poetic art have probably been the subject of less disagreement than his ideas. Any appraisal of his technique should take into account what he himself thought of as the inner (rather than the merely external) music of verse. From a somewhat mechanical point of view M. Kado's *Swinburnes Verskunst* (1911) makes an inventory of metrical forms such as "lyric," "song," "ballad." A few pages in Saintsbury's *History of English Prosody* (1910) are more instructive. Lafourcade describes the meters used in *Poems and Ballads.* R. H. Fletcher's "The Metrical Forms Used by Certain Victorian Poets" (*JEGP*, 1908) furnishes some statistics, estimating that Swinburne used 420 metrical and stanzaic forms, almost twice as many as Tennyson (240) and Browning (200).

Swinburne's diction has been considered, not always in relation to his poetic effects, by Thomas, Drinkwater, Reul, Nicolson, Lafourcade, Chew, and others. An old-fashioned treatise, G. Serner's *On the Language of Swinburne's Lyrics and Epics* (1910; "epics" seems an odd part of the title), brings out the extent of the poet's archaisms and coinages in archaic patterns, as well as his fondness for compounds, especially participial compounds. Serner used an earlier study by H. W. F. Wollaeger. J. R. Firth's "Modes of Meaning" (in the English Association *Essays and Studies*, 1951) has a section on Swinburne, "the most phonetic of all English poets," emphasizing "idiosyncrasies which make it [Swinburne's language] so personal that it can be called Swinburnese." T. S. Eliot (*The Sacred Wood*, 1920) explains why Swinburne's "diffuseness" may, as in "The Triumph of Time," be considered a peculiar artistic achievement.

Many of Eliot's followers have been anti-Romantic; perhaps partly for this reason and partly because of the nature of Swinburne's language, with an alleged lack of progression and correlation in his imagery, "explications" of his poems have not been numerous, though the first volume of the *Explicator* (1943) does contain a discussion of "Autumn in Cornwall." "Swinburne's 'A Nympholept,'" by P. F. Baum (*SAQ*, 1958) stands out as an excellent critique of one of Swinburne's successful poems: a poem whose author seeks no mystical contemplation or communion with nature but "complete ecstatic absorption—the pure realization of the unattainable, the possession for its own sake, when heaven and earth, man and God are united, melted into one"; a poem in which the poet assumes the dramatic character of an ancient Greek, "a dramatic creation of the feelings—doubt, fear, and finally happy surrender—of one submitting himself to the physical circumstances of still noon and intense heat, yielding to them, and achieving through them the ecstatic state of trance." The most curious and misguided explication for many years, in contrast to Baum's, is one of "Hertha," in E. M. W. Tillyard's *Five Poems* (1948). Tillyard assumes that "Hertha" and other poems were "called forth" by Swinburne's "fury" against the Ecumenical Council (see, however, Lafourcade, *Swinburne*, 1932, pp. 170–177). Though Tillyard's approach emphasizes historical backgrounds, some of his assertions are clearly anachronistic. Swinburne's metaphor based on the Life-tree Yggdrasill[16] be-

---

[16]Wendell Stacy Johnson's "Swinburne and Carlyle" (*ELN*, 1963) suggests that a speech by Hertha in Swinburne's poem may owe something to Carlyle's lecture on "The Hero as Divinity." His view that elsewhere the imagery of clothing is reminiscent of *Sartor Resartus* disregards the importance in everyday speech, as well as in the Bible, of words like *vesture* or *girdled*. The subject is still challenging.

comes an excuse for accusing him of "something that would have appealed to Hitler and Rosenberg," though Tillyard could hardly deny that the general tenor of the poem, which insists on the freedom of the soul, would have been repugnant to both. The author of "Liberty and Loyalty" (Bonchurch Edition, XVI) was always a sincere believer in individualism—a point of difference between his views and Mazzini's. The attitude behind Tillyard's assault on "the cult of Truth"—Victorians who followed the leadings of conscience were unaware that it was a "cult"—is at least as likely to foster social irresponsibility as reverence for what Tillyard calls "the great abstraction." He is not judging Victorian thinkers in their own historical context but in accordance with a personal interpretation of what has happened since their time. One returns with relief to the explication of "Hertha" in Lafcadio Hearn's *Interpretations of Literature* (1917).[17]

VI. GENERAL CRITICISM

Among the more general critical works on Swinburne, those by Theodore Wratislaw, Edward Thomas, G. E. Woodberry, and John Drinkwater are mainly of historical interest and have been briefly considered elsewhere.[18] Paul de Reul's *L'Œuvre de Swinburne* (1922) is still worth consulting on such subjects as Swinburne's relation to French authors. It contains sections on his music, imagination, and ideas and discusses the narrative

[17]Gwen A. Jones, "Notes on Swinburne's 'Song of Italy' " (*MLN*, 1917), helps to elucidate the historical allusions in the poem.

[18]In *Swinburne's Literary Career and Fame* (1933; the issue of 1963 by another publisher, being printed by offset, takes no account of what is now known about T. J. Wise's forgeries and Gosse's errors), the bibliography of which lists books and articles not mentioned here.

poems, dramas, and criticism. Reul was earlier the author of "Swinburne et la France" (*La Grande Revue,* 1904). Alice Galimberti's *L'Aedo d'Italia* (1925) discusses, translates, and adapts Swinburne for Italian readers, as Reul does for the French, but is of less importance to English-speaking students.

Harold Nicolson's *Swinburne* (1926), like other studies, leans too heavily on Gosse's *Life* for its facts. Nicolson's thesis that the key to Swinburne's temperament lies in a pendulum-like oscillation between "the impulse towards revolt and the impulse toward submission" has at least as much plausibility as most of the formulas fashionable in biographical writing, but occasionally it restricts his view of Swinburne's personal and literary qualities, as when he declares that *Love's Cross-Currents* illustrates "a curiously un-Swinburnian element of the mundane, the analytical, almost of the cynical"— a statement that hardly does justice to Swinburne's complexity. The most successful chapter is on *Atalanta.* Though for reasons of temperament Nicolson must have found his subject not entirely compatible, his critical emphases are mostly sound.

T. E. Welby's *A Study of Swinburne* (1926), not to be confused with the same author's earlier and less satisfactory book, was based on more research than Nicolson's *Swinburne* and is more sympathetic, though it contains some repetition and other faults of organization. Like Nicolson, Welby believes that Swinburne's work is a "multiple, many-mooded offering to liberty apprehended in very many ways"; but he adds that "freedom for Swinburne is not a riot of impulses in a vacuum. It is that condition in which man becomes the conscious, voluntarily dedicated . . . instrument of the supreme purpose." He calls the author of *Songs before Sunrise* "a profoundly religious poet," since "a religious poet does not become irreligious" because he says " 'dear city of man' instead of 'dear city of Zeus.' " Welby is less reticent than Gosse's *Life* about Swinburne's pathological side but declares, "With all his childishness, impishness, extravagance, all his freakishness and weaknesses, he was a very great man and a very great gentleman."

Volume I, *La Vie,* of Lafourcade's *La Jeunesse de Swinburne* has been discussed above, along with his later biography in English. Volume II, *L'Œuvre,* is, in spite of inaccuracies and an

annoying number of misprints, a work not to be ignored. Lafour-
cade has outlined at length Swinburne's apprenticeship and the
evolution of his ideas. If the time limit (1867) seems arbitrary
and the space accorded to certain juvenilia disproportionate, the
book is usually informative. Lafourcade called attention to the
manuscript of *The Unhappy Revenge* and quoted from some
unpublished poems, as well as from letters at the time unpub-
lished. One may question the soundness of a critical stance reaf-
firmed in his "Swinburne Vindicated" (*London Mercury*, 1938),
one of many articles prompted by Swinburne's centenary. Lafour-
cade insists on the genuineness of Swinburne's sexual experience
and therefore of the poems based on that experience—and he re-
minds us that Swinburne sang of many forms of love. He quotes
from *Chastelard* "the most beautiful and moving lines [Swin-
burne] ever wrote," since "to show how he turned to account the
strange though genuine material which lay at his disposal is to
vindicate both the man and the artist." But if emotions are pe-
ripheral rather than central in human experience, will the au-
thor who expresses them seem less remote from humanity?

S. C. Chew's *Swinburne* (1929) appeared too soon after *La
Jeunesse* to make use of its materials, though it is remarkable
for a richness of detail due not only to assimilation of earlier
researches but also to the author's broad knowledge of Swinburne's
milieu and of literature. It excels other general studies in appreci-
ation of *Songs before Sunrise* and in judicious and scholarly
treatment of the Arthurian poems, the dramas, and the criticism.
The comments on "Ave atque Vale" deserve special mention.
Chew assigns to Swinburne the highest position among poets
whose work belongs exclusively to the second half of the nine-
teenth century. His article on Swinburne in *A Literary History
of England* (1948), edited by Albert C. Baugh, is both knowl-
edgeable and succinct.

Of the many short critiques of Swinburne, Oliver Elton's
estimate in his *Survey of English Literature, 1780–1880,* IV
(1920) still deserves high rank. This, together with some other
twentieth-century criticism, is discussed in the last chapter of
C. K. Hyder's *Swinburne's Literary Career and Fame* (1933),
the concluding section of which summarizes the history of Swin-

burne's reputation to 1932. The book gives attention to Swinburne's response to criticism, especially in his invective.[19]

There is still no adequate account of Swinburne's fortunes in Europe. In his centenary article (*RLC*, 1937), Henri Peyre writes of Swinburne's pre-eminence as a European poet, who, like Byron and Poe, deserves a place in the history of comparative literature—not only because he did much for the recognition of French poetry in England but also because he influenced such authors as Mallarmé, Verlaine, and Gide. Eileen Souffrin's "Swinburne et sa legende en France" (*RLC*, 1951) contains fresh material about the poet's reputation among French literary men, some of whom considered him "un Edgar Poe 'fin de siècle' "; curiously, while in England Swinburne was denounced as borrowing from the wicked French, in France he was sometimes regarded as the representative of a vice characteristic of the English.[20] Mario Praz's *The Romantic Agony* (revised edition, 1951) mentions Swinburne's influence on D'Annunzio and others. In "More Swinburne-D'Annunzio Parallels" (*PMLA*, 1940), C. S. Brown, Jr., deals with the extensive borrowings—more accurately, plagiarisms—of D'Annunzio, chiefly from Gabriel Mourey's prose translation of *Poems and Ballads*. Beulah B. Amram's "Swinburne and Carducci" (*Yale Review*, 1916) is primarily a comparison of the English and the Italian poet.

Lafourcade thought Swinburne's affiliations to be with the moderns. Though the poet was responsible for some innovation, more often, perhaps more justly, his art has been considered a culminating point in the great century of Romanticism. The last generation has been one of anti-Romantic reaction, doubtless to some extent because of literary fashion and because of a misunderstanding of what Romanticism stood for, as Ernest Bernbaum and B. Ifor Evans (see especially the latter's *Tradition and Romanticism*, 1940) have convincingly argued.

But what is "modern?" If one accepts conventional or rather provincial notions of time, is not Swinburne a spokesman for

[19]A few articles appearing since 1933 are listed in *Victorian Poets: A Guide* (1956), note 20, pp. 158-159.

[20]See also Baldensperger and Friederich's *Bibliography of Comparative Literature* (1950). Daniel A. de Graaf's "L'influence de Swinburne sur Verlaine et Rimbaud" (*Revue des sciences humains*, 1960) may be added to the articles listed there.

"modern" views on grounds other than those suggested by La-
fourcade, whose findings have greatly influenced the critics?
Swinburne's poems will hardly shock a generation in which, as
has been remarked, even the Marquis de Sade is treated as a
sort of culture hero. Long before the time of the "God is dead"
school of theologians, Swinburne perceived, too, like his wise
contemporary Matthew Arnold, that "the fact" is unfortunately
ever failing supernatural revelation. But the humanistic Swinburne
also knew that truth is not the sole possession of the new theo-
logians of science; the opening passage of *Under the Microscope*
may suggest some such awareness, and "The Pilgrims" is, after
all, one of the most profoundly religious of modern poems.

Like Charles Lamb, a poet can write for antiquity as well as
for posterity. Critics may as well admit the limitations and
eccentricities of the poet's experience, but they will insist that
a tree is not to be judged by its roots or a flower by the ordure
that nourished it; nor will they dwell on an aspect of that
experience and neglect the whole. They will not admit that
Swinburne lacked loftiness of thought or a sweep of imagination
worthy of his great poetic resources. In a world besotted by
specious pleaders for putting the human race into shackles, they
will not concede that his vision of freedom as the very condition
of the soul's growth is lacking in value. If a world-view such as
is expressed in what may be one of the most Lucretian of nine-
teenth-century poems, "Genesis," seems to offend orthodoxies,
what of that? The poetry of Lucretius himself, who may be re-
garded as "modern" or "ancient" or neither, has lasted during
ages that have seen the decline and fall of many orthodoxies.

The Pre-Raphaelites

WILLIAM E. FREDEMAN

Like other literary taxonomical labels such as Neo-Classic, Romantic, and Naturalistic, Pre-Raphaelite belies its own definition by impressing itself on the reader with a precision and a denotative positiveness that seduces him into believing that he comprehends its complexity merely by his knowledge of the term. The principal critical limitation of such terms is that they become catchall labels descriptive of many contradictory forces. The convenience of the label cannot, however, absolve the critic from the responsibility of definition. In the strictest sense—and many contemporary critics, especially art critics, still insist on a tightly circumscribed use of the term—Pre-Raphaelite refers to that Brotherhood of seven painters who, in 1848, challenged the aesthetic conformity and the sterile rules of the Royal Academy. Of these seven Pre-Raphaelite Brothers—Dante Gabriel Rossetti, William Holman Hunt, John Everett Millais, Frederic George Stephens, James Collinson, William Michael Rossetti, and Thomas Woolner—only the first and last two are discussed among the Pre-Raphaelite poets in this chapter. If the initial question that must be posed is "what is Pre-Raphaelitism as applied to poetry?" the prelude to an answer must be sought in the artistic movement out of which developed a corpus of poetry that can be labelled critically Pre-Raphaelite.

A history of Pre-Raphaelitism would not be irrelevant to a discussion of the poetry of the movement, but it would be digressive. Unfortunately, there is no single objective and factually reliable history to recommend. The popular books on the movement, such as Francis Bickley's *Pre-Raphaelite Comedy* (1932), Frances Winwar's *Poor Splendid Wings* (1933), and William Gaunt's *Pre-Raphaelite Tragedy* (1942), are amusingly written but semifictionalized accounts. The one history by a PRB, Holman Hunt's *Pre-Raphaelitism and the Pre-Raphaelite Brotherhood* (1905; second edition revised by M. E. Holman Hunt, 1913), is a massive compilation and an invaluable document, but the work is vitiated both by Hunt's personal and artistic prejudices and by the distance separating the writing of the book from the events it reports. D. S. R. Welland's *The Pre-Raphaelites in Literature and Art* (1953) is a useful introductory handbook to the movement, but it attempts far too much within the compass of a small volume. Graham Hough's chapters in *The Last Romantics* (1949), among the most reliable criticism on the Pre-Raphaelites, of necessity assume some familiarity with the history of the movement. And William E. Fredeman's "Commentary" in *Pre-Raphaelitism: A Bibliocritical Study* (1965), though it traces the history of the movement through a critical examination of the major scholarship and seeks to establish a working definition, cannot be construed as a practical introduction for the beginning student. The most recent book on the PRB, G. H. Fleming's *Rossetti and the Pre-Raphaelite Brotherhood* (1967) provides a reliable history of the early movement, but as its emphasis is on Rossetti it will be discussed in a later section. Lacking a definitive history of the movement—one of the immediate desiderata of Pre-Raphaelite scholarship—the student must at the present time either rely on encylopedia or anthology accounts, which are greatly oversimplified, or take the longer and more tedious route of re-creating the history for himself.

Central to any study of Pre-Raphaelitism are the formidable memoirs and diaries (most of them in two volumes) and the writings of the indefatigable William Michael Rossetti. Indispensable in the first category are not only the memoirs of the Brotherhood—William Holman Hunt, John Everett Millais (1899), D. G. Rossetti (1895), W. M. Rossetti (1906), and Thomas Woolner (1917)—but also those of the later Pre-Raphaelites, both "Brothers" from the second (or Oxford) phase such as Edward Burne-Jones (1904) and minor associates and affiliates such as William Bell Scott (1892). And this list must be supplemented by memoirs, biographies, and letters of writers and artists of lesser importance if a complete picture is to be formed.

William Michael Rossetti planned a series of volumes which would chronicle the Rossetti family throughout the century. In three published books—*Præraphaelite Diaries and Letters* (1900), *Ruskin: Rossetti: Preraphaelitism* (1899), and *Rossetti Papers* (1903)—he brought his materials to 1870. He completed the preliminary editing for some of the later volumes for which he failed to find a publisher; the balance of these Rossetti family papers is now in the Special Collections of the University of British Columbia Library. William Rossetti was an extremely decorous editor, often bowdlerizing his materials unconscionably, but without his efforts, it is safe to say that Pre-Raphaelite scholarship could never have made a beginning.

There has been an unfortunate tendency to disassociate visual and literary Pre-Raphaelitism in an either-or way, as if the two were mutually exclusive phenomena, but the student of literary Pre-Raphaelitism must initially familiarize himself with the artistic side of the movement. The best place to begin is with a close study of the paintings themselves, and there are several good collections of reproductions. The best is Robin Ironside's *Pre-Raphaelite Painters* (1948), with an outstanding catalog by John Gere. An expensively produced and genuinely representative edition of color reproductions of Pre-Raphaelite art would prove of inestimable use to students of both the literature and art of the movement. The two best accounts of the history and influence of Pre-Raphaelite painting are A. P. Oppé's chapter in *Early Victorian England*, edited by G. M. Young (1934), and T. S. R. Boase's survey in the Oxford History of English Art, *English Art, 1800–1870* (1959).

The PRB began as a rebellion against the tyrannical hold of the Royal Academy on British art. It was the belated counterpart in painting of the romantic revolution in literature that began at the turn of the century. The Pre-Raphaelites, with their oversimplified and ambiguous dictum "follow nature," were neither the only nor the best exponents of this revolution, but because the movement they inaugurated became so expansive, incorporating many of the related arts and crafts and recruiting to its ranks such a diversified group of artists and writers, it is not an exaggeration to say, with Stephen Spender, that Pre-Raphaelitism was "the greatest artistic movement in England during the nineteenth century" (*New Writing and Daylight*, 1945). In "The Pre-Raphaelite Literary Painters," one of the most perceptive articles on the movement, Spender correctly observes that the "inspiration of Pre-Raphaelitism was verbal, literary, poetic, rather than of painting." One may go further and assert that while the movement began as a reform in painting, its greatest impact was made in English letters.

The student coming to the Brotherhood for the first time should proceed with three elementary observations clearly in mind. First, the PRB was an exceedingly transitory event in the history of art, which by 1854 had for all practical purposes disbanded. Second, the Pre-Raphaelite Brothers were all excessively young, as is shown by their self-conscious preoccupation with their own activities, their strong sense of high purpose, and the seriousness with which they pursued their (to us, now) not so revolutionary art. The truly remarkable fact about the Pre-Raphaelite Brotherhood is that what Rossetti once called "the visionary vanities of half-a-dozen boys" should have left its impress so markedly on the world of British art. Finally, there is virtually no formal aesthetic creed which can be educed from either the statements or from the visual and literary works of the Brotherhood that will explain satisfactorily the term Pre-Raphaelitism. Ruskin (with whom the PRB shared many basic views on art), Holman Hunt, William Michael Rossetti, and a host of subsequent commentators have attempted to rationalize the label, all unsuccessfully. The distinction made by Holman Hunt and nineteenth-century critics between Pre-Raphaelitism and Pre-Raphaelism is merely specious. Whether applied in derision or adopted consciously by the Brotherhood, the term is an unfortunate misnomer. This reservation does not, of course, preclude the use of the term Pre-Raphaelite in a critical context, but it does underscore the obvious qualification that the denominator common to the Pre-Raphaelites is romanticism.

No simple catalog of external characteristics can convey the complexity of the Pre-Raphaelite aesthetic or carry the burden of the term's definition. Such catalogs are easy enough to compile—a realism derived from the literal observation and truthful rendering of nature; a preoccupation with external detail for its own sake; the reintroduction of vivid coloration into painting; a predisposition to medieval themes and subjects, with overtones of an "Early Christian" ethic; artistic sincerity in the treatment of subjects and emotions; the use of obvious literary sources as the inspiration for art—but inevitably they are misleading. More important is the recognition of the several paradoxes operative within the Pre-Raphaelites' working aesthetic: the conflict inherent in the choice of realistic techniques to portray essentially romantic subjects; the unreconciled contradiction between their mimetic ("follow nature") and expressive ("fidelity to inner experience") theories of art; and the attempt to fuse the literary and visual media by utilizing reciprocal techniques. Oswald Doughty, in his "Rossetti's Conception of the 'Poetic' in Poetry and Painting" (*EDH,* 1953), recognizes this aspect as crucial to an understanding of Rossetti's work; and Stephen Spender sees it as one of the cardinal weaknesses of Pre-Raphaelite art: "... the attempt to paint poetry according to the Pre-Raphaelite formula of truth makes the mistake of *copying* poetry in painting" (p. 127).

"What is Pre-Raphaelitism?" was the title of one of the earliest monographs on the Pre-Raphaelites, by John Ballantyne (1856). The perennial question, it was extended to "What is Pre-Raphaelism in Poetry?" by Anna Janney De Armond (*Delaware Notes,* 1946). For Ballantyne, Pre-Raphaelitism was synonymous with Ruskinism—an association that persists to the present day. Without minimizing in any way the importance of Ruskin in fostering the reputation of the movement by his letters to the *Times* and the later pamphlet *Pre-Raphaelitism* (1851), it can safely be stated that Ruskin's understanding of the movement as a whole, not just of the PRB, was too literal and far too suffused with his own moral and didactic concepts. Any study of the Pre-Raphaelites, however, must account for Ruskin's historical and aesthetic significance. The Library Edition of *The Works of John Ruskin,* edited by E. T. Cook and A. D. O. Wedderburn (1903–1912) is monumental and a gold mine of incidental information relating to the Pre-Raphaelites. Most works on Ruskin treat his involvement with Pre-Raphaelitism. Indispensable are H. A. Ladd's *The Victorian Morality of Art: An Analysis of Ruskin's Esthetic* (1932); Derrick Leon's *Ruskin: The Great Victorian* (1949), perhaps the finest biography; and John D. Rosenberg's *The Darkening Glass: A Portrait of Ruskin's Genius* (1961). Graham Hough's chapter in *The Last Romantics* (1949) traces the seminal relationship between Ruskin's theories and those of Rossetti, Morris, and the Pre-Raphaelites; while Frank Daniel Curtin's "Aesthetics in English Social Reform: Ruskin and his Followers"

(*Nineteenth Century Studies,* 1940) offers a convenient summary of this important aspect of nineteenth-century thought.

If it is difficult to define Pre-Raphaelitism in art, it is infinitely harder to apply the term with precision to a body of poetry. Few scholars have tackled the problem in a serious way. Professor De Armond's essay, already mentioned, goes scarcely beyond the poetry of *The Germ* and provides a most unsatisfactory answer to the question posed in its title. She attempts to show that any definition (accounting for poets as disparate as Rossetti and Morris) "must explain . . . not a single, static movement, but an actual development in poetic theory and poetic practice" (p. 86). Recognizing the problems involved in terminology, Professor De Armond concludes that "Pre-Raphaelitism is certainly an arbitrary term and one fundamentally empty of content; but the group which applied the name to itself gave it, both by precept and example, a definite meaning" (p. 86). What that "definite meaning" is, however, is never quite revealed. Both R. L. Mégroz (*Modern English Poetry,* 1933) and John Heath-Stubbs (*The Darkling Plain,* 1950) regard dream poetry (in the unallegorical sense) as the hallmark of the Pre-Raphaelites, dream poetry built on a romantic foundation. Heath-Stubbs, whose book is subtitled "A Study of the Later Fortunes of Romanticism in English Poetry from George Darley to W. B. Yeats," discusses Pre-Raphaelitism as an "aesthetic withdrawal" "into the contemplation of purely decorative beauty." For him their dream-poetry, more than the "formal peculiarities of their style or their mediaevalism," characterizes the literary Pre-Raphaelites.

The best single analysis of Pre-Raphaelite poetry is Humphry House's in *All in Due Time* (1955). House never elaborated on the ideas which he introduced in this brilliant essay, mainly concerned with the medievalism of the movement, which he sees as merely "one aspect of Pre-Raphaelite naturalism." At its simplest level, Pre-Raphaelite poetry, House says, was a "searching through the mixture of modernism and medievalism after deeper purposes" (p. 153). The Pre-Raphaelite preference for the medieval lay principally in the absence of what may be called a "sacramental view of things" in the modern world. In an earlier "Essay on the Decorative Art of the Pre-Raphaelites," Stephen

Ullmann in his "Synaesthetic Metaphors in William Morris" (*Studies in English Philology,* 1937) made some tentative suggestions about the use made by the Pre-Raphaelites of synaesthesia as a means for creating realistic effects in their painting and poetry. He pointed out that since synaesthesia is more "plastic than any single sensation," it is especially adapted to the realistic treatment of nature in art. The greatest part of the article is devoted to a tabular analysis of synaesthetic metaphors in Morris' poetry, but many of his general conclusions, such as the "decorative power of synaesthetic imagery," point to a qualitative distinction that may well be organic to the whole of Pre-Raphaelite poetry. W. W. Robson's chapter on Pre-Raphaelite poetry in volume six of the Pelican Guide to English Literature, *From Dickens to Hardy,* edited by Boris Ford (1958), is totally unsympathetic; Pre-Raphaelite poetry, for him, bears "a derivative and subordinate relation to that of the great Romantics" (p. 353). His catalog of superficial characteristics is stock: particularization, e.g., of sensory (both visual and auditory) detail, the use of archaisms and medievalisms for decoration, an autumnal mood or habit of feeling, religiosity, and literariness. The "Pre-Raphaelite key" he defines as "the static, dreamy atmosphere, which has not the transitory vividness of real dreams, but rather the insubstantiality of a waking dream or reverie" (p. 364).

The Pre-Raphaelite aesthetic was essentially romantic, and in the poetry and painting of the movement there are twin manifestations of romantic escapism which look simultaneously backward to a medieval world of the imagination and forward to a utopian dream of the future. Dissatisfied with the present, both aesthetically and socially, the Pre-Raphaelites enisled themselves in a world remote from contemporaneity, a timeless "literary" world of beauty and art. The paradox of their technical adherence to naturalism and corresponding detail at a time when the ultra-realistic medium was in its infancy, has led many commentators to label them "photographic," but a careful study of their work reveals that not even their technique, let alone their concern with particularity, bears the slightest resemblance to photography. If they seldom produced what F. G. Stephens in "Modern Giants" (*Germ,* No. 4) called "the poetry of things about us," the "Subject in Art" that J. L. Tupper (*Germ,* No. 3) took such pains to belabor, it was because as Tupper says, anticipating Arnold, "all things of the past . . . come down to us with some poetry about them," while "incidents of the present time are well nigh barren in poetic attraction."

Pre-Raphaelitism has always presented a contradiction to both its adherents and antagonists. On the one hand, its importance as an aesthetic force throughout the last half of the century is demonstrable and easily documented. What should be the essential documentation of the movement's significance, on the other hand —the pictures, poems, and artifacts produced by the individual Pre-Raphaelites—has always seemed unequal to the movement's general reputation and influence. Even allowing for differences in taste and sensibility between the Victorian and modern period, which led most critics to condemn the recent retrospective exhibition of Millais' works at the Royal Academy (1967), the art and poetry of the Pre-Raphaelites does not, with some rare exceptions, measure up to the work of their greatest contemporaries, certainly not to that of their romantic predecessors.

In part, this contradiction is attributable to the failure of the Pre-Raphaelites to clarify their initial aims and principles and to their willingness to acquiesce in vague and half-formed ideas. Critics such as Geoffrey Grigson (*The Harp of Aeolus*, 1947) have tended to see the movement as a cult of personality, but despite the magnitude of Rossetti's influence on the PRB, on the Oxford group, and on the minor poets, the inherent energy of Pre-Raphaelitism belies this oversimplification. Clearly—and the hostility of the artistic establishment to the Pre-Raphaelites confirms this point—Victorian art was ripe for revolution when the Pre-Raphaelites seized their advantage at mid-century. The opportunity and the obligation they had was to revitalize an art that had become stale and stereotyped. Had they been equal to the articulation required to win sufficient talented converts to their numbers, the history of the movement might have been radically different. But it was all, in the PRB stage anyway, too self-conscious. The few positive utterances they did make were merely clichéd romanticisms, and the visual manifestations of their limited principles seemed to their contemporaries either eccentric or perverse. "Coterie glory," someone later called it, thereby reducing the Brotherhood to the level of a mutual admiration society.

It is perhaps this failure of the Pre-Raphaelites to clarify their aesthetic intentions that explains why so frequently the impressionistic critics such as Ford Madox Ford, Laurence Housman, and Arthur Symons seem to come so much closer to capturing the essence of the movement than the scholars. "You would do well," Chauncey B. Tinker once said, "not to press too ardently for pre-Raphaelite explanations" (*Essays in Retrospect,* 1948). But the spirit of the Brotherhood, what can be called its quintessential poetry, was contagious, and the messianic urge that led the Brotherhood to call their weak manifesto *The Germ* proved prophetic. Their ideas served as a bulwark for the avant-garde of the century against the forces of conservatism and conformity. The aestheticism of the nineties is a long remove from the PRB— in fact, superficially there is little resemblance—but the real meaning of the term Pre-Raphaelitism and the ultimate explanation of its influence lies in the generic extension that made it accessible to later artists and writers.

GENERAL BIBLIOGRAPHY

The only bibliography of the Pre-Raphaelite Movement is William E. Fredeman's *Pre-Raphaelitism: A Bibliocritical Study* (1965). Intended as a "critical reference guide to the whole subject of Pre-Raphaelitism," the volume comprises a commentary and a bibliography. In the commentary, consisting of an introduction and a survey of scholarship, the author traces, through an examination of selected books and articles, both the history of the movement and its critical reputation.

The bibliography is divided into four parts and one hundred

sections. Part I, "Sources for Bibliography and Provenance" (sections 1–21), contains brief descriptions of the general holdings of the major public and private repositories of Pre-Raphaelite materials; checklists of important exhibitions and sales, the catalogs of which are so vital in locating particular pictures, drawings, and manuscripts, are also included. Part II is the "Bibliography of Individual Figures" (sections 22–65). Items relating to Dante Gabriel Rossetti are classified by subject into thirteen sections (22–34) which together constitute the most extensive bibliography of Rossetti to date. The bibliographies of the other two major Pre-Raphaelite poets—William Morris (section 43) and Christina Rossetti (section 44)—are purposely selective. Those sections treating the minor poets—William Allingham (section 46), Thomas Gordon Hake (section 48), Philip Bourke Marston (section 50), Arthur O'Shaughnessy (section 51), John Payne (section 54), William Bell Scott (section 56), and Thomas Woolner (section 40)—are in most instances the only bibliographies available, apart from the listings in the *CBEL*. The sections devoted to Coventry Patmore (section 52), John Ruskin (section 45), Algernon Swinburne (section 62), and Theodore Watts-Dunton (section 64) are limited in the main to those items which demonstrate the association of these authors directly or indirectly with Pre-Raphaelitism. Part III, the "Bibliography of the Pre-Raphaelite Movement" (sections 66–87), is also subdivided by subject and traces the history and reputation of the Movement in all its phases and activities. Part IV, the "Bibliography of Pre-Raphaelite Illustrations" (sections 88–100), is subdivided by illustrators and is less likely than the other sections to be of immediate interest to the student of literature.

Pre-Raphaelitism renders obsolete most earlier checklists. However, the only serious bibliographical survey antedating *Pre-Raphaelitism*—Howard Mumford Jones's chapter in the first edition of *The Victorian Poets* (1956)—remains of great value for its critical insights. For individual authors, Ehrsam, Deily, and Smith's now outdated *Bibliographies of Twelve Victorian Authors* (1936) contains many items in the sections on Dante Gabriel Rossetti, Christina Rossetti, and William Morris *not* in Fredeman. For Rossetti's primary works, William Michael Rossetti's *Bibliography* (1905) is still important, and his *Classified Lists* of

Rossetti's writings (1906) should be compared with the chronological table of contents in his edition of the *Works* (1911) and the survey in *Dante Gabriel Rossetti as Designer and Writer* (1889). The two book-length bibliographies of Morris by H. Buxton Forman and Temple Scott (both published in 1897) have never been superseded, but R. C. H. Briggs's *Handlist of the Public Addresses of Morris* (1961) is a convenient supplement. Forman's *Books of William Morris* is especially useful for its incidental information relating to the publication of Morris' books; Temple Scott's *Bibliography* contains, in addition to Morris' own writings, including his contributions to periodicals, a checklist of writings on Morris, both articles and reviews and criticism. Both volumes treat the publications of the Kelmscott Press. For current research on the Pre-Raphaelites, the standard serial bibliographies are those in *Victorian Studies* and *PMLA*, but these listings should be supplemented by the biennial selective and annotated bibliography of "William Morris & his Circle" compiled by William E. Fredeman for the *Journal of the William Morris Society*, two instalments of which have appeared to date covering the years 1960 to 1965 (1964, 1966).

DANTE GABRIEL ROSSETTI

Rossetti is unique in being the one poet whose claim to be called a Pre-Raphaelite requires no defence, though he himself had reservations about the label. Whether he founded the PRB or not matters little; he was the inspired catalyst without which there would have been no Pre-Raphaelite reaction. What Rossetti had was raw enthusiasm coupled with artistic faith and the capacity for encouraging talent, however minuscule. He was imaginative, intelligent, and generous both of his time and praise. Without him the PRB would have been even more short-lived, the Oxford phase would probably never have materialized, and the continuance of Pre-Raphaelitism as an aesthetic force throughout the century would have been precluded.

Rossetti's role is ultimately ambiguous. Many critics deny him a significant position in the histories of either British art or poetry, and it may be that his real importance lies rather in the influence he exerted on fellow artists and poets than in his actual productions. It is not easy in Rossetti's case to decide whether his talent was too great or too small to achieve success in two media. Certainly his output in both is impressive, but one wonders what he might have produced had he limited himself to either poetry or painting. The conflict between these two expressive forms is apparent in his earliest youth, though his strongest inclinations seem to have been poetic. His natural tendency was to confuse the two, as his pictures and poems, and his recorded comments, make instantly clear. Rossetti regarded himself primarily as an artist, and he explained in one of the published "Scraps" preserved by his brother that he had "never hoped to produce in poetry more than a small amount of quintessential work" (*Works*, p. 638).

That "quintessential work," involving what he elsewhere called "fundamental brainwork" constitutes a substantial, and a difficult, canon. He is today more admired as a painter than as a poet, though his professional grasp of the painter's craft was infinitely inferior to his mastery of poetic technique. Rossetti's poetry was not widely read in his own time, and it is unlikely that it will ever command a large and enthusiastic audience. However, because an increasing number of readers have learned to overcome the obstacles inherent in the poetry—succinctness, compression, ellipsis—it is slowly beginning to be revalued. In time, perhaps, its critical worth may come to be recognized in and for itself, independent of the biographical element which for most readers has been its principal appeal.

I. WORKS

The dominance of Rossetti among the Pre-Raphaelite poets has not yet produced a complete critical text of his poetry and prose. Many of the materials for such an edition—both manuscripts and the so-called "Trial Books"—are in the collection of Mrs. Janet Camp Troxell (New Haven, Connecticut), who has done much of the preliminary research. In her article on "The 'Trial Books' of D. G. Rossetti" (*Colophon,* 1938), Mrs. Troxell gave the first detailed indication of the complexities facing the editor who wished to account for Rossetti's final text of the *Poems* (1870), through no less than six proof stages previous to the first edition. Some sense of Rossetti's tendency toward intense revision was available from his letters, especially those to his publisher, F. S. Ellis, edited by Oswald Doughty in the centenary year, and from Paull F. Baum's variorum edition of *The Blessed Damozel* (1937), and Mrs. Troxell demonstrated that his revises of the several "Trial" and proof stages of *Poems* amount virtually to manuscripts, so heavily corrected are they.

Until an edition based on available manuscript and "trial" stages is forthcoming, the standard edition must be W. M. Rossetti's fourth major edition of his brother's writings, *Works* (1911). This edition, though excluding his first poem, the privately printed *Sir Hugh the Heron,* and the unpublished juvenile ballad "William and Mary," prints almost all Rossetti's known writings and translations, including selections from the versicles and fragments and from the juvenilia contained in the notebooks. Essentially complete and in the main textually reliable, *Works,* prefaced by a memoir and containing full notes by the editor, has a revised chronological table of contents giving date of composition and first printing of each of Rossetti's poems and prose pieces.

Two separate publications of Rossetti's translations should be noted, although both are reprinted in *Works:* Burger's *Lenore,* edited with an introduction by W. M. Rossetti (1900), and the Bibliophile Society's edition of Hartmann von Aue's *Henry the Leper,* edited by William P. Trent (1905), the second volume of which is a facsimile of Rossetti's translation "paraphrase." *Works* (1911) must be supplemented by three further publications: William Rossetti's "Some Scraps of Verse and Prose by Dante Gabriel Rossetti" (*Pall Mall Magazine,* 1898), two of which were not reprinted in *Works;* Paull F. Baum's *Dante Gabriel Rossetti: An Analytical List of Manuscripts in the Duke*

University Library, with hitherto Unpublished Verse and Prose (1931); and J. R. Wahl's edition of *Jan Van Hunks* (1952). Of greatest interest among the Duke manuscripts are the juvenile ballad "William and Mary" (which Baum does not print) and thirteen *bout-rimé* sonnets (which he does). Baum's attribution of some of these sonnets to Dante Gabriel rather than to William Michael was challenged by Frances Winwar in "Dante Gabriel's or William Michael's?" (*PMLA,* 1933).

In addition to Wahl's edition of *Jan Van Hunks* mentioned above, four separate editions of Rossetti's poems have appeared. P. F. Baum's *The House of Life* (1928) must be regarded as nearly definitive, though he does not utilize to any degree the manuscripts of the poem. His text, based on the 1881 version, accounts for revisions between the partial texts of 1869 (in the *Fortnightly Review*) and 1870. Prefaced by a thorough introduction treating the composition, characteristics, and autobiographical qualities of the poem, the edition also contains full notes and two important appendices on the dating and prosody of the sonnets in the series. Baum's later variorum edition of *The Blessed Damozel: The Unpublished Manuscript, Texts and Collation* (1937), comparing the versions of the poem published in *The Germ* (1850), *The Oxford and Cambridge Magazine* (1856), and *Poems* (1881) with the fair-copy manuscript in the Pierpont Morgan Library, is introduced by an essay of admirable clarity and thoroughness. Not all critics, however, have agreed with Baum's ascription of authority to the Morgan Library manuscript, and his essay should be compared with K. L. Knickerbocker's (*SP,* 1932), the first to utilize the manuscript, and J. A. Sanford's (*SP,* 1938), in which it is regarded as "worthless for scholarly purposes."

Janet Troxell's edition of *Rossetti's Sister Helen* (1939) is based principally on the proofs and "Trial Books" in her own collection. The major texts of the poem, from its first appearance in the *Düsseldorf Artists' Album* (1854) through the final version in *Poems* (1881), are collated to demonstrate Rossetti's revisions. Full notes, facsimiles, and a careful introduction are provided. The last separate edition of importance is J. R. Wahl's *The Kelmscott Love Sonnets of Dante Gabriel Rossetti* (1954), based on an album containing twenty-eight sonnets from *The House of*

Life in fair-copy manuscripts given by Rossetti to Jane Morris and now in the Bodleian. In his introduction, Wahl argues for the relevance of these manuscripts as documents elucidating Rossetti's relationship with Jane Morris. While one may agree that these sonnets are, in fact, the ones "which Rossetti wrote during the months he spent at Kelmscott with Mrs. Morris during the summer of 1871, while her husband was in Iceland, and that it is his love for her which inspired these poems," Wahl's emotional interpretation of the literary history of the sonnets is less convincing: "It is as if a manuscript of Petrarch's later love sonnets were to come to light, carefully copied in his own hand and presented by him to Laura" (p. ix). Wahl's edition of these love sonnets pursues too exclusively, as does Doughty's biography, which will be discussed later, the biographical context of *The House of Life,* at the expense of the poetic.

Of collected reprints of Rossetti's works, ranging from those of the Kelmscott and Mosher Presses to special Christmas gift books, there is seemingly no end, but most of these reprints have no textual significance. Four student anthologies may be mentioned as offering wide and representative selections, with introductions of varying significance. F. L. Lucas' edition in the "Poets in Brief" series (1933) is prefaced by essentially the same essay that appears in the editor's *Ten Victorian Poets* (revised edition, 1940). Lilian Howarth's edition of *Poems* (1950) is designed for the Australian reader. Oswald Doughty's *Poems* (1957) is the most readily procurable anthology and it does contain all of Rossetti's poetry from his three major collections (*Poems,* 1870; *Ballads and Sonnets,* 1881; and *Poems: a New Edition,* 1881). However, in choosing to follow the structure of Rossetti's own volumes, the editor was reduced to breaking *The House of Life,* Rossetti's major work, into two halves rather than presenting it as a complete poem, and thereby unconsciously encouraging, perhaps, a reading of the poem that has been perpetuated in too many critical examinations. P. F. Baum's *Poems, Ballads and Sonnets* (1937) is by far the most useful anthology. Long unprocurable, this edition desperately wants reprinting in order to make again accessible not only Baum's important introductory background to Rossetti the poet but also the rich notes that accompany his selection.

II. LETTERS

The publication of *Letters of Dante Gabriel Rossetti* (1965–1967), edited in five volumes by Oswald Doughty (Rossetti's ablest biographer) and John Robert Wahl, makes available to the student the largest single collection of letters by the painter-poet. It supplants four separate editions, another four volumes containing sizable groups of his letters, four privately printed pamphlets by Thomas J. Wise, at least four articles devoted exclusively to the correspondence, and many articles and books in which single letters or smaller groups of the correspondence are scattered.

At the time of writing, the announced Index volume (Five), which may or may not contain supplementary letters, has not appeared, and the scope of the whole edition can only be estimated; 2,615 letters, written between 1835–1882, are included in the four volumes. The completed *Letters* will thus be the standard work, replacing more than twenty earlier sources and including hundreds of letters (nearly sixty percent of the total) never before published or only published in part.

While *Letters* preempts earlier editions, it does not necessarily make totally redundant the volumes edited by George Birkbeck Hill (to William Allingham, 1897), Oswald Doughty (to F. S. Ellis, 1928), Janet Troxell (*Three Rossettis*, 1937), and P. F. Baum (to Fanny Cornforth, 1940), or the many volumes edited by W. M. Rossetti—*The Family Letters with a Memoir* (1895), *Ruskin: Rossetti: Preraphaelitism: Papers 1854 to 1862* (1899), *Præraphaelite Diaries and Letters* (1900), *Rossetti Papers, 1862–1870* (1903)—which remain useful reference books for their introductory material and notes.

Letters is not, as Professor Doughty claims in his too-brief introduction, "comprehensive." At least two major collections of letters—belonging to Sir Derwent Hall Caine and Mrs. Troxell—were inaccessible to the editors. Several published letters have been inadvertently overlooked. The matter of completeness must be the principal concern of the scholar for this edition, and the exclusion of one group of published and three library collections of unpublished letters is a serious weakness. Doughty states in his Preface that Rossetti's letters to Jane Morris (which were removed from reserve at the British Museum in January 1964) became available when this edition was already in proof. Presumably, the same qualification explains the absence of the twenty-nine letters in Lona Packer's *Rossetti-Macmillan Letters* (1963), and the many letters in Gale Pedrick's *Life with Rossetti* (1964) not printed in this edition, but no editorial explanation is given to account for the missing letters from Rossetti to Frederic George Stephens in the Stephens Papers in the Bodleian, nor for the more than six hundred letters in the Humanities Research Center at the University of Texas. The letters to Jane Morris have not as yet been published but R. C. H. Briggs's "Letters to Janey" (*JWMS*, 1964) is a thorough documentary account of their contents, which proved less sensational than many Rossetti students had expected, or hoped.

The *Letters of Dante Gabriel Rossetti*, despite its limitations, will be, when the projected index volume makes the letters accessible, a useful edition. It hardly approaches the level of excellence of Cecil Y. Lang's magnificent *Swinburne Letters* (six volumes, 1959–1962); but the convenience of having such a quantity of Rossetti's correspondence dependably edited in a single edition will partially compensate for its deficiencies.

III. BIOGRAPHIES

It is impossible within the scope of the present survey to discuss in detail the forty books — sixteen of which are full-scale biographies — on Dante Gabriel Rossetti that may be construed, in part at least, as biographical. Several facts of Rossetti's life account for the biographical curiosity and speculation that has been the prominent concern of students with his works: his foreign background, his magnetic personality which attracted so many writers and artists; the tragic denouement of his engagement and marriage to Elizabeth Siddal and the mysterious circumstances surrounding her death; the burial of his poems with his wife and their eventual exhumation; and the ambiguous nature of his relationship with Jane Morris, the wife of his best friend. Rossetti sought to forestall the scandal-mongers by delegating to his old friend Theodore Watts-Dunton the role of biographer. The nearest Watts-Dunton came to writing the official life was in an article consisting of personal recollections which he published the year after Rossetti's death, deceptively entitled "The Truth about Rossetti" (*Nineteenth Century*,

1883). Readers who remembered Hall Caine's comment that it was to Watts-Dunton that Rossetti "unlocked the most sacred secrets of his heart" must have found the article anticlimactic. William Michael Rossetti waited a discreet thirteen years before publishing his *Memoir* (to accompany the *Family Letters*, 1895). Oswald Doughty lays the responsibility for the "ridiculous, idealized, public image of the poet" as a "darkly brooding, mysterious, mystical, poet recluse, a Byronic hero who was also a *Vates Sacer*, a Poet-Seer," at the doorstep of Watts-Dunton and Hall Caine, acolytes of Rossetti's declining years.

Two biographies were published in the year of Rossetti's death (1882), both by friends from the later part of Rossetti's life: Hall Caine's *Recollections* and William Sharp's *Dante Gabriel Rossetti: A Record and a Study*. Caine's book consists of personal recreations of conversations with Rossetti on literary and artistic subjects, and the volume is liberally sprinkled with excerpts from Rossetti's many letters to the young litterateur. Rossetti, who by 1880 had alienated many of his old friends, clung in later years to the new generation of literary aspirants who sought his company, and there is no doubt from the *Recollections* that he regarded Caine as a confidant. Whether he revealed as much as William Bell Scott suspected must await the eventual publication of the poet's correspondence to his come-lately friend. Though Caine's volume is more personal, William Sharp's *Record and Study* is not without value. B. Ifor Evans' evaluation of it as an "undertaker's" biography is patently unfair. Sharp discusses fully Rossetti's contributions to both poetry and art, and the level of many of his critical observations is exceptional for the period. Still useful as a summary is the "Artistic Record" listing Rossetti's paintings and drawings, though H. C. Marillier's *Dante Gabriel Rossetti: An Illustrated Memorial of His Art and Life* (1899) is a fuller and more reliable account, which will remain the standard monograph until Mrs. Virginia Surtees' *catalogue raisonné* is completed. A valuable supplement to Marillier's study is W. M. Rossetti's *Dante Gabriel Rossetti as Designer and Writer* (1889).

Of the remaining books on Rossetti previous to the centenary year, only a few need be singled out. Joseph Knight's *Life* (1887) is unexceptional save for the bibliography appended by J. P. Anderson. W. M. Rossetti's *Memoir* (1895) has defects which the author recognizes as inherent in brotherly biographies. Many of these early biographies, especially the foreign works (seven of which appeared before 1928), deal primarily with Rossetti's art. Most of these volumes are derivative; several, such as Ford Madox Hueffer's *Critical Essay* (1902) and Arthur Symons' *Rossetti* (1909), are impressionistic. A. C. Benson's biography (*EML,* 1904) is unoriginal but still readable.

The centenary year launched a new interest in Rossetti's life, though neither of the two volumes published in that year was particularly distinguished. R. L. Mégroz' *Dante Gabriel Rossetti: Painter Poet of Heaven in Earth* (1928) is divided into a section "Mainly Biographical" and another "Mainly Critical." Mégroz overemphasizes the mystical qualities of Rossetti's life and art, and he presses too hard the romantic love element in the poetry and art toward a formal philosophical system. Evelyn Waugh's biography (1928), concentrating on Rossetti's art, with detailed analyses of individual paintings, is unsympathetic, but his book is relatively free from the anecdotal obsessions of so many early biographies. Waugh's concern to strip away the story-book aspects of the Rossetti legend was prompted by his suspicions about Rossetti's reputation as "supreme man," "king," and "master of the moment," which, he said, "can be achieved by anyone who is dogmatic, plausible, and vain" (p. 13).

A fair number of the Rossetti biographies are popular; many, by the most charitable appraisal, can only be described as sensational. The three historical surveys of Pre-Raphaelitism (by Bickley, Winwar, and Gaunt), which are to so great an extent biographies of Rossetti, all fall into the popular category. Two sensational biographies published during the thirties are Violet Hunt's *The Wife of Rossetti: Her Life and Death* (1932) and David Larg's *Trial by Virgins* (1933). Violet Hunt's book, nominally on Elizabeth Siddal, is in reality a biographical attack on Rossetti. Built on hearsay, scandal, and downright fabrications, this volume, a veritable handbook of quidnuncery, is as much a work of fiction as Nerina Shute's *Victorian Love Story* (1954) or Paula Batchelor's *Angel with Bright Hair* (1957), both novels based on the life of Rossetti.

Almost without exception, biographies of Dante Gabriel Rossetti begin with an introductory chapter on the poet's Italian background, which serves as a prelude to the history of the Rossetti family fortunes in England and provides the backdrop against which the life-story of the principal subject is set. The best account is R. D. Waller's *The Rossetti Family* (1932), a full examination of both the Polidori and Rossetti lines, with separate chapters on Dante Gabriel Rossetti and the other children, to 1854. A volume unique for its concentration on Gabriele Rossetti is the admirable scholarly study by E. R. Vincent, *Gabriele Rossetti in England* (1936). The documentary source for most subsequent treatments of this phase of the Rossetti biography, these two books contain supplementary material essential to an understanding of Rossetti's life and career.

The two outstanding biographical examinations of Rossetti appeared in 1949: Signora Helen Rossetti Angeli's *Dante Gabriel Rossetti: His Friends and Enemies;* and Oswald Doughty's *A Victorian Romantic: Dante Gabriel Rossetti* (second edition, 1960). As the niece of Dante Gabriel and the daughter of William Michael Rossetti, Signora Angeli drew on both family papers and tradition. She writes with unique authoritativeness, bringing to her material a spontaneity and wit relatively unclouded by the pious familial concerns that too often characterize her father's treatment of his relations. After three introductory chapters—the first, entitled "Denigration," a survey of previous biographies—the author considers, in separate chapters, fifteen friends and enemies of her uncle, including Charles Augustus Howell, on whom she has done a separate biography, *Pre-Raphaelite Twilight* (1954). Lesser associates are considered in seven further chapters. In the main judicious, these chapters on individuals represent a more organized approach than is normally found in conventional biographies, both a strength and a weak-ness of this book. A total view of the complexity of the man Rossetti comes through, but the effect is harder to sustain in vignette form, and the volume is more useful as a work of reference than as a pure biography.

The standard biography of Rossetti is by Oswald Doughty, who also wrote the pamphlet in the Writers and Their Work series (No. 85, 1957). *A Victorian Romantic* was a welcome departure from the sensational biographies of the thirties when it appeared in 1949 (the second edition is so little revised that it is more accurate to regard it as a reprinting). The author's lack of sympathy with his subject presents its own kind of bias and special pleading, but the book is a brilliant synthesis of an amazing wealth of materials. Doughty's was the first biography to explore in detail Rossetti's passion for Jane Morris, which has become the *idée fixe* of subsequent biographies and of much of the nonbiographical literature. However, Doughty was merely the first biographer to render her articulate as the innominata of *The House of Life.* Elaborating on speculations first advanced by Hall Caine (*My Story,* 1908) and P. F. Baum, in his edition of the sonnet sequence (1928), Doughty makes the Rossetti-Jane Morris relationship the biographical referential for the critical re-examination of Rossetti's poetry; and by a kind of reciprocal illumination the poetry becomes a tool for restoring the palimpsests in Rossetti's life. Later critics, such as J. R. Wahl, have followed Doughty's lead, and Jane Morris has been relegated to the status of a "mournful Pre-Raphaelite pin-up." In 1958, to celebrate the purchase by the University of Kansas of Rossetti's *La Pia,* which formed the centerpiece of a small Pre-Raphaelite exhibition held at the University's art museum, W. D. Paden published a long monograph tracing the biographical relevance of the picture, especially as it applies symbolically to Rossetti's increasing physical and psychological decline, the result of his combined guilt and frustration stemming from his involvement with Jane Morris.

The name and nature of Rossetti's mistresses is not vital to the critical evaluation of either the poetry or the paintings of Rossetti, but because the relationship between Rossetti and Jane Morris remains obscure, it continues to be the preoccupation of many writers. The thinness of the reserved letters in the British Museum seriously impaired Rosalie Glynn Grylls's *Portrait of Rossetti* (1964). The principal virtue of *Portrait of Rossetti* is its authoress' sympathy with her subject, but even this restorative value is mitigated by her intemperate attack on Professor Doughty, whose book this volume in no sense replaces.

Three further studies of Rossetti remain to be examined, though none of the three can be regarded as a major biography. Jacques Savarit's *Tendances mystiques et ésotériques chez Dante-Gabriel Rossetti* (1961), a psychological biography, overemphasizes the aberrant aspects of Rossetti's life to explain his controlling, essentially mystical, aesthetic. The bias of Gale Pedrick's *Life with Rossetti, or, No Peacocks Allowed* (1964) is "towards the domestic rather than the romantic." The main interest of the book lies in the many letters which the author, a great-nephew of Dunn, reproduces. As a supplement to his father's earlier edition of Henry Treffry Dunn's *Recollections of Dante Rossetti and His Circle (Cheyne Walk Life)* (1904), Pedrick's detailed account of the Cheyne Walk period of Rossetti's life is not without biographical significance. G. H. Fleming's *Rossetti and the Pre-Raphaelite Brotherhood* (1967), the first of a two-volume study, has already been mentioned as one of the most convenient historical surveys of the movement to 1854. Fleming's book exposes the vulnerable underside of present-day Rossetti studies: until new material is either discovered or released, there is simply no room for yet another biography. Fleming speaks of the "ponderable barrier" which Doughty's *A Victorian Romantic* has erected "on the path of potential biographers of the most famous Pre-Raphaelite" (p. xii), but this is merely an open admission that Doughty's book predisposes other biographies toward redundancy. Paradoxically, interest in Rossetti's biography is more compulsive than ever. One critic, David Sonstroem, has recently gone so far as to state (in a review of the Doughty-Wahl letters) that "the world no longer cares about the poems and paintings of Rossetti. . . . But the reputation of Rossetti the personality continues to thrive (it owes much to his erratic love-life), and the collected letters will surely increase interest in the man about town" (*VS*, December 1966, p. 222). If this is true—and the proliferation of books on the poet-painter gives no indication of having reached ebb-tide—then the embarrassment of scholarship in 1968 in knowing more about the poets than it does about the poetry is immeasurably greater than it was in 1956 when Professor Jones indicted the biographical imbalance that characterizes the voluminous writings on the English Pre-Raphaelites.

IV. SCHOLARSHIP AND CRITICISM

Rossetti scholarship and criticism, like biography, suffers from a disorder that Marshall McLuhan might diagnose as "information overload." That Rossetti has fared better at the hands of the scholars than the critics may point to telling limitations in his poetry; for, while there is virtually only a handful of seminal critical articles, the scholarship on the poetry is extensive.

Besides the textual studies discussed above under editions, many of the manuscript sources and variant versions of Rossetti's poems have been written up. The forty-five manuscripts of poems in the Bancroft Collection have been described in two articles by Ruth Wallerstein (*MLN*, 1929), who provides texts of two previously unpublished sonnets, and by P. F. Baum (*MP*, 1941). The ambiguous status of the Pierpont Morgan Library manuscript of "The Blessed Damozel" has already been mentioned, together with publications relating to it. A variant in that manuscript is the subject of Joseph F. Vogel's " 'White Rose' or 'White Robe' in 'The Blessed Damozel' " (*ELN*, 1963). Other poems have been treated in considerably less detail. Merill L. Howe's "Some Unpublished Stanzas by Dante Gabriel Rossetti" (*MLN*, 1933) recorded as by Rossetti and reproduced the text of "A Border Song," which was not included in *Works* (1911); a decade later, S. N. Ray (*MLN*, 1943) traced the discovery of the ballad (signed "D. G. R." and published in volume II of *Once A Week*, 1860) through the columns of *Notes and Queries* (1894). "The Full Text of Rossetti's Sonnet on *Sordello*" (one of the *bout-rimé* sonnets), only the octave of which was published in *Works* (1911), was restored by Robert F. Metzdorf (*HLB*, 1953). A minor textual comment is Jon Bracker's "Notes on the Texts of Two Poems by Dante Gabriel Rossetti" (*LCUT*, 1963), on emendations of "The Carillon" (later "Antwerp and Bruges") and "The Orchard Pit," based on readings in Doughty's anthology (see editions). Finally, there are two studies of early versions of "Sister Helen" by Otto Jiriczek (*GRM*, 1911) and M. Forster (*Die Leipziger Neunundneunzig*, 1929), but both have been taken into account in Mrs. Troxell's edition of the poem (1939).

It was as a translator that Rossetti made his first major incursion into literature. Superseding an earlier article by W. N. Guthrie (*SR*, 1909), important for two appended letters from W. M. Rossetti dealing with his brother's translations, is Oswald Doughty's "Dante Gabriel Rossetti as Translator" (*Theoria*, 1953), which concentrates on *The Early Italian Poets* (1861) and concludes that "Rossetti's attitude as translator and editor was that of an artist, not of an academic" (p. 105). Although P. F. Baum's "Rossetti's 'The Leaf' " (*MLQ*, 1941) treats a specific poem, the author is also interested generally in the poet as a translator; Albert E. Trombly, in "A Translation of Rossetti's" (*MLN*, 1923), deals exclusively with "The Leaf," which he shows to derive from Arnault, though it purports to be a translation from Leopardi. Both Cecil Y. Lang and Rossiter Bellinger have examined Rossetti's "John of Tours" and "My Father's Close": Lang provides the probable French originals from Gérard de Nerval (*PMLA*, 1949), and Bellinger, in "Rossetti's Two Translations from 'Old French'" (*MLN*, 1950) evaluates their literary worth. Finally, Anne Paolucci compares "Ezra Pound and D. G. Rossetti as Translators of Guido Cavalcanti" (*RR*, 1960).

Rossetti's early interest in languages produced two precocious translations (of Burger's *Lenore* and of Hartmann von Aue's *Henry the Leper*), both of which are discussed in L. A. Willoughby's *Dante Gabriel Rossetti and German Literature* (1912). Rossetti's reading in Italian literature after 1844 was enormous—see Albert M. Turner's "Rossetti's Reading and his Critical Opinions" (*PMLA*, 1927)—leading to translations, to imitations of Italian verse forms, especially the sonnet, and to original composition, the subject of R. C. Simonini, Jr.'s "Rossetti's Poems in Italian" (*Italica*, 1948). The influence of Dante was paramount in Rossetti's early poetry and art, and he expropriated themes as well as subjects from Dante. His attitude toward the primacy of love, the source of what many critics see as his essential mysticism, can be traced directly to the *Vita Nuova*, the "auto-psychological" aspects of which are apparent in *The House of Life*. There are several studies of Rossetti and Dante: *Dante Gabriel Rossetti in Relation to Dante Alighieri*, by Walter Butterworth (1912); B. J. Morse's "Dante Gabriel Rossetti and Dante Alighieri" (*Englische Studien*, 1933); and Nicolette Gray's *Rossetti, Dante and Ourselves* (1947). While all three authors treat both the literary and artistic influence of Dante, Miss Gray's book, an "interim essay," is devoted principally to establishing the basic differences between the two poets, particularly in their respective views on love. Of his illustrations, Rossetti once said that his method was to "allegorize on my own hook." Miss Gray shows convincingly, through an examination of Rossetti's direct translations, that for him Dante was essentially another literary rather than a spiritual source; in interpreting (and translating) him, Rossetti tended to transform the original to fit his own purposes.

Of Rossetti's indebtedness to other Italian poets little investigation has been made, although R. D. Waller's " 'The Blessed Damozel' " (*MLR,* 1931) traces the influence of Dante and other Italian poets on Rossetti's poems; and Federico Olivero, in *Il Petrarca e Dante Gabriele Rossetti* (1933), sees the sonnets of Petrarch as a model for Rossetti's love sonnets. The whole problem of Rossetti's development occupies Kurt Horn's *Zur Entstehungsgeschichte von Dante Gabriel Rossettis Dichtungen* (1909). Other examinations of Rossetti's non-Italian sources are Dwight and Helen Culler's "The Sources of 'The King's Tragedy' " (*SP,* 1944) and P. F. Baum's "Rossetti's 'The White Ship' " (*Library Notes,* 1948).

"With Rossetti," Baum asserted, "hardly any of the forms of Quellenforschung can have any interest; for he was always careful, and even anxious, to avoid the appearance of borrowing" (*The Blessed Damozel,* p. xxxv). While this is not an uncontested opinion, the truth of Baum's statement is supported by the paucity of parallel studies of Rossetti's poetry. Ferdinand Holthausen detailed Biblical echoes in two articles (*GRM,* 1925–1926). James Routh's "Parallels in Coleridge, Keats and Rossetti" (*MLN,* 1910) were nonexistent, and his negative findings were challenged by Wesley Hill Shine, who cites a number of interesting parallels in "rhythm, in subject matter, or in sentiment" which Routh was unable to find, in "The Influence of Keats upon Rossetti" (*Englische Studien,* 1927).

Blake, Poe, and Keats are usually regarded as the three poetic mentors of Rossetti. It is not easy to be profound when comparing poet-artists of the caliber and complexity of Blake and Rossetti. The obvious ranges of comparison—use of dual media, mysticism, decoration—have been explored in a German dissertation by Johanna Bassalik-de Vries (1911), and in a good introductory article by B. J. Morse (*Englische Studien,* 1932); but there is no study in depth of the real aesthetic affinities between the two artists, either in their poetry or painting. Kerrison Preston's book, *Blake and Rossetti* (1944), is jejune. The claims for Poe's influence have always seemed inflated. Ultimately, they are probably based on biographical rather than literary similarities.

Oddly, for all the attention given to Poe by writers on Rossetti, the only extensive comparison of the two has been a German dissertation by H. H. Kühnelt (published in *Bedeutung von Edgar Allan Poe für die englische Literatur,* 1949) and a brief note on "Rossetti and a Poe Image" by John P. Runden (*N&Q,* 1958). Alan D. McKillop's *"Festus* and *The Blessed Damozel"* (*MLN,* 1919) cites parallel passages and suggests that Philip James Bailey's poem, introduced to Rossetti by the American, Charles Ware, in 1845, was more influential on Rossetti's poem than Poe's "The Raven." A contrasting view is presented by Paul Lauter, in "The Narrator of 'The Blessed Damozel' " (*MLN,* 1958), who draws a close parallel between the two poems.

As G. H. Ford says in his excellent *Keats and the Victorians* (1944; reprinted, 1962) —which replaces the only other book on the subject, Leonie Villard's *The Influence of Keats on Tennyson and Rossetti* (1914) — "early biographers of Rossetti . . . took for granted that he had drawn from Keats" (p. 123). Ford's own "contention is that the reader who senses the influence of Keats in certain passages and the scholar who examines the passages minutely and often finds *exact* parallels absent, are both right" (p. 124). It is not unusual to encounter the claim that Keats was the first Pre-Raphaelite, but such a claim merely confounds both criticism and literary history.

Rossetti's greatest influence on contemporary and later writers was obviously on his fellow Pre-Raphaelites. One comparison of the poetry and poetic theory of Morris and Rossetti is unpublished and (it is rumored) restricted; the chapter in Albert J. Farmer's *Le Mouvement esthétique et "décadent" en Angleterre (1873–1900)* (1931) examines both the visual and literary contributions of the Pre-Raphaelites, especially Morris and Rossetti, to the *fin de siècle.* The whole matter of Rossetti's influence remains to be explored. The few studies to date are either excessively general or suspiciously eccentric. Rossetti's impact on the Imagists might prove a rewarding pursuit; T. Wilson West's "D. G. Rossetti and Ezra Pound" (*RES,* 1953) is restricted to a few parallel passages and similarities in diction in Pound's early poetry. The two German studies of Rossetti and Stefan George (1868–1933), by Adelheid Klinnert (1933) and Ralph Farrell (*Stefan Georges Beziehungen zur englischen Dichtung,*

1937), are less surprising than two recent articles by Yao Shen and Clyde de L. Ryals. The first, "Accident or Universality," indicates a similarity in theme between Rossetti's "The Blessed Damozel" and Pai Chü Yi's "Song of a Guitar" (*WHR*, 1955–56); Ryals, in "The 'Inner Experience': The Aesthetic of Rossetti and Isak Dineson" (*RLV*, 1960), compares Dineson's "The Young Man with the Carnation" with Rossetti's "Hand and Soul," both of which, with differences that appear more significant than their similarities, proclaim that "art is a religious activity" (p. 373).

Scholarship has solved many—but by no means all—of the problems (textual, source, generic, influence) associated with Rossetti's poetry. However functional such research may be, it fails, as Professor Jones remarked, "to represent the application of modern criticism to a poet in many ways astonishingly contemporary in his psychological processes" (p. 186).

Although Rossetti's poetry has attracted considerable critical attention, there exists no modern full-scale analysis of the canon to replace Mrs. F. S. Boas' historical survey, *Rossetti and his Poetry* (1914); Kurt Horn's systematic but superficial *Studien zum dichterischen Entwicklungsgange Dante Gabriel Rossettis* (1909); and Albert E. Trombly's *Rossetti the Poet: An Appreciation* (1920). Renato Lo Schiavo's *La Poesia di Dante Gabriele Rossetti* (1957), though more current in its documentation, depends too heavily on secondary sources and shares the historical and biographical weaknesses of its predecessors. B. Ifor Evans' survey in *English Poetry in the Later Nineteenth Century* (1933; revised, 1966), for all its generalizations, is as dependable as any introductory account of the poetry.

Nineteenth-century commentary on the poetry tended to be extreme either in its adulation or condemnation. The reviews of *Poems* (1870)—and all the evidence points to Rossetti's having manipulated them—were so consistently eulogistic (Swinburne's, reprinted in *Essays and Studies*, 1875, is a good example) that the volume eventually evoked the infamous attack by Robert Buchanan in *The Fleshly School of Poetry and Other Phenomena of the Day* (1872). The details of Buchanan's attack have been fully surveyed by John A. Cassidy in "Robert Buchanan and the Fleshly Controversy" (*PMLA*, 1952), and in G. G. Storey's "Reply" (*PMLA*, 1953). What is important in this belated diatribe-review is Buchanan's singling out from Rosetti's poetry that one element of sensualism, or (as he phrased it) "Fleshliness," that has subsequently become the greatest obstacle to an objective examination of Rossetti's life and work. It is this quality, imperfectly understood, that gave rise, in the later part of the century, to the identification of Rossetti as the father of Aestheticism. This view—promulgated by Pater's essay (1880; revised and reprinted in *Appreciations,* 1889), by Walter Hamilton in his *The Aesthetic Movement in England* (1882), and by F. W. H. Myers in his perceptive "Rossetti and the Religion of Beauty" *(Essays: Modern,* 1883)—still persists in modern criticism. Barbara Charlesworth, in limning the "Decadent Consciousness in Victorian Literature," in *Dark Passages* (1965), begins her analysis with an extended discussion of Rossetti in which she attributes to him the same escapist fragmentation or splintering of experience that characterizes the "Decadent Moment."

Works dealing with Rossetti's ideas, with what many writers loosely label his philosophy—of love, women, religion—far outnumber critical examinations of his poetry. Rossetti's conception of "Fundamental Brainwork" refers, however, not to the content of poetry but to the particular textural and structural synthesis that is working within the poem. Of studies treating this aspect there are almost none. Among the best work done on his general poetry, and vital to a complete understanding of his art, are the *Malerdichter*-type analyses, which concentrate on the dynamic interrelationship between his poetry and his painting, the reciprocal techniques of the dual media, and aesthetic advantages and limitations that accrue either from imposing one art on another or synthesizing the two. Among such studies, three are outstanding. The earliest is Eva Tietz's "Das Malerische in Rossettis Dichtung" *(Anglia,* 1927). Dr. Tietz's study, focusing on visual elements, goes beyond both the *ut pictura poesis* theory of the eighteenth century and the rather naive studies of the nineteenth to examine the technical way in which the particular painterly qualities such as perspective, linear forms, and color, function in the poetry. Oswald Doughty, in "Rossetti's Conception of the 'Poetic' in Poetry and Painting" *(EDH,* 1953), emphasizes that Rossetti "was not only a poet-painter, he was a 'poetic'-painter and a poet as well." His "poetry" is "common to both the arts he practised" (p. 91). Freely paraphrased, Doughty's thesis is that this "poetic" element in Rossetti derived from an ideal or "dream-world of beauty, both sensuous and emotional [in which] he lived his 'real' life, his most significant existence" (p. 98). The intellectual aspect of Rossetti's "poetic" is found in the medieval Platonic and Neo-Platonic ideas which evoke in him an "emotional energy and sensuous imagery."

The *Malerdichter* studies often stress different qualities. Dr. Tietz emphasizes the technical aspects of artistic composition in the poetry; Doughty enlarges on the poetic idea central to Rossetti's dual media. The third study, Wendell Stacy Johnson's "D. G. Rossetti as Painter and Poet" (*VP*, 1965) is concerned with subject matter and imagery. After a brief review of the "sister arts" in the Victorian period, Johnson compares the imagery in the paired poem-pictures of Rossetti "to demonstrate the degree of relationship between picture and poem" (p. 13). As might be expected, the largest part of the article is devoted to "The Blessed Damozel" (of which there are several pictorial and poetic versions). Johnson's final statement puts nicely the dilemma involved in using the phrase "poet-painter" to classify Rossetti: " . . . the accent hovers between the two words in that ambiguous phrase when we consider his work as a whole" (p. 18).

An incidental value in Johnson's essay is his retort (in a brief footnote) to Harold L. Weatherby's article, "Problems of Form and Content in the Poetry of Dante Gabriel Rossetti" (*VP*, 1964). Weatherby argues that despite Rossetti's "conscious efforts at the creation of poetic forms, his content, which in the final analysis is the only thing that can validate form, often failed him. Or he failed it" (p. 19). While he often writes good poetry, Weatherby contends, "he wrote only a few good *poems*." Johnson's rebuttal is deft and well taken: Rossetti's "inability to merge form and reality completely, to merge the heavenly ideal with the earthly flesh, can be both a cause of incoherence in his poetry and—in certain poetic moments, as in some early pictures —a source of tension that is formally controlled" (p. 11, n. 6).

Reflecting that Rossetti is almost a one-poem poet, it is somewhat surprising to realize that most of the explicatory articles on Rossetti have been written on *The House of Life*. Even more startling is the fact that "The Blessed Damozel" has received not one serious and detailed analytical study. Nor, indeed, have most of Rossetti's other works. Stanley Williams' brief chapter on "Two Poems by Rossetti" (*Studies in Victorian Literature*, 1924) is a pleasant essay on "The Blessed Damozel" and "Jenny," but it is hardly criticism, let alone explication. The only other essay on "The Blessed Damozel," besides those mentioned earlier under editions and textual studies, is Elizabeth Jackson's technical "Notes on the Stanza of Rossetti's 'The Blessed Damozel' " (*PMLA*, 1943). W. C. DeVane, in his "The Harlot and the Thoughtful Young Man: A Study of the Relation between Rossetti's 'Jenny' and Browning's 'Fifine at the Fair' " (*SP*, 1932), sees "Fifine," as Rossetti himself saw it, as an attack on "Jenny." A brief analysis of "The Staff and Scrip" appeared with a translation of the poem by Kurt Horn (*ZFEU*, 1927). There is an article in Japanese by Sanechika Kodama on Rossetti's "One Dream Alone" (*Dóshisha Daigaku Jimbungaku*, 1958). Clyde K. Hyder's "Rossetti's *Rose Mary*: A Study in the Occult" (*VP*, 1963) is almost unique in being one of the few genuine explications of a Rossetti poem other than *The House of Life*. In this erudite article, Hyder demonstrates that "the occult is so successfully interwoven with the story as to obscure the degree of the poet's originality" (p. 197). He examines Rossetti's probable sources, the narrative, imagery, and external trappings of the poem, and finally relates motifs in "Rose Mary" to recurring themes and devices in other of Rossetti's poems. A detailed analysis of one poem in which Rossetti successfully "resolves his intellectual-emotional dichotomy" is Ronnalie R. Howard's "Rossetti's *A Last Confession*: A Dramatic Monologue" (*VP*, 1967).

To encounter *The House of Life* critically is to engage with what P. F. Baum once called the "biographical imperative." Most critics seem incapable of disassociating the poem from what they believe to be its autobiographical nature, and the poem has become more a document than a work of art. *The House of Life* is not unlike two other works by Rossetti in this respect, except that both "The Blessed Damozel" and the prose allegory "Hand and Soul" tend to be read as biographically anticipatory, foreshadowings of eventuality confirming Rossetti's essential mysticism. Colin Franklin's " 'The Blessed Damozel' at Penkill" (*EIC*, 1964), and B. J. Morse's "A Note on the

Autobiographical Elements in Rossetti's 'Hand and Soul' "
(*Anglia*, 1930) are in this sense conventional readings.

Besides the major studies of *The House of Life,* there are
several short explications of individual sonnets and smaller divi-
sions within the poem. Of these lesser studies, Douglas J.
Robillard's "Rossetti's 'Willowwood' Sonnets and the Structure of
The House of Life" (*VN,* 1962) is by far the most important.
Robillard considers the four "Willowwood" sonnets as "central
. . . to the pattern of the work, . . . a pivot on which the whole
structure turns" (p. 6). His discussion focuses on the 1869 and
1870 fragmentary versions of the poem, however, and his reading
is less secure when applied to the whole of the sequence. John
Lindberg's "Rossetti's Cumaean Oracle" (*VN,* 1962) treats the
concluding sonnet of *The House of Life,* "The One Hope,"
which, in his reading, "implies that Rossetti's theme is inexhaus-
tible, not to terminate in a round century of rimes. The sequence
might continue in recurring cycles as an aesthetic extension of
personality." Three *Explicator* articles on individual sonnets are
those of Joseph F. Vogel, on Sonnet 87, "Death's Songsters" (1963),
and Sonnet 81, "Memorial Thresholds" (1964); and Helen Buttel,
on Sonnet 2, "Bridal Birth" (1964). John Masefield's brief notes
on the sonnets in *Thanks Before Going* (1947) should also be
cited.

In the first extended critical study of *The House of Life,* by
Frederick M. Tisdel (*MP,* 1917), the sonnets are considered as
occasional poems reflecting some incident or emotion in the
poet's life. Tisdel's main contribution was to the chronology of
the composition of the sonnets. Ruth Wallerstein, in "Personal
Experience in Rossetti's *House of Life*" (*PMLA,* 1927), was not
concerned, as was Tisdel, with the identity of the "new love";
she reads the sequence as "autobiographical, telling in various
forms the story of Rossetti's love for his wife" (p. 494). Opposed
to the biographical critics who read *The House of Life* either
as literal biography reflecting the known facts of Rossetti's life
or "as a kind of anagrammatical sonnet-memoir," William E.
Fredeman, in his "Rossetti's 'In Memoriam': An Elegiac Read-
ing of *The House of Life*" (*BJRL,* 1965), examines the poem as
a "finished work of art." In three sections, the structure of the
poem is discussed; the biographical claims made about the poem

are examined; and a reading of the poem based on the two previous sections is suggested, "concluding with an interpretive analysis of the [poem] as a kind of 'In Memoriam,' a retrospective review of Rossetti's life 'transfigured' in artistic terms that are essentially elegiac" (p. 302). Fredeman sees the structure of the entire cycle as a large sonnet, to which the Introductory Sonnet serves as prologue. A major analysis of the poem, appearing in the same year, J. L. Kendall's "The Concept of the Infinite Moment in *The House of Life*" *(VN)*, concentrates on the sonnets in Part I, though he advocates a total view of the poem. "The best key to the unifying imaginative concept is Rossetti's pre-occupation with time," which he abhors. Love and Time are at odds to preserve the infinite moment, a term Kendall borrows from Browing criticism.

The two most recent studies of the poem (both in French) are by Henri A. Talon. The first, "Dante Gabriel Rossetti, peintre-poète dans *La Maison de Vie*" *(EA,* 1966), belongs to the *Malerdichter* class discussed above. Talon is more subtle in his comprehension of the poet-painter than most previous critics. His distinction between Rossetti the landscape painter and Rossetti the portraitist is crucial to the thesis of his article, for not only does it de-emphasize the presence of the two beloveds in the poem, it also subordinates them to the natural imagery. Rossetti's principal subject is woman, but she is never particularized: "Le portraitiste est vaincu par le paysagiste . . . " (p. 4). Rossetti unites in his word-paintings "sa vision et son amour de la femme qui sont l'âme de son esthétique" (p. 5). Talon's second and much longer study, *D. G. Rossetti: The House of Life: Quelques aspects de l'art, des thèmes, et du symbolisme* (1966), is divided into two parts. The first is an extended analysis of seven individual sonnets from the sequence all chosen because they clarify " 'l'art poétique' de Rossetti, la virtuosité du sonnettiste et certains thèmes de l'oeuvre." Part II is devoted to short essays on four aspects of the symbolism in *The House of Life:* personal experience, natural imagery ("L'arbre et la fleur"), the circle which unites the temporal with the eternal, and the transference of personal to universal or archetypal symbols. Talon's work on *The House of Life* restores to the poem some of the integrity which, because of the misplaced emphasis of the biographical critics, it has been in constant danger of losing.

Concluding his excellent general discussion of *The House of Life* in *The Romantic Imagination* (1949), C. M. Bowra says that the poem "presents what was most powerful in Rossetti's creative being": "Though Rossetti lacks the sweep and the scope of the great Romantics, though at times he seems remote or exotic, too enclosed in his special outlook and too careless of the world about him, he stands in the true Romantic tradition because of his belief in the mystery of life" (p. 220).

CHRISTINA ROSSETTI

Of Christina Rossetti, H. Buxton Forman remarked in his essay in *Our Living Poets* (1871), "the first thing that strikes us on going through this lady's works is that she is a poet: this impression is the earliest, because we *feel* it; and the second thing which comes forward prominently — second, because we find it out by *thinking*, not *feeling* — is that she is a Preraphaelite poet, profoundly influenced by the Preraphaelite movement in literature, and perfectly conscious of certain principles in workmanship" (p. 235).

Christina Georgina Rossetti has been grossly misrepresented as the "high-priestess of Preraphaelitism" (Edmund Gosse, *Critical Kit-Kats,* 1896), as a Pre-Raphaelite "Saint by Chance" (Z. E. Green, *English Review,* 1936), and most recently as "la vierge sage des préraphaélites" (C. Murciaux, *Revue de Paris,* 1964); but her role in the movement is more tenuous and less self-conscious than these epithets imply. "For me, as well as for Gabriel," Christina wrote to Edmund Gosse, "whilst our

284

'school' was everything, it was no one definite thing"; herself she regarded as "the least and last of the group." As a *Germ* poet, the sister of two PRB's and the fiancé of another, it is not surprising that Christina has been regarded as a satellite of the Brotherhood. Certainly *Goblin Market* was the most successful of the early Pre-Raphaelite volumes, and its title poem evinces strong Pre-Raphaelite affinities in its marked pictorial detail applied to an exotically fanciful narrative. But, as Sir Maurice Bowra has shown, Christina Rossetti's poetic talent was so natural that she could use Pre-Raphaelitism without "surrendering any of her originality" (*The Romantic Imagination*, 1949, p. 247). Her nephew, Ford Madox Ford (*Memories and Impressions*, 1911), regards her as transcending the limitations of Pre-Raphaelitism, expecially the Ruskinian sort. She was, he asserts convincingly, more modern than the rest.

By almost universal consensus, Christina Rossetti is regarded as a serious and significant poet, and she "has a place not far from the highest among English religious poets" (Bowra, p. 246). The secret of her style, said Arthur Symons (Miles, VII, pp. 418-419), "which seems innocently unaware of its own beauty," is its sincerity, "yet not sincerity only, but sincerity as the servant of a finely touched and exceptionally *seeing* nature. A power of seeing finely beyond the scope of ordinary vision: that, in a few words, is the note of Miss Rossetti's genius." Christina Rossetti's dual personality found expression in two distinct canons, and the reader who restricts himself exclusively to the secular poetry misses the complexity and subtlety of her aesthetic-cum-religious syntheses. Thus, it may be unenlightening to press too closely the Pre-Raphaelitism of Christina Rossetti, who "presents . . . the case of a poet whose naturally Romantic tendencies were turned into a different channel by the intensity of her religious faith" (Bowra, p. 269).

I. WORKS AND LETTERS

The standard edition of Christina Rossetti, *The Poetical Works*, edited with a memoir and notes by William Michael Rossetti (1904), is a most exasperating volume to use. When Christina Rossetti collected her *Poems* in 1890, she arranged them into two series, removing a few poems and adding others previously unpublished. In 1896, W. M. Rossetti edited a volume of *New Poems,* primarily unpublished poems existing only in manuscript; he also restored some of the poems which his sister had dropped from her own collection. He did not, however, either in 1896 or 1904, rake "together all that I could find" but "left unused a considerable number of compositions that were at my disposal," a decision with which Swinburne heartily concurred (see Lang, VI, 179). In an appendix to the Table of Contents, W. M. Rossetti conveniently lists the titles of excluded poems for "some future editor, who might really be minded to carry to its utmost limit the 'raking-together' process." William Michael's editorial decision to limit his sister's canon according to his own lights emphasizes the critical disparity between literary sensibilities a half-century apart; but the existence of more than sixty poems not incorporated into the *Poetical Works* (see pp. xli-xliii) makes all the more desirable a complete edition.

Exclusion is not the only basis for faulting William Michael's edition, however. The arrangement of the poems under six arbitrary headings makes location difficult, a handicap which the Index of First Lines does little to assuage. Since the poems are arranged neither alphabetically nor chronologically, the volume inhibits both a systematic study of the poet's artistic development and easy reference to a given poem by title. The introductory memoir and notes to the volume are useful, however, and lacking a definitive edition, the 1904 *Poetical Works* is indispensable.

Christina Rossetti's letters have never been brought together in a collected edition. The title given by W. M. Rossetti to the one volume of her letters that has been published (*Family Letters,* 1908) was literally interpreted. Apart from this volume, William Michael made few of his sister's letters public — there are several hundred among the Angeli Papers — confining himself to the handful in *Ruskin: Rossetti: Preraphaelitism* (1899) and *Rossetti Papers, 1862–70* (1903). He did, however, allow Mackenzie Bell to use unpublished letters in his *Christina Rossetti* (1898). Three further groups of correspondence have been made available, by Janet Troxell, S. G. Putt, and Lona Packer. In *Three Rossettis* (1937), Mrs. Troxell devotes two chapters to Christina Rossetti's letters in her own collection. The first, concerned with the publication of *The Prince's Progress*, contains three letters to Dante Gabriel; the second is a general discussion of Christina Rossetti's correspondence in which nearly thirty letters to various recipients are reproduced. S. Gorley Putt's "Christina Rossetti, Alms-giver" (*English,* 1961) examines nine letters (at Yale) from the poetess to William Bryant of Clerkenwell, a professional leech whose frequent "begging letters" taxed sorely the patience of even Christina's charity. The largest collection of Christina Rossetti's letters to be published in recent times is that in *The Rossetti-Macmillan Letters* (1963), edited by Lona Packer, which includes ninety-six letters from Christina. Most of these letters were discovered in the files of Macmillan and Company, but the author also used the letters to F. S. Ellis in the British Museum. These letters, while not sensationally revealing, provide an illuminating account of the literary and business practices of the Rossetti family and they underscore the reciprocal interest of the Rossettis in one another's activities. At the same time, they are useful for their commentary on Christina Rossetti's poetic career. Professor Packer also edited two other groups of Christina Rossetti's unpublished letters: to Alice Boyd of Penkill Castle (*TLS,* 26 June 1959), and to her nephew, Arthur Rossetti (*N&Q,* December 1959). She made use of these primary materials both in her biography of the poet (see below) and in such articles as "F. S. Ellis and the Rossettis: A Publishing Venture and Misadventure, 1870" (*WHR,* 1962), and "Swinburne and Christina Rossetti: Atheist and Anglican" (*UTQ,* 1963). From the letters that have been published to date, it is clear that a complete edition of her correspondence should have a high priority among the desiderata of scholarship on Christina Rossetti.

II. BIOGRAPHY AND CRITICISM

It must surely be no accident that Christina Rossetti has appealed almost exclusively to female biographers and critics. With the lone exception of the first major study of her life and work, Mackenzie Bell's *Christina Rossetti: a Biographical and Critical Study* (1898), every biography of the poet has been written by a woman. The magnet of their attraction has normally been the extremes of religion or frustrated love. F. L. Lucas' tantalizing comment, in an otherwise drab essay on Christina Rossetti (*Ten Victorian Poets,* 1940), that "this Mariana of Albany Street was born to have been one of the great lovers of history," might easily serve as the epigraph for a dozen books and articles. The roster of lady-biographers between Mackenzie Bell and Lona Mosk Packer — some more critical than others — includes Justine F. de Wilde (*Poet and Woman,* 1923), Mary F. Sanders (1930), Dorothy Stuart (*EML,* 1930), Sara Teasdale (1932), Marya Zaturenska (*A Portrait with a Background,* 1949), and Margaret Sawtell (*Her Life and Religion,* 1955). As examples of the feminine bias that controls so much of the writing about Christina Rossetti, the essays by Elizabeth Parker ("The Love Affairs of Christina Rossetti," *University Magazine,* 1919), Irene M. Shipton ("The Poetess of the Oxford Movement," *Church Quarterly Review,* 1933), and Zaidee E. Green ("Saint by Chance," *English Review,* 1936) may be mentioned as characteristic. Finally, and in keeping with the tradition, the recent Writers and their Work pamphlet on Christina Rossetti (No. 189, 1965) is also by a woman, Georgina Battiscombe, the biographer of Charlotte Yonge.

These biographies are not uniformly bad or uncritical, but they are incrementally repetitive, depending almost exclusively for their documentation on Mackenzie Bell, W. M. Rossetti, or one another. The occasional intuitive insight into the poetry does not, unfortunately, compensate for the lack of new material, which enabled Bell's volume to remain unsurpassed, at least until 1963. Bell's five chapters on Christina Rossetti's life are unquestionably superior to their counterparts which purport to be critical. Factual rather than speculative, Bell tells a dull and unenlivened story that fails to satisfy readers of a more romantic bent.

The truth is that Christina Rossetti's external life was dull and uneventful, and Bell was unconcerned with recreating, let alone hypothesizing, her inner or "secret" life. Failing to find in the known biographical details an adequate explanation for the tensions, frustrations, and passions apparent in her poetry, her biographers too frequently resort to playing games, making of her poems gnomic biographical anagrams to define the boundaries of a psycho-sexual existence sublimated in terms of religious experience. Religion, in this context, becomes for Christina Rossetti what chloral was for Dante Gabriel. "No woman," Sir Maurice Bowra observes, "could write with this terrible directness if she did not to some degree know the experience which she describes" (p. 261). But if Charles B. Cayley (and by extension James Collinson) was "but a weak prop on which to hang such love poetry as Christina's," as Georgina Battiscombe says (p. 20), who is the source of all this ardor? Two explanations are possible. One is that framed by Bowra (but implicit in many interpretations) that "Only in God could she find a finally satisfying object for the abounding love which was the mainspring of her life and character" (p. 270). To this view, Miss Battiscombe subscribes, explaining that Christina's refusal of love was not an expression of horror at the thought of sexual intimacy; "it was not the nature but the inadequacy of the demands of the flesh which made her turn away to another love" (p. 21), which in her case was divine. "It was," says Bowra, "this conflict between her human self and her divine calling which created her most characteristic poetry" (p. 269). Insofar as this thesis posits a sensuality that frequently accompanies the mystical, Bowra's theory does provide critical access to Christina Rossetti's poetry, though it hardly satisfies his qualification about the necessary directness of the experiences described. And this qualification leads to the second possible explanation: that lurking beneath the surface of this intense love poetry hides an unidentified object of affection and yearning, an innominate lover whom the poet has chosen to leave unrevealed. He might, of course, be an idealization, a sublimation of the poet's frustrated desires, but feminine intuition is unlikely to be satisfied by vagaries on this score. Since a real-live man has more to recommend him than an imaginary one, candidates must be sifted and subjected to a "scholarly" scrutiny which the Louis Parensells of biographical romance lack the substance to withstand.

Female biographers — especially female biographers of other females — often seem possessed of an intuitional capacity inaccessible to men, the biographers of Christina Rossetti's brother Dante Gabriel notwithstanding. Every good biographer needs what may be called the empathic faculty — the ability to project himself into the actual life situations and even the emotions of his subject. But to extend this faculty toward a literal parody of Virginia Woolf's " 'I am Christina Rossetti' " (*Second Common Reader*, 1932) is apt to result in what R. H. Super has justifiably called "novel writing for the uncreative."

The most recent, distinctly the best, and certainly the most extreme book in the long line of lady-biographies is *Christina Rossetti* (1963) by the late Professor Lona Mosk Packer, the most distinguished Christina Rossetti scholar yet to appear. Professor Packer's book is a serious study of the poet but it depends too heavily on unsupported speculation for its major thesis. Drawing on a variety of previously unused and unpublished manuscript sources, Professor Packer arrives at a reading of Christina Rossetti's life and poetry that is psychologically of major importance. She identifies William Bell Scott, the minor Pre-Raphaelite poet, painter, and intimate associate of her two brothers, as the innominate lover in Christina Rossetti's life. Most of the "evidence" marshalled by Professor Packer to support her theory that William Bell Scott was her secret lover and the inspirational source of her passionate love poetry was either speculative or drawn directly from the poetry itself. There is no documentation among extant literary papers to substantiate the liaison. In fact, William E. Fredeman offered counterevidence against the Scott theory from the recently discovered Penkill Papers, now in the Special Collections of the University of British Columbia Library (*VS*, 1964). R. D. Waller, in his chapter on Christina Rossetti in *The Rossetti Family* (1932), observed that "like her brother in *The House of Life*, Christina is often too enigmatic to escape questioning" (p. 235). This enigmatic quality — the sadness of her verse and her early preoccupation with the theme of the lost lover, even in the poems of 1847 — has tempted biographers to explain externally experiences which (to use Waller's phrase out of context) were "distilled from her inner life, and not usually visable on the surface" (p. 240). Professor Packer's intuition in seizing on an emotional relevance in Christina's poetry not explained by the "traditional biographical line" fostered by W. M. Rossetti is almost certainly viable, adding dimension and meaning to much of the canon; but in linking this emotional relevance so inextricably to the Scott theory she weakened her major thesis. Her biography is, never-theless, with this important qualification, an essential book for any serious student of Christina Rossetti, and it makes redundant — because it is the apogee of this particular genre — the seven or eight lady-biographies which precede it.

Biographical has long outstripped critical interest in Christina Rossetti, and the body of valuable criticism on the poetry is not extensive. The only two book-length studies — Edith Birk-head's *Christina Rossetti and Her Poetry* (1930) and Fredegond Shove's *Christina Rossetti: A Study* (1931) — are semi-biograph-ical and are no more penetratingly critical than most of the biographies discussed above. In her discussion of *Monna Innominata*, for example, Fredegond Shove notes that though the sonnets are "called after some imaginary and forgotten Italian lady," they "bear really, of course, the impress of Christina Rossetti's own heart": "Read without biographical re-ference... the sonnets... do not bear the stamp of her highest talent and cannot be rated with her best purely lyrical work" (p. 48).

It is difficult to find early studies of Christina Rossetti that emphasize the poetry as poetry. Mary Breme's book (in German) on the influence of the Bible on her poetry (1907), which is concerned with both parallels and stylistic analysis, is almost ex-clusive in this category, though Walter de la Mare — with whom Christina Rossetti shares many obvious qualities — in his essay in *Transactions of the Royal Society of Literature* (1926), con-centrated on her poetry, assuming, as H. M. Jones remarked that "she was an artist and not a moral convalescent." The cen-tenary fervor produced few critical articles of note, most of them being either familial, general, or impressionistic. Morton D. Zabel's "Christina Rossetti and Emily Dickinson" (*Poetry,* 1931) sounds comparisons between the two poets, principally in an isolation from direct experience which culminates in what he calls "the fulfilment of high lyric impulse." B. J. Morse, in "Some Notes on Christina Rossetti and Italy" (*Anglia,* 1931), denies the insularity generally ascribed to Christina Rossetti and points out that in her canon there is not a single impassioned poem on England. Friedrich Dubslaff's *Die Sprachform der Lyrik*

Christina Rossettis (1933) has all the limitations associated with German dissertations, but his is one of the few studies focusing directly on the poetry.

Two post-centenary general studies are those in B. Ifor Evans' *English Poetry in the Later Nineteenth Century* (1933; revised, 1966) and Maurice Bowra's *The Romantic Imagination* (1949). Bowra has already been discussed. Evans' chapter is a general survey of the canon which seldom rises above the critical level of his bland conclusion that Christina Rossetti united "poetry with Pre-Raphaelite décor and the poetry of religious sensibility" (p. 103). In the revised edition, Evans incorporates his own important article on the sources of "Goblin Market" (*MLR*, 1933), in which he traced the antecedents of the poem to Thomas Keightley's *Fairy Mythology*, Allingham's "The Fairies," and the *Arabian Nights*, but except for his recognition of Professor Packer's volume, he has not brought the scholarship up to date. Two other studies of interest are Hoxie N. Fairchild's chapter in volume four of *Religious Trends in English Poetry* (1957), a careful examination of the poetry limited only by the exclusiveness of the author's point of view; and the section on Christina Rossetti in Nesca Robb's *Four in Exile* (1948). Miss Robb's thematic analysis is provocative throughout, the more so because in examining the "doubly lost" paradise that becomes "the burden of a two-fold exile" in Christina Rossetti's "lost lover" poems, she consistently avoids making the biographical concession.

Surprisingly, there is only a handful of articles treating individual poems by Christina Rossetti. Barbara Garlitz, in her examination of " 'Sing Song' and Nineteenth Century Children's Poetry" (*PMLA*, 1955), focuses on an aspect of Christina Rossetti's writing which has always attracted readers and which is central to a recent book on the poet — Thomas B. Swann's *Wonder and Whimsey: The Fantastic World of Christina Rossetti* (1960). Lona Packer's "Symbol and Reality in Christina Rossetti's *Goblin Market*" (*PMLA*, 1958) is a major study of the poem but the stress given to the love-allegory — the Scott theory was first introduced in this article — should be corrected by the reading suggested in Winston Weathers' "Christina Rossetti: The Sisterhood of Self" (*VP*, 1965). Recognizing as "one of the major motifs" in Christina Rossetti's "mythic fabric" the "fragmented self moving or struggling toward harmony and balance," Weathers examines in detail those poems of "sisterhood" in which the poet allegorizes her struggle for identity. "Goblin Market" justifiably commands greatest attention, but Weathers also discusses other poems in the canon which treat this dilemma. Weathers identifies three stages in the poetry — division, conflict, integration — which together lead to a "total mythic picture" that opens up a new "dimension of meaning" in Christina Rossetti's poetry, a dimension "that will lift her work out of the net niche it has occupied for the last century" (p. 89).

Neither Weathers not Richard D. Lynde, in his brief note on "A Birthday" (*VP*, 1965), takes into sufficient account the critical explications of individual poems in Lona Packer's *Christina Rossetti* (1963). Although many, if not most, of her readings of the poems are colored to some extent by the author's forcing them to meet the Scott theory, one of the permanent values of this biography resides in the original and illuminating insights Professor Packer brought to the poetry. If read in the light of their relevance to the poet's general emotional life rather than as documentary evidence of her devotion to a specific person, Professor Packer's explications are certainly among the most important and, indeed, almost the only serious criticism which the poetry of Christina Rossetti has ever received.

WILLIAM MORRIS

In an obituary article entitled "William Morris: Poet, Artist and Craftsman, and Social Reconstructor" (*Progressive Review,*

1896), Walter Crane said that Morris "united Pre-Raphaelite viv-
idness with dream-like wistful sweetness and flowing narrative,
woven in a kind of rich medieval tapestry of verse." Few
critics writing on Morris today would give prominence of place
to Morris the poet; as Jack Lindsay has observed (*William Morris,
Writer*, 1961), "the multifarious activities of William Morris in
art, craft, and design, and in the political expression of his ideas,
have tended to put his role as a writer in the background" (p. 5).
Even Morris' daughter, when she came to edit the two-volume
supplement to the *Collected Works* in 1936, subordinated Morris
the writer to Morris the artist in her subtitle ("Artist, Writer,
Socialist"). Yet as Lindsay has correctly shown, "there is a very
real sense in which it was Morris the poet who provides the
continuity and the dynamic force in all aspects of his develop-
ment." Morris' introduction to Pre-Raphaelitism dated from his
Oxford days, when, together with Burne-Jones and other mem-
bers of the "Set" or "Brotherhood," he came under the influence
of Rossetti. Initially, Morris was overwhelmed by the dominance
of Rossetti's personality, but his period of slavish imitation was
short. The principal attraction of early Pre-Raphaelitism for
Morris was almost certainly its concern with medievalism, which
Walter Gordon has called "the major leitmotif of the Victorian
period — the self-conscious critical appraisal of the present in
terms of the past" ("Pre-Raphaelitism and *The Oxford and Cam-
bridge Magazine*," *JRUL*, 1966, p. 42). Certainly, an intense
medievalism characterized all three of the principal productions
of the Oxford phase of Pre-Raphaelitism: the painting of the
Union murals, *The Oxford and Cambridge Magazine*, and *The
Defence of Guenevere*, in many respects the most Pre-
Raphaelite volume of poetry the movement produced. Morris
gave both a new dimension and direction to Pre-Raphaelitism,
however, and he extended the aesthetic of the movement to
areas of revolt and reform never envisioned by the original PRB's
— the arts and crafts, interior decoration and design, furniture,
tapestries, stained glass, printing, even aesthetic socialism. By
this extension he also altered radically the definition by which
Pre-Raphaelitism was to be recognized; the seminal conception
was Rossetti's, but the triumph of the Morris Movement, in all
its far-reaching manifestations, was, in time, to obliterate the
literal, restrictive definition which Holman Hunt insisted on

until his death.

After *The Earthly Paradise* (1868–70), there is little of Pre-Raphaelitism evident in Morris' literary work, which is largely dominated by his translations, his lectures, and his socialistic writings. It is almost as if, having delineated the search for an earthly paradise and having concluded that if it existed at all it did so only in art, Morris turned to the fundamental task of reshaping, both by precept and example, a world which socially, politically, and aesthetically was inferior to that ideal world of *The Earthly Paradise,* about which he had "idly" sung.

I. WORKS AND LETTERS

With few exceptions, the complete writings of William Morris are available in two standard works, both edited by Morris' daughter: *The Collected Works* in twenty-four volumes (1910–1915), and *William Morris: Artist, Writer, Socialist,* two volumes (1936). Both collections were reprinted in 1966. Although many of Morris' lectures are included in the supplementary volumes to the *Collected Works,* several have never been collected; those unpublished will shortly appear in an edition prepared by Professor Eugene D. Le Mire, which will also contain a Calendar of Morris' complicated career as a public lecturer. Three lesser poems of Morris have been recently discovered and printed: an early sonnet written some time after 1867, in *William Morris and his Praise of Wine,* edited by Ward Ritchie (1958); a poem entitled "Lonely Love and Loveless Death," treating triangulated love, edited by David J. DeLaura (*MP,* 1965); a poem in Eddic meter addressed to Jane Morris, edited by R. C. Ellison (*English,* 1964). Each poem, according to its respective editor, has biographical significance.

Morris students are fortunate in having several good anthologies of his poetry and prose writings to choose from. The poems are selected in the World's Classics (1914), and the Oxford Standard Authors series includes both poetry and prose to 1870 (1920). Both have long been out of print. Since 1930, four important collections have appeared, each with valuable introductory material. A. H. R. Ball's *Selections from the Prose Works* (1931) devotes a disproportionate amount of space to chapters from the major prose works, and in attempting to present a complete picture of the man, the editor is forced into fragmenting his selections. The best of the anthologies is the Nonesuch Centenary Edition, edited by G. D. H. Cole (1934). Widely representative of Morris' works this selection is free from the crippling effects of excerption; and the carefully edited and textually reliable volume is prefaced by a tactful and balanced introductory essay that emphasizes Morris as both creative artist and Socialist. The interrelationship of Morris' artistic and Socialist theories is the informing bias of Holbrook Jackson's anthology of Morris' essays and lectures, *On Art and Socialism* (1947), the only collection of Morris' lectures apart from those published by the writer himself. Spurred by the increasing interest in Morris stimulated by the three Morris exhibitions sponsored by the William Morris Society — *The Typographical Adventure Of William Morris* (1958), *Morris and Company* (1961), and *The Work of William Morris* (1962) — Asa Briggs prepared his anthology of *Selected Writings and Designs* (1962), with a supplement by Graeme Shankland on Morris as designer. Illustrated with twenty-four plates, this Penguin book is not only the most easily procurable collection of Morris' writings; it also reflects, by minimizing the poetry, the new emphasis on Morris as Socialist-craftsman which has in the past decade dominated Morris studies.

A complete edition of Morris' letters has been undertaken by Norman Kelvin for the Stanford University Press. Since an edition of such magnitude must inevitably span years of preparation, it is unlikely that students will have access to Morris' letters in the immediate future. The urgency of this project is readily evinced, both by the paucity of Morris' letters already in print and by the immense importance of those few that are to the advancement of scholarship. The letters are widely scattered, but concentrations are located in the British Museum (see R. Flower, "The William Morris Manuscripts," *BMQ*, 1939–40), the Victoria and Albert Museum, the William Morris Gallery (Walthamstow), the Fitzwilliam Museum, and the University of Texas. "The Morris Letters at Texas" from the Fairfax Murray collection were described by E. E. Stokes, Jr., for the William Morris Society in 1963 (*JWMS*). The only edition of Morris' letters is that by Philip Henderson to Morris' family and friends

(1950), with a biographical and critical introduction. This edition, containing over four hundred letters, includes those printed in Mackail, in May Morris' two collections of her father's writings, and in other sources such as T. J. Wise's privately printed *Letters on Socialism* (1894), but the largest proportion of the letters are published here for the first time. Unfortunately, few early letters of Morris appear in Henderson's edition. R. Page Arnot's *William Morris: The Man and the Myth* (1964), while not exclusively an edition of Morris' letters, publishes the full texts of forty-six letters from Morris to John Lincoln Mahon and John Glasse, Morris' companions in the Socialist League. Fourteen of the eighteen letters to Glasse appeared first in *Unpublished Letters of William Morris* introduced by Arnot (Labour Monthly Pamphlet, 1951). Five letters from Morris to Fred Henderson are published in Appendix III of E. P. Thompson's biography.

II. BIOGRAPHY AND CRITICISM

"Everyone who writes about him is just a little silly," Sir Walter Raleigh once said about William Morris (*Letters*, 1926, II, 396). What this distinguished man of letters may have had in mind is the uncritical adulation and reverence that characterize so much of the writing on Morris. The late Sir Sydney Cockerell, in the introduction to the World's Classics edition of Mackail's famous biography (1950), confirmed that by him and his friends Morris was regarded as flawless. Something of the same total acceptance persists in Morris scholarship to this day: one is either a Morris devotee or in the main ignorant of his works and accomplishments.

Few of the more than twenty biographies of William Morris add substantially to the knowledge of his life and works. The earliest books emphasized his essential duality as artist-craftsman and writer; later studies have tended to stress the political theory underlying his activities in several fields. With some exceptions, most of these studies are derivative, drawing heavily on the standard and official biography, *The Life of William Morris* by J. W. Mackail (1899). Mackail's *Life*, the *Memorials of Sir Edward Burne-Jones*, edited by his wife Georgiana (1904), and

May Morris' prefaces to the individual volumes of the *Collected Works* (1910–1915) are the primary sources for biographical material on Morris.

Mackail's biography, which has always been considered something of a classic (as E. P. Thompson, Morris' most important recent biographer, notes, it is not likely to be superseded as a "year-by-year narrative of the main events in Morris' life"), is deficient in three specific ways. First, in style it is typical of scores of late Victorian commemorative biographies; second, Mackail's hostility to socialism motivated him to minimize and almost ignore this vital stage in Morris' career; and, third, because of his intimate family associations, he was forced to be deferential about certain aspects of Morris' personal relationships.

A corrective to Mackail's deficiencies as biographer is not found in many books before E. P. Thompson's *William Morris: Romantic to Revolutionary* (1955, Second edition, 1961). The aim of R. D. Macleod's *Morris Without Mackail* (1954; reprinted as *William Morris [As Seen by his Contemporaries]*, 1956) was "to endeavour to find the real Morris by going beyond Mackail." Reacting against the sentimental, pious, and threnodic qualities of Mackail's biography, Macleod sought to illuminate corners of Morris' life which Mackail was content (or forced) to leave in the shadows, such as the situation between Rossetti and Jane Morris. He was also concerned to point out how Mackail has misled subsequent biographers who slavishly elaborated his observations on Morris. Unfortunately, Macleod's pamphlet is so clearly biased against Morris as to negate any salutary benefits that might accrue from presenting Morris without Mackail.

It is unnecessary to give more than a cursory survey of most of the intervening biographies between Mackail and Thompson. Most of them now seem both dated and superficial. Holbrook Jackson's *William Morris: Craftsman-Socialist* (1908) was for many years the best of the single-volume studies. Revised with four additional chapters in 1926, the volume is still a useful and reliable introduction, though it is weighted rather heavily toward a hagiological presentation of its subject. The various "series" biographies — English Men of Letters by Alfred Noyes (1908), Home University Library by Arthur Clutton-Brock (1914), Great Lives by Montague Weekley (1934) — have all been superseded, as has Arthur Compton-Rickett's *Study in Personality* (1913). But these volumes, however redundant as biography, all treat Morris' works, including his poetry, and they do offer occasional insights, as do the other two centenary biographies by Paul Bloomfield and H. V. Wiles (1934).

Several early works remain important because they treat specific aspects of Morris' life, art, and thought. G. Vidalenc's *William Morris* (1920) concentrates on Morris' decorative art and on his aesthetic and social theories; Morris' Socialism is also the subject of Anna A. von Helmholtz-Phelan's *The Social Philosophy of William Morris* (1927). Still a central book to Morris studies is John Bruce Glasier's *William Morris and the Early Days of the Socialist Movement* (1921), with a preface by May Morris. Glasier's association with Morris in the Socialist League should lend authority to his reminiscences; however, E. P. Thompson has shown in Appendix IV of his biography, "William Morris, Bruce Glasier and Marxism," that "passages which refer to Morris's attitude to Marxism, to religion, and his relations with Glasier himself, cannot be accepted as trustworthy evidence" (p. 889). *The Kelmscott Press and William Morris, Master-Craftsman* by Henry Halliday Sparling (1924) is the best treatment of Morris' career as a printer and publisher. As a co-editor with Morris on the *Commonweal,* Secretary of the Kelmscott Press, and husband of May Morris, Sparling rightly claimed to be "especially qualified as an interpreter of his teaching." Two lesser studies of Morris may also be mentioned: W. R. Lethaby's *Philip Webb and his Work* (1935), and T. Earle Welby's discussion of Morris in *The Victorian Romantics* (1929; reprinted, 1966). Finally, George Bernard Shaw's *William Morris as I Knew Him* (1936) is an amusing, impressionistic account of Shaw's early acquaintance with the Morris household.

Three further books antedate Thompson. Lloyd W. Eshleman's *A Victorian Rebel: The Life of William Morris* was felt to be inadequate when it appeared in 1940. Its aim, said C. F. Harrold, was to be readable and it failed to be substantial. That general stricture was no less valid when the book reappeared in 1949 as *William Morris, Prophet of England's New Order* by Lloyd Eric Grey, printed apparently from the same plates. Edward and Stephani Godwin's *Warrior Bard: The Life of William Morris*

(1947) is a sentimental biography which makes of Morris' activities a series of moral exempla eulogizing socialism. Esther Meynell's *Portrait of William Morris* (1947), intended as a "study of Morris himself, and not of his work as craftsman or author," is undistinguished but readable.

Sufficient reference has perhaps been made to E. P. Thompson's biography to indicate its original contribution to Morris studies. Indeed, Thompson's is the first book on Morris since Mackail to introduce such a wealth of new biographical material. The author's overwhelming preoccupation is with Morris' Communism and, though his emphasis becomes at times oppressive, it is particularly his treatment of Morris' years of "practical Socialism" that is new in this biography. In the same tradition is R. Page Arnot's *William Morris: The Man and the Myth* (1964), an expansion of his *Vindication* (1934). Arnot distinguishes, in his first chapter, two myths about William Morris—the bourgeois (or "establishmentarian") myth and the Menshevik (or "gentle Socialist") myth. Arnot sets himself the task of destroying both, the first a legacy of Mackail, the second of Bruce Glasier, both bitterly anti-Marxist. Thus, Arnot defines in the latest study the extremes of Morris biographies between Mackail and Thompson. Both Thompson and Arnot represent a divergence from these two mainstreams. It remains to be seen what direction subsequent studies will take. The three most recent books on Morris — *The Work of William Morris* by Paul Thompson, *William Morris, His Life, Work and Friends* by Philip Henderson, and *William Morris as Designer* by Ray Watkinson (all published in 1967) — appeared too late for inclusion in this survey.

Even more than the other two major Pre-Raphaelite poets, Morris has been transformed from an "idle singer" into what R. F. Fleissner has called a "neglected singer." There is no full-scale assessment of his poetry save the short *William Morris and His Poetry* (1925), which the author, B. Ifor Evans, has more or less updated in his *English Poetry in the Later Nineteenth Century* (revised edition, 1966) and the little-known pamphlet by James Ormerod on the *Poetry of William Morris* (1938). Neither John Drinkwater's *William Morris: A Critical Study* (1912) nor Stopford A. Brooke's discussion in *Four Victorian Poets* (1908; reprinted, 1964) can seriously be recommended as even adequate introductions. Critical interest in Morris the poet has been distracted by the intense concern with other areas of his creative genius. Recently there have been signs of a resurgence of interest, but modern critics seem no more disposed than were their forerunners to examine the canon beyond *The Defence of Guenevere, Jason,* and *The Earthly Paradise.*

It may be true, as Professor Jones argued, that the limited number of inquiries into Morris' work as a poet-craftsman is due to a general feeling that "the simplicity of his verse offers no cruxes to interpretation," but if indeed Morris' poetry were as thin as this comment suggests, critical oversight would be perfectly justifiable. A more probable explanation is to be found in Morris' complexity. Evans is right in stating that "the whole of Morris is not in his poetry" (p. 126); but the corollary to this statement is that the whole of Morris is incomprehensible without the poetry, and the literary romances and translations which are complementary to it.

It was Morris' "profounder mediaevalism" that led Walter Pater in the first major analysis of his poetry to call it "aesthetic" (*Appreciations,* 1889). Pater instinctively recognized the affinity of sentiment in the poetry of Rossetti and Morris, what may be called the "aesthetic" — or better, the Pre-Raphaelite — quality common to them both. Identifying the parallel between medieval asceticism and sensualism which results in the imaginative and psychological paradox whereby the artist can employ the symbols and sentiments of Christianity and at the same time rebel against them to produce an essentially pagan effect, Pater explained one of the most complex syntheses in the poetry and at the same time accounted for the special kind of medievalism that Pre-Raphaelitism adopts. As Humphry House astutely saw, the medievalism of the Pre-Raphaelites is an essential aspect of their naturalism. But their medievalism defines more than just the natural landscape; it also transfigures, usually symbolically, the psychological landscape in the poetry and the painting.

Morris, as Pater recognized, is less intense, less subtle than Rossetti. His delight in part is with mere profusion, with the simple, pristine abundance of a world which he is delineating from his own imagination. It was this exuberance which impressed Yeats, in "The Happiest of the Poets" (*Ideas of Good and Evil,* 1903). There is an earthy, realistic, almost elemental quality in Morris' poetry that is not present in Rossetti's, which may be what C. S. Lewis meant in saying that "you can go on from Morris to all sorts of subleties, delicacies, and sublimities, which he lacks. But you can hardly go behind him" (*Rehabilitations,* 1939, p. 55).

Pater's and Yeats's essays are among the earliest and best responses to Morris' poetry. Most serious criticism dates from the centenary year (1934), when a wave of interest in all aspects of Morris' work was generated. This criticism falls into three major categories: source studies including the translations, studies tracing influences on Morris and comparative analyses, and explications of individual works. Good general discussions are lacking. B. Ifor Evans' chapter (already mentioned) surveys the major volumes and indicates the main line of development in the poetry, but his criticism is unpenetrating; so is F. L. Lucas' in *Ten Victorian Poets* (1940). An important background examination of Morris' aesthetic theory is that by Graham Hough in *The Last Romantics* (1949), but he is less concerned with specific problems in the poetry than with Morris' total participation in the arts. Philip Henderson, who edited the *Letters* and has recently completed a biography of Morris, also prepared the survey in the Writers and Their Work series (No. 32, 1952; second edition, 1964), which is a convenient, if elementary, introduction.

It was Swinburne, reviewing *The Life and Death of Jason* in 1867, who stressed the complete originality of Morris' *The Defence of Guenevere.* Swinburne was obviously referring to Morris' handling of his materials and to his vision of the medieval world rather than to the originality of his subjects. For Morris is one of the most "literary" writers in the language. The origins of his writings and his use of sources form one of the largest groups of studies. There are two major works on Morris' broader sources: Elisabeth Kuester's *Mittelalter und Antike bei William Morris* (1928) examines Morris' treatment of the Middle Ages in his early poetry; Margaret Grennan, in her *William Morris: Medievalist and Revolutionary* (1945), "attempts to define and develop the inter-relations of Morris' medievalism and his socialism and to place him in a tradition that has undoubtedly left its mark on modern thought." The leading scholar to explore Morris' use of Norse myth and literature is Karl Litzenberg, whose articles (many of them published in *Scandinavian Studies and Notes,* between 1935 and 1938) are too numerous to detail. One major essay of Litzenberg's, which goes well beyond source study and the Norse tradition, should be specified, however— "The Diction of William Morris" (*Archiv för Nordisk Filologi,* 1937). Morris' sources attracted early critical attention. J. Riegel's *Die Quellen von William Morris' Dichtung "The Earthly Paradise"* appeared six years before Morris' death. Among other early studies are H. Bartels' *William Morris, The Story of Sigurd the Volsung and the Fall of the Niblungs: Eine Studie über das Verhältnis des Epos zu den Quellen* (1906); C. H. Herford's *Norse Myth in English Poetry* (1919); and G. T. McDowell's "The Treatment of the Volsunga Saga by William Morris" (*SS,* 1923). A later source study important because of its value to explication is Oscar Maurer, Jr.'s "Some Sources of William Morris's 'The Wanderers'" (*Studies in English,* 1950).

Morris' general indebtedness to the Norse sagas is the subject of J. N. Swannell's *William Morris & Old Norse Literature* (1961). As the inspiration for "The Lovers of Gudrun," which Swannell has called the "least typical of the Earthly Paradise poems," the *Laxdôela Saga* has received much attention. Oscar Maurer, Jr. has discussed Morris' translation and literary use of the saga (*TSLL,* 1963). John Robert Wahl, in *No Idle Singer* (1964), examines the sources and the manuscripts of both "The Lovers of Gudrun" and *Sigurd the Volsung,* but Wahl's reading of Morris' treatment of his sources tends to be more autobiographical than literary. Certainly Morris' introduction to Icelandic literature around 1868 marked a turning point both in his life and art; his reading and translations, and his two trips to Iceland in 1871 and 1873, came, as John Purkis has shown in *The Icelandic Jaunt* (1962), "at a crucial stage in Morris' development" (p. 28). Dorothy M. Hoare, in *The Works of Morris and Yeats in Relation to Early Saga Literature* (1937), demonstrates that neither Yeats nor Morris was faithful to his sources; each used this new material in an original way, stamping it with his own personality. How vital the total experience was for Morris, he himself made plain in one of his letters in which he says (to

Mrs. Coronio), "it was no idle whim that drew me there, but a true instinct for what I needed." Morris' translations occupied him sporadically for a quarter-century. With Eríkr Magnússon he translated the major sagas, culminating in the publication of *The Saga Library* (1891–1895) ; he made English verse translations of both the *Aeneid* and the *Odyssey;* he rendered into English various medieval French romances; and, finally, with A. J. Wyatt, he brought out his version of the *Beowulf* at the Kelmscott Press (1895). Many of the books and articles already cited offer evaluations of Morris as translator but there are few formal discussions such as G. B. Riddehough's two articles on the translations of the *Aeneid* and *Odyssey* (*JEGP,* 1937, 1941). "The fact that Morris's 'Beowulf' is for most people unreadable and *Sigurd the Volsung* far too long," writes Professor Jones, "should not obscure his great services as a conduit between the present and the past, and between the rest of the world and Great Britain" (p. 194).

The problems of sources and influence are inextricable, especially in a writer who draws heavily on older literature for his raw material. Morris' indebtedness to the Middle Ages and to the corpus of Norse literature has been sufficiently indicated. Stella P. Wilson's "William Morris and France" (*SAQ,* 1924) is a general review; needed are more specialized studies such as T. Walton's "A French Disciple of William Morris" (*RLC,* 1935), on Jean Lahor. There have been many articles comparing Morris with other artists and practising craftsmen, but literary comparisons have been limited in the main to Keats, Yeats, and Shaw. The basis of Shaw's debt to Morris places it outside the purview of the present survey. Of the two essays on Keats and Morris, that by Clarice Short (*PMLA,* 1944) covers much the same ground as George H. Ford's more thorough chapter in his *Keats and the Victorians* (1944; reprinted, 1962). Both Short and Ford discuss Morris' use of Keatsian imagery and color, particularly in the poetry subsequent to *The Defence of Guenevere.* Ford points out that as one of the "few great English poets who wrote narrative verse," Keats was an immediate model for Morris. A more direct comparison can be made between Morris and the early Yeats, whose admiration, unlike Shaw's, was not grounded in socialism. Yeats was greatly encouraged by Morris, and the two poets were attracted by similar materials. Peter Faulkner is the modern critic who has concentrated on this influence. In two articles (*Threshold*, 1960; *JWMS*, 1963) and in a small monograph, *William Morris and W. B. Yeats* (1962), he has explored this comparison, commenting interestingly that "the weight of the pre-Raphaelite prestige must have been tremendous" on the young Yeats of the Celtic Twilight, "who occurs to me to have been more the Yeats of the pre-Raphaelite twilight" (p. 7). As Faulkner shows, Yeats outgrew Morris in becoming a great poet, but the impact of Morris' personality, his vigorous social criticism, and his intensely narrative poetry exerted a significant influence on Yeats' poetic development.

Before turning to explicatory articles on individual poems, reference should be made to five works relevant to a literary account of Morris. A. K. Davis' "William Morris and the Eastern Question, with a Fugitive Political Poem by Morris" (*Humanistic Studies in Honor of J. C. Metcalfe*, 1941), is important here largely for its addition to the canon. Donald Gray's "Arthur, Roland, Empedocles, Sigurd, and the Despair of Heroes in Victorian Poetry" (*BUSE*, 1961) discusses Morris' hero in the context of other Victorians who are unable to realize their ambitions to reshape the world. The work of one of the most active modern Morris critics, Jessie Kocmanová, is always penetrating, and her recent "The Aesthetic Purpose of William Morris in the Context of his Late Prose Romances" (*BSE*, 1966) deserves mention because in the first chapter she recapitulates and expands many of the points made in her previous article, "The Poetic Maturing of William Morris" (*BSE*, 1964), which stresses the essential development evident in Morris' poetry. She takes issue with the conventional interpretation, stemming from Dixon Scott (*Primitiae: Essays*, 1912), that in his later works Morris betrayed his poetic gifts, and that the "*Guenevere* volume is the main fruit of the poet's creative struggle." Professor Kocmanová's "Some Remarks on E. P. Thompson's Opinion of the Poetry of Morris" (*PP*, 1960) may also be noted at this point; further observations concerning Thompson's evaluation of the dramatic shift in Morris' poetry after *Guenevere* are made in her article on the romances. An excellent (but generally unknown) introduction to Morris' writings, which stresses the necessity of reading them "in terms of symbolic image and not in terms of allegory," is Richard Stingle's "William Morris" (*Association of Canadian University Teachers of English Report*, 1960).

Only two of Morris' volumes have been subjected to explication. For a brief account of "Sir Peter Harpdon's End" see Frank J. Davies' discussion of the poem (*PQ*, 1932). There are two pairs of articles relating to the title poem of *The Defence of Guenevere* volume. Laurence Perrine's "Morris's Guenevere: An Interpretation" (*PQ*, 1960) compares Morris' treatment of his heroine with that by other writers, notably Malory and Tennyson. "The poem," he argues, "is not Morris's defence of Guenevere, but Guenevere's defence of herself." Mother Angela Carson (*PQ*, 1963) counters that Guenevere is the guilty queen in Mellyagraunce's castle, that Morris implies her guilt. Her infidelity with Launcelot is a false charge in Malory, Tennyson, and Morris. That the queen nearly loses her life on the wrong charge is a fine irony in the poem. Meredith B. Raymond's "The Arthurian Group in *The Defence of Guenevere and Other Poems*" (*VP*, 1966) is an expansion of an earlier reading advanced by Curtis Dahl in his "Morris's 'The Chapel in Lyoness': An Interpretation" (*SP*, 1954). Dahl, stressing Launcelot's gift of grace to Ozana, sees the poem as a "spiritual drama"; Raymond argues that not only "The Chapel in Lyoness," but also "The Defence of Guenevere," "King Arthur's Tomb," and "Sir Galahad" form together a larger spiritual drama with an "observable structure." The effect of the four poems is one of fragmentation, but "the device of seeing a set of four poems in two pairs strengthens a reading of the entire group as a unified compostion" (p. 218).

There have been three major examinations of *The Earthly Paradise*, discounting Otto Löhmann's "Die Rahmenerzählung von Morris' 'Earthly Paradise' " (*Archiv*, 1937), which is a study in technique. The earliest, Oscar Maurer, Jr.'s "William Morris and the Poetry of Escape" in *Nineteenth Century Studies* (1940), considers the question whether *The Earthly Paradise* is escape poetry or sociological commentary. Maurer concludes that "when evasion became impossible for him," Morris "left his generation behind." R. F. Fleissner, in *"Percute Hic:* Morris' Terrestrial Paradise" *(VP,* 1965), has utilized the British Museum manuscripts to establish variant readings. An understanding of the nature of Morris' moral quest will, he feels, shake most conventional readings of the poem. Fleissner regards the question of whether the poem is, "in the words of Oscar Maurer, Jr., a 'manifesto of "escapism" ' " as "self-answering." Fleissner is too dogmatic in his retrieval of the poem from the clutches of the escapists, but his article offers a positive alternative to the usual interpretations; and his suggestion that there is an intentional relationship (something more than a pun) between Morris' reference to the "Idle singer" and the form of the "idyll" is one not before advanced.

John Robert Wahl's "The Mood of Energy and the Mood of Idleness: A Note on *The Earthly Paradise" (ESA,* 1959) is indirectly refuted in Fleissener's article. Wahl's contention that "any careful reading of *The Earthly Paradise* can . . . lead to one conclusion only: that its true major themes are the impotence of the human will and the bitterness of frustrated love" (p. 94) is immediately at variance with Fleissner's emphasis on the moral worth and clarity of the tales, which also clashes with Wahl's comments about the ambiguity of the poem, what he calls "blurred imprecision." Wahl's criticism, as has been noted several times, tends to be consistently biographical. Increasingly, Morris' poetry is being impressed—as Rossetti's has been for so long—to serve the biographer. E. P. Thompson's biography is to a large degree modeled on Oswald Doughty's *A Victorian Romantic,* which Philip Henderson once annotated as "the first attempt to penetrate the mystery surrounding Morris's private life." Like Doughty, Thompson frequently uses the poetry and other writings to document, and sometimes to recreate, the emotional crises of Morris' life. The persistency of the biographical critics will almost certainly prevail in Morris' case, the moreso perhaps because of his recorded abomination of introspective poetry.

THE MINOR POETS

Given the reservations about Pre-Raphaelite poetry suggested earlier in this chapter, it is axiomatic that as applied to the minor poets of the movement, Pre-Raphaelite is, at best, a neutral critical term. In large measure, the label is used associationally, though clearly it implies an influence (especially Rossettian), certain technical affinities, the recurrence of themes and literary forms, and at least token commitment to those qualitative aspects of Pre-Raphaelitism already outlined. Precisely which poets are regarded as Pre-Raphaelite depends on the definition posited by the individual critic. In H. Buxton Forman's contemporary *Our Living Poets* (1871), Dante Gabriel and Christina Rossetti shared honors with "those genuine children of the Pre-Raphaelite movement," Coventry Patmore and Thomas Woolner, and with William Bell Scott as Pre-Raphaelite poets, while Morris and Swinburne (together with O'Shaughnessy and Payne, in an Appendix) were classed as Renaissance poets, although "having both been profoundly influenced at first by Mr. Rossetti, and being the obvious historic successors to the Pre-Raphaelite group," Forman conceded, "their names might naturally have been looked for after the names in that group." A decade later, for Walter Hamilton (*The Aesthetic Movement in England,* 1882), whose categories were no more soundly based than Forman's, the Pre-Raphaelites were the "Poets of the Aesthetic School" and among their numbers were counted, besides Dante Gabriel Rossetti and Woolner, W. M. Rossetti, Morris, Swinburne, and O'Shaughnessy. R. L. Mégroz, in his chapter on Pre-Raphaelite poetry (*Modern English Poetry,* 1933), succumbs to the inclusive view: "Thus Hopkins is the only important English poet of the last three decades of the nineteenth century who remains outside the Pre-Raphaelite movement, for even Meredith was affected by it" (p. 18). Even Hopkins is brought into the circle by a later critic, Elizabeth Rothenstein (*Month*, 1949), who argues convincingly that Hopkins was "the one man who did realize to the full the P.R.B. ideal." His preoccupation with the "thisness" of natural objects afforded to "Hopkins' view of nature an insight and a depth that the Pre-Raphaelites never enjoyed."

In the only extended critical and historical treatment of the Pre-Raphaelite minors, B. Ifor Evans' chapter in *English Poetry in the Later Nineteenth Century* (1933; revised, 1966), seven poets are linked in what the author recognizes as a "lightly fitting formula," poets "who had some personal or technical allegiance to one of the three major poets." Since William Sharp (1856 –1905) did not even meet Rossetti until 1881, it is difficult to regard him seriously as a Pre-Raphaelite, even by Professor Evans' loose criteria. Sharp, and his feminine alter-ego, Fiona Macleod, clearly garnered, as Evans notes, the poetic leavings of the century's romanticism from Ossian to the "Celtic Twilight," and he expropriated qualities of "aesthetic" Pre-Raphaelitism but added little to the narrow corpus of poetry that may be labeled distinctly Pre-Raphaelite. Generally there are four groups of poets whose purview may be described as Pre-Raphaelite: the *Germ* poets, the poets of the second or Oxford "Brotherhood," the poets who came directly under the influence of Rossetti around 1870, when his *Poems* was published, and a few fringe poets whose work is demonstrably "Pre-Raphaelesque." Fifty-one poems by twelve writers (not to say poets) appeared in the pages of *The Germ* which was altered in title in the last two issues to *Art and Poetry,* conveying thereby a literary emphasis that was apparent in the earliest stages of the Brotherhood.

William Michael Rossetti (1829–1919) never regarded himself as a true poet, and it is not unlikely that many of his poems in *The Germ* were included by default — editorial expediency to compensate for dilatory contributors. He did write one deliberate Pre-Raphaelite poem, "Mrs. Holmes Grey" (published in *The Broadway Annual,* 1868), and he continued to compose verse throughout his life, issuing one collection, his *Democratic Sonnets,* in 1907. There has been no published examination of William Rossetti's poetry, the paper on him by H. Buxton Forman in his "Criticisms on Contemporaries" series (*Tinsley's Magazine*, 1869) having been dropped from *Our Living Poets* (1871). He has, however, attracted some attention—as an editor of Shelley, as an early champion of Whitman, and as the amanuensis of the Pre-Raphaelites and Rossetti family. Outside his own publications (cited previously), his letters are published in R. S. Garnett's *Letters about Shelley Interchanged by Three Friends* (1917), Clarence Gohdes and P. F. Baum's *Letters of William Rossetti Concerning Whitman, Blake, and Shelley to Anne Gilchrist and Her Son, Herbert Gilchrist* (1934), Janet Troxell's *Three Rossettis* (1937), and Lona Packer's *The Rossetti-Macmillan Letters* (1963). Harold Blodgett has surveyed his part in the Whitman revival in *Walt Whitman in England* (1934). Basic biographical material can be found in R. D. Waller's *The Rossetti Family* (1932), and in Jerome Thale's somewhat satirical article "The Third Rossetti" (*WHR*, 1956). Three dissertations have been done on William Michael, two of them unpublished on his criticism, Lawrence H. Chewning's (University of Virginia, 1951) and Roger W. Peattie's (London, 1966); the third, Wilhelm Justus' *William Michael Rossetti im Kreise der Präraphaeliten* (1934) treats his role in the Brotherhood. Lona Packer's "William Michael Rossetti and the Quilter Controversy: 'The Gospel of Intensity' " (*VS*, 1963) discusses William Rossetti's defense of the Pre-Raphaelites against Quilter's charge that the aesthetic poets and painters inherited their Art for Art's Sake tendencies from the Pre-Raphaelites.

As a member of the PRB, Thomas Woolner's (1825–1892) claim to be classed with the Pre-Raphaelites is unchallengeable; his claim to be remembered at all as a poet is, however, much less secure. Woolner never attained popularity, although he published five volumes of poems, *My Beautiful Lady* going through three editions. Deservedly, he has been ignored critically, for as Evans amusingly puts it, his vein was "a thin one, with almost as little gold as he himself found in the Australian diggings" (p. 137). John Lucas Tupper (1826–1879) was a *Germ* poet in recognition of his printer-father's generosity in carrying the journal financially. Between the PRB period and the publication of W. M. Rossetti's posthumous edition of *Poems by the Late John Lucas Tupper* (1897) all is silence, and the edition itself,

Oswald Doughty says, was "an act of piety stimulated by the poet's widow." It is ironic that so nondescript a poet as Tupper should have commanded notice in recent times. Doughty does not, however, magnify Tupper's abilities in his biographical study, "A Minor Pre-Raphaelite: John Lucas Tupper" (*EM*, 1960).

Of the seven casual contributors to *The Germ*, only William Bell Scott (1811–1890) can be identified with the Pre-Raphaelites in any permanent way. In his early poetry, Scott reached for themes that were beyond his meager poetic ability and produced pseudo-philosophical tracts, but in *Poems by a Painter* (1854), itself a significant title, and his collected *Poems* (1875) he showed in a handful of poems genuine lyrical ability. Rossetti was, characteristically and uncritically, enthusiastic about Scott's early work, and there is no doubt from extant correspondence that the two poets had a reciprocal influence on each other. The debt was perhaps principally in one direction, but Scott certainly played a salient role in encouraging Rossetti to publish his *Poems* (1870). Scott has had some critical attention but in the main his reputation has depended on the sensationalism of his *Autobiographical Notes* (two volumes, 1892), on Swinburne's excessive attack on him following its publication, and, more recently, on Lona Packer's immortalization of him as the "demon-lover" in Christina Rossetti's life. The recently discovered Penkill Papers have already cast considerable doubt on the identification of Scott as Christina's lover; they may also eventually restore to him some of his former prestige as the "moving spirit among those connected with the Pre-Raphaelite Movement" (Cosmo Monkhouse, *Academy*, 1890).

The remainder of the *Germ* poets, with the exception of Coventry Patmore, were poets by accident who shared the literary enthusiasm of the PRB's but who lacked either the talent or the emotional and intellectual energy to sustain the experiment. The principal poets of the second or Oxford "Brotherhood" were Morris and Swinburne, together with one distinctly minor poet, Richard Watson (later Canon) Dixon. Swinburne research can properly be left to Professor Hyder, but some notice ought here to be given to Swinburne's Pre-Raphaelite poetry. Despite John Heath-Stubbs' categorical assertion that "Swinburne is, rightly, classed with the Pre-Raphaelite poets," Swinburne was himself categorical in denying an affinity between his poetry (after

1861) and that of the Pre-Raphaelites. Pre-Raphaelitism is clearly only a phase in Swinburne's poetic development, but it might be argued that, in its own way, *Poems and Ballads* is a volume equally as Pre-Raphaelite as Morris' *Defence of Guenevere,* Christina Rossetti's *Goblin Market and Other Poems,* and Rossetti's *Poems.* Like those volumes, it is one of the cornerstones of literary Pre-Raphaelitism, introducing to the common body of Pre-Raphaelite poetry the elements of eroticism and paganism which, coupled with the medievalism of Morris, the exoticism of Christina Rossetti, and the limp aestheticism of Rossetti, ushers in the poetry of romantic decadence. For the painterly qualities associated with the other three, Swinburne substitutes that aural diffuseness which T. S. Eliot rightly saw as so essential to a poetry that is vague by intent, to a poetry in which "the meaning and the sound are one thing" (*Selected Essays,* 1950, p. 283).

Rossetti was long overdue in print when his volume of *Poems* appeared in 1870. Following it, and to a lesser degree influenced by the poetry of Morris and Swinburne, appeared Arthur O'Shaughnessy's *An Epic of Women,* John Payne's *The Masque of Shadows* (both 1870), and Philip Bourke Marston's *Song-Tide and Other Poems* (1871). Each of these volumes is derivative, yet, significantly, each poet has taken something different from the poetry of the movement. For O'Shaughnessy (1844–1881), the appeal was the sensuality and decorative quality of Rossetti's verse, which finds its outlet in his cynical love poetry. From Rossetti, Payne (1842–1916) borrows the sonnet and ballad forms. He is also preoccupied, as is O'Shaughnessy, with melancholy and with death. His successful early poems treating medieval themes derive, in their simplicity and directness, from Morris. Marston (1850–1887), the blind poet, writes almost exclusively in the sonnet form in his early poetry, directly under the spell of Rossetti. As a result of his physical limitation, his poetry tends to be hyper-synaesthetic rather than visual in its detail, and in place of the external decoration of most Pre-Raphaelite poetry Marston substitutes a heightened melancholy and nostalgia combined with an intensified sensuality, which is, as William Sharp long ago noted, his only subtlety.

Little of real merit has been written on these three poets. O'Shaughnessy and Marston were seriously espoused for a time by the American poetess, Louise Chandler Moulton, who prepared an edition of Marston with a memoir (1892), and a small monograph and anthology on O'Shaughnessy (1894), whose poetry was reprinted in this century, edited by W. A. Percy (1923). John Payne, who lived until 1916, found in the antiquarian Thomas Wright of Olney a disciple who undertook a biography (1919) and an edition of his *Autobiography* (1926). C. R. McGregor Williams' *John Payne* (in French, 1926) is the lone critical study of Payne's poetry and translations. A small, privately printed biographical study of Marston by Charles C. Osborne appeared in 1926. W. D. Paden has done two of his characteristically thorough papers on O'Shaughnessy, one treating his public life as a civil servant ("Arthur O'Shaughnessy in the British Museum; or the Case of the Misplaced Fusees and the Reluctant Zoologist," *VS*, 1964), the other dispelling the myth that O'Shaughnessy was the natural son of Lord Lytton ("Arthur O'Shaughnessy: The Ancestry of a Victorian Poet," *BJRL,* 1964).

Besides the poets discussed here, Ifor Evans included William Allingham (1824–1889) among the minor Pre-Raphaelites, and indeed the melancholy of many of his mood poems and the sense of transiency that motivates much of his poetry does indicate a link with the poets of the movement. Evans is right, however, in indicating that Pre-Raphaelitism only "entered into" some of Allingham's lyrics; it "does not explain him fully as a poet" (p. 136). The qualities he shares with the Pre-Raphaelities are almost all those of romanticism itself, translated through the alembic of his Celtic origins. It is as an Irish poet that Allingham has attracted the greatest interest, and he is the only one of the minor poets with his own bibliography, albeit an inadequate one, by P. S. O'Hegarty (1945).

A final word must be said of the fringe poets. Among these "Pre-Raphaelesque" poets may be mentioned Thomas Gordon Hake (1809–1895), whose *Memoirs of Eighty Years* (1892) is a valuable source book for its commentary on Rossetti; R. W. Dixon (1833–1900); Noel Paton (1821–1901), author of *Poems by a Painter* (1861); Sebastian Evans (1830–1909); G. A. Simcox (1841–1905); and, of course, Elizabeth Siddal (1834–1862). Of these, only Dixon has been studied in detail, in James Sambrook's recent *A Poet Hidden: The Life of Richard Watson Dixon*

(1962). Sambrook acknowledges for Dixon a Pre-Raphaelite phase, the result of his association with Rossetti, Morris, and Burne-Jones at Oxford. The impact of Pre-Raphaelitism almost diverted him permanently from orders and did convert him to a brief novitiate as a Pre-Raphaelite artist. In many of the poems in his first volume, *Christ's Company and Other Poems* (1861), "we find that dreamy, decorative medievalism, with heraldry, emblems, elaborate pictorial detail and more than a hint of the 'aesthetic swoon,' which characterised the later stages of Pre-Raphaelitism" (p. 33). Dixon's later work was saved from the "exclusive aestheticism" of Morris and late Pre-Raphaelitism by the religious quality which distinguished his poetry from that of his fellow poets.

The Pre-Raphaelite minor poets are not likely ever to be rediscovered. Though several of them produced volumes of some slight distinction, and many of them attract, and deserve, biographical attention, it is hardly feasible that scholarship will ever attempt to reclaim permanently a Noel Paton or a Thomas Gordon Hake or a G. A. Simcox from the limbo of nineteenth-century literary history, though the dissertational mill may ultimately find in them—as indeed it already has in O'Shaughnessy, Allingham, Payne, and William Bell Scott—grist for "original" research. Like minor stage characters they serve primarily to illuminate the principal actors, and any attempt to magnify their importance would be a distortion of the first order. The general unavailability of their work, even in modern anthologies, is a regrettable instance of a distortion at the other extreme, which makes doubly timely the recent "anthology of the finest Pre-Raphaelite poems" by James D. Merritt (*The Pre-Raphaelite Poem,* 1966) and the forthcoming Pre-Raphaelite anthologies by Cecil Y. Lang and Jerome H. Buckley. Merritt's attractive paperback is weakened by an introduction which does little more than turn up old ground. In a remarkable avoidance of any definition of Pre-Raphaelite poetry, he confines himself to bland and sometimes contradictory generalizations. In all, Merritt includes seventeen poets, seven of whom are represented only by their poems in *The Germ.* Leaving aside cavils about his choice of poems by the majors, most of the minor poets are inadequately represented.

Lesser and later Pre-Raphaelites tend to proliferate as scholarship on the men and the movement advances. Writers who a few decades ago were alien to the Pre-Raphaelite camp have been shown to have had Pre-Raphaelite affinities or to have been influenced substantially by the movement. Elizabeth Rothenstein's treatment of Hopkins has already been discussed, but she is not alone in ascribing to Hopkins the fulfilment of Pre-Raphaelite doctrines. "It is no accident," writes Humphry House in *All in Due Time* (1955), "that Gerard Manley Hopkins was devoted to [Christina Rossetti's] poems in his youth; for it was he, not the aesthetes, who truly developed Pre-Raphaelite aims" (p. 158). Even Professor Saintsbury in his *History of Nineteenth Century Literature* (1896) had recognized Hopkins as one of the "outlying" members of the Pre-Raphaelite school.

What Kineton Parkes in an early history of the movement called the "Pre-Raphaelite measles" seem to have been caught by some writers considerably more "outlying" than Hopkins. Wayne Burns has made a convincing case for a strong Pre-Raphaelite influence on the "matter of fact" style of Charles Reade's *Christie Johnstone,* which he sees as "A Portrait of the Artist as a Young Pre-Raphaelite" (*From Jane Austen to Joseph Conrad,* 1958). George Bernard Shaw, who had what Geoffrey Mander once called "Pre-Raphaelite links," stated cryptically in the Preface to *Plays Pleasant* (1898) that in *Candida* his intended aim was to "distill the quintessential drama from Pre-Raphaelitism." Having already identified himself as a Pre-Raphaelite dramatist ("Art Corner," *Our Corner,* May 1886), Shaw set out in *Candida* to test the dramatic potential of Pre-Raphaelite principles as he interpreted them. In her recent article, "Bernard Shaw's Pre-Raphaelite Drama" (*PMLA,* 1966), Elsie B. Adams attempts to sort out precisely what Shaw meant and to trace the common elements in Shavian and Pre-Raphaelite theories. By relating Shaw's essentially religious view of Pre-Raphaelitism (especially as held by Holman Hunt) to his concept of "Creative Evolution" and to his view of the theater as "the temple for the modern religion," Miss Adams disposes of the superficialities of *Candida*'s Pre-Raphaelitism, and she concludes (rather startlingly) that "all of Shaw's plays which are devoted to suggesting the infinite possibilities of the ever-changing and progressing Life Force . . . may be considered such Pre-Raphaelite drama" (p. 437).

If the modern student is surprised by an article such as Euralio De Michelis' "Un Poeta d'Autunno" (*NA,* 1963) which explores D'Annunzio's indebtedness to the Pre-Raphaelites, there are many areas of Pre-Raphaelite influence that might profitably be investigated. A full examination of the movement's importance to a succession of literary isms—Aestheticism, English Symbolism, Imagism, and even Surrealism—may lead to the eventual recognition of Pre-Raphaelitism as one of the most dynamic movements of the nineteenth century and perhaps the most aesthetically fecund progenitor of the twentieth.

Gerard Manley Hopkins

JOHN PICK

I. BIBLIOGRAPHICAL MATERIALS

Although Gerard Manley Hopkins was rejected and neglected during his lifetime and although his single slim volume of poems was not published until 1918, almost thirty years after his death, the generations of critics since 1918 have probably directed more attention to him than to any other Victorian poet. As *TLS* has remarked, "No modern poet has been critically commented on in more detail ... Rarely has a poet attracted such a burden of documentation and commentary."

The most complete bibliographies appear in *Immortal Diamond: Studies in Gerard Manley Hopkins* (edited by Norman Weyand, 1949), which extends with thoroughness through 1944; in "Forty Years of Criticism. A Chronological Check List of Criticism the Works of Gerard Manley Hopkins from 1909 to 1949," (*Bulletin of Bibliography,* 1950) ; and in Jean-Georges Ritz's *Le Poète Gérard Manley Hopkins* (1963), which is fairly complete to the early 1950's, though less definitive after that. The ten-page bibliography in W. A. M. Peters' *Gerard Manley Hopkins: A Critical Essay towards the Understanding of His Poetry* (1948) is unreliable and inaccurate. The most discriminatingly selective bibliography appears in "A Bibliographical Study of Hopkins Criticism, 1918–1949" (*Thought,* 1950) by Maurice Charney, who presents one hundred items.

The history, still tinged with mystery, of the Hopkins manuscripts now largely in the Bodleian and at Campion Hall, Oxford, as well as a catalog of unpublished manuscripts, is given by D. Anthony Bischoff in two articles: "The Manuscripts of Gerard Manley Hopkins" (*Thought,* 1951) and "Gerard Manley Hopkins" (*VN,* 1958) .

Several surveys of Hopkins criticism have appeared: Elgin W.

Mellown has devoted one article to the critical reception of Hopkins from his death until 1918 and another to the reaction to his poems, 1918 to 1930 (*MP* 1959 and 1965). W. H. Gardner, in the first volume of his *Gerard Manley Hopkins: A Study of Poetic Idiosyncrasy in Relation to Poetic Tradition* (1944), devotes a chapter, "Critics and Reviewers," to an evaluation through 1942. Maurice Charney's "A Bibliographical Study of Hopkins Criticism, 1918–1949" (*Thought,* 1950) is carefully critical and usefully subdivided into such topics as trends, themes, sources and analogues, prosody, and style.

A useful anthology of Hopkins criticism is Geoffrey H. Hartman's edition, *Hopkins A Collection of Critical Essays* (1966).

Because Hopkins often used words in their unfamiliar meanings or occasionally employed words in their provincial or dialectical usages, and even revived archaisms or coined new words, a helpful aid is Raymond V. Schoder's "An Interpretive Glossary," in *Immortal Diamond: Studies in Gerard Manley Hopkins* (1949).

A Hopkins concordance is projected by Charles W. Hagelman, Jr.

II. EDITIONS AND SELECTIONS

The first edition of *Poems of Gerard Manley Hopkins,* 1918, edited by Robert Bridges, was followed by a second edition in 1930, with an introduction by Charles Williams and an appendix of additional poems. The second edition has been pirated. In 1948 this was superseded by the third edition, retaining Bridges' Preface and Notes for their historical importance, but edited

with additional poems, notes, and a critical and biographical intro-
duction by W. H. Gardner. This printing includes nearly twice
as many poems as the 1918 edition, but most of the additions are
minor. Gardner, working with the manuscripts, corrects the chrono-
logy of earlier editions, makes additional collations and emen-
dations, and restores some of the readings that Bridges has altered.
The third edition was reprinted in 1961 with further additions
and corrections. A fourth edition, in which W. H. Gardner was
aided by N. H. MacKenzie, appeared in 1967.

Almost fifty years have now passed since the first edition, and
a final definitive edition giving all the cancellations and variants
and all the reading marks Hopkins used—even if somewhat spor-
adically and inconsistently—has long been needed. This has now
been undertaken by N. H. MacKenzie for the Oxford English
Texts series.

The first edition of the *Poems* appeared in 1918, but evalu-
ations of Hopkins' character and of his objectives remained peri-
lous until the middle and late thirties when four additional
volumes of primary materials were published. Claude Colleer
Abbott meticulously edited in 1935 (reprinted, 1955), *Letters of
Gerard Manley Hopkins to Robert Bridges* and *The Correspon-
dence of Gerard Manley Hopkins and Richard Watson Dixon*,
and in 1938, *Further Letters*. The bulk of the latter volume is
devoted to letters to Alexander Baillie and correspondence with
Coventry Patmore, in addition to some letters to Newman and
his school and college friends, but includes only a few family
letters. A second edition of *Further Letters* in 1956 added half
a dozen letters of Hopkins to his father, some seventy to his
mother, and other miscellaneous correspondence.

In 1937, Humphry House edited *The Note-Books and Papers
of Gerard Manley Hopkins*. The volume, which became a mine
for succeeding Hopkins scholars, included generous portions of
his diaries and journals, his essays, and examples of his sermons
and commentaries. It was a model of editing and contained
sketches, drawings, and even maps of the English and Welsh
districts associated with Hopkins. The House edition was later
split into two volumes, each expanded considerably by much new
material, including, for instance, 20,000 hitherto unpublished

words in three copybooks discovered in 1947 by D. Anthony Bischoff in a war-damaged room in London. As a result we now have *The Journals and Papers of Gerard Manley Hopkins* (edited by Humphry House, completed by Graham Storey, 1959) and *The Sermons and Devotional Writings of Gerard Manley Hopkins* (edited by Christopher Devlin, 1959).

The search for Hopkinsiana has been strenuous, and one has learned long ago to avoid such expressions as "the last of Hopkins." Only recently the discovery of unknown letters and new versions of familiar poems, all in the poet's autograph, was announced (*TLS*, 1965).

The various volumes of correspondence and notebooks were expensive and sometimes out of print. These facts, along with the widening acceptance of Hopkins, resulted in the appearance of three different volumes of selections in 1953.

An inexpensive *Selected Poems of Gerard Manley Hopkins*, edited with an introduction and notes by James Reeves, includes all the mature poems as well as two examples of earlier work and three specimens of later unfinished poems. Convinced that "readers of modern poetry are now so accustomed to accentual verse and 'the rhythm of common speech' that the marks may now be considered an unnecessary blemish," Reeves removed all accent marks, and in doing so, unfortunately also removed the meaning from some of the poems. The edition is therefore not recommended.

The other two volumes of selections attempt to present representative poems and portions of the diaries, journals, letters sermons, and commentaries. *Poems and Prose of Gerard Manley Hopkins*, edited by W. H. Gardner, has a chronological arrangement, while *A Hopkins Reader*, edited by John Pick (revised and expanded 1966), arranges the selections under various headings: observation of nature, poetic theory, practical criticism, religion, and the like. Gardner's book gives more space to the poems, while Pick's offers more of the prose.

III. BIOGRAPHICAL STUDIES

No satisfactory biography of Hopkins exists, though the habit of quoting haphazardly from his letters and other sources of information about his life has seldom been resisted.

Certain special studies, such as Martin C. D'Arcy's "Gerard Manley Hopkins" (in *Great Catholics,* edited by Claude Williamson, 1939); Pick's *Gerard Manley Hopkins: Priest and Poet* (1942); Martin C. Carroll's "Gerard Manley Hopkins and the Society of Jesus" (in *Immortal Diamond: Studies in Gerard Manley Hopkins,* 1949); and sections of two books by David A. Downes, *Gerard Manley Hopkins: A Study of His Ignatian Spirit* (1959) and *Victorian Portraits: Hopkins and Pater* (1965) are helpful for the interpretation of separate aspects of the poet's life. This list could be extended considerably.

For some years following its publication in 1930, G. F. Lahey's *Gerard Manley Hopkins* had both the advantages and disadvantages of being a pioneering work. But in attempting to do everything within the space of 150 pages, the book was merely an introduction. Quoting frequently and liberally from primary sources, this study whetted appetites while it left them unsatisfied and many found it sketchy, fragmentary, and disappointing.

The year 1944, the centenary of Hopkins' birth, evoked innumerable critical studies and Eleanor Ruggles' *Gerard Manley Hopkins: A Life.* The latter is semipopularized and has the quality of vivid readability. In its readability also lies its danger. Hopkins' Life is fluently fictionalized and dramatized, though it would be too harsh to say that the work is a frustrated historical novel.

The most balanced and carefully constructed brief biographies of the poet are those of Austin Warren in his introductory chapter to *Gerard Manley Hopkins by the Kenyon Critics,* (1945) and

W. H. Gardner's introduction to the third edition of the *Poems* (1948). More detailed but not definitive are the biographical chapters scattered through both volumes of W. H. Gardner's *Gerard Manley Hopkins.*

Jean-Georges Ritz's monumental *Le Poète Gérard Manley Hopkins, S. J. 1844–1889: Le Homme et l'oeuvre* (1963) unfortunately remains in French.

A further important biographical contribution by the same scholar is his *Robert Bridges and Gerard Hopkins 1863–1889: A Literary Friendship* (1960). It is greatly to Ritz's credit that he manages to construct a significant study of the friendship of the two poets in spite of the fact that Bridges destroyed his own side of their correspondence and took great care to leave directions that no biography of him ever be written. Though Ritz tries to be scrupulously fair to both men and feels—unlike many previous critics—that to praise one does not mean he must disparage the other, nevertheless his impartiality brings out more forcefully than ever the relative stature of Hopkins.

A one-volume life of Hopkins is being written by Anthony Bischoff. For many years there have been plans for a two-volume definitive biography, the first devoted to his early life and the second to his Jesuit years; the unexpected death of Humphry House, who was working on the first, brought progress on that volume to a halt, but Anthony Bischoff has been writing the second. Some of the problems and questions facing his ultimate biographer or biographers have been challengingly raised in an article "The Hopkins Enigma" (*Thought,* 1961).

IV. HISTORY OF HOPKINS CRITICISM

The advantage of a chronological survey of Hopkins criticism is that it is almost a history of the transition from Victorian to modern poetry. Above all, we learn again the truth of the observation that a poet often has to create the taste by which he is to be appreaciated.

Hopkins died in 1889, and his poems were not published until 1918. But the criticism of his poetry started during his life among his small circle of friends, the three poets who constituted his public. The varying attitudes of Robert Bridges, Richard Watson Dixon, and Coventry Patmore are important and may be reconstructed in some detail by studying the various volumes of letters and correspondence already listed.

The least of these was the one who was most understanding and appreciative, for Dixon read the poems with "delight, astonishment, and admiration." He found them "amazingly original." He urged immediate publication. He felt the "power" of "The Wreck of the Deutschland," a poem which came to be a test for each of Hopkins' friends. Dixon perceived that something in Hopkins' life and character gave his poem a "rare charm," "something I cannot describe, but known to myself by the inadequate word *terrible pathos*—something of what you call temper in poetry: a right temper which goes to the point of the terrible: the terrible crystal."

Very different was the reaction of Patmore, a fellow-Catholic and experimentalist in verse, who preferred those poems least typical of Hopkins and most nearly approximating what he called "the ordinary rules of composition." Patmore granted that the "obscuring novelties" in time might became "additional delights" but yet "I do not think I could ever become sufficiently accustomed to your favourite poem, 'The Wreck of the Deutschland' to reconcile me to its strangeness."

But Bridges became for a long period the most influential and controversial critic of Hopkins. His lifelong friendship was very important to Hopkins in spite of the fact that there was little sympathy, either in religion or in poetry, beween the two. Hopkins was conscious that, in a sense, Bridges was his most important audience; and Bridges' almost constant and discouraging criticism had the effect of making Hopkins consider with double care the effects he was trying to produce.

Hopkins apparently had to plead with Bridges to read "The Wreck of the Deutschland" a second time, and Bridges retorted that its sprung rhythm was "presumptuous jugglery." Hopkins clearly hoped to convert Bridges to sprung rhythm; the degree to which he influenced Bridges' own experiments in sprung rhythm has been studied by Ritz, and there has even been the suggestion that Bridges delayed the edition of Hopkins' poetry to put critics off the scent.

The only two poems that Hopkins submitted for publication were sent to the Jesuit periodical, *The Month*, which rejected them, and Bridges became during his lifetime the custodian of the poems, carefully preserving them.

The story of the posthumous disposition of Hopkins' other manuscripts is involved; scholars are relying on D. Anthony Bischoff to clarify this area of Hopkins studies. The discovery of Hopkins' will in 1947, almost sixty years after his death, has added a note of drama to an already complicated situation (see "Hopkins' Manuscripts," by D. Anthony Bischoff, *Thought*, 1951).

Between the death of Hopkins in 1889 and the appearance of the first edition of his poems in 1918, Bridges managed to introduce several of Hopkins' poems—though sometimes is truncated versions—into anthologies. (See Simon Nowell Smith's "Bridges, Hopkins and Mr. Daniel," *TLS*, 1957, and Elgin W. Mellown's "Gerard Manley Hopkins and His Public, 1889–1918," *MP*, 1959). This method of attempting to win a public for his dead friend seems commendable, except that he adopted the habit of frightening away readers by warning them in these anthologies that the poems "not only sacrifice simplicity, but very often, among verses of the rarest beauty, show a neglect of those canons of taste which seem common to all poetry."

In 1909, probably embarrassed by the neglect of Hopkins during his lifetime, and having tried to collect the scattered manuscripts, Joseph Keating published a series of three articles in *The Month*. And it has recently been revealed that correspondence exists in which Father Keating was thwarted by Bridges in publishing an edition of Hopkins' poems in 1909.

Nearly a decade later, in 1918, Bridges, then Poet Laureate, published the first edition of Hopkins' poems, and it bacame Bridges' most important piece of Hopkins criticism: he summarized his reflections after forty years of acquaintance with Hopkins' poetry. He had collated the manuscripts in his possession, had written notes for the poems, helpfully drawing on explanations from Hopkins' letters, and it must be noted in Bridges' favor that not a single poem of major literary importance has been added in succeeding editions.

In his famous—to many later critics, infamous—"Preface to Notes" (reprinted in all subsequent editions), the Poet Laureate set down in orderly fashion his final judgement of the poetry of Hopkins. It is no exaggeration to say that it presents the outlines of Hopkins criticism ever since that time, because all the scholarship since 1918 has tended either to accept Bridges' position, to quality it, or eventually completely to reverse it. Future critics were to weigh every word and phrase of the "Preface to Notes."

Bridges hoped that readers could be led "to search out the rare masterly beauties that distinguish his work," but he felt it necessary "to put readers at their ease" by defining the "bad faults" of Hopkins.

The indictment starts with "faults of taste" under which he specifies "affectation in metaphor" and "perversion of human feeling" which he contends "are mostly efforts to force emotion into theological or sectarian channels" as in "the exaggerated Marianism of some pieces, or the naked encounter of sensualism and asceticism which hurts the 'Golden Echo.' "

Then he turns to "the rude shocks of his purely artistic wantonness . . . which a reader must have courage to face." These he classifies as "Oddity and Obscurity." The chief cause of the obscurity was "his habitual omission of the relative pronoun," a "license" Hopkins abused "beyond precedent." Another source of obscurity was "that in aiming at condensation" he used "words that are grammatically ambiguous"; he was insensitive "to the irrelevant suggestions that our numerous homophones cause"; and he "would seem even to welcome and seek artistic effect in the consequent confusion." Finally, some of the rhymes are "repellent," "freaks," and in these "his childishness is incredible" and "appalling." All these "blemishes . . . are of such quality and magnitude as to deny him even a hearing from those who love continuous literary decorum and are grown to be intolerant of its absence."

In the notes which followed, Bridges gave almost no help

with Hopkins' first great poem. "The Wreck of the Deutschland," except to say, "The labour spent on this great metrical experiment must have served to establish the poet's prosody and perhaps his diction: therefore the poem stands logically as well as chronologically in the front of his book, like a great dragon folded in the gate to forbid all entrance, and confident in his strength from past success." And the editor admits, disarmingly enough, that "he was himself shamefully worsted in a brave frontal assault, the more easily perhaps because both subject and treatment were distasteful to him." Later one of Bridges' critics was to say that it was Bridges himself who "stands like a great dragon folded in the gate to forbid all entrance" to a sympathetic approach to Hopkins.

But Bridges' "Preface to Notes" fortunately had been tucked away at the back of the book while at the front stood a warmly lyrical prefatory sonnet of dedication addressed to Hopkins and concluding:

> Go forth: amidst our chaffinch flock display
> Thy plumage of far wonder and heavenward flight!

Had the "Preface to Notes" stood in place of the sonnet it is difficult to see how reviewers would have dared pass the gate at all.

This little volume of 1918 was destined to affect deeply the course of modern poetry. Hopkins himself had written to Bridges, "If you do not like it, it is because there is something you have not seen and I see ... and if the whole world agreed to condemn it or see nothing in it I should only tell them to take a generation and come to me again."

Hopkins' premonition proved to be correct. Looking back at the 1920's, Sir Herbert Read in 1933 could write, "When the history of the last decade comes to be written by a dispassionate critic, no influence will rank in importance with that of Gerard Manley Hopkins."

Yet the first edition of 750 copies took ten years to exhaust. During the 1920's Hopkins was chiefly a "poets' poet" and the small sale appears to have been chiefly to writers; thus his influence was felt very soon on a generation that was rejecting both the Victorians and the Georgians. Between his death and the publication of his poetry a revolution had taken place: the imagists and *vers-libristes* had gained the ascendancy; and so, paradoxically, a poet was welcomed as a leader whose dates made him chronologically Victorian but whose poetry seemed at first sight a rejection of all traditions.

Reviews of first editions are seldom definitive. The one thing on which the critics were agreed was that Hopkins was difficult. But they varied widely, holding that he was not worth struggling over, or contending that the more his poetry was studied the more beauty was discovered. Bridges, too, was praised and attacked. One reviewer wrote of him as "the perfect devoted editor. Bouquets all go to him. Bridges is trying to breathe life into that which cannot live" (*Oxford Magazine,* 1919). To another his "Preface to Notes" was "This frank, lucid and just summary which makes appreciation easy" (*Everyman,* 1919). But one critic cried out, "From our best friends deliver us, O Lord!" (Edward Sapir, 1921).

The quarrel of the critics was on, and on such a variety of fronts as to be bewildering (see Elgin W. Mellown's "The Reception of Gerard Manley Hopkins' Poems, 1918–1930," *MP,* 1965). Some were convinced that Bridges held a priori that emotion was forced if it "ran in theological channels" and that to complain of "exaggerated Marianism" was like complaining of the "exaggerated Beatricity of the *Divina Commedia*" (Frederic Page, *DubR,* 1920). Hopkins' sprung rhythm evoked the comments: "Any reader is to be forgiven who feels that life is too short to work through torment to the understanding of prosody" (Louise Imogen Guiney) ; and "The metrical effects which Hopkins studies with such assiduity do not seem to us to be worth the pains bestowed upon them" (*Spectator,* 1919). Yet other critics hailed him: "As a metrist he has no equal in English" (*Ave Maria,* 1919) and found in him "a rhythm which explicates meaning and makes it more intense" (John Middleton Murry, *Athenaeum,* 1919). To still another, "It is doubtful if the freest verse of our day is more sensitive in its rhythmic pulsations than the sprung verse of Hopkins" (Edward Sapir, *Poetry,* 1921).

The predominant note of the first reviews was frank confusion. Thus in a single review one could come across the remark that his poetry "produces the effect almost of idiocy" but that there are also "authentic fragments that we trust even when they bewilder us" (*TLS*, 1919).

The 1920's therefore tended to become years of violent rejection or of enthusiastic but often uncritical acceptance. It was also the decade during which Hopkins' poems began to be reprinted in anthologies of contemporary poetry and to be included in such surveys of recent writing as Laura Riding and Robert Grave's *A Survey of Modernist Poetry* (1927).

But the major historians of prosody tended to dismiss him with brief comment. T. S. Omond in a postscript classified Hopkins' sprung rhythm among the "fantastic new would-be developments of metre" (*English Metrists*, 1921). Saintsbury disposed of him in *The Cambridge History of English Literature* with a footnote, and in his *History of English Prosody* (1923), it is quite clear to him that Hopkins' poems "all were experiments," of rather doubtful importance.

There are many curiosities among this avalanche of early critiques of Hopkins. The younger poets tended to welcome him, but such a writer as T. Sturge Moore edited one of Hopkins' poems and congratulated himself on having cut it in half: "Though as you may decide, his lavish outlay in words attained more music, my spare recension has retained most of his felicities, discarded his most ludicrous redundancies" (*Criterion*, 1930).

The most important and influential criticism of Hopkins starts with an article in 1926 by I. A. Richards (*Dial*, 1926; see also *Practical Criticism*, 1930) and with William Empson's *Seven Types of Ambiguity* (1930).

Richards trained on Hopkins those methods of close examination of the text and critical exegesis for which he is famous. Hopkins "may be described, without opposition, as the most obscure poet of English verse writers," but unlike many previous critics, Richards welcomed the difficulty. Indeed, obscurity has a positive value and allows for "resistance" and hence for more complex responses in the sensitive reader. Consequently he approaches Hopkins enthusiastically as a poet to be wrestled with, convinced that his subtleties will yield great riches through careful critical analysis, and he made "The Windhover" the focus of Hopkins criticism. Richards had a profoundly salutary effect on later students of Hopkins, though he probably misled them by dismissing Hopkins' explanations of his prosody as excuses to allow himself "complete rhythmical freedom," and by approaching his religious beliefs as "bundles of invested capital."

With the publication of Empson's *Seven Types of Ambiguity,* the poetry of Hopkins took on a new dimension and became the happy hunting ground for the ambiguity seekers. It cannot be denied that they made the text take on a richness that critics had not hitherto discovered. "The Windhover" for Empson illustrates "a clear sense of the Freudian use of opposites, where two things thought of as incompatible but desired intensely by different systems of judgment" are brought into conjunction and "forced into open conflict before the readers."

The year 1930—the year of the second edition of his poems and of the first volume devoted to a study of his life and art —became a turning point in Hopkins criticism. The reviewers' reception of the second edition differed markedly from that of the first, and it ran rapidly through more than a dozen printings. The number of articles produced in 1930 to 1931 equalled the number produced during the entire preceding decade, and Hopkins was firmly established.

The second edition, adding a few early poems and later translations and fragments but nothing of major importance, was prefaced by a sympathetic and enthusiastic introduction by Charles Williams, in direct contrast to the attitude of Bridges a dozen years before. In Hopkins' poetry, said Williams, "it is as if the imagination, seeking for expression, had found verb and substantive at one rush" and the defect is not with the poet but with the reader whose mind "cannot work at a quick enough rate." Hopkins "breaks now into joy, now into inquiry, now into a terror of fearful expectation, but always into song. . . . He was unique among the Victorians . . . because his purely poetic energy was so much greater." And more in the same vein.

Hardly a reviewer took issue with such assertions, and several of them made irreverent allusions to Bridges. *TLS* (1930) called Hopkins "a true genius," "one of the major poets," "the most original of the poets of the nineteenth century," and for the young contemporary poet "full of strong powers (and an unexhausted technical prowess) which he feels he must assimilate and possess." In America, Malcolm Cowley said: "He has more to teach the poets of today than either Tennyson or Browning" (*New York Herald Tribune Weekly Book Review*, 1931.) Another reviewer went so far as to say, "...a careful reading yields at once the poet's thought and the justification of his tortured syntax" (Justin O'Brien, *Bookman*, 1931). There was less loose talk about oddity, obscurity, and twisted prosody; some of the critics began to point out a relationship between his neologisms, his "contorted grammar, his startling and baffling rhetoric" and his effort to inscape his emotions. They began to realize his poetry as an integrated whole: "... a purposive colliding and jamming, an overlapping and telescoping of images and words in an effort towards sustained music and sense" (Hildegarde Flanner, *New Republic*, 1931).

Gerard Manley Hopkins (1930) by G. F. Lahey was the first critical-biographical volume, and about it some remarks have already been made. Introductory rather than definitive, it aroused deeper interest in his life and character. For the first time it made available a larger group—for some had been published in *The Month* (1909) and in *DubR* (1920)—of extracts from his letters and diaries. The critical sections are the least adequate, and Lahey seems, surprisingly enough, to echo Bridges in condemning some of Hopkins' rhymes, tmesis, omissions of relatives, syncopation of words, and marooning of prepositions. Indeed Lahey gallantly pays as high tribute to Bridges as has ever been paid.

In the most controversial sentences in the book, Father Lahey spoke of the Dublin sonnets: "The celebrated 'terrible sonnets' are only terrible in the same way that the beauty of Christ is terrible. Only the strong pinions of an eagle can realize the cherished happiness of such suffering. It is a place where Golgotha and Tabor meet. Read in this light his poems cease to be tragic" (p. 143).

Comments on and quarrels with this passage echo through criticisim for many years and take on several variations. Sir Herbert Read in an important essay ("Gerard Manley Hopkins," *English Critical Essays, Twentieth Century*, edited by P. M. Jones, 1933; reprinted in *Defence of Shelley and Other Essays*, 1936, and in *Collected Essays in Literary Criticism*, 1938) built up a theory of poetry, elaborated with references to Hopkins (*Form in*

Modern Poetry, 1933) , that poetic sensibility is consistent only with a state of spiritual tension and acuity and that "true originality is due to a conflict between sensibility and belief." He went on to the conclusion that the tension is bridged by doubt. Hence he classified Hopkins' greatest poems, the "terrible sonnets," as poems of doubt. To him " 'The Windhover' is completely objective in its senseful catalogue, but Hopkins gets over his scruples by dedicating his poem 'To Christ our Lord.' "

Sir Herbert's thesis that poetic activity is primarily the result of a conflict (or coexistence and counter-action) of sensiblity and belief led him to suggest that Hopkins' Jesuit allegiance had a profound effect on his poetry: "Perhaps in actual intensity his poetry gained more than it lost by this step but one cannot help regretting the curtailment it suffered in range and quantity." Later Read withdrew the implication that there was "an open conflict between the poetic impulse and theological faith in Hopkins" (Gardner, *Gerard Manley Hopkins: A Study of Poetic Idiosyncrasy in Relation to Poetic Tradition,* I, 237) , but presumably he continued to hold in modified form that the intensity of the later poetry had its origin in some kind of tension between sensibility and spirituality.

Sir Herbert's book, *Form in Modern Poetry* (1933) , and his essays contained other valuable contributions, especially on Hopkins' use of language. He decided that "nothing could have made Hopkins's poetry popular in his day: it was necessary that it should first be absorbed by the sensibility of a new generation of poets," and after surveying contemporary poetry he concluded of Hopkins that "no influence whatsoever is so potent for the future of English poetry."

Probably even more influential on a generation of critics was F. R. Leavis, who in a chapter of *New Bearings in English Poetry* (1932) extended the work of Richards and presented what may be called the first thoroughgoing defence of Hopkins' style. He opens his essay with enthusiasm: "He was one of the most remarkable technical inventors who ever wrote, and he was a major poet. Had he received the attention that was his due the history of English poetry from the 'nineties onward would have been different." After fifty pages of analysis he concludes, equally enthusiastically, "He is likely to prove, for our time and the future, the only influential poet of the Victorian age and he seems to me the greatest." Almost everything that Leavis says is a direct contradiction to Bridges, of whom he comments, "What Dr. Bridges calls 'blemishes' are essential to Hopkins's aim and achievement," and he feels that Hopkins was a master in exploiting the resources and potentialities of English as a living language. The essay, including careful exegesis of half a dozen poems, remains more than thirty years later one of the best short introductions to the poetry of Hopkins.

In 1933, one of I. A. Richards' students, Elsie Phare, published her book, *The Poetry of Gerard Manley Hopkins: A Survey and Commentary*, a volume long out of print. Like Richards and Levis the author tends to disregard Hopkins' prosody. Miss Phare's method is loose, rambling, and informal, but she makes a number of contributions. By a multitude of comparisions she tries to determine the "school" or "tribe" to which he belongs, and her book has many paraphrases of the poems. Her exegesis is frequently skillful though occasionally subjective or merely impressionistic. Some poems are spoiled by the "naked encounter between sensousness and asceticism." However, Miss Phare's most frequently recurring criticism is that Hopkins artificially forces and exaggerates his emotional responses. She confesses that her tendency is to think "that becoming a Jesuit must involve some unnatural or undesirable deformation." Hopkins' emotions, therefore, tend to be unnatural to her, and yet she very frequently attempts critical sympathy.

Yeats in his preface to *The Oxford Book of Modern Verse* (1936) was not enthusiastic and confessed that he "read Gerard Manley Hopkins with difficulty." Yet he granted that Hopkins' sprung rhythm "has given new vitality to much contemporary verse." T. S. Eliot never reversed his very qualified estimate of Hopkins which he made briefly in *After Strange Gods* (1934), the same year that Edith Sitwell in *Aspects of Modern Poetry* was to praise him so highly. Still another poet during the same year, C. Day Lewis, called him "among the great technical innovators in verse" and his sprung rhythm "one of the best gifts to posterity" (*A Hope for Poetry*, 1934). To Day Lewis, "He is a true revolutionary poet, for his imagination was always breaking up and melting down the inherited forms of language, fusing them into new possibilities, hammering them into new shapes."

Ever since 1918 this emphasis on Hopkins the revolutionary had been the predominant note of criticism. To Day Lewis, for instance, his poetry "is difficult to connect with anything in the past . . . Hopkins remains without affinities." It was not until the Kenyon critics (1944) and Gardner (1944) that a balance was struck.

In 1935 several important contributions appeared in a Hopkins issue of *New Verse*. In addition to Humphry House's "A Note of Hopkins' Religious Life," suggesting that Jesuit discipline intensified an already scrupulous strain, especially notable is Christopher Devlin's essay, "Gerard Hopkins and Duns Scotus," the first article to explore the parallelism between the medieval Franciscan philosopher and the nineteenth-century poet. Charles Madge and Geoffrey Grigson contributed articles on Hopkins' imagery with important comparisons, developed for the first time, between Hopkins and Whitman, and there was also an article by Ll. Wyn Griffith on Welsh influences, a topic to be further developed by later critics.

The Hopkins issue of *New Verse* is very difficult to obtain, as is a little book also published in 1935 in an edition of three hundred copies: *The Mind and Poetry of Gerard Manley Hopkins* by Bernard Kelly. Humphry House in *New Verse* had pointed out what critics were reluctantly coming to realize, that Hopkins' religious experience was "the direct origin of some of his greatest poems"; Kelly concentrates on the intensity and psychological actuality of his spiritual vision and opposes both Bridges and Read in holding that a true asceticism welcomes both the delight of the senses and of transcendant reality. And continuing the study of Hopkins' religious experience, Christopher Devlin, in "The Ignatian Inspiration of Gerard Manley Hopkins" (*Blackfriars*, 1935) discussed the pervading influence, barely mentioned heretofore, of the *Spiritual Exercises* of St. Ignatius on the poet's character and verse. Devlin held that the *Exercises* "were not the occasion but the origin of Hopkins' poetic experience."

All of Hopkins scholarship was put on a firmer footing in the middle thirties by the publication of *The Letters of Gerard Manley Hopkins to Robert Bridges* and *The Correspondence of*

Gerard Manley Hopkins and Richard Watson Dixon in 1935, *The Note-Books and Papers of Gerard Manley Hopkins* in 1937, and *Further Letters of Gerard Manley Hopkins in* 1938. These volumes raised his stature considerably. In his letters and other prose works many critics now found the same disciplined honesty and intensity of conviction as in his poems. Now scholars could study his diaries and see in them the raw materials of his poetry. They offered adequate explanations of his prosody, his literary methods, and his ideals of poetry. Now they might discover a new Hopkins in his literary criticism and they learned about the multiplicity of his interests, much about his struggles, and a good deal about his character. Hopkins scholarship has by no means as yet exhausted these volumes. In the flood of reviews and short articles which appeared almost immediately there was a new admiration. Bonamy Dobrée, for instance: "The more one reads Hopkins the more complex does he become, and the greater in stature" (*Spectator*, 1938).

During this period the two most articulate voices of dissent were those of G. M. Young and D. S. MacColl. To the former, Hopkins was an admirable poet "but his theories on metre [seemed] to be as demonstrably wrong as those of any speculator who has led a multitude into the wilderness to perish." Indeed Young found Hopkins' ignorance on the subject of meter "so profound that he was not aware there was anything to know" ("Forty Years of Verse," *London Mercury*, 1936; reprinted in part in G. M. Young, *Daylight and Champaign,* 1937).

No less forthright was MacColl's statement after reading *Further Letters:* "It is high time that the bubble so assiduously blown around Hopkins' mistaken views on prosody should be pricked" ("Patmore and Hopkins: Sense and Nonsense in English Prosody," *London Mercury*, 1938). It was not until later that critics became more aware of the high degree to which his aesthetic theory was in harmony with his creative practice.

One has only to acquire a cursory knowledge of Hopkins scholarship to realize the possibilities it affords for conflicting estimates of his poetry. But if the publication of his poetry had stirred controversy, the publication of his letters added fuel to the flames.

The storm that centered on his prose was almost entirely

devoted to some aspect of a single problem: did his Jesuit life kill the poet in him or did it enrich his poetry? Abetted by Abbott's introductions to the volumes with such statements as, "It is our good fortune that his name belongs to literaure and not to hagiography," and "But what is possible to the resolved will of Milton the heretic was beyond the power of Hopkins the priest," and with the new mass of evidence, the critics dashed in to quote now one passage, now another. The battle over Bridges' "Preface to Notes" had not been hotter. C. Day Lewis dismissed the problem bluntly: "His religious vocation puts a wall between his life and ours only reminiscent of the wall of madhouse" (*New Republic,* 1935) .

There were those who took the postion of G. W. Stonier: "Religion did not stifle the poet in Hopkins for without religion he could hardly have written many of his best poems" (*New Statesman and Nation,* 1935) ; and of Egerton Clarke: "The habit of mind and will which was fostered in his life as a Jesuit transformed his work. Under that influence it developed, changing from mere experimental versification into an authentic utterance . . . " (*DubR* 1936) . David Daiches, who also gives a reasoned explanation of Hopkins' innovations in language, implied that his religious values were so secure that he was enabled to concentrate on expression, communication, and the art of poetry (*New Literary Values,* 1936) .

The most trenchant voice of opposition to such views was that of John Gould Fletcher: "To an artist of Hopkins's sort, dogmatic theology, though it may be of assistance in first orientating and disciplining his mind, always ends by finally destroying it. Art, and perhaps more particularly poetry, is a heresy which ends in being more valuable to a man than any orthodoxy whatsoever . . ." (*American Review,* 1936) .

In the midst of all the talk about the unhappy, repressed, and frustrated Jesuit, an essay particularly outstanding for taking a multiplicity of factors into consideration is Martin C. D'Arcy's "Gerard Manley Hopkins" in *Great Catholics,* edited by Claude Williamson, 1939. D'Arcy does not shy away from "unresolved tensions" and the tendency in Hopkins toward scrupulousness, nor does he minimize "the war within" which was so evident in his letters and which found expression in his greatest poetry.

Minor stirs were created in the 1930's by critics quick to pick up references to Communism in his letters (for instance, Babette Deutsch, *This Is Modern Poetry*, 1935), which often were linked with the suggestion that he started out as a young Communist and eventually conformed to a Tory conservatism. While such views were extreme, they had the virtue of bringing attention to Hopkins' social thought, briefly but well summarized by F. O. Matthiessen (*American Renaissance*, 1941), who also dealt perceptively with the recurring comparison between Whitman and Hopkins, emphasizing Hopkins' more highly disciplined art. A recent treatment of the subject, suggesting more actual and positive influence of Whitman on Hopkins than former critics had found, is by William Darby Templeman ("Hopkins and Whitman: Evidence of Influence and Ethics," *PQ*, 1954).

There were those also, who, after reading the letters and going back to the poetry, detected Freudian phrases everywhere (already noted in *New Verse*, 1935, by Grigson and Madge) and by isolating these elements built up interpretations of Hopkins as a martyr to torture accepted masochistically at the hands of severe Jesuit discipline—and worse. Philip Henderson (*The Poet and Society*, 1939) not only sees Communism everywhere, but detects in Hopkins obvious Freudian significances.

John Pick's *Gerard Manley Hopkins: Priest and Poet* (1942; anticipated by his articles in *Month*, 1940) was an attempt to make a thoroughgoing study of the relationships between Hopkins' life and poetry on the one hand, and his religous ideals and standards on the other. The latter, Pick contended, are expressed in *The Spiritual Exercises*, which became the chief formative influence on attitudes expressed in the mature poetry. He grants that the poet's dedication to Jesuit life was at least in part responsible for the small quantity of his production but asserts that it correspondingly gained in intensity and in those very qualities which every critic has granted as constituting his greatness.

In 1944 one hundred years had passed since the birth of Hopkins, though barely twenty-five had elapsed since his poems were available to the public. Eleanor Ruggles' *Gerard Manley Hopkins: A Life* has already been commented on. The centenary year was signalized, as might be expected, by the major periodicals, which carried nearly a hundred anniversary articles and

337

reviews. Special issues of *Kenyon Review* were devoted to Hopkins, and the articles were reprinted, with the addition of an introductory biographical sketch by Austin Warren and an article by F. R. Leavis from *Scrutiny* (1944), in a collected volume called *Gerard Manley Hopkins by the Kenyon Critics* (1945).

Several generalizations may be made about this notable book. The assumption behind each of the contributions is that Hopkins has assumed a permanent postion in English letters and that what remains is to define exactly his place. Next, all of the critics take almost for granted that his religion contributed to his greatness. Leavis, for instance, brings the volume to a close with: "Hopkins's religious interests are bound up with the presence in his poetry of a vigour of mind that puts him in another world from the other Victorians. It is a vitality of thought, a vigour of thinking intelligence, that is at the same time a vitality of concreteness."

A further observation may be made: while the predominant tendency of earlier critics had been to think of Hopkins as almost totally lacking in any Victorian elements, the Kenyon contributors emphasize those aspects in which he was a poet of his own time. This is not true merely of Arthur Mizener's essay, which is labeled "Victorian Hopkins."

Still another centenary tribute took the form of a collection of articles, *Immortal Diamond: Studies in Gerard Manley Hopkins,* edited by Norman Weyand, though this collection by a dozen American Jesuits was delayed, because of wartime conditions, until 1949. Like many symposia, it is uneven in quality. The importance of the "Glossary of Difficult Words" and the Bibliography has already been pointed out. "Gerard Manley Hopkins and the Society of Jesus" by Martin C. Caroll, in the absence of a definitive life of Hopkins, is valuable for sketching the typical training of a Jesuit, though it may oversimplify the problems of the priest and the poet. As might be expected, it is where doctrinal points are concerned that the book makes important contributions, and helpful aid is given in Maurice M. McNamee's "Hopkins: Poet of Nature and of the Supernatural," and in Robert B. Boyle's "The Thought Structure of 'The Wreck of the Deutschland.' " The editor has contributed an appendix entitled "The Historical Basis of 'The Wreck of the Deutschland' and 'The Loss of the Eurydice,' " giving the newspaper and eyewitness accounts of the two tragedies. As is almost inevitable there is one chapter devoted to an analysis of what has been Hopkins' most discussed poem, "What Does 'The Windhover' Mean?" by Raymond V. Schoder, who gives a thoroughly Ignatian interpretation. The article summarizes most of the previous interpretations, principally those by Richards, Empson, Leavis, Phare, Sargent, Kelly, Pick, Ruggles, McLuhan, and Grady. Schoder's own position is that the poem is not so much one of renunciation, stoic sacrifice, indecisive inner conflict, as of victory and triumph.

An eighty-page chapter, the longest and one of the best in the volume, is "Hopkins' Sprung Rhythm and the Life of English Poetry" by Walter Ong, an essay built up with great care and with a multiplicity of examples. According to Ong, Hopkins found the source of sprung rhythm running like an undercurrent in English poetry and speech wherever sense stress or interpretive stress was found. It was "a rhythm still inherent in the language and only suppressed by an artificially sustained tradition"—a rhythm deeply rooted in the genius of the English language.

Ong's emphasis on the organic quality of Hopkins' poetry is one that critics had been increasingly emphasizing. This essay was written during the year both Whitehall (in *Gerard Manley Hopkins by the Kenyon Critics*) and Gardner put forth the same thesis. The introduction, for instance, of rhyme into sense-stress verse gives it a different function from that in ordinary running rhythm; the line endings are less marked and exact rhymes therefore have less purpose. Further, sense-stress or sprung rhythm calls for alliteration, assonance, crowding out of relatives and the dramatic suppression of words, the telescoping of grammatical structure—not ornamentally but because with these devices the interpretive stress mounts in value. Bridges failed to appreciate Hopkins, Ong contends, because he refused to regard Hopkins' rhythm as an organic whole, hence the kind of "bickering" that was evidenced in his "Preface to Notes" in 1918.

The centenary year also brought forth the first installment of a two-volume study which is the most definitive work on Hopkins thus far, the work by W. H. Gardner entitled, accurately if awkwardly, *Gerard Manley Hopkins (1884-1889): A Study of Poetic Idiosyncrasy in Relation to Poetic Tradition*. Volume I appeared in England in 1944 and in America in 1948; volume II, ın both countries in 1949. Both have been reprinted several times since.

Gardner had himself been the author, starting in 1935, of several of the most significant articles on Hopkins. His new study took into careful consideration not only these articles but all that critics had to say about Hopkins up to this time.

The key to his comprehensiveness is indicated by the subtitle of his work: "A Study of Poetic Idiosyncrasy in Relation to Poetic Tradition." His purpose is to show that Hopkins was both traditionalist and revolutionary; that his poetry, at first sight so odd and eccentric in matters of style and rhythm, is in fact deeply rooted in European traditions. For example, Hopkins called most of his poems "sonnets," and in a chapter on "Sonnet Morphology" Gardner demonstrates how Hopkins did not abandon the Petrarchan form but developed its latent possibilities. Thus his practice was "to infuse a new spirit into the old form without destroying its identity." The same comment, Gardner would hold, can be applied to his metrics, his imagery, and his thought. Primarily critical rather than biographical, the book has adequate chapters on Hopkins' life, relating him to his family and friendships, to his social, cultural, artistic, political, economic, and religious backgrounds. Gardner also deals with the influences of Scotus and *The Spiritual Exercises* and with the evolution and growth of his poetry.

His chapters on prosody and on meter are very detailed and especially significant because he refuses to isolate sprung rhythm not merely from the semantic rhythm but from all the numerous highly wrought devices which Hopkins used to fuse his poems into organic wholes. Gardner treats the usually emphasized influences of Old English metrics and makes a detailed study of the impact of Greek melic and choral verse which influenced the poet in the direction of syntactic dislocation or interruption, thus imparting vigor and dramatic immediacy to poetry.

Particularly valuable is Gardner's emphasis on the disciplined quality of Hopkins' poetry and on the means he used to try to avoid the pitfalls usually accompanying sprung rhythm: "Sprung rhythm tends to degenerate into doggerel or even bad prose" when it is written "without the strict architectonic and elaborate phonal devices which Hopkins employs." Further chapters are devoted to his diction and syntax, his themes and his imagery, along with careful examination of his vocabulary.

A whole series of chapters is devoted to a chronological survey of his poetry, from the earliest verse (the first study of these poems to make clear Hopkins' early ability to handle conventional forms) to his final and last production, and including even the more important fragments. Occasionally an entire chapter is devoted to a single poem, as in the case of "The Wreck of the Deutschland." Here Gardner's distance from Bridges can be judged by his assertion that it "stands like a great overture at the beginning of his mature work, rich in themes which are taken up, developed and varied, sometimes more than once, in the subsequent poems."

In these chapters, with exegesis accompanied by sensitive paraphrase, he gives frequent scansions, and there are elaborate footnotes and appendices. Gardner tries to qualify the comments of such critics as those who have made Hopkins the only Victorian influential in modern poetry, pointing out in a chapter devoted to "Hopkins and Modern Poetry" the importance of Browning, of Whitman, and of several other figures and movements just as formative as Hopkins. Significant, too, are his comments on the difference between sprung rhythm and free verse, whence came a confusion of which critics and poets had alike been guilty.

A final "Epilogue" attempts to summarize Hopkins' limitations and failures, his contributions and accomplishments. For Gardner the later far outweigh the former: "After an intensive reading of Hopkins, most other English poetry seems outwardly facile and in varying degrees inadequate."

It would be folly to contend that the fifteen chapters of the two volumes are equally successful. "Hopkins as Reader and Critic," for instance, falls short, but no subsequent work on the subject of Hopkins as a literary critic has superseded it, and this subject is worthy of a book-length study. Gardner's is a reasoned admiration, and in his enthusiasm he has discovered much that escaped previous critics.

The chief defect of Gardner's two volumes is an organizational one. Separate chapters are really separate essays, and there is repetition and backtracking. But it does remain the most comprehensively inclusive work that has been published on Hopinks and the best summation of Hopkins' basic contributions to poetry.

The third edition of the *Poems,* which Gardner edited in 1948, draws on the findings of these two volumes and together they have established Gardner as perhaps the leading Hopkins scholar of our time.

In 1948 an almost useless book appeared, *Gerard Manley Hopkins: The Man and the Poet* by K. R. Srinivasa Iyengar, published by the Indian Branch of the Oxford University Press. Much of the book had originally appeared in 1938 in *The New Review* of Calcutta, and the book was ready for press in 1939. Publication was delayed by the war, and the author resisted too firmly the temptation to revise extensively so that he might take advantage of the numerous special critical studies which appeared during the ten years from 1938 to 1948.

However, the book does stand as an instance of how widespread interest in Hopkins has become in countries other than England or America; for instance, in the same year, 1948, appeared *Gerard Manley Hopkins: Gedichte,* with a long introduction by Irene Behn. Among the more recent examples of the acceptance of Hopkins in other countries are *Hopkinsiana: la vida, la obra y la supervivencia de Gerard Manley Hopkins* by José Manuel Gutierrez, which resulted in an extended interchange of letters in *TLS* during 1954 and 1955; French translations by Pierre Leyris (*Gerard Manley Hopkins: Reliquae 1958*); Georges Cattaui's *Trois Poètes: Hopkins, Yeats, Eliot,* (1947) ; and Jean-Georges Ritz's *Le Poète Gérard Manley Hopkins, S. J. 1884–1889: L'Homme et l'oeuvre* (1963) which runs to some seven hundred pages.

In 1948 a major critical work appeared, *Gerard Manley Hopkins: A Critical Essay towards the Understanding of His Poetry* by W. A. M. Peters, dealing in detail with a single aspect of Hopkins and making this aspect the key to all of his poetry. Much had been written previously of "inscape" and Duns Scotus; important earlier studies had been Christopher Devlin's "Gerard Hopkins and Duns Scotus," W. H. Gardner's "A Note on Hopkins and Duns Scotus" (*Scrutiny,* 1936) , and Devlin's "An Essay on Scotus" (*Month,* 1946) ; but here was an entire book devoted to showing that inscape explains why Hopkins wrote exactly as he did.

Peters sets out to show that his "obscurity and oddity," his deviations from common usage, his syntactical or grammatical idiosyncrasies, and all that is baffling to the ordinary reader are not the result of "artistic wantonness," as Bridges contended, but are the logically integrated outcome of his theory of inscape.

Peters chooses to ignore the factor of literary tradition and thus inevitably exaggerates the uniqueness of Hopkins. While W. H. Gardner had attempted to suggest the complexity of "idiosyncrasy in relation to poetic tradition," Peters isolates the absolute individuality of the poet, and he seems unaware of the solipsistic subjectivity toward which his thesis carries him.

However, even if he insists too strongly on making everything in Hopkins fit his central thesis, he has explored so thoroughly certain aspects of Hopkins' use of language that whoever will finally write the balanced and comprehensively definitive book about Hopkins' poetry will have to draw on Peters.

The relation of Duns Scotus to Hopkins has continued to interest critics. Marjorie D. Coogan introduced minor qualifications in a redefinition of inscape ("Inscape and Instress: Further Analogies with Scotus," *PMLA*, 1950). Far-reaching in its implications is a tentative article by Christopher Devlin ("Time's Eunuch," *Month*, 1949) which relates Scotus so intimately to Hopkins' inspiration that the falling-off of his productivity is attributed to his abandonment of Scotism as a speculative system and is conjecturally used as an explanation for much of the feeling of frustration in his later poems.

Related problems are tenuously and subtly explored by Devlin in two further articles of the following year ("The Image and the Word I & II," *Month*, 1950; see also the interchange of correspondence on these articles between Devlin and Gardner, *Month*, 1950).

Devlin's edition of *The Sermons and Devotional Writings of Hopkins* (1959) contains an appendix, "Scotus and Hopkins," as well as important remarks on the influence of Scotus in his introductions. He sees Scotus as related to Hopkins' Victorian conscience and to his almost crippling sense of duty.

Two articles by John Abraham entitled "The Hopkins Aesthetic" (*Continuum*, 1963) are largely concentrated on Scotism, and he emphasizes the contradictory conclusions of Peters and Devlin.

Scotus was one of the most abstruse of philosophers—there was good reason for calling him "Doctor Subtilis"—and these are difficult articles. However, they are far-reaching in their implications and eventually someone who is both philosopher and literary critic must attempt a definitive treatment of Scotus and Hopkins.

Abraham holds that it is not inscape but instress that is the equivalent of the Scotist *haecceitas*. Bell Gale Chevigny more recently in "Instress and Devotion in the Poetry of Gerard Manley Hopkins" (*VS* 1965) seems unaware of all the controversy that has stormed around the implications of the term "instress," but he creatively relates it to three major phases of Hopkins' mature poetry.

The 1950's saw further important contributions to Hopkins scholarship, undoubtedly spurred by the new edition of *Letters to Robert Bridges, Correspondence with Dixon,* the augmented edition of *Further Letters,* and the publication of both *The Journals and Papers of Hopkins* and *The Sermons and Devotional Writings of Hopkins.*

The general trend from 1918 had been toward the growing acceptance of Hopkins, and at mid-century, for instance, the only extended and violent attack on his poetry was that of Yvor Winters ("The Poetry of Gerard Manley Hopkins," *HudR,* 1949; reprinted in *The Function of Criticism,* 1957; for an extended reply see J. H. Johnston, "Reply to Yvor Winters," *Renascence,* 1950). After fifty deflating pages in which Hopkins is characterized by "an unrestrained indulgence in meaningless emotion," Winters grudgingly places Hopkins among "the twelve or fourteen best British poets of the nineteenth century." Even this is an index to the change that had taken place in criticism since 1918.

In 1954 appeared Geoffrey H. Hartman's *The Unmediated Vision: An Interpretation of Wordsworth, Hopkins, Rilke and Valery,* in which the Hopkins chapter is concentrated on "The Windhover," exemplifying Hartman's critical method "to show that a unified multiple interpretation of poetry is textually justified, even required . . . since the poem brings the complete man into activity."

Geoffrey Grigson's little booklet, *Gerard Manley Hopkins,* published the following year in the "Writers and Their Work" series is not so much a rounded and balanced introduction to Hopkins as the enthusiastic tribute of another poet to Hopkins as one dedicated to the "passionate science" of careful nature observation.

Alan Heuser's *The Shaping Vision of Gerard Manley Hopkins* (1958) is stimulating and suggestive but undeveloped. In fifteen short chapters he sketches the growth of Hopkins' "shaping vision," soundly suggesting how complex, even in Hopkins' earliest days, were all the factors that went into his constantly and continually changing and evolving views.

Not only does Heuser take into account many of the Ignatian and Scotist influences, but he also emphasizes the contribution of the Pre-Raphaelites, hardly remarked on before, and the Greeks. He considers that Hopkins moved from naturalistic idealism through a philosophy of inscape and instress to a Scotist voluntarism and a Pythagorean Platonism.

Heuser concludes that of all the influences on Hopkins, the Pre-Raphaelites were the most significant, and, if a distinct label for Hopkins is needed, it is "baroque," and that in this Hopkins was a new expression of the old Jesuit ideal.

The volume, condensed and difficult, is not an introduction to Hopkins for the ordinary reader. It does offer a map of territory for further critics to explore.

For several decades scholars have increasingly recognized the importance of the Ignatian impact on the life and art of Hopkins, and in 1959 David A. Downes published a full-volume study of this influence, *Gerard Manley Hopkins: A Study of His Ignatian Spirit*. He sees even the pre-Catholic verse of Hopkins as an anticipation of Ignatian attitudes and almost all his mature poetry—except possibly the "terrible sonnets"—as structured by Ignatian spiritual methods. Central to his thesis is that Ignatian influence provided Hopkins with emotional and mental dispositions convertible to poetic techniques.

Some points raised by Downes are worthy of still further examination. Was the tradition of the Jesuits in the nineteenth century a Suarism which might be considered as close to Scotism as to Thomism? And Downes himself seems unable to decide whether the "terrible sonnets," probably the greatest of Hopkins' poems, are "the least Ignatian" or whether "Nothing could be more Ignatian."

Downes published still another book on Hopkins in 1965, *Victorian Portraits: Hopkins and Pater*. Heretofore the Pater-Hopkins relationship had not received much more than an occasional allusion. For a brief but impressionable period at Oxford in the 1860's the two were friends and there are only a few scattered references to Pater in Hopkins' diaries and letters. This would seem an extremely slight foundation for building a book, yet Downes has produced a many-layered study by suggesting contrasts as well as affinities between the two men. The book is sounder in its treatment of Hopkins than of Pater.

The 1950's would have been incomplete without a comparison of Hopkins and Dylan Thomas, who died in 1953. Henry Treece had included a chapter intitled "The Debt to Hopkins" in his *Dylan Thomas* back in 1949. J. H. B. Peel in an article, "The Echoes in the Booming Voice" (*N. Y. Times Book Review*), in 1957 wrote, "Hopkins was not only the original of Thomas' booming voice; he was also its master in that he boomed better . . . the difference between Hopkins and Thomas is fundamentally a difference btweeen a major and a minor poet."

Just as the 1930's would have been incomplete without attempts to find social protest or Freudian echoes in Hopkins, so the 1950's would have been incomplete without hailing him as an earlier Angry Young Man. John Wain's *Gerard Manley Hopkins: An Idiom of Desperation* (*Proceedings of the British Academy*, 1959; reprinted in *Essays in Literature and Ideas*, 1963) singled out Hopkins as "the greatest of the Victorian poets," whose isolation from the establishment gave him his bold originality. He broke new ground in staying close to ordinary speech, while Bridges ("that monumentally deaf eardrum") "by comparison, has no pipe-line to living, informal speech." Wain's essay, brashly bristling with fresh ideas, is by no means trivial or without significance.

Two important studies appeared in 1960, Jean-Georges Ritz's *Robert Bridges and Gerard Manley Hopkins 1863–1889: A Literary Friendship*, already referred to, and Robert Boyle's *Metaphor in Hopkins*.

Hopkins has not always been fortunate in his critics, but Boyle succeeded in uncovering an important dimension of the poetic accomplishment of Hopkins. Belonging to that group of contemporary critics following Cleanth Brooks and John Crowe Ransom, he sees in metaphor the key to significant poetry. Boyle further extends this to include "metaphorical rhythm" to which he finds the sprung rhythm of Hopkins especially suited.

The central metaphor of all of Hopkins' mature poetry is Christ's life "divinizing the heart of acquiescent humans, reaching even to animals, birds, trees, the good earth itself." Boyle traces the chronological deepening of this vision and chooses eight significant images which have a vital influence in eight important poems which further express eight themes pervasive in Hopkins' mature poems. Hopkins emerges from Boyle's book with newly discovered height, depth, and breadth.

A chapter of forty pages in *Studies in Structure: The Stages of the Spiritual Life in Four Modern Authors,* (1964) , by Robert Andreach, is devoted to Hopkins. Employing the traditional stages in the spiritual life, he holds that Hopkins' early poems represent a false direction, neither truly mystical nor genuinely ascetical. His later poetry embodies a genuine ascetic purgation. The study is helpful in directing attention to the early poems and also in counteracting the facile tendency to label Hopkins a mystical poet.

Almost inevitably the climate of the 1960's, which echoed Nietzsche's "Gott is tot," found expression in J. Hillis Miller's *The Disappearance of God: Five Nineteenth-Century Writers* (1963). Purporting to use the critical methods of the "Geneva School" and of recent Parisian structualist critics, Miller sees much of contemporary literature as involving a nihilism which is covert in nineteenth-century literature: "In nihilism the disappearance of God becomes the death of God. This death is the presupposition of much twentieth-century literature."

The five authors he presents—DeQuincey, Browning, Emily Brontë, and Hopkins—heroically attempt to recover immanence in a world of transcendance. This is what Miller really means by the rather misleading term "disappearance."

Easily the longest chapter, one of nearly a hundred pages, studies Hopkins and partly incorporates two of his other articles ("The Creation of Self in Gerard Manley Hopkins," *ELH,* 1955, and "The Theme of the Disappearance of God in Victorian

Poetry," *VS* 1963). For Miller, "Neither Arnold, nor Tennyson, nor Browing is able to transcend so completely the spiritual condition of his age. Hopkins alone recovers a world like that of Eden before the fall." But this applies only to the poetry of his central period, and Miller traces the breakdown in his precarious last years. Following Devlin, Miller sees this collapse as due to Hopkins' Victorianism, abetted by Scotus. In his last period, "Hopkins has, beyond all his contemporaries the most shattering experience of the disappearance of God." Yet at the very close of his life, God, transcendant not immanent, reappeared—but across an unbridgeable gulf.

The book occasioned widely varying opinions. While one scholarly reviewer wrote, "This is the best book on Victorian literature I have ever encountered, and the only really good one," another referred to it as "monstrously overlong, arrogantly idiosyncratic, and undeniably important... his prolixity is largely inseparable from his moments of vibrancy and vision."

The book is both brilliantly right and brilliantly wrong. Miller worked carefully with the recent new editions of primary materials, but many will hesitate to follow him in his insistence on the identity of poetry and prayer ("When there is a failure of grace there is a failure of poetry") and this makes difficult the explanation of the Dublin or "terrible" sonnents.

By the mid-1960's it was widely recognized that Hopkins was deeply rooted in tradition, but Todd K. Bender in his *Gerard Manley Hopkins: The Classical Background and Critical Reception of His Work* (1966) has given a new twist to this emphasis. To Bender, many of the apparent innovations were at least partially derivative. The source for his syntactical and structural distortion, disjunctive diction, ambiguity, far-fetched imagery, and basically nonlogical patterns of hyperbaton as well as his interest in "underthought" and "overthought" is to be found in Hopkins' creative modification of Latin and Greek practices. Bender's special contribution is that he suggests that the assumptions behind these things are precisely those demanded of poetry by the critics (Richards, Read, Empson, and their followers) responsible for the critical reception of Hopkins after 1918. In other words, Hopkins, deeply grounded in the past, precociously foresees by some forty years the assumptions behind the critical taste which in the 1920's and 1930's enthusiastically welcomed him.

The most recent useful introduction to Hopkins is *Gerard Manley Hopkins* by Jim Hunter (1966), containing short chapters dealing with important aspects of the poet and numerous suggestive paraphrases of most of the poems. Elementary and sometimes uneven, it can be recommended to undergraduates.

Innumerable articles have appeared over the years in reference to sprung rhythm, and the work of Gardner and Ong has already been mentioned. Two recent contributions suggest that there is still a considerable lack of unanimity. Paull F. Baum's thesis ("Sprung Rhythm," *PMLA*, 1959) is not new: sprung rhythm is not so much a modification of conventional verse as a new creation; Hopkins wrote better than he theorized; and his prosodic terminology is often confused and confusing. On the other hand, Elisabeth W. Schneider ("Sprung Rhythm: A Chapter in the Evolution of Nineteenth-Century Verse," *PMLA*, 1965) holds that sprung rhythm was part of the nineteenth-century search for fresh metrical forms, and that Hopkins' meter does not depart widely from conventional metrical forms. However, she points out that about the only thing critics agree on is that Hopkins invented the term "sprung rhythm."

Recent years have seen an increasing number of articles and even chapters of books relating Hopkins to the metaphysical poets, especially to Herbert, Donne, or Crashaw—in spite of the virtual absence of recorded references to them in his letters, journals, or notebooks. See, for instance, David Morris' *The Poetry of Gerard Manley Hopkins and T. S. Eliot in the Light of the Donne Tradition* (1953) or Joseph E. Duncan's *The Revival of Metaphysical Poetry: A History of a Style, 1800 to the Present* (1959) on this subject. There has been also a growing tendency to stress the baroque elements in Hopkins, as do two articles appearing in 1961: "Hopkins Again," by David Sutherland (*PrS*, 1961), and "The 'Barbarous Beauty' of Gerard Manley Hopkins," by Rosana Zelocchi (*Convivium*, 1961).

After fifty years of closer and closer reading of Hopkins, the bibliographical list of separate articles devoted to individual poems and even particular lines or images is ever expanding. In such periodicals as *Explicator* and *Notes and Queries*, "God's

Grandeur" and the Dublin sonnets seem to be the favorites for exegesis, one article often evoking another in reply.

A considerable literature has grown up around "The Wreck of the Deutschland" which many readers have found, as did Bridges, to be "like a great dragon folded in the gate to forbid all entrance" to the poetry of Hopkins. The best of the earlier evaluations of this poem may be found in Gardner's contribution to *Essays and Studies by Members of the English Association* (1935), which he incorporated as a chapter into his *Gerard Manley Hopkins (1884–1889): A Study of Poetic Idiosyncrasy in Relation to Poetic Tradition;* in " 'The Wreck of the Deutschland': An Introduction and a Paraphrase," by Francis Ryan (*DubR,* 1948) ; and in Boyle's and Weyand's contributions to *Immortal Diamond: Studies in Gerard Manley Hopkins* (1949). M. B. McNamee's later "Mastery and Mercy in 'The Wreck of the Deutschland' " (*CE,* 1962) is a short and readable introduction to the content of the poem.

Two nearly book-length studies of the poem have appeared in the past decade. *Mastery and Mercy: A Study of Two Religious Poems,* 1957, by Philip M. Martin, attempts a rather thin and casual running commentary on the religious content. It is rather elementary for those of a generation who have become accustomed to careful textual exegesis. Far more complex is the treatment in *The Wreck of the Deutschland: An Essay and Commentary* (1963), by Joseph E. Keating, who devotes a hundred pages to wrestling with the basic paradoxes in the poem.

One of the best studies of the poem appeared most recently. Elisabeth W. Schneider's *"The Wreck of the Deutschland: A New Reading"* (*PMLA,* 1966) ranks the poem "among the great odes of the English language." Stressing the tension and reconciliation of passion and asceticism, freedom and law, idiosyncrasy and control, she attributes the poem's effectiveness to the "peculiarly explosive character of these oppositions inherent in the detail as well as the whole design."

But of all the poems, "The Windhover"—which Hopkins himself once called the best thing he ever wrote—easily has continued to attract most attention. Undoubtedly the day is not far off when an entire book—or at least a doctoral dissertation—will be written about these fourteen lines.

Helpful summaries of earlier criticism of the poem may be found in the essay "What Does 'The Windhover' Mean?" by Raymond Schoder (in *Immortal Diamond: Studies in Gerard Manley Hopkins,* 1949), and in Boyle's *Metaphor in Hopkins* (1960). Every comma and hyphen and indeed every spelling has been examined, and the sonnet has been interpreted as everything from an exercise in ornithology to a Freudian revelation of divine masochism. Articles and counter-articles and counter-replies have proliferated. A sampling of the titles of recent articles on the poem is suggestive: "The Return of 'The Windhover,' " " 'The Windhover' Revisted," "Once More into 'The Windhover,' " "Another Look at 'The Windhover,' " and " 'The Windhover': A Further Simplification."

"Hopkins," wrote a reviewer recently in *TLS,* "has survived the long process of his literary resurrection," and there seems no letup in Hopkins scholarship. One thing seems certain: he continues to be one of the most controversial of figures, the only nineteenth-century poet claimed by both the Victorians and the Moderns.

The Later Victorian Poets

LIONEL STEVENSON

The perspective of time is still strangely uncertain with regard to the significance of the many competent poets who flourished during the final third of the nineteenth century. Instead of two or three dominant figures, there were a score or more of varied writers, whose reputations both then and now are difficult to define and to correlate. Research scholars of the present generation have concentrated on a few of the poets and have done little with others. One group, in particular, who may be called the "Tennysonians" and who were unquestionably the most widely admired in their own day, are now virtually forgotten. This group included Robert Buchanan, Lewis Morris, Edwin Arnold, Alfred Austin, and William Watson. Austin, the prolific laureate, has been made the subject of a thorough biographical study, which attempts to place him in his literary and political milieu (*Alfred Austin: Victorian,* by Norton Crowell, 1953). But otherwise the school of Tennyson remains unexplored territory.

In the present chapter, fourteen of the "late Victorians" are considered. Several fairly distinct "schools" or "groups" or "movements" are recognizable; but the effort to classify the fourteen poets in any way has proved impracticable, in view of the overlapping and complex relationships among them. Francis Thompson, for instance, belongs primarily in the Roman Catholic group with Patmore, and yet he has much in common with the Aesthetic group that stemmed from Pater and included Wilde, Dowson, and Johnson. Accordingly the poets are arranged merely in the chronological order of age, from Patmore to Dowson—a span of forty-four years.

COVENTRY PATMORE (1823–1896)

The biography of Coventry Patmore has gone through several distinct phases. Soon after his death he was made the subject of a ponderous two-volume "official" biography, *The Memoirs and Correspondence of Coventry Patmore,* by Basil Champneys (1900). This book provided the formal picture of the poet's life, and quoted liberally from his letters and journals; but its author, an architect, was unskilled in writing and was further handicapped by the fact that the widow and children of his subject were alive. The whole emotional life of this highly emotional poet was therefore slighted: his relations with his three wives were mentioned in the most conventional terms, and his senile infatuation for Alice Meynell was ignored.

Five years later Edmund Gosse did a short biographical sketch for the series Literary Lives (1905). Not for the first or last time, Gosse was torn between his instinct to make an incisive biographical portrait and his respect for discretion, and hence he was not able to make full use of his knowledge of Patmore's complex personality.

During the next generation Patmore perhaps more intensely than any of his contemporaries suffered from the general contempt toward all things "Victorian," because as author of *The Angel in the House* he was regarded as the extreme spokesman of sentimental domesticity. Thirty years after Gosse's book, a young writer named Derek Patmore awoke to the fact that his great-grandfather had been a man of some literary stature, and in 1935 he published *Portrait of My Family,* confessing frankly that "it was not until I went to New York, at the age of nineteen, that I became interested in the subject. Over there, everybody seemed to know more about my family than I knew myself! . . . In mortification at my own ignorance and partly in self-defense,

355

I determined to read his poems, and learn something about his life" (p. 2). After discovering Champneys' biography in the Columbia University Library, the young Patmore became so fascinated that he searched for family documents after his return to England. His book was youthfully naive and unnecessarily jaunty, but it used many of Patmore's letters to his third wife and revealed several new aspects of the poet's character.

During the next dozen years Victorianism grew respectable and the late-Victorian school of Roman Catholic poetry came into fashion. Besides, Derek Patmore matured; and his great-uncle, the last surviving son of the poet, died. Hence a complete revision of the biography was undertaken and came out in 1949 as *The Life and Times of Coventry Patmore*. It is based on much more extensive research than its predecessor, and maintains a soundly objective attitude. "When this book first appeared," the author remarks, "the revival of interest in Coventry Patmore and his poems had only just begun after a long eclipse. . . . A new generation has now arisen. . . . For them, Coventry Patmore is no longer the slightly ridiculous poet of matrimony, but a mystic and a religious poet of the highest order."

A few influential critics had paid some attention to Patmore during the decades of his eclipse, mainly to praise his sequence of odes, *The Unknown Eros,* at the expense of *The Angel in the House.* Arthur Symons led the way with an essay in *Studies in Two Literatures* (1897) and added a supplementary one, written in 1906 and reprinted in *Figures of Several Centuries* (1916). Arthur Quiller-Couch's essay, first printed as a review of Champneys' biography in 1900, was included in the third series of his *Studies in Literature* (1929). Of the odes, Quiller-Couch declares, "gradually the opinion gains that we possess in them one of the rarest treasures of Victorian poetry."

The change in critical estimation was started mainly by two books that appeared during Patmore's general disfavor. The first was *The Idea of Coventry Patmore,* by Osbert Burdett (1921). With somewhat ponderous thoroughness Burdett expounded his thesis that Patmore

is one of the few poets who had a system of thought . . . Though the fact has been admitted, his theory has not been studied, partly because no one has given serious attention to his idea, partly because the detail which it introduced into his epic has been judged adversely by his critics on the ground that poetry, even on the grand scale of the epic, was incapable without degradation of assimilating the contemporary atmosphere which it was his main endeavour to express. He is one of the few poets who have tried to build a philosophy of life out of the experiences of love; and his attempt is original because it is not, as were previous attempts, based upon any disregard or arbitrary manipulation of the facts, but was inspired by an unusually frank admission of them. If we value this poetical honesty, we shall study the attempt in a fair light. If not, the difficulties resulting from the honesty will appear unnecessary because they could have been evaded (p. vii.)

The second important critical work was *Patmore: A Study in Poetry* (1933). It was written by Frederick Page, an enthusiast who had devoted years to collecting information about Patmore and his circle and who had contributed useful facts and acute criticism both to Burdett's book and to Derek Patmore's. The gentle irony of Page's style can be illustrated by his introductory allusion to Burdett's pretentious claims: "Patmore's poetry lends itself to the facile and intricate systematization by the summarist and the student that one may maliciously and usefully disturb and postpone.... Whether his poetry is seen through the reversed telescope of writers of handbooks, or through Mr. Osbert Burdett's microscope, equally it is not seen as poetry" (p. 12). To correct this imbalance, Page devotes much of his attention to Patmore's artistic technique in *The Angel in the House* and *The Unknown Eros*. He asserts that "The alternation of preludes and idyls constitutes an art-form unique in English, although perhaps owing something to Wither's *Faire Virtue*." Page suggests that "the very close connexion of *The Angel in the House* and *Faire Virtue*" would repay a more thorough analysis than he was able to give it.

The revival of critical appreciation became clear early in the thirties. Perhaps the best essay on Patmore is the one which Herbert Read contributed to *The Great Victorians*, edited by H. J. and Hugh Massingham (1932), and which was later reprinted in Read's volume, *In Defence of Shelley, and Other Essays* (1936). Admitting "the intermittency of his inspiration" and the "ugly inversions and elisions" even in his best poems, Read nevertheless concludes that in the odes "the thought is

357

irredeemably fused in the expression, and the result is true poetry of the rarest and perhaps the highest kind—metaphysical poetry such as has been written by Lucretius, Dante, Donne, Crashaw, and Wordsworth." At the same time as Read's essay, Desmond MacCarthy's came out in his *Criticism* (1932). MacCarthy calls Patmore "a more magnificent poet and a more interesting 'prophet' than even the literary seem as yet able to believe, . . . the greatest religious poet in English literature since the seventeenth century and perhaps greater than Crashaw." Other essays that discuss Patmore and his poetry with some authority are by Shane Leslie, in *Studies in Divine Failure* (1932), and by F. L. Lucas, in *Ten Victorian Poets* (1940). A stimulating essay, though cranky and exaggerated, as its subtitle implies, is "Patmore and Hopkins: Sense and Nonsense in English Poetry," by D. S. MacColl (*London Mercury*, 1938). Attacking Hopkins' "mistaken views on prosody," MacColl asserts that "Coventry Patmore is the only English poet who has understood what he himself and his brother poets were doing when they wrote verse." Patmore's great innovation was to discard the concept of the metrical "foot" and substitute that of the musical "bar," measured from stress to stress. MacColl insists that Bridges and Hopkins made a "theoretical mess" of Patmore's principle, and that Hopkins only gradually grasped its true import as he grew older.

A noteworthy phenomenon is the recognition of Patmore in France and Italy. Paul Claudel translated nine of the odes about 1900 and his versions were published in 1911 with an extensive introduction by Valéry Larbaud, which was reprinted, slightly revised, in Larbaud's *Ce vice impuni: La lecture, domaine anglais* (*Oeuvres complètes*, III, 1951). Marius-François Guyard's article "De Patmore à Claudel: Histoire et nature d'une influence" (*Révue de littérature comparée*, 1959) gives a good account of the relationship. Another excellent French study is "L'Amour selon Coventry Patmore," by Charles Du Bos, in his *Approximations* (7th series, 1937). In Italy, Augusto Guido published a book on Patmore in 1946. Influenced by Claudel's admiration for Patmore, Mario Praz wrote "The Epic of the Everyday," which is rather illogically appended to his book, *The Hero in Eclipse in Victorian Fiction* (translated by Angus Davidson, 1956). Though *The Angel in the House* is the epitome of what Praz scorns as "Biedermeier," he links the poem to the Wordsworthian tradition: he finds in it "Wordsworth's loftiest note, and . . . also his pedestrian side, his bathos, carried to the point of the most deliberate carelessness." Praz adds that "Patmore drew far more inspiration from the English poets of the seventeenth century than has been recognized even by our own contemporaries."

Two modern books on Patmore came out almost simultaneously. *Coventry Patmore,* by E. J. Oliver (1956), is a concise and readable account of his life and works emphasizing the "extravagant contradictions" and intransigent independence of his character. Oliver divides Patmore's writings into three distinct periods, corresponding with his three marriages. A more important book is *The Mind and Art of Coventry Patmore,* by J. G. Reid (1957), which is "an attempt to see Patmore whole, in his prose as well as in his poetry, and to present as complete an exegesis of his thought as possible." The investigation of his sources is particularly thorough, though Reid shows also "the degree to which Patmore's thought, while deriving in great part from the philosophers and mystics in whom he read, is original and represents the vehicle of a deeply-felt personal experience." The bibliography of both primary and secondary sources is the best available, and the book as a whole is the most extensive and scholarly study of Patmore's work yet published.

Since Patmore's rehabilitation, he has not been the subject of many significant articles. Paul Turner's "Aurora and the Angel" (*RES,* 1948) compares his poem and Mrs. Browning's as specimens of the novel in verse. There is some value in "Prophet without Responsibility: A Study of Coventry Patmore," by J. M. Cohen (*Essays in Criticism,* 1951), and in three articles by W. H. Gardner in *The Month* (1952, 1958). The most enthusiastic recent essay is "Patmore, Donne, and the 'Wit of Love,'" in *The Charted Mirror,* by John Holloway (1960). Going farther than others in defending *The Angel in the House,* Holloway asserts:

> Within limits, modern readers will admire the neatness and humour and dramatic detachment of parts of the poem; and sometimes Patmore deserves admiration for the dexterity, and the intrinsic rightness and truthfulness, with which he has made these down-to-earth incidents grow into powerful and disturbing realities. . . . Often

enough Patmore displays a good deal of Donne's exploring subtlety, his close yet unforced argumentation, and even his fondness for recondite yet telling astronomical metaphors ... But also like Donne, Patmore could explore his subject, and subtly, through the metaphor which is not recondite at all, save in the sense that it is disconcertingly humdrum. . . . It is clear that Patmore was not only a deeply thinking poet, seeking sexual love, in its fulness, as a paradigm of man's essential quality and his characteristic relation with God; but also a poet whose thought regularly entered the fibre of his language, and grew into a concrete embodiment of itself (pp. 56-57).

The technical subtlety of *The Angel* is defended also by William Cadbury in "The Structure of Feeling in a Poem by Patmore" (*VP*, 1966).

GEORGE MEREDITH (1828–1909)

Students of George Meredith are abundantly supplied with bibliographical data through two monumental volumes compiled by Maurice Buxton Forman: *A Bibliography of the Writings in Prose and Verse of George Meredith* (1922) and *Meredithiana* (1924), the latter listing most of the secondary material that had appeared in print up to the date of its publication. The latter listing has been extended thirty years by H. Lewis Sawin in "George Meredith: A Bibliography of Meredithiana, 1920–1953" (*Bulletin of Bibliography*, 1955).

One of the immediate desiderata in the study of Meredith is a dependable edition of the letters, and Professor C. L. Cline of the University of Texas is preparing one. The two volumes edited by Meredith's son (1912) suffer from every sort of editorial misdemeanor—misreadings, misdatings, unindicated omissions, suppressed names. A number of letters in the largest extant collection of Meredithiana were printed in *A Catalogue of the Altschul Collection of George Meredith in the Yale University Library,* edited by Bertha Coolidge (1931), but this, too, is not free of errors and many letters have come into the Altschul Collection since the catalog was compiled. Phyllis Bartlett has provided a valuable analysis of Meredith's early manuscript poems in the Berg Collection *(Bulletin of the New York Public Library,* 1957).

The first book which offered any biographical information about Meredith was *George Meredith in Anecdote and Criticism,* by J. A. Hammerton (1909), reissued two years later, with revisions, as *George Meredith: His Life and Art in Anecdote and Criticism.* This was a scissors-and paste job, made up largely from reviews of his books and from other articles in periodicals. A serious attempt at a biography was made by S. M. Ellis, who had experience in writing about other Victorian novelists; both the merits and the defects of his book—*George Meredith: His Life and Friends in Relation to his Work* (1919)—spring from the fact that his father had been Meredith's first cousin. He was able to supply many details of family history not previously available, but this led to undue emphasis on Meredith's early life and to distortion of trivial details in order to exalt the Ellis family at Meredith's expense. Under threat of a suit for infringement of copyright, the book was recalled and a new edition was issued, reduced about sixty percent by omission of quoted passages.

French academic thoroughness and accuracy marked the book by René Galland, *George Meredith: Les cinquante premières années (1828–1878)* (1923). Galland had worked on the book for years, and consulted surviving members of the family, who supplied him with authentic details. Nothing so favorable can be said about *The Life of George Meredith,* by "R. E. Sencourt" (R. E. Gordon George), which came out in the centennial year, 1928. It contains fantastic errors of fact and of interpretation, and is colored throughout by its writer's idiosyncrasies. There is better writing in Siegfried Sassoon's book, *Meredith* (1948), but as a biography it is ill-proportioned and sketchy, in consequence of Sassoon's lack of experience in methods of research. He had access to the large collection of data assembled by M. Buxton Forman and then owned by the publishing firm of Constable, but he seems to have dipped into it at random instead of making a systematic study. Jack Lindsay's *George Meredith: His Life and Work* (1956) is inaccurate as to facts and ideologically biased. The only full-scale biography based on extensive investigation of all available evidence is *The Ordeal of George Meredith,* by Lionel Stevenson (1953).

For the study of Meredith's reputation there are two helpful volumes: *George Meredith: Some Early Appreciations,* compiled by Maurice Buxton Forman (1909), and *George Meredith and British Criticism,* by René Galland (1923).

Most of the general studies of Meredith's writings have concentrated on his novels and need not be discussed here. The only book devoted solely to his poetry is *The Poetry and Philosophy of George Meredith,* by George Macaulay Trevelyan (1906), which retains its value after more than half a century and is indispensable as an introduction to Meredith's poetical work. Nevertheless, its title reveals an emphasis which was prevalent at the time but which has contributed to a surviving notion that Meredith's poetry was solemnly didactic. The same point of view dominated the book by Constantin Photiadès, *George Meredith: Sa vie, son imagination, son art, sa doctrine* (1910), translated by Arthur Price as *George Meredith: His Life, Genius, and Teaching* (1913); the references to Meredith's poems in this book deal mainly with their philosophic content. In *George Meredith, Novelist, Poet, Reformer,* by M. Sturge Henderson (1907), four chapters on Meredith's poetry were supplied by Basil de Sélincourt, three dealing with the ideas in his poems and one on "Meredith as artist and craftsman." Mrs. Sturge Henderson herself wrote the chapter on *Modern Love,* almost the first to deal perceptively with that important poem. Twenty years later this book was revised and reissued as *The Writings and Life of George Meredith,* by Mary Sturge Gretton (1926), with some of de Sélincourt's comments absorbed into the main body of the book, which now received a chronological arrangement. The chapter on "Meredith's Poetry" in *George Meredith,* by J. H. E. Crees (1918), is totally commonplace. The most recent book on Meredith, *A Troubled Eden,* by Norman Kelvin (1961), includes a discussion of *Modern Love* in the second chapter, and the whole of the extensive fourth chapter is devoted to Meredith's late poems, after 1883. Kelvin does a useful job with this difficult poetry by defining "a number of casually distributed themes that can be rearranged into an intelligible, hierarchical order." The poems after 1883 are also the subject of an essay in M. R. Ridley's *Second Thoughts: More Studies in Literature* (1965).

Essays of general appreciation include two by Sir E. K. Chambers in *A Sheaf of Studies* (1942), "Meredith's *Modern Love*" and "Meredith's Nature Poetry" (both originally printed in journals many years earlier), and one by Chauncey B. Tinker in *Essays in Retrospect* (1948), "Meredith's Poetry," which first came out as preface to the catalog of the Altschul Collection. Leo C. Robertson's "Meredith the Poet" (*English Review*, 1927) is of minor merit.

The connection between the ideas in Meredith's poetry and the current scientific thought of his day is explored in a chapter of *Darwin among the Poets*, by Lionel Stevenson (1932), and in a chapter of *Scientific Thought in Poetry*, by Ralph B. Crum (1931). Further relevant points can be found in an article by James Stone, "Meredith and Goethe" (*TQ*, 1952).

Meredith's highly idiosyncratic use of symbolism and other figurative devices ought to be of interest to modern critics; but the only extant study of it is to be found in a dissertation by Hildegarde Littman, *Das dichterische Bild in der Lyric George Merediths und Thomas Hardys im Zusammenhang mit ihrer Weltanschauung* (1938). The same book was issued also as volume VI of *Schweizer anglistische Arbeiten* under the simpler title of *Die Metapher in Merediths und Hardys Lyrik*. It classifies the principal symbols used by each poet.

The special notice accorded to *Modern Love* among Meredith's poems, first observable in the chapter on his poetry in Richard Le Gallienne's early book, *George Meredith: Some Characteristics* (1890), and reiterated by Harriet Monroe in an article on "Meredith as a Poet" in *Poetry* (1928), in which she terms that poem his "one masterpiece," gained new impetus from the introduction supplied by C. Day Lewis for an edition of the poem published in 1948. There is a useful article by William T. Going, "A Note on

'My Lady' of *Modern Love"* (*MLQ,* 1946), which challenges
Sencourt's assertion that the "lady" was Janet Duff Gordon;
Going argues that this portion of the poem is not to be interpreted
as literally autobiographical. The two subsequent studies of *Modern
Love* have focused on the pattern of recurring images: "The
Jangled Harp: Symbolic Structure in *Modern Love,"* by Norman
Friedman (*MLQ,* 1957), and "The Significance of the Image
Patterns in Meredith's *Modern Love,"* by Elizabeth Cox Wright
(*VN,* 1958). Separate studies of other poems by Meredith are
astonishingly few. Outstanding is "Meredith's 'Periander,'" by
J. M. S. Tompkins (*RES,* 1960). Two useful studies appeared in
Victorian Poetry in 1963: "The Growth of Meredith's 'Lucifer
in Starlight,'" by John W. Morris, and "Meredith and the Wilis,"
by Carl H. Ketcham. Much critical investigation of Meredith's
poems remains to be done.

JAMES THOMSON (1834–1882)

The first biographical information about Thomson was provided
by his loyal friend Bertram Dobell in an introduction to the
posthumous volume of Thomson's work, *A Voice from the Nile,*
in 1884. This memoir was enlarged when prefixed to the complete
edition of the *Poetical Works* in 1895. Meanwhile Henry S. Salt
had written *The Life of James Thomson* (1889), a book which
printed a good deal of material from Thomson's letters and jour-
nals. By 1910 this biography had long been out of print, and so
Dobell reissued his own sketch in a small volume, *The Laureate
of Pessimism,* omitting some passages but also adding a good
many.

A conventional German doctoral dissertation came out in 1906, *James Thomson der jungere, sein Leben und seine Werke,* by Josefine Weissel (*Wiener Beitrage zur englischen Philologie,* 24). J. E. Meeker's book, *The Life and Poetry of James Thomson* (1917), is undistinguished and sometimes undependable; and David Worcester's Harvard thesis, "James Thomson the Second: Studies in the Life and Poetry of B. V.," is available only in abstract in *Harvard University Summaries of Theses* (1934).

The most thorough book is *James Thomson (B.V.): A Critical Study,* by Imogene B. Walker (1950). She announces her intention, somewhat portentously, thus:

> I have considered the influences on, events in, and conditions of Thomson's life; his honest, analytical, philosophic cast of mind; his sympathetic and imaginative temperament; his works both as outgrowths and as evidence of the above; and the development and final statement of his philosophy. This philosophy, as expressed in his writings, is the result of his life, his cast of mind, and his temperament, plus the times in which he lived. . . . These five strands I have endeavoured to weave into a whole that the relations between them may become apparent, letting first one and then another dominate as chronology dictates (p. vi).

Mrs. Walker was given access to unpublished notebooks, diaries, and letters in the possession of Percy Dobell, and she produced an adequate and intelligent book, though some areas of the author's biography are left without much detail.

One of these areas had already received full treatment in a special study of real value and interest by Marjorie L. Reyburn: "James Thomson in Central City" (*University of Colorado Studies,* Series B, 1940). Using previously unpublished material from Thomson's personal diary and business journal and from the court records of Gilpin County, along with the recollections of an old inhabitant, Miss Reyburn gives a full account of Thomson's fantastic expedition to Colorado.

James Thomson, by Charles Vachot (1966), is an exhaustive French treatise, dealing with Thomson's prose as well as his poetry and discussing both genres as to subjects, forms, and emotional moods. With deep admiration for Thomson, Vachot concentrates on aesthetic and psychological interpretation and pays much attention to his literary antecedents. Thomson's prose work is again related to his poetry in William David Schaefer's *James Thomson (B.V.): Beyond "The City"* (1966), a briefer and less laudatory study. Dismissing "The City of Dreadful Night" as not "worth serious study," and discounting the sentimental legend of Thomson's beloved Matilda, Schaefer seeks to trace the development of the poet's thought under three heads: "Theist to Atheist," "Optimist to Pessimist," and "Romantic to Realist." In an article in *PMLA* (1962), "The Two Cities of Dreadful Night," Schaefer displays the evolution of the poem out of what were originally two separate works written three years apart. Schaefer has also edited a selection of Thomson's prose writings under the title, *The Speedy Extinction of Evil and Misery* (1967).

Probably the best brief consideration of Thomson is the chapter in *Genius and Disaster* (1925), by Jeannette Marks. Also helpful is "James Thomson and His *City of Dreadful Night*," by N. Hardy Wallis, in *Essay by Divers Hands* (1935). Another significant essay is "The Vanity of Rhetoric," by R. A. Foakes, in *The Romantic Assertion* (1958). Foakes deals with Thomson as the final figure in his book because *The City of Dreadful Night* marks the disintegration of the Romantic assertion. It "inverts the rhetoric and the images of the Romantic vision, and applies them to an assertion of despair, the negation of that vision."

Using an approach much like Foakes's, Jerome L. McGann, in "James Thomson (B.V.): The Woven Hymns of Night and Day" (*SEL*, 1963), interprets *The City of Dreadful Night* in terms of the Romantic mythic vision and contrasts it with Thomson's other poems. While Thomson was a disciple of Shelley, what he created in *The City* "is not a myth but an anti-myth... Such a vision of reality has one serious drawback: it mitigates [militates] against life, any form of life—for example, poetic creation... Thomson brought *The City of Dreadful Night* into being and gave unity to his own experience; but by so doing he dammed up the springs of his creative energy."

There have been several studies of the origins of Thomson's pessimistic philosophy: "Les Sources du pessimisme de Thomson," by Henri Peyre (*Revue Anglo-Américaine*, 1924–25); "Poets and Pessimism," by Benjamin M. Woodbridge (*Romanic Review*, 1944); and "Leopardi and *The City of Dreadful Night*," by

Lyman A. Cotten (*SP*, 1945). R. A. Forsyth emphasizes the scientific element in "Evolutionism and the Pessimism of James Thomson (B.V.)" (*Essays in Criticism*, 1962). An exhaustive monograph is *The Pessimism of James Thomson (B.V.) in Relation to His Times*, by Kenneth Hugh Byron (1965), which suggests that Thomson's gloomy outlook is a microcosm of a contemporary mood resulting from religious doubts, the decline of philosophical idealism, and the apparently incurable social evils consequent on the industrial revolution. Two other academic studies deserve mention. "An Angel in the City of Dreadful Night," by H. Hoffman (*SeR*, 1924), deals with the influence of Shelley. "Blake's Nebuchadnezzar in *The City of Dreadful Night*," by George M. Harper (*SP*, 1953), suggests that both the imagery and the ideas in Thomson's Canto xviii are derived from Blake's poems and his drawing of Nebuchadnezzar.

Attention should be directed to the introduction by Gordon Hall Gerould in *Poems of James Thomson (B.V.)*) 1927, and the one by Edmund Blunden in an edition of *The City of Dreadful Night and Other Poems* (1932). Anne Ridler provides a useful biographical and critical introduction, as well as textual notes, to *Poems and Some Letters of James Thomson* (1963).

THOMAS HARDY (1840–1928)

An earlier bibliographical source for Hardy, *A Bibliography of the Works of Thomas Hardy*, by A. P. Webb (1916), has been replaced by *Thomas Hardy: A Bibliographical Study*, by Richard Little Purdy (1954), a thorough, accurate, and well-organized work, which also supplies many details of Hardy's life not to be found in the biographies. For secondary material, an excellent compilation is *The First Hundred Years of Thomas Hardy, 1840–1940: A Centenary Bibliography of Hardiana,* by Carl J. Weber (1942).

The official biography of Hardy was nominally by his widow, Florence Emily, and came out in two volumes, *The Early Life* (1928) and *The Later Years* (1930). Actually it seems to have been written wholly by Hardy himself and left for posthumous publication. Although it supplies much essential information, it is exasperating because of its omissions and evasions, and the style is undistinguished. The first published biography, *The Life of Thomas Hardy,* by Ernest Brennecke (1925), was handicapped by lack of data, being an unauthorized work written within the subject's lifetime. For scholarly accuracy and a well-balanced survey of the available facts, the only dependable book is *Hardy of Wessex,* by Carl J. Weber (1940). The revised edition (1965) incorporates recently discovered data. New information that affects an understanding of Hardy's poetry mainly concerns his early love affair with a cousin and the incompatibility of his marriage to Emma Gifford. The story of the abortive engagement is presented, with some melodramatic coloring, by Lois Deacon in *Tryphena and Thomas Hardy* (1962). The record of the discordant marriage can be found in two books edited by Weber in 1963: *Dearest Emmie,* consisting of Hardy's letters to his wife, and *Hardy's Love Poems,* a selection of 116 poems that reveal the emotional tensions of the relationship.

Most of the books on Hardy's writing deal primarily with the novels, but since 1920 several have included discussion of his poetry also. Samuel C. Chew entitled his book *Thomas Hardy, Poet and Novelist* (1921; revised, 1928). A chapter on the poetry, written by J. E. Barton, was added to a new edition of Lionel Johnson's book, *The Art of Thomas Hardy,* in 1923. The poems supplied most of the material for Ernest Brennecke's account of the author's philosophical ideas, *Thomas Hardy's Universe: A Study of a Poet's Mind* (1924). H. C. Duffin had published a book in 1916 entitled *Thomas Hardy: A Study of the Wessex Novels;* when a third and revised edition came out in 1937, the subtitle was changed to read "A Study of the Wessex Novels, the Poems, and *The Dynasts.*" One of the better general books on his writings is *Thomas Hardy: A Study of His Writings and Their Background,* by W. R. Rutland (1938). Discussion of the poetry occupies almost half of Edmund Blunden's *Thomas Hardy* in the English Men of Letters series (1942). There is a good deal of reference to the poems in the book by Harvey C. Webster, *On a Darkling Plain: The Art and Thought of Thomas Hardy* (1947). A group of modern American critics announced their opinions of both the prose and the poetry in the "Hardy Centennial Issue" of the *Southern Review* (1940). The latest long book, *Thomas Hardy: A Critical Study* (1954), by Evelyn Hardy (no relation), makes some use of manuscript sources, but is not noteworthy for accuracy of detail, acuteness of judgment, or mastery of recent research in the field. Its main value for students of Hardy's poetry is the careful linking of individual poems with events of his life and passages in his novels. She also makes some good comments on his poetic imagery.

It was the era of disillusionment after the First World War that brought recognition to Hardy as a poet, and consequently the studies devoted exclusively to his poetry began to appear at that time. In 1919 John Middleton Murry, in the *Athenaeum,* declared that Hardy's poetry is at least as important as his novels. This influential essay was reprinted, with the title "The Poetry of Thomas Hardy," in Murry's book, *Aspects of Literature* (1920). Robert M. Smith wrote a good article on "Philosophy in Thomas Hardy's Poetry" (*North American Review,* 1924). John Livingston Lowes contrasted Hardy's attitude toward Nature with Meredith's in "Two Readings of Earth" (*Yale Review,* 1926; reprinted in *Essays in Appreciation,* 1936). F. L. Lucas included Hardy among his *Ten Victorian Poets* (1940). One of the best general essays on the subject is the introduction by G. M. Young to *Selected Poems of Thomas Hardy* in the Golden Treasury series (1940). There are two essays on Hardy's poetry in R. P. Blackmur's volume, *The Expense of Greatness* (1940), one of them reprinted from the recent *Southern Review* centennial issue; another of the essays from that issue, by Allen Tate, was included in Tate's *Reason in Madness* (1941). V. H. Collins contributed an essay on "The Love Poetry of Thomas Hardy" to *Essay and Studies by Members of the English Association* (1942). "The Dramatic Element in Hardy's Poetry" was dealt with by Marguerite Roberts in *Queen's Quarterly* (1944).

There was a gap of some years before a new crop of significant articles began to sprout. In "Hardy and the Poetry of Isolation" (*ELH*, 1959) David Perkins emphasizes the "urgent preoccupation" with "aloneness" in the poems. "One may describe many of Hardy's poems," he says, "as a fingering of the theme of isolation and an exploring of roads out of the dilemma—roads which are inevitably obstructed by a nagging honesty to his own experience. It is precisely in his sensitivity to the frustration and tragedy of human life that Hardy feels himself cut off from other men. Much that is usually termed his 'pessimism' is a way of looking at things which he felt to be unshared and which prevented him from entering whole-heartedly into the state of mind of his fellows."

Carl Van Doren's essay on "The Poems of Thomas Hardy" in *Four Poets on Poetry* (edited by D. C. Allen, 1959) asserts the uniformity of Hardy's work: "The modern critic [cannot] decide with readiness which poems of Hardy's are the best, let alone the most characteristic. No poet more stubbornly resists selection. And this has not been to Hardy's advantage in the field where reputations are made. There is no core of pieces, no inner set of classic or perfect poems which would prove his rank. Perhaps no poem of Hardy's is perfect; indeed, there is not great poet in whom imperfection is easier to find. Yet he is a great poet, and there are those who love him without limit even though they will admit his thousand failures and defects. With such persons it is the whole of him that registers and counts."

Similar praise is expressed by C. M. Bowra in "The Lyrical Poetry of Thomas Hardy," in his *Inspiration and Poetry* (1965): "At his best . . . he is the most representative British poet between Tennyson and Yeats . . . Hardy did not write poetry to exhibit a scheme of the universe, but he did in fact reveal such a scheme in the only way that poetry can, that is in concrete instances where the individual case raises questions of vast import beyond itself and becomes an example and a symbol of universal laws . . . Just because he was essentially a dramatic poet, for whom the individual situation counted for so much that he must present it in its realistic details, he could never be a 'pure' poet like some of his contemporaries. . . . He was a man among other men, not a visionary or a mystic or a seer."

Another favorable essay is John Crowe Ransom's "Thomas Hardy and the Religious Difficulties of a Naturalist" (*Kenyon Review*, 1960) : "Fresh as these little poems were, they were in an ancient grand manner which betokened a largeness of mind. . . . We could not have foreseen the valor or the ingenuity of his imagination. It was a metaphysical imagination, in the service of a theological passion. In verse he could indulge frankly in speculation, which he could only intimate darkly in the Wessex novels . . . If we look for the genre most likely to describe them, we may call them fables." Ransom also praises the "extremely clean and formal workmanship" in the best of the poems.

The philosophical base of the poetry is considered more specifically by J. O. Bailey in "Evolutionary Meliorism in the Poetry of Thomas Hardy" (*SP*, 1963). Bailey demonstrates that the poetry reveals Hardy's thought in three phases: "first, a phase of bleak pessimism when he read Darwin in the 1860's and reluctantly rejected religious faith; second, influenced by Schopenhauer and von Hartmann, a phase of meditation about an Unconscious Will that might become conscious and amend the world; and third, the phase of evolutionary meliorism."

More emphasis is laid on technique in "The Illusion of Simplicity: The Shorter Poems of Thomas Hardy," by Albert J. Guerard (*SeR*, 1964) :

> Something about Hardy's poetry — perhaps its peculiar blend of plainness and eccentricity, perhaps the uninhibited directness of its sad and tired wisdom, perhaps the surface simplicity — disarms the critic . . . Why does this "simple" poetry, with its transparency of statement and shameless reiteration, have such a considerable appeal for readers bred on ambiguity and paradox? . . . A rare accent of sincerity, then, and a sense of expression fully realized — These are initial grounds for the poems' appeal. . . . A refusal to permit an easy correspondence of spoken phrase and written line . . . is a common source of Hardy's roughness. The reader who respects the speech rhythms of the phrase repeatedly finds himself in awkward metrical situations. The resulting tension is one of the several reasons why the "simple" Hardy is not so simple after all.

A useful though rather superficial essay (written to serve as introduction to a paperback selection) is "The Poetry of Thomas Hardy," by John Wain, in *Critical Quarterly* (1966). Wain

points out Hardy's affinity with Wordsworth, his influence on
subsequent poets, and the "unselfconscious" autobiographical ele-
ment. Wain remarks that the poems "are very like the work of a
village craftsman."

The origins and possible dates of some poems in relation to
similar episodes in the novels are discussed by R. W. King in
"Verse and Prose Parallels in the Work of Thomas Hardy" (*RES*
1962), with the discouraging conclusion that "we must hesitate
to assign priority in time to either member of related pairs. Each
case must be considered in the light of such positive evidence
as may be available."

Restricted studies of particular poems or topics include "Hardy's
'Afterwards,' " by Charles Mitchell (*VP*, 1963), "Thomas Hardy
on the Evidence of Things Unseen," by John E. Parish (*VP*,
1964), "When There Is Nothing: Hardy's 'Souls of the Slain,' "
by Barton R. Friedman (*Renascence*, 1965), and "Dialectical
Structure in Hardy's Poems," by D. E. Moyer (*VN*, 1965).

E. C. Hickson published a University of Pennsylvania disser-
tation, *The Versification of Thomas Hardy* (1931), and Hilde-
garde Littman analyzed his metaphors in the Bern dissertation
which is described above in the section on Meredith. The first
important book devoted wholly to Hardy as a poet is *The Poetry
of Thomas Hardy,* by James G. Southworth (1947). While
attempting to keep an impartial attitude, Professor Southworth
admits that he became less enthusiastic about Hardy as a poet
as he wrote the book: "I belong to a different age from those
who have written largely about Hardy, and I cannot share their
exuberance. Where they see victory, I sense defeat; where
they see vision, I sense short-sightedness."

The first part of Southworth's book undertakes "to synthesize
Hardy's poetic aesthetic as well as his poetic thought.... It be-
comes increasingly clear that Hardy formulated no philosophical
system, nor did he intend to do so." Part II is devoted to the
poet's technical methods, examining his prosody in detail and
attempting to define his prosodic theory. The author claims to be
the first to study the revisions that Hardy made in the manuscripts
of his poems. The final section of the book is "an attempt at a
general evaluation of Hardy's achievement as a poet, not as a
thinker." Expressing the opinion that *The Dynasts* is "fragmentary

as a work of art," Southworth did not treat that work in detail, in order to avoid overlapping with the book by Amiya C. Chakravarty.

A detailed analysis of Hardy's poetic methods is offered in *The Pattern of Hardy's Poetry*, by Samuel Hynes (1961). Like Southworth, Hynes qualifies his praise, explaining that "in Hardy's work, more perhaps than in the work of most poets, good poems and bad poems resemble each other, rather as the family beauty resembles the ugly duckling—you see the same bone-structure, even though the flesh is arranged differently. Frequently a bad poem has seemed to offer a better example than a good poem would, simply because its bone-structure *is* so clear, its 'pattern' so overt: I have tried to maintain a reasonable balance by also including analyses of a number of the poems which I consider Hardy's best." In preliminary chapters Hynes indicates some of Hardy's poetic predecessors, particularly William Barnes, and summarizes Hardy's ideas as a preliminary to showing how the author's techniques are appropriate to his subjects. He then investigates structure, diction, and imagery to demonstrate how the poetry reveals the eternal conflict between irreconcilables that was in Hardy's view the only principle of universal order.

In recent years the greatest attention has centered on Hardy's epic-drama. Amiya C. Chakravarty devoted a whole volume to *"The Dynasts" and the Post-War Age in Poetry* (1938); about two-thirds of the book gives a detailed analysis of the poem, and the remaining portion advances the theory that the work gained great significance through the events of the first World War and the subsequent rise of dictators—significance that Hardy could not have foreseen when writing what he considered to be the reconstruction of a past era and of a vanished system.

Two subsequent books also examine the epic-drama. *Thomas Hardy and the Cosmic Mind,* by J. O. Bailey (1956), concentrates on the influence of von Hartmann's *Philosophy of the Unconscious,* leading to examination of Hardy's "interest in psychic phenomena, to a new interpretation of the Spirits in his drama, to reconsideration of the Immanent Will as Mind, to definition of Hardy's evolutionary meliorism, and to understanding his treatment of Napoleon as servant of the Will." Harold Orel's short book, *Thomas Hardy's Epic Drama: A Study of "The Dynasts"* (1963), seeks "to re-emphasize the meaning behind Hardy's descriptive epithet," by relating it to the epic conventions, especially to *Paradise Lost*. There are somewhat digressive chapters on Hardy's troubles with critics, on his concept of the universe, and so forth; the value of the book is in the contrasts between Milton's stable universe and Hardy's painfully evolving one, and between Milton's celestial hierarchy and Hardy's phantom intelligences.

Annette B. Hopkins dealt with *"The Dynasts* and the Course of History" (*SAQ*, 1945). George Witter Sherman suggested one of the imaginative sources for it in "The Influence of London on *The Dynasts"* (*PMLA*, 1948). A specific origin, in *The Drama of Kings*, by Robert Buchanan, was proposed by Hoxie Neale Fairchild, in "The Immediate Source of *The Dynasts"* (*PMLA*, 1952); and a sequel to this article, in the same journal (1954), "The Original Source of Hardy's *Dynasts*," by John A. Cassidy, went back to Hugo's *Legende des siécles*. Further suggestions of literary sources are to be found in "Hardy's Shelley," by Phyllis Bartlett (*Keats-Shelley Journal*, 1956), and *"War and Peace* and *The Dynasts,"* by Emma Clifford (*MP*, 1956). Miss Clifford also traces the development of the Napoleonic theme in Hardy's work in "The Trumpet-Major Notebook and *The Dynasts"* (*RES*, 1957). Another element in the epic-drama was discussed by E. A. Horsman, "The Language of *The Dynasts"* (*Durham University Journal*, 1949). As 1954 was the semicentennial of the first volume of *The Dynasts*, several articles undertook a general reassessment. A leading article in *TLS* (15 January 1954), "Hardy after Fifty Years," declared that the time has now come when his poetry can be judged fairly. Richard Church wrote on "Thomas Hardy as Revealed in *The Dynasts"* in *Études Anglaises* (1954). In *"The Dynasts,* a Prophecy" (*SAQ*, 1954), Jacob Korg followed the main idea of Chakravarty's book (without mentioning it) by saying that Hardy's theory that "war, which has always been considered as an instrument of human policy, was itself making an instrument of men . . . was practically unintelligible to the Edwardian world which received it," but "has gained authority from recent history."

Later articles include J. M. Stedmond's "Hardy's *Dynasts* and the 'Mythical Method' " (*English*, 1958), which suggests that "the ambiguous form of *The Dynasts* allows him to use the best of both sides of his literary intent." Pointing out "the ironic over-tones inherent in Hardy's use of the Aeschylean superstructure," Stedmond remarks that "he must have been aware of the contrast between his answers and those of Aeschylus . . . A great deal of the flavour of Hardy's epic drama is missed if one reads *The Dynasts* without juxtaposing the views of the ancient and the modern writer." Roy Morrell's *"The Dynasts* Reconsidered" (*MLR,* 1963) challenges the assumption that Hardy really form-ulates in this poem a creed of absolute determinism. Taking issue with strictures by John Laird in his *Philosophical Incursions into English Literature* (1946) , Morrell asserts that "Hardy might be *trying* to give the reader a 'troubled perspective,' that he might be *refusing* to hand out a 'clue and a philosophy,' " and that therefore he should not be condemned for inconsistency. A somewhat similar line is followed by Emma Clifford in "The Impressionistic View of History in *The Dynasts*" (*MLQ,* 1961) . She believes that Hardy's view of life, "often vague and even inconsistent in the various expressions that he gives to it, leads him so inevitably to the formation of impressions rather than the assertion of dogma or the adumbration of 'law' that, if we are fully to appreciate *The Dynasts,* we should consider the content of the work in relation to the impressionism that apparently meant so much to him."

ROBERT BRIDGES (1844–1930)

Robert Seymour Bridges is one of the few minor Victorian poets to be accorded a full and accurate bibliography, that by George L. Mackay (1933) . On the other hand, Bridges' long life was so uniformly pleasant and uneventful that an extensive account of it is not seriously needed, and therefore no attempt has been made to defy the request in his will that no biography should be written. His richest satisfactions, and perhaps his greatest significance, lay in his relationships with literary friends; hence the truest picture of his life can be derived from his correspondence with them and his generous tributes to their memory. His recollections of Digby Mackworth Dolben, Richard Watson Dixon, and Henry Bradley were assembled in a small volume under the title *Three Friends* (1932). *The Correspondence of Robert Bridges and Henry Bradley, 1900–1927* came out in 1940. And the first volume of *The Letters of Gerard Manley Hopkins,* edited by Claude Colleer Abbott (1940), consisted wholly of "Letters to Robert Bridges." A few years later, another batch of correspondence was edited by Derek Patmore in "Coventry Patmore and Robert Bridges: Some Letters" (*Fortnightly Review,* 1948).

Several of Bridges' younger contemporaries have recorded their acquaintance with him. One of these is Edward Thompson, whose slim book, *Robert Bridges, 1844–1930,* came out in 1945. This book offers a general survey of Bridges' poetry, with copious quotations, but it is the personal anecdotes that make it interesting. Logan Pearsall Smith wrote his recollections of Bridges in Tract XXXV of the Society for Pure English (1931). George Gordon gave some agreeable memories and comments in two lectures which were later published: the Rede lecture of 1931, printed in *The Lives of Authors* (1950), and his final lecture in the Oxford Chair of Poetry, 1938, printed in *The Discipline of Letters* (1946), the latter discussing Bridges' relations with Hopkins. Simon Nowell-Smith traced the special topic of Bridges' long association with the Clarendon Press in "A Poet in Walton Street," in *Essays Mainly on the Nineteenth Century Presented to Sir Humphrey Milford* (1948). Appreciations of Bridges by Hopkins, Patmore, Lionel Johnson, Laurence Binyon, Arthur Symons, Cyril Connolly, and others are included in *Poetry and Prose of Robert Bridges,* edited by John Sparrow (1955).

The first separate monograph on Bridges was by F. E. Brett Young, *Robert Bridges: A Critical Study* (1914). It was a useful defense of Bridges as a lyric poet at the time when his appointment as Poet Laureate had invoked a deluge of stupid journalistic abuse, but it showed little understanding of his dramatic work. A very sketchy book by T. M. Kelshall, *Robert Bridges, Poet Laureate* (1924), was inaccurate as to facts and indiscriminate in its praise.

The appearance of *The Testament of Beauty* in 1929 resulted in an immediate re-estimation of Bridges' importance and of his essential qualities. The philosophical content of the book, its wide range of learned reference, and its experiments in prosody all combined to render it a challenge to scholars. Nowell C. Smith brought out a very useful guidebook, *Notes on "The Testament of Beauty,"* in 1931 and revised it for a new edition in 1940. Smith did not get very far in analyzing the philosophic theme of the poem, but he traced a great many sources and explained obscure allusions with accuracy and thoroughness. Mabel L. V. Hughes adopted a different approach in *Everyman's "Testament of Beauty"* (1942); her earnestly religious disquisition adds nothing for a genuine understanding of the poem. Finally, a detailed study of its technical aspects has been made in the University of Pennsylvania dissertation of Elizabeth Cox Wright, *Metaphor, Sound, and Meaning: A Study of Robert Bridges' "Testament of Beauty"* (1952).

The one indispensable book on Bridges, however, is that by Albert J. Guerard, *Robert Bridges: A Study of Traditionalism in Poetry* (1942). With scholarly thoroughness, critical acumen, and a luminous style, Gerard offers not only "the first exhaustive critical study of Bridges' poetry," but also "a study and defence of traditionalism." His thesis is that "far from being a learned formalist, primarily interested in prosodic exercises, Bridges seems to me to have been one of the most impressive as well as one of the most serious poets of the last hundred years ... The way in which Bridges used very diverse masters in his lyrics, plays, and philosophical poems may illustrate not only the manner in which a poet perfects his style but also some of the workings of the creative imagination" (pp. vii–viii). Guerard presents precise evidence as to sources and analogues, much of it embodied in the text of his chapters, and further data in an appendix. Another appendix gives a detailed study of Bridges' prosody.

Of strictly academic studies, the earliest in date is a German dissertation by Alfred Gilde, *Die dramatische Behandlung der Rückkehr des Odysseus bei Nicholas Rowe, Robert Bridges, und Stephen Phillips* (1903), and the most meticulous is *On the Language of Robert Bridges' Poetry*, by Tatsu Sasaki (1932). On his general philosophy, the most careful articles are those by J. Gordon Eaker on "Robert Bridges' Concept of Nature" (*PMLA*, 1939), and by Andrew J. Green on "Robert Bridges and the Spiritual Animal" (*Philosophical Review*, 1944). "Bridges' Classical Prosody: New Verses and Variants" was the subject of an article in *TLS* by Simon Nowell-Smith (28 August 1943), quoting material from manuscript copies made by Lionel Muirhead, a friend of Bridges. A dissertation by Sister Mary Gretchen Berg, OSF, *The Prosodic Structure of Robert Bridges' "New Miltonic Syllabics"* (1962), is a more detailed study of this technical matter.

Several good general appreciations of the poet came out about the time when *The Testament of Beauty* was published or at the time of his death a year later. Edward Davison's essay "In Praise of the Poet Laureate" was in *Fortnightly Review* (1928) ; Arthur Waugh's "Robert Bridges" was in the same periodical (1930) ; and Oliver Elton's "Robert Bridges and *The Testament of Beauty*" (English Association Pamphlet, 1932) was reprinted in his *Essays and Addresses* (1939). A professional philosopher, John Laird, deals with *The Testament of Beauty* in a chapter in his *Philosophical Incursions into English Literature* (1946).

A short article by Adam Fox on "English Landscape in Robert Bridges" (*English*, 1942) emphasized that "Bridges was not a romantic, and at the same time he was not a reactionary. He thought new effects might be got in poetry by mastering the medium, that is the words with which poets work, and he came in course of time to feel that new effects could only be had through new methods . . . The scene for him brings its own enjoyment, and that enjoyment he seeks to communicate" (no. 21, p. 75).

The same point of view appears in a more recent essay, "The Road Not Taken: A Study of the Poetry of Robert Bridges," by J. M. Cohen (*Cambridge Journal*, 1951). Dwelling on Bridges' essential classicism, Cohen asserts that "as a lyric poet he remains to be rediscovered; a succeeding generation may find his the outstanding poetry published between Thomson's *City of Dreadful Night* (1880) and Yeats' *Green Helmet* volume (1910)....

The Shropshire Lad is the product of a much less profound and anonymous emotion than Bridges'."

Almost the only recent article on Bridges' work is "Profundity Revisited: Bridges and His Critics," by Robert Beum (*Dalhousie Review*, 1964). There is also a helpful brief introduction to Bridges by John Sparrow in the Writers and Their Work series (1962). Sparrow declares categorically that "he is surely the author of the largest body of entirely beautiful poetry in the language. . . . For him, poetry was essentially an affair of making rather than expressing, an art rather than an outlet."

WILLIAM ERNEST HENLEY (1849–1903)

A full biography of Henley was long planned by his friend and disciple, Charles Whibley, who collected a mass of material for the purpose but died in 1930 with only a rough draft of three chapters written. Henley has therefore received his first significant study only within the past quarter of a century. Two earlier books about him were brief sentimental tributes—*William Ernest Henley*, by L. Cope Cornford (1913), and *W. E. Henley: a Memoir*, by Kennedy Williamson (1930). In 1945 Jerome H. Buckley published *William Ernest Henley: A Study in the "Counter-decadence" of the 'Nineties*, and four years later came *W. E. Henley* by "John Connell" (John Henry Robertson). These two volumes, one American, the other English, complement each other effectively. Buckley, attempting "the first general criticism of Henley's life and work," announces that he has "deliberately slighted anecdote and personal melodrama, in order to relate Henley to a broader social, aesthetic, and intellectual background." He starts with a good chapter on "The Victorian Activist Philosophies" and uses Henley as the outstanding representative of this school. Connell, on the other hand, had access to Whibley's notes and drafts and to the six large volumes of Henley's letters that Whibley had bound in chronological order. Accordingly his book is largely biographical, with much quotation from letters. The incompleteness of his data, however, was soon proved to him; in consequence of a talk that he gave on the BBC he came into possession of a large collection of Henley correspondence that Henley's widow had left to a friend. Connell reported on this new material in three articles in the *National and English Review* (1951). There is also an article by J. H. Hallam, "Some Early Letters and Verses of W. E. Henley" (*Blackwood's*, 1943), recounting a friendship between the poet and a London coffee-house keeper in 1872 to 1879, which gave Henley his knowledge of Cockney slang. Hitherto unpublished poems in the National Library of Scotland were edited by W. M. Parker under the title, "W. E. Henley: Twenty-five New Poems: A Centenary Discovery" (*Poetry Review*, 1949).

Critical essays include one by Marietta Neff on "The Place of Henley" (*North American Review*, 1920), which points out that though Henley regarded himself as a rebel and innovator he was influenced by many forces. W. B. Nichols took a similar line in "The Influence of Henley" in *Poetry Review* (1921), declaring that Henley could have had little or no effect on the Georgian generation in their free-verse experiments because none of them seemed to be acquainted with his work. Alfred Noyes contributed an appreciation of "Henley—Last of the Buccaneers" to the New York *Bookman* (1916). This reappeared with slight changes in the *Contemporary Review* (1922), and in his book, *Some Aspects of Modern Poetry* (1924). Noyes praised Henley as "our first, our only, our unapproachable portrait-painter in English verse." On the other hand, a strongly antagonistic evaluation was given by Arthur Symons in "The Revival of Henley" (*London Quarterly Review*, 1922).

Dealing with Henley's prose and his journalism are two essays of some value, one by Horace Gregory, "On William Ernest Henley's Editorial Career," in *The Shield of Achilles* (1944), and one by Morris U. Schappes, "William Ernest Henley's

Principles of Criticism," in *PMLA* (1931). Fuller study of this topic must depend on the identification of the great quantity of reviews and essays that Henley published anonymously in many papers.

ROBERT LOUIS STEVENSON (1850–1894)

A veritable library of books and articles about Robert Louis Stevenson has accumulated during the past half century, but relatively little of it can be accorded the name of "research" and far less of it can be regarded as bearing directly on his poetry. The standard bibliography was compiled by William F. Prideaux (new edition, edited and enlarged by Mrs. Luther S. Livingston, 1917). George L. Mackay edited a monumental five-volume catalog of the works by and about Stevenson in the Beinecke collection, Yale University Library (1951–1961). A general report on the "The Edwin J. Beinecke Collection of Robert Louis Stevenson," by Marjorie Gray Wynne, appeared in the *Yale University Library Gazette* (1952).

The cornerstone of Stevenson biography is still the two-volume *Life* by Graham Balfour (1901), and the principal walls are the four volumes of *Letters,* edited by Sidney Colvin (1912). A new and complete collection of the letters is now being edited by Professor Bradford A. Booth. In recent years assiduous admirers have devoted whole books to each epoch of Stevenson's life—Edinburgh, Switzerland, California, Samoa. The adulation of earlier biographers and critics rendered Stevenson a natural target for the debunkers during the twenties, and his life was subjected to a combination of psychoanalysis and gossip-mongering by George

S. Hellman in *The True Stevenson* (1925) and by J. A. Steuart in *Robert Louis Stevenson, Man and Writer* (two volumes, 1926). Some of the scandalous rumors that they unearthed are now discounted, but a better-balanced portrayal of Stevenson was made possible by their assault on the old sanctification of him. An extensive recent biography is *Voyage to Windward*, by J. C. Furnas (1951), and an intelligent modern estimate of Stevenson's work can be found in the volume on him by David Daiches in the Makers of Modern Literature series (1947).

For the study of Stevenson's poems, it is essential to use the edition prepared by Janet Adam Smith (1951). The need for a thorough revision of his text with recourse to manuscripts was clearly shown through a correspondence in *TLS* (29 August 1929; 26 December 1929; 30 January 1930), which brought out a few of the misreadings in *New Poems and Variant Readings* (1918). Miss Adam Smith has established a text that often differs significantly from previous printings of the poems.

The one modern scholar who has spoken out strongly on the significance of Stevenson's poetry is H. W. Garrod. His essay on "The Poetry of Robert Louis Stevenson," in *The Profession of Poetry and Other Lectures* (1929), completely rewritten for *Essays Mainly on the Nineteenth Century Presented to Sir Humphrey Milford* (1948), makes several interesting assertions:

> For the secondary account in which the poetry of Stevenson is held, Lang, I fancy, has some responsibility. Yet the real mischief began, perhaps, with Stevenson himself. Stevenson practiced self-depreciation as an art; and it is an art which no poet can afford. . . .
> It can hardly, I think, be accident that the three Victorian poets who wrought the disintegration of Victorian poetic diction were all of them novelists. The greatest of them I take to be Stevenson. But "prosators" they are, all of them . . .
> He took from [Matthew Arnold] his blank verse. I am bold to say that it is the best part of his poetry. . . . Of the blank-verse lyric . . . I count Stevenson . . . a supreme master.
> The poems . . . influenced deeply two poets who, till the other day, counted a good deal with the young — Housman and Rupert Brooke . . When I am asked what poets we have had since Matthew Arnold, I say still always, Stevenson, Housman, Brooke.

One of Stevenson's poetic disciples, Alfred Noyes, included an essay on him in his book, *Some Aspects of Modern Poetry*

(1924), and Hugh Richards contributed an article on "Robert Louis Stevenson and His Poetry" to the *London Quarterly and Holborn Review* (1932). A Marburg dissertation by Hermann Alberts, *Der Optimismus des englischen Dichters Robert Louis Stevenson* (1928), presents the fairly obvious facts about his philosophic attitudes. The historical authenticity of the story used in his poem "Ticonderoga" is dealt with in an article by David A. Randall in *New Colophon* (1949).

OSCAR WILDE (1854–1900)

The prolific output of books on Oscar Wilde shows little sign of diminishing. It is true that the last of his personal friends is now dead, and so presumably there is an end to the string of controversial books of recollections, wherein Shaw, Sherard, Harris, Douglas, Ross, and others gave their conflicting reports. But a new generation continues to be fascinated by the man's psychological peculiarities and by his paradoxes and epigrams.

A Bibliography of Oscar Wilde was compiled by "Stuart Mason" (C. S. Millard) in 1914, and has been reprinted, with a new introduction by T. d'A. Smith (1967). There is a specialized bibliographical study of "The Ballad of Reading Gaol" by Abraham Horodisch (1954). *The Letters of Oscar Wilde,* edited by Rupert Hart-Davis, came out in 1962. But in spite of extensive records printed by Wilde's associates and acquaintances, no thorough and objective biography of him has as yet been published. *Oscar Wilde,* by Gustaf J. Renier (1932), gives a reasonably well-balanced study of the principal influences that shaped his career. *Oscar Wilde and the Yellow Nineties,* by Frances Winwar (1940), and *Oscar Wilde: His Life and Wit,* by Hesketh Pearson (1946), are popular works designed for easy reading. The background of his boyhood is vividly presented in *The Wildes of Merrion Square,* by Patrick Byrne (1953), and an intimate picture of his tragic later life can be found in *Son of Oscar Wilde,* by Vyvyan Holland (1955).

George Woodcock's book *The Paradox of Oscar Wilde* (1949) presents the view of a clever young modern. In it and in most of the works mentioned above his poetry is discussed incidentally, but specialized studies of it in English are few. An article by Edouard Roditi, "Oscar Wilde's Poetry as Art History" (*Poetry,* 1947), was later used as the first chapter of Roditi's book on Wilde in the Makers of Modern Literature series (1948). In emphasizing the influence of Whistler and the Impressionists, Roditi followed the same line as Gerda Eichbaum in her article, "Die impressionistischen Fruhgedichte Oscar Wildes unter besonderer Berücksichtigung des Einflusses von James MacNeill Whistler" (*Die neueren Sprache,* 1932).

It is remarkable that virtually all the detailed investigation of Wilde's poetry that has been made is in German. Bernhard Fehr published "Studien zu Oscar Wildes Gedichten" in *Palaestra* (1918). Helene Richter dealt with most of the poems in a long and exhaustive article, "Oscar Wildes Persönlichkeit in seinen Gedichten" (*ES,* 1920). In spite of its title, an article by Stefan von Ullman, "Synästhesien in den dichterischen Werken von Oscar Wilde" (*ES,* 1938), deals mainly with the prose; but its analysis of certain types of imagery is also applicable to the poetry. Rudolf Stamm contributed "W. B. Yeats und Oscar Wilde's 'Ballad of Reading Gaol'" to *Studies in English Literature Presented to Professor Dr. Karl Bunner,* edited by Siegfried Kroninger (1958).

Only one of Wilde's poems has been subject to separate examination. Bernhard Fehr wrote on "Oscar Wildes 'The Harlot's House'" (*Archiv für das Studium der neueren Sprachen und Literaturen,* 1916), tracing the influence of Poe and of various French authors; and J. D. Thomas presented evidence as to the date and circumstances in which the poem was written in "The Composition of Wilde's 'The Harlot's House'" (*MLN,* 1950). Thomas is also the author of "Oscar Wilde's Prose and Poetry" in *Rice Institute Pamphlets* (1955).

JOHN DAVIDSON (1857–1909)

In John Davidson's will he requested the destruction of his letters and prohibited the writing of his biography. Though his life was a picturesque and tragic one, the ban was respected until 1961, when J. Benjamin Townsend published *John Davidson, Poet of Armageddon,* an exhaustively diligent study. The only other academic treatment of Davidson in English is a University of Pennsylvania dissertation by Hayim Fineman, *John Davidson: A Study of the Relation of His Ideas to His Poetry* (1916). It is a relatively brief and superficial treatise. Fineman links him with the imperialistic swagger of his time and with the realistic poetry about London slums, but makes claims for his originality: "He had a point of view and a depth of emotion altogether his own; he tried to stem the tide of French influence and endeavored to construct a new basis for English poetry. Out of his own experience and the scientific thought of his own time he attempted to create 'a new dwelling place for the human imagination.' This he did with a passion and energy in the presence of which the writings of most of his contemporaries pale" (p. 4). Much of Fineman's essay is concerned with Davidson's interpretation of Nietzsche, which Fineman considers to be a subjective and sometimes inconsistent affiliation: "in his later work he passes the Nietzschean ideas through a materialistic crucible so that they practically become amplifications of his own point of view." This aspect of his work is examined more fully in *John Davidson und sein geistiges Werden unter dem Einfluss Nietzsches,* by Gertrud von Petzold (1928).

An essay by Milton Bronner, "John Davidson: Poet of Anarchy" (*Forum,* 1910), emphasizes the autobiographic element in his poetry and deplores the megalomania that affected his later work: "Both by actual performance and by what is here foreshadowed and indicated, one sees what a powerful poet of the masses Davidson might have become had his attention remained concentrated on this phase of existence."

Edward J. O'Brien wrote an introduction to *The Man Forbid,* a collection of Davidson's critical essays (1910), in which he suggested that Davidson "succeeded in founding a school in contemporary English composition . . . whose chief exponent to-day is Mr. Gilbert Chesterton." He attributed Davidson's attitude to his innate Scottish individualism and love of disputation. This idea was carried out more fully by R. M. Wenley in an intro-duction to the Modern Library edition of Davidson's poems (1924). Wenley had known Davidson when they were fellow-students, and he elaborates the early formative influences of Scottish Calvinist theology and of the philosophical ferment at Glasgow University under Nichol and the Caird brothers. A selection of his poems made by Maurice Lindsay in 1961 includes a valuable introduction by the editor, an appreciative essay by Hugh MacDiarmid, and a preface by T. S. Eliot.

"The Religious Significance of John Davidson" was discussed by A. J. Maries in the *Westminster Review* (1913). An essay by D. R. Lock, "John Davidson and the Poetry of the 'Nineties' " (*London Quarterly and Holborn Review,* 1936), reappeared (under the pen name of "Petronius Applejoy") as "A View of John Davidson against a 'Nineties Background" in the *Catholic World* (1942). Lock emphasizes the stylistic influence of Henley and asserts that all of Davidson's best imaginative work was done before the close of the nineties. John A. Lester dealt with "Prose-Poetry Transmutation in the Poetry of John Davidson" (*MP,* 1958), and in the same year issued *John Davidson: A Grub-Street Bibliography* as "Secretary's News Sheet, no. 40" of the Bibliographical Society of Virginia.

The largest and richest collection of Davidson material is at Princeton and is described in "The Quest for John Davidson," by J. Benjamin Townsend (*Princeton University Library Chron-icle,* 1952). These papers were utilized by Townsend in writing his biography of Davidson.

FRANCIS THOMPSON (1859–1907)

The basic reference source on this poet is "A Critical Bibliography of Works by and about Francis Thompson," by Myrtle P. Pope, serialized in four issues of the *Bulletin of the New York Public Library* (1958–1959). There is a larger body of writing about Thompson than about most of his contemporaries of comparable stature, but some of it is of limited scholarly value. The chief biographical source was the Meynell family, who wrote about him with literary grace and sensitive affection but were influenced by their intricate personal relationship with him. Other writers have been sentimentally moved by Thompson's pathetic life and unworldly charm. Some others approach his work strictly from the direction of Roman Catholic doctrine and liturgy.

The official *Life of Francis Thompson*, by Everard Meynell (1913), is one of the best-written biographies of its generation and gives an attractive picture of the poet's personality. The biographer's sister, Viola Meynell, added further documentation and revealing details in *Francis Thompson and Wilfrid Meynell: A Memoir* (1952). It was not until the centenary of the poet's birth, however, that dispassionate and scholarly studies began to appear. *Francis Thompson, Man and Poet*, by J. C. Reid (1960), is a careful and well-balanced biography, cautious about the picturesque view of Thompson's poverty and narcotic addiction and not over enthusiastic about the literary merit of his poetry. Father Terence L. Connolly delivered a blistering attack on Reid's book in "Laudanum or Poetry," a long review article (*Renascence*, 1961). A book by Paul van K. Thomson, *Francis Thompson: A Critical Biography* (1961), is perhaps more sympathetic than Reid's, but here again the unevenness of his inspiration and the neurotic excesses of his behavior are candidly admitted.

Specific aspects of Thompson's life are taken up in the chapter about him in *The Milk of Paradise,* by Meyer H. Abrams (1934), a study of the influence of narcotics on poetry, and in an article by Doyle Hennessy, "Did Francis Thompson Attempt Suicide?" in *Catholic World* (1950), a somewhat specious effort to refute a commonly accepted episode. There are useful biographical details in a book by the Rev. Terence L. Connolly, S. J., *Francis Thompson: In His Paths* (1944); in a first-personal narrative of a pilgrimage "to persons and places associated with the poet" Father Connolly records interviews with surviving acquaintances and includes previously unpublished extracts from Thompson's notebooks, etc.

Father Connolly is unquestionably the leading American authority on Thompson and has accumulated a large collection of his works at Boston College. His notes to the revised edition of Thompson's poems (1941) can give valuable help to students, and he has edited four volumes of Thompson's previously unpublished or unreprinted writings: *The Man Has Wings: New Poems and Plays* (1957) and three collections of book reviews from periodicals—*Literary Criticisms by Francis Thompson* (1947), *Minor Poets* (1949), and *The Real Robert Louis Stevenson and Other Critical Essays* (1959).

General studies of Thompson's work are of varying value. *Francis Thompson, Poet and Mystic,* by John Thomson (1923, a revised and enlarged third edition of a book first published in 1913), and *Guidance from Francis Thompson in Matters of Faith,* by J. A. Hutton (1926), are conventional and trite. The title of a book by R. L. Mégroz, *Francis Thompson: The Poet of Earth in Heaven* (1927), is misleading; its subtitle, "A Study in Poetic Mysticism and the Evolution of Love Poetry," gives a clue to its real contents. Mégroz undertakes such a vast perspective that he has little space left for his announced topic. "The work of Francis Thompson," he explained "seemed to me to call for an unusually comprehensive picture of its wide background in poetry and religion. I chose a succession of poets whose work has significant affinities or contrasts with Thompson's." He could thus include whole chapters on Patmore, Crashaw, Shelley, Donne, St. Augustine, and others.

Thompson's poetry has exerted a peculiar fascination for Continental scholars. There are two German dissertations: one by George Ashton Beacock at Marburg in 1912 made a detailed study of his metrical techniques and of his vocabulary; the other is *Francis Thompsons dichterische Entwicklung: ein biographische-psychologischer Versuch,* by Alfons Martz, at Münster (1932). John Kingsley Rooker's Paris dissertation (1913), while inaccurate in many respects, has a good discussion of Thompson's meter. A French book by Agnès de la Gorce, *Francis Thompson et les poètes Catholiques d'Angleterre,* first issued in Paris in 1932, achieved an English version by H. F. Kynaston-Snell the next year. Written from an orthodox Romanist point of view, the book emphasizes the theological element throughout, and is not free from errors of fact. Its thesis is that "The Hound of Heaven" is the flower of the "Catholic Renaissance" that grew out of the Oxford Movement. Pierre Danchin's *Francis Thompson: La vie et l'oeuvre d'un poète* (1959) is a typically thorough French dissertation, including new biographical data. Danchin added further details in his article, "Francis Thompson (1859–1907): A propos d'un centennaire" (*Etudes Anglaises,* 1960). The book and the article are indispensable sources of accurate information.

An Italian scholar, Federico Olivero, published *Francis Thompson* in Brescia in 1935; an English translation by Dante Milani came out in Turin in 1938. It contains detailed chapters on Thompson's religious thought, his poetic theory, his images, style, choice of words, meter, etc. It is marred by indiscriminate enthusiasm and a tendency to vague generalities, while the discussion of details is weakened by the author's imperfect grasp of English connotations. The list of possible sources and analogues is useful, though some of the suggestions are far-fetched. A later Italian study, by Emilia D'Alessio (1937), is a slight sketch of minor importance.

Several works by Roman Catholic scholars concentrate on the symbolic and mystical interpretation of Thompson's major poem. *A Study of Francis Thompson's "Hound of Heaven,"* by the Rev. J. F. X. O'Conor, S.J. (1912), is brief and sketchy, its chief point being a paralleling of the poem with the *Spiritual Exercises* of St. Ignatius Loyola. A more extensive study is *"The*

Hound of Heaven": *An Interpretation,* by the Rev. Francis P. Le Buffe, S.J. (1921). The author explains that "this little volume is offered as an ascetical and scriptural interpretation of the poem. The author refrains almost entirely from literary questions. His one aim has been to attempt to clarify obscure passages and to give all passages the atmosphere that is required for them from Sacred Scripture and from standard ascetical principles."

The first article that applied modern critical analysis to Thompson's poetic technique, going farther than Beacock, Rooker, and Olivero into the study of his diction, is "The Praetorian Cohorts: A Study of the Language of Francis Thompson's Poetry," by Frederick B. Tolles (*English Studies,* 1940). Challenging the often-repeated statement—which originated with Geoffrey Bliss's article, "Francis Thompson and Richard Crashaw" (*Month,* 1908) and was developed by Arthur Symons in *Dramatis Personae* (1925)—that Thompson was strongly influenced by the Metaphysical poets, Tolles demonstrated that "his characteristic practices in the use of words spring directly from the work of certain of his immediate predecessors and contemporaries." Donald H. Reiman traces a particular literary pedigree in "Shelley, De Vere, and Thompson's 'Hound of Heaven'" (*Victorian Newsletter,* 1961). Irving H. Buchen goes more deeply into the lineage of the poem's symbolism in "Source Hunting versus Tradition: Thompson's 'The Hound of Heaven'" (*VP,* 1964). In another article in the same journal (1965), "Francis Thompson and the Aesthetics of the Incarnation," Buchen examines the relationship between the poet's religious belief and his literary criterion of "rich faultiness."

A different aspect of his work was considered by W. G. Wilson in "Francis Thompson's Outlook on Science" (*Contemporary Review,* 1957). Shortly after that date, the centennial year evoked a crop of articles offering general evaluations of the poet's achievement: John Quinlan's "The Centenary of Francis Thompson" (*Contemporary Review,* 1959); Reginald J. Dingle's "Francis Thompson's Centenary: The Fashionable Reaction" (*Dublin Review,* 1960); F. N. Lee's "Francis Thompson, 1859–1902" (*Bulletin of the John Rylands Library,* 1960); Peter Butter's "Francis Thompson" (*REL,* 1961); Louis L. Nichols' "Francis

Thompson: Flight and Fall" (*Thought,* 1961) ; James D. Brophy, Jrs.' "Francis Thompson and Contemporary Readers: A Centennial Appraisal" (*Renascence,* 1962). Finally, Peter Butter supplies a convenient introduction to Thompson in his brochure for the Writers and Their Work series (1962).

ALFRED EDWARD HOUSMAN (1859–1936)

There is an almost comic contrast between the dearth of published material about A. E. Housman prior to 1936 and the deluge that has poured out ever since his death in that year. His poems had begun to receive their belated recognition in the twenties; but the slender total of them and their pellucid simplicity offered no challenge to scholars, and his obdurate reticence was an obstacle to any biographical study—though presumably his cloistered life offered as little grist for the biographer as his poetry offered for the annotator.

Now, thirty years later, the poems bear a staggering load of critical apparatus. He is the only poet of his generation to have been concordanced: Clyde Kenneth Hyder published *A Concordance to the Poems of A. E. Housman* at Lawrence, Kansas, in 1940. Unfortunately Hyder did not always use the most reliable texts. The bibliography of his few poems has proved unexpectedly complex: T. G. Ehrsam brought out an exhaustive but incomplete and inaccurate *Bibliography of A. E. Housman* in 1941, and later came an excellent work by John Carter and John Sparrow, *A. E. Housman: An Annotated Hand-List* (1952), based on an earlier list printed in *The Library* (1940). Another useful work is the edition of *A Shropshire Lad* published by the Colby College Library in 1946 with notes and a semicentennial bibliography by Carl J. Weber.

Study of variant drafts of Housman's poems, as well as the addition of unpublished pieces to the corpus, began when his manuscript notebooks became available. In *TLS* (12 June 1943), John Carter reported on "A Poem of A. E. Housman," using "The Sage to the Young Man" as a specimen to show how the study of the manuscripts throws light on the textual evolution of his work. A fuller report was given by Maurice Plautner, who examined the manuscripts of *A Shropshire Lad* and *Last Poems* in the Cambridge University Library and discussed "Variants in the Manuscripts of the Poems of Rupert Brooke and A. E. Housman" (*RES*, 1943). A similar study is "*A Shropshire Lad* in Process: The Textual Evolution of Some A. E. Housman Poems," by William White (*The Library*, 1954). A correspondence between White and John Carter with regard to textual variants in *A Shropshire Lad* appeared in *TLS* (12 February, 5 March, 15 May 1954).

Soon, however, the examination of the notebooks became the special province of Tom Burns Haber. His published findings include "A New Poem on an Old Subject from a Notebook of A. E. Housman" (*TQ*, 1951); "A Poem of Beeches from the Notebooks of A. E. Housman" (*Dalhousie Review*, 1951); "Some New Poems from A. E. Housman's Notebooks" (*CE*, 1951); and a more general article, "How 'Poetic' is A. E. Housman's Poetry?" (*MLN*, 1952), in which are listed many "poetic" phrases which the poet excised during revision. Haber deals with another stage of the revising process in "A. E. Housman's Printer's Copy of *Last Poems*" (*Papers of the Bibliographical Society of America*, 1952). The culmination of all this research was Haber's book, *The Manuscript Poems of A. E. Housman* (1954). But a long article, "The Housman Dilemma," in *TLS* (29 April 1955), charged that there were various editorial deficiencies in this volume, both in the textual transcription and in the commentary. Haber's response and the reviewer's rebuttal were printed in the *TLS* issue of 1 July 1955, and the debate was reopened in letters by John Carter and the anonymous reviewer in the issues of 15 and 22 June 1956, with Haber retorting again in that of 20 July.

A centennial edition of Housman's *Complete Poems* was brought out in 1959, edited by Haber, with a detailed "history of the text." Again an acrimonious debate broke out when Carter attacked the editor's accuracy and Haber defended himself at great length (*TLS,* 29 May, 24 July, 14 August 1959). Undeterred by his adversaries, Haber wrote about "A. E. Housman's Notebooks and his Posthumous Poetry" in *Iowa English Yearbook,* 1963, and in 1965 he published *The Making of "A Shropshire Lad": A Manuscript Variorum,* using elaborate typographical devices to show all the cancellations and alternatives in every draft of the poems.

A full record of "all evaluations of Housman's poetry and poetic theory" published between 1920 and 1945 was provided by R. W. Stallman in "Annotated Bibliography of A. E. Housman: A Critical Study" (*PMLA,* 1945). In view of Stallman's invaluable work, I need here only to mention a selection of the most important or most typical research prior to 1945, and then to cover the additional publications of the past twenty years.

Before any full-length biography appeared, the poet's life and habits had been thoroughly revealed in print by many of his friends. Shortly after his death the magazine of his old school, *The Bromsgrovian,* issued a special supplement containing important recollections by his brother (Laurence Housman), his sister (Katherine E. Symons), A. W. Pollard, R .W. Chambers, Alan Ker, A. S. F. Gow, and John Sparrow. Several of these people also wrote on the subject at greater length: A. S. F. Gow published *A. E. Housman* in 1936; Laurence Housman provided both family episodes and unpublished documents in *A. E. H.: Some Poems, Some Letters, and a Personal Memoir* (1937); and an article by R. W. Chambers, which first appeared in the *London University College Magazine,* was included in Chambers' book, *Man's Unconquerable Mind* (1939), as part of an essay entitled "Philologists at University College, London." His publisher, Grant Richards, contributed his memories in *Housman, 1897–1936* (1942).

The first approach to a full biography is the book by Percy Withers, *A Buried Life* (1940). This was followed in 1957 by *A. E. Housman: A Divided Life,* by George L. Watson, which provoked controversy by its emphasis on his abnormal devotion to a male friend. Perhaps more blameworthy than the psychological speculations is the padding out of the meager life story with pretentious clichés. Housman's devotion to Moses Jackson figured largely again in Maude M. Hawkins's *A. E. Housman: Man behind a Mask* (1958). A rather sentimental book, it is riddled with errors of detail, as indicated by William White in *TLS* (1 August 1958).

More commendable is the restrained biographical section in Norman Marlow's *A. E. Housman, Scholar and Poet* (1958). Apart from brief chapters on language and meter, the juvenilia, and the nonsense verse, the book is devoted mainly to tracing a wide range of literary antecedents. Articles offering general studies of Housman's poetry include a typically wise and witty one by H. W. Garrod in *Essays and Studies by Members of the English Association* (1939). "Collected and canonized," Garrod remarks, "Housman waits now only the scholiast, and that 'academic appreciation which is the second death.'" Chauncey B. Tinker's *Essays in Retrospect* (1948) contains an essay on "The Poetry of A. E. Housman," part of which first appeared in the *Yale Review* in 1935; for its publication as a book, Professor Tinker added a section vigorously protesting the posthumous publication of inferior poems by Housman. Edmund Wilson, in *The Triple Thinkers* (revised edition, 1948), gives a stimulating discussion of Housman's poetry, emphasizing his classical scholarship and linking him with other author-scholars—Gray, Fitz-Gerald, Pater, Hopkins, and Lewis Carroll. Other general discussions are "The Essential Housman," by Stephen Spender (*Horizon*, 1940); "The Poetry of A. E. Housman," by A. F. Allison (*RES*, 1943); "A. E. Housman: His Outlook and Art," by Robert Hamilton (*London Quarterly and Holborn Review*, 1950); and "The Elegiac Theme in Housman," by Michael Macklem (*Queen's Quarterly*, 1952). Tom Burns Haber discussed "Housman's Poetic Ear" in *Poet Lore* (1948), arguing that his technical mastery of poetic melody had been inadequately recognized: "For this poet, as for all great lyrists, sound was not the mere handmaiden of sense but an intimate and equal companion." Other articles by Haber are "Housman's Poetic Method: His Lectures and His Notebooks" (*PMLA*, 1954), and "A. E. Housman's Downward Eye" (*JEGP*, 1954), a discussion of autobiographical implications in Housman's love poetry. John W. Stevenson has also contributed several useful articles: "The Pastoral Setting in the Poetry of A. E. Housman" (*SAQ*, 1956), "The Martyr as Innocent: Housman's Lonely Lad" (*SAQ*, 1958), and "Housman's Lyric Tradition" (*Forum* [Houston], 1963). Further general studies are "Housman's Shropshire," by Ralph Franklin (*MLQ*, 1963), "The Nature of Housman's Poetry," by Christopher Ricks (*Essays in Criticism*, 1964), and "The Irony and Ethics of *A Shropshire Lad*," by Eugene D. Le Mire (*University of Windsor Review*, 1965). Ian Scott-Kilvert supplied the pamphlet on Housman to the Writers and Their Work series (1956), and there is a graceful essay, "Housman, Professor Paradox," in Gilbert Highet's *Powers of Poetry* (1960). An American poet's impressions of "Epitaph on an Army of Mercenaries" can be found in "Round about a Poem of Housman's," by Richard Wilbur (*The Moment of Poetry*, edited by D. C. Allen, 1962).

Three efforts have been made to define Housman's philosophic attitude by comparing him with other pessimistic poets: one by Hugh Molson, "The Philosophies of Hardy and Housman" (*QR*, 1937); another by Arnold Whitridge, "Vigny and Housman: A Study in Pessimism" (*American Scholar*, 1941); and a third by G. Singh, "A. E. Housman and Leopardi" (*English Miscellany*, 1962). Tom Burns Haber discussed "The Spirit of the Perverse in A. E. Housman" (*SAQ*, 1941), and the poet's scientific background is suggested in Haber's article, "A. E. Housman, Astronomer-Poet" (*English Studies*, 1954). "A. E. Housman's Use of Astronomy," by J. N. Wysong (*Anglia*, 1962), is a mechanical listing of all references to stars and planets in the poems.

The "scholiasts" have devoted themselves enthusiastically to identifying the sources of poems or of individual lines and allusions. That modest journal, *The Explicator*, devoted a whole issue to Housman in March 1944, and has contained many other notes on his poems since that date. *Notes and Queries* is equally hospitable to Housmaniana. The names most frequently recurring as contributors of these notes are William White and Tom Burns Haber, but other scholars have been represented from time to time.

John Sparrow led the way in this direction with his essay on "Echoes in the Poetry of A. E. Housman" (*NC*, 1934). Another inclusive study was that by G. B. A. Fletcher, "Reminiscences in Housman" (*RES*, 1945), which cited parallels with the Bible, Lucretius, Dr. Johnson, and Bridges. Classical sources, strangely enough, have been the least often reported—can it be because of inadequate classical knowledge on the part of students of English poetry? "Vergil and A. E. Housman," by Ralph E. Marcellino (*Classical Journal*, 1941), is a brief note on *Last Poems II*, and "Two Paraphrases by A. E. Housman," by Paul R. Murphy (*Classical Journal*, 1941), deals with *More Poems X–XI* and their source in Sappho. Haber wrote about "Housman and Lucretius" in *Classical Journal* (1963). Two articles in *VP* (1964, 1966) link him with the pastoral tradition: "A. E. Housman's Modification of the Flower Motif of the Pastoral Elegy," by Jules Paul Seigel, and "Horatian Tradition and Pastoral Mode in Housman's *A Shropshire Lad*," by R. L. Kowalczyk. His indebtedness to the Bible, particularly in *More Poems XXII*, has been examined by Charles E. Mounts, "Housman's Twisting of Scripture" (*MLN*, 1946); by D. P. Harding, "A Note on Housman's Use of the Bible" (*MLN*, 1950); and by Vincent Freimarck, "Further Notes on Housman's Use of the Bible" (*MLN*, 1952). Haber traced "The Influence of the Ballads in Housman's Poetry" (*SP*, 1942), and also offered abundant illustration of his debt to Shakespeare in "What Fools These Mortals Be! Housman's Poetry and the Lyrics of Shakespeare" (*MLQ*, 1945). Charles Norman pointed out an interesting parallel in "Dr. Johnson and Housman" (*Poetry*, 1942). A more obscure English poet, the Victorian G. A. Simcox, was suggested by Haber in "The Poetic Antecedents of Housman's 'Hell Gate'" (*PQ*, 1952); but his theory was queried by John Sparrow in "G. A. Simcox, Mr. T. Burns Haber, and Housman's 'Hell Gate'" (*PQ*, 1954). E. H. S. Walde and T. S. Dorch deal admirably with "A. E. Housman and Matthew Arnold" in *Boston University Studies in English* (1960). The influence of Heine was dealt with by Herman Salinger, "Housman's *Last Poems XXX* and Heine's *Lyrischer Intermezzo*" (*MLN*, 1939), and by Haber, "Heine and Housman" (*JEGP*, 1944). Everett B. Gladding proposed a parallel with another German lyrist in "Housman's *More Poems VII* and Dehmel's Trost" (*MLN*, 1941); but this suggestion was later minimized by C. B. Beall, "Housman, Dehmel, and Dante"

(*MLN,* 1942) . Many of these sources and analogues are assembled in Marlow's book (*supra*) , but lynx-eyed critics will probably continue to trace connections between this essentially bookish poet and his predecessors.

RUDYARD KIPLING (1865–1936)

Rudyard Kipling's reputation plummeted so violently before the close of his lifetime that few literary scholars of the present generation have ventured to deal with his work. Not his importance as a subject for research, but his high prestige as a "collectable" author, was responsible for the elaborate *Bibliography of the Works of Rudyard Kipling,* compiled by Flora V. Livingston in 1927 and supplemented in 1936. "The Kipling Collection at the University of Texas" (said to be the third largest in this country) is described by A. W. Yeats in the *Library Chronicle of the University of Texas* (1952) . These are superseded, however, by James M. Stewart's *Rudyard Kipling: A Bibliographical Catalogue* (1960) .

The authorized biography of Kipling is that by C. E. Carrington, 1955. Two books which have tried to estimate his career and work without prejudice are *Rudyard Kipling: A Study in Literature and Political Ideas,* by Edward Shanks (1940) , and *Rudyard Kipling: A New Appreciation,* by Hilton Brown (1945) . Bonamy Dobrée has an intelligent chapter on Kipling in *The Lamp and the Lute* (1929) .

In the special field of Kipling's poetry, a useful reference book is *A Handbook to the Poetry of Rudyard Kipling,* compiled by Ralph A. Durand (1914) . General critical articles include

"The Poetry of Rudyard Kipling," by J. De Lancey Ferguson (*Forum*, 1913); "La Poésie de Rudyard Kipling," by André Chevrillon, in his *Trois études de littérature anglaise* (1921; English translation by F. Simmons, 1923); and a chapter on Kipling in André Maurois's *Prophets and Poets* (1935). The interesting opinions of the leading poet of modernism can be found in the introduction which T. S. Eliot wrote for *A Choice of Kipling's Verse* (1943) and which was reprinted in his *On Poetry and Poets* (1957). Eliot advances the theory that "his verse and his prose are inseparable; that we must finally judge him, not separately as a poet and as a writer of prose fiction, but as the inventor of a mixed form." A memorial address by Eliot in honor of Kipling was printed in French translation in *Mercure de France* (1959). An attempt to define the prevailing elements in Kipling's poetic outlook was made by Lionel Stevenson in "The Ideas in Kipling's Poetry" (*TQ*, 1932).

The technique of his verse forms was examined in *Beiträge zur Metrik Rudyard Kiplings*, by Ernst Löwe (*Marburger Studien zur englischen Philologie*, 1906). The only book-length study of his verse is *Le poétique de Rudyard Kipling*, by François Léaud (1958). The poetry is perceptively discussed and related to the prose fiction in *The Art of Rudyard Kipling*, by J. M. S. Tompkins (1960), and in *Rudyard Kipling, Realist and Fabulist*, by Bonamy Dobrée (1967). Relevant comments on poems are to be found in Robert Escarpit's *Rudyard Kipling: Servitudes et grandeurs impèriales* (1955) and C. A. Bodelsen's *Aspects of Kipling's Art* (1964). The fact that he was essentially a literary poet rather than a rough-and-ready rhymester is thoroughly demonstrated in a University of Pennsylvania dissertation by Ann M. Weygandt, *Kipling's Reading and Its Influence on His Poetry* (1939). In particular, his kinship with Latin poetry has been pointed out in two articles, "The Classical Element in the Poems of Rudyard Kipling," by Harold W. Gilmer (*Classical Weekly*, 1921), and "Two Imperial Poets: Horace and Kipling," by Louis E. Lord (*Classical Journal*, 1921). Finally, a widely-known and dramatic anecdote about the composition of one of his best-known poems is set right by A. W. Yeats in "The Genesis of 'The Recessional'" (*University of Texas Studies in English*, 1952).

LIONEL JOHNSON (1867–1902)

Biographical material on Lionel Johnson was slow in appearing. A small volume dealing with his schooldays, *Some Winchester Letters of Lionel Johson,* which came out in 1919, was withdrawn from circulation under pressure from Johnson's family, who were offended by certain allusions. Not until 1939 did a substantial biography appear, but it was worth waiting for. Written by Arthur W. Patrick, it is a Sorbonne dissertation fulfilling the best French standards: *Lionel Johnson (1867–1902), poète et critique.* Patrick had access to many unpublished letters of the poet, provided by his sister, and was able to identify a large number of Johnson's unsigned book reviews. Patrick explains: "Cette étude est la première consacrée à Lionel Johnson. . . . Cela expliquera la place importante donnée à partie biographique, place qui autrement semblerait disproportionnée. Parce que son oeuvre est peu connue, il semble que la façon la plus féconde de la traiter soit l'explication et la description. Il s'ensuite donc que j'ai parfois agi, non en critique, mais en chroniqueur" (p. 5). In spite of this modest disclaimer, the book offers useful insights into Johnson's poetry and criticism, and is provided with a full bibliography.

A quantity of Johnson's schoolboy poetry was edited by Ian Fletcher in "Seven New Poems by Lionel Johnson" (*Poetry Review,* 1950), and "Fifteen New Poems by Lionel Johnson" (*Poetry Review,* 1952). Fletcher analyzes one of Johnson's poems, "The Dark Angel," in *Interpretations: Essays on Twelve English Poems,* edited by John Wain (1955).

Some of the most interesting critical essays on Johnson have appeared as introductions to volumes of his poetry, notably that by Ezra Pound in the 1915 edition of *The Poetical Works of Lionel Johnson* (omitted from subsequent editions of this collection). Others are by Clement K. Shorter in *Selections from the*

Poems of Lionel Johnson (1908), Wilfrid Meynell in *Religious Poems of Lionel Johnson* (1917), and H. V. Marrot in *A New Selection from the Poems of Lionel Johnson* (1927). Louise Imogen Guiney's sensitive appreciation, "Of Lionel Johnson," first published in the *Atlantic Monthly* (1902), was used as introduction for *Some Poems of Lionel Johnson* (1912).

Probably the best critical study is the one by Milton Bronner, "The Art of Lionel Johnson," in the New York *Bookman* (1912). His opinion is that "Johnson's verses stand off by themselves in their virginal purity and spotlessness . . . Serenity, gravity—those terms might well apply to all he ever wrote . . . Johnson was hampered by his very knowledge. He was too scholarly." An article by Arthur Waugh, "The Poetry of Lionel Johnson" (*NC*, 1916), later reprinted in his book, *Tradition and Change* (1919), begins with some personal recollections of Johnson as an undergraduate and goes on to expound the thesis that his poetry "was in a very special sense the sincere and deep expression of his spiritual life. For Johnson's mind and taste were less affected by contact with the world of actions than any man's I ever met. It was the classical inspiration, bred of the Wykhamist cast of thought, which was responsible for every idea and every form of expresssion that he was to develop later on."

There is a pleasant essay on "Lionel Johnson, English Irishman," in *Tuesdays at Ten,* by Cornelius Weygant (1928). A later article, "The Art of Lionel Johnson," by A. Bronson Feldman (*Poet Lore,* 1953), has some use as a general survey of Johnson's life and work, but is marred by sloppy writing and uncritical hyperbole. The special question of Johnson's relationship with the aesthetic movement is treated in John Pick's article, "Divergent Disciples of Walter Pater" (*Thought,* 1948). A good essay by Barbara Charlesworth, "The Gray World of Lionel Johnson," appeared in a rather obscure journal, *Carrell* (Miami, Florida, 1963).

ERNEST DOWSON (1867–1900)

For a generation after his death, the figure of Ernest Dowson appeared in numerous volumes of reminiscences about the nineties as a stereotyped example of the decadent poet, a ragged, childlike victim of drink, drugs, and tuberculosis. The originator of the portrait was Arthur Symons, who first sketched it in an obituary notice of the poet, reprinted as the preface to the first collection of Dowson's poems (1905) and in various volumes of Symons' essays. The surviving family and intimate friends of Dowson were annoyed by Symons' portrayal, but had only slight success in contradicting it. The most important attempt was made by one of Dowson's closest associates, Victor Plarr, in a brief volume—*Ernest Dowson, 1888–1897: Reminiscences, Unpublished Letters, and Marginalia* (1914); he made so many excisions in the letters, however, and evaded so many crucial issues that the book was not effective in combatting the accepted impression. Perhaps its chief value was an appended bibliography compiled by H. Guy Harrison. The legend was made all the more melodramatic when Plarr's daughter Marion used it as the theme of a novel, *Cynara: The Story of Ernest Dowson and Adelaide* (1933). She printed eight letters of Dowson that had been omitted from her father's book; but the fictional treatment of the story ruins its value. Incidentally, a novel is said to have been suggested by Dowson's life and character—*The Divine Fire,* by May Sinclair (1904). Other conspicuous contributions to the legend were those by Frank Harris in *Contemporary Portraits,* second series (1919), and by W. B. Yeats in *The Trembling of the Veil* (1922).

A turn of the tide could be recognized in the preface by Desmond Flower for the first definitive edition of Dowson's *Poetical Works* (1934), which included about forty poems and drafts not previously printed; but the real challenge to the traditional portrait was given by John Gawsworth in an address to the Royal Society of Literature, printed as "The Dowson Legend" in *Essays by Divers Hands* (1938). Gawsworth traced the development of the legend in detail, and marshaled the evidence in favor of a less degrading portrayal, supporting his argument with quotations from twelve previously unpublished letters from Dowson to an Oxford friend, chiefly dealing with his love for Adelaide Foltinowicz. A thorough review of the whole problem is provided in "The Dowson Legend Today," by Russell M. Goldfarb (*SEL*, 1964).

Finally, a full and balanced study of the poet's life and work was brought out by Mark Longaker in *Ernest Dowson* (1944). He consulted many hitherto unpublished letters, and accumulated a mass of personal recollections from surviving friends of the poet, by personal interviews as well as by correspondence. The introduction stated that "it is Dowson's life and personality . . . which are the chief objects of consideration. His poetry and prose were of highly subjective quality, and, as a result, many of the lineaments of his character can be illuminated by a careful interpretation of his works; but it is equally true that much of the dark beauty of his poetry finds expression only in the circumstances which shaped his life" (p. vii). Longaker's style is wordy and heavy-handed, and his approach lacks the imaginative sympathy needed for a fully convincing portrayal of Dowson's elusive character; but as an exhaustive marshaling of factual evidence his book is of basic importance.

Longaker admitted that "there exist some of Dowson's letters which are inaccessible to me at present, and there are stages in his life which remain almost totally unilluminated"; yet the two decades since this was written have added little to the supply of information. Longaker provided a long critical introduction and useful notes to his edition of *The Poems of Ernest Dowson* (1963), which is now the standard text, except that it excludes the rejected pieces that are to be found in Flower's edition.

"A Note on Ernest Dowson," by L. Birkett Marshall (*RES*, 1952), gives some details about Dowson's friend Sam Smith. A brief note by Bruce A. Morisette in *MLN* (1943), "The Untraced Quotation of Ernest Dowson's Dedication," finds its source in Flaubert's *Education sentimentale*. There are stimulating suggestions as to Dowson's relationship to other poets in an article by Geoffrey Tillotson which first appeared in *TLS* and was subsequently reprinted in Tillotson's *Essays in Criticism and Research* (1942) :

> Dowson . . . is a poet who is characteristic of his time and who, because of that modernity, is as closely allied with other good poets coming after him as he is with the good poets who preceded him and with the good poets who were his contemporaries. Like all good poets he epitomizes significant developments in the poetical history of perhaps a hundred years . . . There are passages in Dowson which are almost "Shropshire Lad" . . . At times Dowson's poetry resembles the extremely individual manner of Hardy's . . . [In his] experiments and achievements in rhythm he stands beside Mr. Yeats . . . The loosening of rhythm connects Dowson with Mr. Eliot, some of whose many roots may be found gripping Dowson's best poem, "Non sum qualis eram" (pp. 153–155).

Tillotson's line of approach might well be extended into a full study of Dowson's sources and influence. His essay is apparently unknown to Thomas Burnett Swann, whose monograph *Ernest Dowson* (1964), in Twayne's English Authors series, is a somewhat naive but useful study, linking Dowson's work with the few events of his life, differentiating his poems from those of his fellow Decadents, and emphasizing his affinity with Horace, Propertius, the Cavalier lyrists, and Verlaine. Swann's portrait tends to revert toward the hapless Dowson of "the legend."

The paucity of information about Dowson was finally mitigated in 1967 by the publication of his collected letters, edited by Desmond Flower and Henry Maas. This book should set many of the disputed matters at rest.

INDEX

411